NAPOLEON III AND THE
CONCERT OF EUROPE

NAPOLEON III

and the Concert

of Europe

WILLIAM E. ECHARD

Louisiana State University Press
Baton Rouge and London

Designer: Albert Crochet
Typeface: Linotron Trump Medieval
Typesetter: G & S Typesetters, Inc.
Printer: Thomson-Shore, Inc.
Binder: John Dekker & Sons, Inc.

LIBRARY OF CONGRESS CATALOGING IN PUBLICATION DATA
Echard, William E., 1931–
  Napoleon III and the Concert of Europe.

  Bibliography: p.
  Includes index.
    1. France—Foreign relations—1848–1870.   2. Napoleon
III, Emperor of the French, 1808–1873.   3. Concert
of Europe.   I. Title.
DC277.E27   1983   944.07   82-12660
ISBN 0-8071-1056-6

To Gwenda

La vérité historique me semble devoir être, après la religion, tout ce qu'il y a de plus sacré au monde.

Louis Napoleon to Mme. Cornu, October 5, 1842

Je crois qu'il y a certains hommes qui naissent pour servir de moyen à la marche du genre humain, comme ces animaux qui naissent, soit pour détruire d'autres animaux plus nuisibles qu'eux, soit pour servir de germes quand ils seront morts à d'autres êtres plus perfectionnés. Je me considère comme un de ces animaux, et j'attends avec résignation, mais avec confiance, le moment, ou de vivre de ma vie providentielle ou de mourir de ma mort fatale, persuadé que des deux manières je serai utile à la France d'abord, à l'humanité ensuite.

Louis Napoleon to Mme. Cornu, September 19, 1845

Contents

Acknowledgments

I wish to express my gratitude to those who have helped in the preparation of this book: to Her Majesty the Queen for permission to work in the Royal Archives at Windsor; to the Canada Council, whose generous grant made possible an additional summer's research in Paris; to York University for the Minor Research Grants that assisted in preparing the manuscript; to Professor Lynn M. Case of the University of Pennsylvania for the many insights into the foreign policy of the Second Empire that I owe to his teaching and to his writings; to *French Historical Studies* and the *Canadian Journal of History* for permission to use articles of mine that they had previously published and that appear here in slightly different form; and to Brenda Williams for the intelligence and efficiency with which she prepared the final typescript.

Abbreviations Used in the Notes

AMAE, CP   Archives du Ministère des Affaires Étrangères, Paris, Correspondance politique. The political correspondence is in bound volumes, identified by country and by date. References cite country, volume number, folios, and document number, if given.

AMAE, MD   Archives du Ministère des Affaires Étrangères, Paris, Mémoires et documents. These files contain a great variety of material. References cite the archival designations.

APP   *Die auswärtige Politik Preussens, 1858–1871: Diplomatische Aktenstücke.* References cite volume, page, and editor's document number.

Archives diplomatiques   *Archives diplomatiques: Recueil mensuel international de diplomatie, d'histoire et de droit international.*

BFSP   *British and Foreign State Papers, Compiled by the Librarian and Keeper of the Papers of the Foreign Office.*

Cavour e l'Inghilterra   Count Camillo Benso Cavour, *Cavour e l'Inghilterra: Carteggio con V. E. d'Azeglio.*

Cavour: Mezzogiorno   Count Camillo Benso Cavour, *La liberazione del Mezzogiorno e la formazione del Regno d'Italia: Carteggi . . . con Villamarina, Scialoja, Cordova, Farini, ecc.*

Cavour-Nigra   Count Camillo Benso Cavour, *Il carteggio Cavour-Nigra dal 1858 al 1861.*

Cavour: Romana   Count Camillo Benso Cavour, *La questione Romana negli anni 1860–1861: Carteggio . . . con P. Pantaleoni, C. Passaglia, O. Vimercati.*

Cavour-Salmour   Count Camillo Benso Cavour, *Il carteggio Cavour-Salmour.*

Clarendon Papers   References cite file number and manuscript page.

Greville Memoirs   Lytton Strachey and Roger Fulford, eds., *The Greville Memoirs, 1814–1860.*

HHSA   Haus-, Hof-, und Staatsarchiv, Vienna. The archival designation for the political correspondence (Politische Aktenstücke) used in this book is IX; thus the citation PA IX. The correspondence with France (Frankreich Berichte [abbreviation Fr. Ber.]) is found in boxes, identified by year, months (in Roman numerals), and box number (Fr. Ber., 1860, VI–IX, Box 66). The documents have both the number given by their writer and a

folio designation assigned by the archivist (no. 78B, folo. 95 97). Each
year also contains a box designated "Varia."

Idées napoléoniennes   Louis Napoleon Bonaparte, *Des idées napoléoniennes.*

Origines   *Les origines diplomatiques de la Guerre de 1870–1871.* References cite volume, page, and the editor's document number.

La politique impériale   Napoleon III, *La politique impériale exposée par les
discours et proclamations de l'Empereur Napoléon III depuis 10 décembre 1848 jusqu'en juillet 1865.*

PRO, FO   Public Record Office, London, Foreign Office. The political correspondence with France is designated PRO, FO, 27; with Italy, PRO, FO,
45; with Prussia, PRO, FO, 64. References cite volume and page number,
and document number, if given.

PRO, FO, 356   Public Record Office, London, Foreign Office, Bloomfield Papers. References cite volume (or box), page, and document number, if
given.

PRO, FO, 519   Public Record Office, London, Foreign Office, Cowley Papers.
References cite volume, page, and document number, if given.

RA   Royal Archives, Windsor. References cite file (*e.g.*, J80) and the document's archival number.

Revue des deux mondes   All references are to the "Chronique de la quin-
zaine" section of this publication and are identified by date.

Russell Papers   References cite the archive file (30/22) and the volume
number.

Victoria Letters, 1837–1861   Christopher Arthur Benson and Viscount
Esher, eds., *The Letters of Queen Victoria: A Selection from Her Majesty's Correspondence Between the Years 1837–1861.*

Victoria Letters, 1862–1878   George Earle Buckle, ed., *The Letters of Queen
Victoria: A Selection from Her Majesty's Correspondence and Journal
Between the Years 1862 and 1878.*

NAPOLEON III AND THE
CONCERT OF EUROPE

Prologue
"Les Idées Napoléoniennes"
1839–1849

A sense of European community still existed in the first half of the nineteenth century. Europe had conquered Napoleon and, under the leadership of Castlereagh, established a congress system to watch over France, the perpetual disturber of peace. The other Europe, that of the "Northern Courts," had drawn together in a Holy Alliance, extending this surveillance to include all foyers of violent change. The champions of nationalism, whose programs were anathema to the defenders of the European order as established in 1815, worked not only in the name of their own nationalities but also for the cause of Europe, a Europe whose peace and unity could only be secured when its peoples had found satisfaction. The "integral nationalism" that was to dominate Europe and the world in the later years of the century had not yet found either voice or force. And, as always, there were those who dreamed of the concert of Europe in terms more sweeping than any of these applications, seeing in it the germs of peace, order, and humanitarian reform.[1] Even Napoleon, in his exile on Saint Helena, brooding no doubt on the forces that had led to his overthrow, became a champion of concepts that in the days of his power he had ignored or opposed—liberalism, nationalism, and a united Europe of free peoples. But myths are as potent in history as realities, and the memorial of Saint Helena would convince those who wished to be convinced. Such a man was Louis Napoleon Bonaparte, nephew of the great Napoleon, and, from 1852, Napoleon III, emperor of the French.

---

1. Holbraad, *The Concert of Europe*. The phrase *concert of Europe* will be used throughout to denote a sense of European community and action. Usually it would manifest itself in conferences or congresses (no clear distinction was made between the two terms, which can therefore be used interchangeably), but the concert could and did act through more conventional diplomatic channels.

The mistake of those who regretted or criticized the policies of Napoleon III, wrote Emile Ollivier more than seventy years ago, "and especially of those who have found him enigmatic, is to have removed him, as it were, from the general ideas in the midst of which his mind was formed and of which he was later to be a reflection." Those ideas rooted themselves early and deeply in a mind whose chief characteristic was neither originality nor changeability, but quiet, gentle, invincible obstinacy. *Mon doux entêté* his mother, Hortense de Beauharnais, had called him, a first description on which it would be difficult to improve. Born in 1808 when his father, Louis Bonaparte, was still king of Holland, educated in Germany and Switzerland, exiled in England, passionately French but attached by ties of family and youth to Italy, grown to manhood in a time when Europe had not yet become merely a word, nurtured on the myths of Saint Helena, Louis Napoleon may well have expressed more than mere propaganda in the writings of his years of exile. "Events have proved and are proving every day," wrote a contemporary in 1861, "that in the writings of Prince Louis Napoleon can be found the explanation of the acts of the Emperor Napoleon III." "We cannot say of these books," Pierre de La Gorce concluded in our own century, "either that they are good or that they are bad; but they are suggestive in the sense that here can be found, in an aspect tangled and almost contradictory, all the guiding ideas which were to inspire the future government." And Louis Napoleon, as exile, prince-president, and emperor, took ideas seriously. "March at the head of the ideas of your time," he wrote in 1841, "these ideas will follow you and uphold you; march in their rear, they will draw you on; march against them, they will overthrow you." Whether, as Palmerston is supposed to have said, ideas proliferated in his head like rabbits in a hutch or, as another contemporary remarked, he had few ideas but those that he had were deeply rooted, certain ideas are distinguished by the persistence with which he clung to them. At home to discipline the French and free them through the agency of Caesarean democracy from their sterile political quarrels, and to develop the French economy, thus bringing a better life to the mass of the people; abroad to restore France to a position of influence and prestige second to none, to revise the treaties of 1815 with full French participation and in general accord with the theory that peoples should be free to dispose of themselves, to break the Holy Alliance, and to gain border rectifications that would allow a reduction in the French army. Perhaps there was more. Perhaps the dark suspicions of his contemporaries were justified. All that we can say with certainty, more than one hundred years after his death, is that no other ambitions have been convincingly demonstrated. Surely it is true, as well, that only within the context of a certain idea of Europe does the foreign policy of Louis Napoleon begin to make sense. France, Victor Hugo said, made two mistakes regarding Napoleon III, the first when it took him for a fool, the second when it took him for a genius. Historians should guard against either error.[2]

Certainly it seems clear that from the publication of *Des idées napoléoniennes* in 1839, an "act of adoration" as Hippolyte Thirria called it, Louis Napoleon was strongly influenced by the Napoleonic legend. Of his uncle he wrote: "Great men have this in common with divinity—that they never die completely. Their spirit survives them; and the Napoleonic idea has sprung from the tomb of St. Helena as the Gospel rose triumphant despite the torment of Calvary." The first Napoleon, his nephew insisted, had been the "Messiah of new ideas" and it was because he represented the true ideas of the century that he had soared so high. And what, in foreign policy, were the ideas that Napoleon I had served? His ultimate aim had been to assure the independence of France and to establish a true peace in Europe, but war had been forced upon him time and again, and Napoleon's ambitions had grown with his exploits. Finally, when the chances of war made him master of the Continent, he dreamed of establishing a confederation of Europe. To this end he would have given up his conquests, established a European law code, a supreme court, uniform coinage and weights and measures. "To replace among the nations of Europe, the state of nature with *l'état social*, this was the thought of the Emperor; and all his political combinations tended toward this immense result." But to establish this new Europe it was necessary first to strike down its enemies. In 1812, Napoleon hazarded all on a single stroke, and lost. He fell, reasoned Louis Napoleon, not because his goals were wrong but because the times had forced him to advance too quickly.[3]

Where, if at all, in *Idées napoléoniennes*, do the thoughts of the pre-

2. Ollivier, "Napoléon III," 49; Molinari, *Napoléon III publiciste*, xiv; La Gorce, *Napoléon III et sa politique*, 4; *Fragments historiques, 1688 et 1830*, in *Oeuvres de Napoléon III*, I, 342.

3. Thirria, *Napoléon III avant l'Empire*, I, 236, 237; *Idées napoléoniennes*, 12, 22, 110, 132, 134, 144.

tender replace those of his predecessor? Perhaps when Louis Napoleon writes convincingly of his opposition to war as a policy, certainly when he addresses himself to the Europe of his ideal. "Let us explain in a few words what we understand to be the Napoleonic idea. . . . Soaring above political factions, exempt from all national prejudice, it sees in France only brothers easily reconciled, and in the various nations of Europe only members of one great family." To fight in Europe, Napoleon had said, is to wage civil war. Louis Napoleon foresaw the process by which this state of civil war might be conjured:

> The more this world grows in perfection the more the barriers which divide men tend to shrink, and the greater the number of those countries which the same interests draw together. In the infancy of society the state of nature existed between man and man. Then a common interest united a small number of individuals, who renounced some of their natural rights in order that the exercise of all others might be guaranteed by society. Thus formed the tribe or clan, an association of men where the state of nature disappeared and law replaced the right of the strongest. The more civilization has progressed the greater the scale upon which this transformation has been worked. At first men fought from door to door, from hill to hill; then the spirit of conquest and the spirit of defense resulted in the formation of cities, provinces, states; and a common danger having united a large part of these territorial fractions, nations were born. Since then, with the national interest embracing all local and provincial interests, men have fought as people against people, and each people in its turn has marched triumphantly upon the territory of its neighbor when it has had a great man at its head and a great cause behind it. The commune, the city, the province have, then, one after the other, enlarged their social sphere and expanded the limits of the circle beyond which exists the state of nature. This transformation has halted at the frontiers of each country, and it is still might and not right that decides the fate of peoples.

If, however, the Napoleonic idea had prevailed, then this transformation of Europe would have continued:

> The last great transformation would then have been accomplished for our continent. And just as in the beginning communal interests were raised above those of individuals, then the interests of the city above those of the commune, those of the province above those of the city, and, finally, the interests of the nation above those of the province, in the same way European interests would have come to dominate national ones and humanity would have been satisfied. For Providence could not wish that one nation be fortunate only at the expense of others and that there should be in Eu-

rope victors and vanquished rather than the reconciled members of a single great family.

Moreover, this reconciliation could not come too soon, for, as Louis Napoleon noted (well before Tocqueville's similar observation), "while our old European center is like a volcano that consumes itself in its crater, the two western and eastern nations [the United States and Russia] march unhesitatingly toward perfection, the one by the will of a single man, the other through liberty." Earlier, in *Rêveries politiques*, Louis Napoleon had indicated what, in his opinion, had to be done. "Men talk of eternal war, of endless conflicts, and yet it would be easy for the sovereigns to consolidate the peace. Let them consult the relationship and customs existing among the various nations; let them give to these their nationality as well as the institutions that they demand; and they will have found the true political balance. Then all peoples will be brothers and will embrace before a tyranny dethroned, a consecrated earth, a satisfied humanity."[4]

And yet, if Louis Napoleon was most attracted by those men whose careers while touching France had transcended its boundaries to embrace all of Europe—Caesar, Charlemagne, Napoleon (he wrote a life of Caesar and projected a study of Charlemagne)—if he dreamed in *Idées napoléoniennes* of a single European family, he remained French above all. To restore the prestige and glory of France, revenge its humiliations, jealously guard its honor and dignity, these were tasks before which other considerations yielded place. France was for him *la grande nation*, the lion whose movements must disturb the world of lesser creatures, the Brennus whose sword would always incline the balance. "It is the destiny of France," he asserted to the National Assembly after his election as president, "to shake the world when she moves, to calm it when she moderates."[5]

Were they reconcilable, the European statesman and the French patriot? "When one has the honor to be at the head of a people like the French people," Louis Napoleon had announced in the proclamation preceding his ill-starred attempt to overthrow Louis Philippe in 1840, "there is an infallible means of accomplishing great things, and that is simply to wish it." For France was not France except in the service of great causes:

4. *Oeuvres de Napoléon III*, I, 9, 24, 154–55, 157–58, 387.
5. Message of the President of the Republic to the National Assembly, June 6, 1849, in *La politique impériale*, 15.

But you, the France of Henry IV, of Louis XIV, of Carnot, of Napoleon, you who have always been for the West the source of progress, you who possess the two bastions of empire—the genius of peaceful arts and the genius of war—have you no longer any mission to fulfill? Are you to exhaust your force and your energy in forever battling your own children? No! That is not your destiny. The day will soon come when, in order to govern you, it will be necessary to understand that your role is to place in all the treaties your sword of Brennus—in the cause of civilization.

Might it not be the destiny of Napoleon's successor, Napoleon III would ask in 1858, to see accomplished by peace those great designs that the Emperor Napoleon conceived during war? Might it not be the new glory of France to lead toward a regenerated Europe, not by arms but by moral influence? "If there are some who do not understand their times," he was to assert a year later, at the moment of his military victory over Austria in Italy, "I am not one of that number. In the enlightened state of public opinion one is greater today by the moral influence that he exercises than by sterile conquests, and this moral influence I seek with pride." Might it not be the destiny of France to exercise a moral hegemony, achieved, as the work of European regeneration would have to be achieved, not on the battlefield but at the conference table, where Europe would unite to ban the specter of war from the Continent?[6]

"I do not doubt," Louis Napoleon wrote to Jacques de Sellon in 1835, "that the Emperor Napoleon had in mind a great project for establishing the peace of Europe on a solid foundation." And he continued: "I am certain he would have accomplished it had he returned the victor from Moscow. He himself says in his memoirs that he wanted to create a Holy Alliance of the peoples. Europe would henceforth have been a single great family and each nation would have decided the great questions by force of words and not of arms. This project has much in common with the one that Sully in his memoirs attributes to Henry IV." And, in 1844, in an article written in prison for *Progrès du Pas-de-Calais*, Louis Napoleon returned to the thought. "Open the memoirs of Sully! . . . In order to establish the European equilibrium, Henry IV foresaw that all nations must be equal in power

6. Thirria, *Napoléon III avant l'Empire*, I, 163; *Oeuvres de Napoléon III*, I, 25–26; address of Napoleon III at the unveiling of the equestrian statue of Napoleon I, Cherbourg, August 8, 1858, in *La politique impériale*, 282–83; proclamation of Napoleon III to the Italians, Quartier général de Milan, June 8, 1859, in *La politique impériale*, 298–99.

and that no one of them should dominate the others by its preponderance. He foresaw that, for the peoples as for individuals, equality alone is the source of all justice. Henry IV had brought the greater part of Europe to second his humanitarian views. . . . He would have established a sort of Areopagus destined to resolve by reason and not by brute force the quarrels of the peoples."[7]

Certainly, then, the concert of Europe as it existed in the years before 1848 could have held no charm for the author of *Idées napoléoniennes*. Not only did that concert effectively exclude from its operation all but the great powers, its purpose was to preserve what existed. The "rules" were such as virtually to preclude—in the Europe of Nicholas I and of Metternich—any significant change, however wise or even necessary.[8] One might infer, therefore, that Louis Napoleon would have seen more advantage than disadvantage to France in the demise of a concert contrived to maintain the status quo and hence the balance of power by mutual recognition of acquired rights. In the first place, he was convinced, and he believed that a majority of Frenchmen were convinced, that the concert of 1815 had been made against France. Second, he believed that true European stability could not be achieved until the nationalities problem was solved, and he knew that no solution was possible if Austria remained invulnerable in its treaty rights, just as he also knew that France of all the great powers had the most to gain and the least to lose from solutions to European problems based on the nationalities principle. If, then, these writings before power were to prove more than mere propaganda, with power must come an effort to reshape the concert of Europe from a passive instrument of conservation to an active agency of change. In February, 1848, the government of Louis Philippe was overthrown by a revolution that none had planned and no one could contain. Europe stood once more at a crossroads. Louis Napoleon, returning to France from

7. Louis Napoleon to Jacques de Sellon, Geneva, March 26, 1835, in Schazmann, *Napoléon III, précurseur*, 5; excerpt from *Progrès du Pas-de-Calais*, November 5, 1844, in *Oeuvres de Napoléon III*, II, 47–48.

8. On this point, see Schroeder, *Austria, Great Britain, and the Crimean War*, 405. Schroeder identifies five rules of the concert: only the five great powers should decide great European questions; no power should wage war in Europe for territorial gain or promote revolution or unrest within another great power's territory or sphere of vital interest; no international question of vital interest to a great power could be raised without its consent; if a major problem did arise, no power could refuse an international conference or exclude any other great power from it; and direct challenges and confrontations between great powers had to be avoided at all costs—mainly by referring the quarrel to the concert.

the English exile that had followed his escape from prison in 1846, was elected president of the Second French Republic on December 10, 1848. The time had come to test whether the writings of this particular pretender were to have more weight than such productions are commonly supposed to have.

CHAPTER I

Prince-President
1849–1852

With his election Louis Napoleon came to office but not to power. Having no true political party of his own, threatened from both Left and Right, dependent upon moderate republicans and the dynastic opposition of the July Monarchy, whose leaders, more inclined to supervise than to serve, were for the most part contemptuous of him, the president could not hope to conduct his own foreign policy during this first year of his presidency. And yet, it was a particularly difficult year. Within France the threat of revolution and of civil war persisted. In northern Italy, Sardinia, defeated the previous year in its efforts to drive the Austrians from the peninsula but still defiant, confronted an Austrian Empire weakened by revolution. The pope had been forced to flee Rome, where a republic would be proclaimed on February 8. An uneasy armistice separated Prussians and Danes, at odds over the question of ownership of the Elbe Duchies. In the south, British and French ships temporarily stood between the Neapolitan government and its rebellious Sicilian subjects while agents attempted mediation. And in the east, Russian armies mobilized along the frontiers of Hungary, ready to intervene if Vienna proved unable to suppress Magyar separatism. In these circumstances it may have meant much or little that the first foreign policy initiative of Louis Napoleon and his foreign minister, Edouard Drouyn de Lhuys, was to suggest to London (on January 17) that the time had come for the two countries to initiate naval disarmament. Nothing came of it. The British foreign secretary, Lord Palmerston, contented himself with stating that Britain, an imperial power, could not regulate the size of its fleet with reference to the size of the fleet of any other single power. Louis Napoleon nevertheless secured reductions in the French military and naval budget of 1849.[1] But increasingly his attention was drawn to events in Italy.

The French provisional government had agreed, before the end of 1848, to attend a conference of mediation at Brussels, where Britain and France would try to arrange peace in northern Italy. During his first months in office Louis Napoleon showed no desire either for a war with Austria or for French intervention at Rome. Probably he wished to avoid both. He accepted the Brussels conference; he urged moderation at Turin; he carefully avoided a commitment to the pope; he persuaded the British ambassador, Lord Normanby, that his government would do everything possible to avoid intervention either in northern Italy or at Rome. Most significant, he insisted that the Roman question be included on the agenda of the Brussels meeting, thus making of that conference an embryo congress on the whole Italian question.[2]

At the beginning of January a special envoy, Baron Jean Baptiste Gros, was sent to London to argue for an extension in scope of the proposed conference. All French efforts, he told Palmerston, ought to tend to prevent an Austrian intervention at Rome "until the moment when the Brussels conference shall open, to which the question of the Papal States will be submitted." And he continued: "We wish, then, that these meetings should be held as soon as possible, and that no isolated fact should prejudice a question which ought to arrive intact at the deliberations of the plenipotentiaries." While the envoy and the foreign secretary were discussing how this matter might best be handled at Brussels, Drouyn de Lhuys combated Madrid's December, 1848, proposal of a congress of Catholic powers. This matter of Rome, he argued, was not exclusively a Catholic concern. Moreover, "as France was already engaged with other powers in treating some of the Italian affairs, he preferred in the first instance making an attempt in the same spot where those powers were about to meet to ascertain whether there really was anything to be done in the pope's favor."

1. Simpson, *Louis Napoleon and the Recovery of France*, 40–41. Henderson, *Crimean War Diplomacy*, 127–28, argues that the peace movement of the time "may at least have influenced the manner in which the [disarmament] overture was made."

2. César Vidal, "La IIe République et le Royaume de Sardaigne," 505–530; François Eugène Gabriel, duc d'Harcourt, to Edouard Drouyn de Lhuys, Gaeta, January 13, 1849, in AMAE, CP, Rome, 989:17 (Harcourt was French representative to the papal court, then at Gaeta); Lord Normanby to Lord Palmerston, Paris, January 15, 1849, in PRO, FO, 27, 840:154. Much of the following discussion of the French intervention at Rome in 1849 may be found in Echard, "Louis Napoleon and the French Decision to Intervene at Rome," 263–74.

Meanwhile another special envoy, Humann, was sent to Vienna with instructions to persuade Prince Felix von Schwarzenberg, the Austrian foreign minister, to send a representative to Brussels and to discuss the Roman question there. Only if it became clear that Austrian intervention (which Paris well knew the pope would prefer) was inevitable was Humann to speak of Franco-Austrian cooperation, by which Paris meant that French forces would act at Cività Vecchia or even Rome itself, while the Austrian army would be restricted to maneuvers on its side of the frontier with the Papal States. Humann's position was weakened, however, by the fact that Schwarzenberg had already received from Austria's ambassador at Paris an indication that France was considering a joint intervention, should it prove necessary.[3]

What could Louis Napoleon have hoped for from an expanded Brussels conference? If successful it would, of course, save him from the possible pitfalls of unilateral intervention. It might even arrange the solution that he most desired and that was the object of French efforts until the end of March—direct reconciliation between the pope and his subjects. Louis Napoleon still thought that if the pope would return to his states the revolt would collapse. Drouyn de Lhuys "seemed to think that such an arrangement might originate with the Great Powers of Europe as should leave to his subjects those concessions which His Holiness had already of his own free will extended to them and should at the same time secure to him, within those limits, perfect liberty of action as their Sovereign." And beyond that? At the end of December, 1848, Normanby had had a conversation with the French president that may provide a clue. Louis Napoleon appeared to think, reported the ambassador, "that the Pope when restored might be placed at the head of such an Italian League or Confederation as should satisfy the desire for nationality now so loudly expressed so far as it was reasonable and practical, and yet leave to the Sovereigns of the separate States that authority over their respective subjects without which no settled Government could again be established within the Peninsula." Time and again over the next ten years Louis Napoleon would attempt to persuade Europe-in-conference to arrange such a confederation for Italy. Perhaps he hoped to begin this work at Brussels

3. Baron Jean Baptiste Gros to Drouyn de Lhuys, London, January 8, 1849, in AMAE, CP, Angleterre, 672:139; Normanby to Palmerston, Paris, January 11, 1849, in PRO, FO, 27, 840:97–98; Drouyn de Lhuys to Humann, Paris, January 3, 1849, in AMAE, CP, Autriche, 437:216–19v; Edouard De la Cour to Drouyn de Lhuys, Vienna, January 16, 1849, in AMAE, CP, Autriche, 437:243–46v.

in 1849. Certainly he intended that the whole Italian question should be discussed there.[4]

At any rate, the French government would attempt, in any conference on the Roman question, to assign the task of intervention—should it prove necessary—to an Italian state or states. At Turin, where Vincenzo Gioberti was president of council until February 20, the possibility of intervention by Spain had led to a counterproposal of Sardinian action. He was himself convinced, Louis Napoleon told Normanby, that the pope would be well advised to accept the king of Sardinia's offer of twelve thousand men. The pope had no intention of accepting such an offer, or Vienna of countenancing it. And so Drouyn de Lhuys began to argue the virtues of a joint Sardinian-Neapolitan intervention. Aside from the clear French intention that Europe should supervise such an operation, and the obvious fact that the French government could not, for political reasons, initiate such a proposal, it would certainly require the authority of a conference to organize joint military action by two states that had only recently severed diplomatic relations.[5]

On February 10 the British and French governments, in a final effort to end Austrian delaying tactics, sent their plenipotentiaries to Brussels. But the king of Sardinia had already left Turin to resume command of his army in the field, and Vienna had stipulated that the Brussels conference should discuss neither territory nor institutions. Drouyn de Lhuys continued to insist on the broadest possible scope for the meeting so that it might consider "all conditions, all guarantees necessary to establish a real and lasting peace in Italy"; but the cause was now hopeless. Palmerston had by February 2 adopted the Austrian point of view, and his reply to the French argument was that "it was not a question, at Brussels, of a congress where the general affairs of Europe or of Italy would be treated, but solely of resolving today the great question of peace." A week later, Vienna took a speech of the Sardinian king, Charles Albert, as pretext for withdrawing en-

4. Normanby to Palmerston, Paris, secret and confidential, January 25, 1849, in PRO, FO, 27, 840:280–83v; Bourgeois and Clermont, *Rome et Napoléon III*, 13; Normanby to Palmerston, Paris, confidential, December 28, 1848, in PRO, FO, 27, 816: 219–20v; Drouyn de Lhuys to Charles Joseph Edmond, comte de Boislecomte, Paris, January 9, 1849, in AMAE, CP, Sardaigne, 323:32–32v; Taylor, *The Italian Problem in European Diplomacy*, 197.

5. Normanby to Palmerston, Paris, secret and confidential, January 25, 1849, in PRO, FO, 27, 840:280–83v; Drouyn de Lhuys to Alphonse Gérard, comte de Rayneval, Paris, February 14, 1849, in AMAE, CP, Naples, 177:145–45v; Drouyn de Lhuys to Harcourt, Paris, February 22, 1849, in AMAE, CP, Rome, 989:48–49v.

tirely from the mediation. Although Drouyn de Lhuys was reluctant to accept the fact, the Brussels conference had lost all reality even before Charles Albert's decision on March 12 to renew the war against Austria.[6]

But thought of a congress did not end at Paris or, for that matter, at Vienna. Since December the Austrian government had shown a preference for bringing together the great-power signatories of the 1815 treaties, obviously for the purpose of reaffirming those treaties in Italy. The concert of Europe as an instrument of the great powers for maintaining the status quo was unpalatable to Louis Napoleon; it was perhaps less so to Drouyn de Lhuys, with his pro-Austrian orientation and his wish to curb the adventurism of the president. When the Austrian ambassador asked if Paris did not think that mediation by a congress of the great powers would be an acceptable alternative to the Brussels conference, Drouyn de Lhuys replied that he could not understand how such a congress could carry out negotiations that Austria had felt were impossible for the Brussels meeting. Come to Brussels, he urged, add the papal question to those already on the agenda, and France might have no objection to considering the possibility of a congress.[7] A short time later, however, Louis Napoleon, most likely without his foreign minister's knowledge, revealed how opposed to those of Austria were his own ideas of what a European congress should be and should do.

On March 5, 1849, Normanby wrote to Palmerston concerning "a very interesting conversation" that he had had that morning with the French president. They had been speaking about the conference of Catholic powers called at Gaeta to consider the Roman question.[8] Louis Napoleon had reviewed the difficulties, listened with his usual courtesy to the ambassador's observations, then had suddenly exclaimed "that the impossibility of treating this separate question satis-

6. Humann to Drouyn de Lhuys, Vienna, January 16, 1849, AMAE, CP, Autriche, 437:237–42v; Drouyn de Lhuys to J. B. Thomas Médée, vice-amiral Cécille, Paris, February 10, 1849, in AMAE, CP, Angleterre, 672:227v–28; De la Cour to Drouyn de Lhuys, Vienna, February 2, 1849, in AMAE, CP, Autriche, 437:267–69v; Cécille to Drouyn de Lhuys, London, February 13, 1849, in AMAE, CP, Angleterre, 672:238–41.

7. Drouyn de Lhuys to De la Cour, Paris, February 20, 1849, in AMAE, CP, Autriche, 438:34–36v; Normanby to Palmerston, Paris, March 12, 1849, in PRO, FO, 27, 842: no. 142.

8. Simpson, Louis Napoleon and the Recovery of France, 41–42, treats this conversation, but he gives only a brief summary of Normanby's dispatch (Normanby to Palmerston, Paris, secret, March 5, 1849, in PRO, FO, 27, 841) and considers it out of context, not relating the proposal to the Roman question.

factorily and the apparent improbability of anything more than a few weeks' delay at best being procured by the conference at Brussels, had at length convinced him that there was no hope of avoiding such a complication of questions as must eventually lead to war, except by the speedy acceptance of a general Congress of the great powers of Europe." Thus was introduced one of the most persistent themes of the future emperor's personal diplomacy, the invitation to the concert of Europe to consider whatever problems might arise, acting not to preserve the status quo but to supervise the changes that time and events had made inevitable:

> From the Sound to the Dardanelles, from Wallachia to Sicily and specially in the very heart and centre of Europe there were questions which were every day assuming a more menacing character.
> The Treaties of 1815 had, over and over again, been violated by almost every one of the contracting parties; and yet the only hope of maintaining order was still in appealing constantly to those obligations.
> It was his duty to consider first the interests of France, the President said, but he did so in this instance in connexion with, and not in opposition to, those of other nations, and above all in the interest of the peace of the world. France had considered these Treaties as made against her, and had always shown an inclination to murmur at the arrangements which had such an origin.
> But if supposing, as a member of the great European Family, taking these arrangements as the existing basis, she met on an equality with others to consider in what respects they might require modification in connexion with the necessities of the existing generation, the whole system, so consolidated, would then be accepted by the French People without the least reluctance.
> If some such measure was not speedily adopted, the President foresaw that whilst trying to patch up matters first in the north and then in the south, a case for war might arise when least expected.
> The President agreed with me completely in thinking that a Congress to consider any beneficial modifications of the Treaties of Vienna could only admit the Representatives of those powers who had signed such Treaties, and that any change in the form of the relations of Germany with other states must be one of the questions to be considered at such Congress.

The French president had not consulted his ministers. The initiative was confidential, entirely his own, and dependent for success upon the willingness of Britain to join with France in a joint proposal. Palmerston was not enthralled at this prospect of a new Areopagus. Neither his efforts at a response nor the dialogue concerning the proposal

within the Foreign Office boded well for Louis Napoleon's concept of
the concert of Europe. Britain would certainly give careful attention
to any specific proposal the French government might make, Palmerston noted in the draft of a response to Normanby, but at the moment the questions threatening European peace were "questions of
internal government," and surely neither Britain nor France "would
be willing to join either actively or by moral support in any measures
which might be proposed in consequence of the resolutions of a Congress for the purpose of dictating to any nation great or small what
should be the form of its government or the nature of its political institutions." Beyond doubt, then, had the French president returned to
the subject with Normanby (and apparently he did not), London's response would have been in the spirit of Palmerston's reflections.
"This notion of a European Congress to settle all pending matters,"
the foreign secretary wrote to the then prime minister, Lord John
Russell, "and to modify the Treaty of Vienna so as to adapt it to the
interests and necessities of the present time sounds well enough to
the ear, but would be difficult and somewhat dangerous in its execution." How, for example, could the decisions of the congress be enforced? "A Congress might not find it easy to give effect to its resolutions without establishing a European *gendarmeries*." Besides, what
of France? Would France not ask for some gains for itself? "On the
whole, therefore, I should be for giving a civil but declining answer,
pointing out the many difficulties which would arise in such a course."
Probably Louis Napoleon never received a response to his initiative
and simply accepted the fact that it had failed.[9] At any rate, although
he took the occasion at the end of March of a visit to Paris by his old
friend, Lord Malmesbury, to discover if the opposition party might

9. Palmerston to Normanby, London, secret, March 5, 1849, in PRO, FO, 27, 841.
This is in Palmerston's writing on note stationery. The date, apparently in another
hand, must be mistaken, as Normanby's report of his conversation with Louis Napoleon was not received until the sixth. This document and a draft made from it, with
some alterations and dated April, are in the Paris to London rather than the London to
Paris correspondence. Moreover, the April draft is marked "not to go." Palmerston to
Russell, March 6, 1849, in Temperley and Penson, *Foundations of British Foreign Policy*, 207–208, no. 60. Apparently there was a disagreement as to the form the British
answer should take. On April 13, Russell wrote to Palmerston: "Some alterations in the
dispatch about the Congress will satisfy me. I only wish the question to be left open"
(Russell to Palmerston, April 13, 1849, in Gooch [ed.], *The later Correspondence of
Lord John Russell*, I, 359). It appears that Normanby was instructed to assume, unless
the president spoke to him again, that what had been said was speculation rather than a
proposal, and that a formal written response was never sent.

prove more amenable to a congress and to revision of the 1815 treaties,[10] events had already led to the channeling of French diplomatic efforts regarding the Roman question into a quite different sort of meeting—that of Gaeta.

On January 31, Paris had accepted without enthusiasm the idea of a conference of Catholic powers. As Drouyn de Lhuys later explained to Normanby, if Austria would not come to Brussels, France had only three choices: actively to oppose a non-French intervention at Rome, but that would imply a willingness to intervene, which France did not want to do; to retire from the affair, but that was politically impracticable, since it would lead to an attack on the government by both Left and Right; or to go to a conference of Catholic states and try to persuade it to sponsor intervention by an Italian force. French interest in such a conference grew as alternatives faded. On Drouyn de Lhuys' initiative it was decided that representatives of France, Spain, Austria, and the Two Sicilies would meet with the pope's secretary of state at Gaeta. But the French foreign minister also insisted that "nothing would prevent a sort of Congress being called [subsequently] to deliberate on the definitive regulations of one of the most delicate questions of European politics."[11] In fact, other powers might well be invited to Gaeta as negotiations advanced.[12] If, however, it was still the intention of the French government to involve Europe in the Roman and Italian questions, events had already made that a virtual impossibility. Austria's victory over Sardinia at Novara on March 23 assured that, when the conference assembled at Gaeta one week later, it would be under the shadow of an Austrian domination of the peninsula, which France could accept only at the cost of its liberal aspirations as well as its desire for prestige and influence. In resisting that domination, the French president would serve the wishes of all parties in France except the most reactionary, no less than his own beliefs.

Nevertheless, the French government seems to have regarded the

10. Malmesbury, Memoirs, I, 256–57, diary entry of March 30, 1849.
11. Normanby to Palmerston, Paris, March 1, 1849, in PRO, FO, 27, 841:197–210, no. 115; Drouyn de Lhuys to Rayneval, Paris, March 3, 1849, in AMAE, CP, Naples, 177:215v.
12. Drouyn de Lhuys broached this idea at Vienna in February (Drouyn de Lhuys to De la Cour, Paris, February 24, 1849, in AMAE, CP, Autriche, 438:61–62v). Schwarzenberg accepted the principle (De la Cour to Drouyn de Lhuys, Vienna, March 2, 1849, in AMAE, CP, Autriche, 438:74–75v) and Drouyn de Lhuys reaffirmed it in a circular to French agents (circular of Drouyn de Lhuys, Paris, March 20, 1849, in AMAE, MD, France, 740:18v–19). Louis Napoleon flatly rejected Schwarzenberg's suggestion that France intervene alone at Rome, preferring the conference (De la Cour to Drouyn de Lhuys, Vienna, March 23, 1849, in AMAE, CP, Autriche, 438:166–68v).

Gaeta meeting as a last chance to avoid French intervention at Rome. Its representatives, Harcourt and Rayneval, were instructed to explore one final time the possibility of a reconciliation between the pope and his subjects. They were to argue adamantly for intervention by Italian powers, if intervention there must be, and they were to insist that the earlier reforms granted by Pius IX should be reaffirmed by him. None of these approaches was acceptable to the conference. One by one the alternatives least repugnant to France were discarded, an Italian intervention (by Naples and Sardinia, or by either one), a mixed Italian-foreign intervention (substitution of Spain for Naples or Sardinia), or a non-Italian intervention excluding Austria and France. Inevitably the balance inclined toward the course of action that Drouyn de Lhuys had, on January 3, declared unacceptable to France, intervention by Austria; and Paris was forced to concede the wisdom of Harcourt's earlier advice: "Probably the conferences will only succeed in making clear the necessity of taking a stand, but only three are possible: either to abandon the pope to his fate, or to let the Austrians act, or to act ourselves." In fact, the pope, who had formally appealed to Austria, France, Spain, and Naples on February 18, had secretly made known at Vienna his preference for unilateral Austrian action. On March 31 the French government prudently obtained (within the context of Anglo-French efforts then being made to mitigate for Sardinia the consequences of defeat) a resolution of the Constituent Assembly authorizing French troops to occupy a part of Italy. At the second meeting of the Gaeta conference on April 14, Harcourt announced that, while Paris had not yet reacted to the results of the first session, it was his personal opinion that the best course would be for the pope to request French intervention. The next day, Drouyn de Lhuys wrote to announce France's decision to act alone, and without waiting to be invited.[13]

It had been a difficult decision to reach (Drouyn de Lhuys' silence during the first two weeks of April attests to the fact), and if we are to believe Normanby, Louis Napoleon was the last to assent to it. His efforts to involve the concert of Europe had been sincere and per-

---

13. Drouyn de Lhuys to Harcourt, Paris, March 6, 1849, in AMAE, CP, Naples, 177:246–51; conférences de Gaëte: compte-rendu de la première séance, March 30, 1849, in AMAE, CP, Naples, 177:385–88; memorandum sur les affaires de Rome, undated, in AMAE, CP, Espagne, 834:310–15; Drouyn de Lhuys to De la Cour, Paris, January 3, 1849, in AMAE, CP, Autriche, 437:210–15v; Harcourt to Drouyn de Lhuys, Rome, March 29, 1849, in AMAE, CP, Rome, 989:110v; conférences de Gaëte: compte-rendu de la seconde séance, April 14, 1849, in AMAE, CP, Naples, 178:41–42v; Drouyn de Lhuys to Rayneval, Paris, April 15, 1849, in AMAE, CP, Naples, 178:31–34v.

sistent, and they would continue. From the moment that the French government confronted Pius IX on the issue of reform, Paris would seek, futilely, the support of any European power that might be willing to accord it. But, fatefully, the French president could not accept joint action by France and Austria. Aside from the traditional rivalry of the two powers in Italy, and Louis Napoleon's almost visceral distaste for the Austrian government and what it represented in Europe, there were other factors that weighed in his mind. Doubtless he would be happy to please the French Catholic party. At the same time, his hope of persuading the pope to establish major reforms at Rome would be easier to realize if Austria were held at arm's length. Moreover, General Louis Lamoricière's words during the debate on credits in the Constituent Assembly (April 16) made clear the political embarrassment that any association with Austria would have entailed:

> I believe that in proceeding to Italy the French forces will go there, if not to save the Roman Republic, which cannot, I regret, be saved, at least to save liberty. . . . If we had believed that France was leagued, engaged with Austria, with Spain, with Naples to intervene in Italy, do you think that we should have come to you to propose the report that we have brought to the tribune? Never! But it is because there have resulted positive affirmations from men of probity, whom we ought to believe, whose word we do believe, that France will act independently.

If Rome became for Louis Napoleon a trap from which he could not escape, even in his days of greatest power, and that in the end would contribute to the final debacle of the Second Empire, it was not a case of deserved retribution for earlier rashness. He had tried and would continue to try to persuade Europe to see Rome and, indeed, Italy as a problem to be resolved in concert. But Austria would use the concert only to reaffirm the status quo; Britain would go to the conference table in extremis, if at all; and the fateful dependence of the new Bonapartism upon public opinion would not permit either abstention or cooperation with Austria. Thus from the beginning the main features of Louis Napoleon's foreign policy were revealed, as were the chief factors that, in the end, would defeat it.[14]

The immediate result of the Roman crisis was, however, to strengthen the authority of the president. At the end of October, 1849, angered

---

14. Normanby to Palmerston, Paris, August 19, 1849, in PRO, FO, 27, 847: no. 443; General Louis Lamoricière, as quoted in *Journal des débats*, cited in Collins, *Catholicism and the Second French Republic*, 219.

by the failure of the cabinet to support his Roman policy, he summarily dismissed it, choosing one more acceptable to himself, and thus escaped for the first time the tutelage to which he had been subject since his election. But there were other restraints less easily shaken. So long as the Radical Left was a threat, Louis Napoleon must cultivate the men of order; so long as Europe started nervously at every rumor of a coup that would once more place a Napoleon on the throne of France, he must tread with caution in his foreign policy. Nor were the foreign ministers between October, 1849, and December, 1851, men without ideas of their own. And, even had they been mere instruments of the president's will, there remained that ambiguous Article 53 of the French constitution: "Il [the president] négocie et ratifie les Traités. Aucun Traité n'est définitif qu'après avoir été approuvé par l'Assemblée Nationale." The coup d'état of December, 1851, changed this, of course, since the new constitution did not permit the Legislative Body to consider treaties, but it also threw much of Europe into a state of apprehension concerning the intentions of Louis Napoleon and thus imposed new restraints on his foreign policy. Small wonder, then, that the intervention at Rome proved to be the last major initiative of French diplomacy before the Crimean War.

In northern Italy, Franco-British efforts probably softened the peace terms imposed upon Sardinia after Novara, and Russia and Austria might have been encouraged to moderation in their attitude toward Turkey by evidence of Anglo-French firmness during the extradition crisis at the end of 1849. But France offered no real obstacle to Russian occupation of the Danubian Principalities and suppression of the Magyar revolt. The French government clearly wanted to withdraw from Rome, but took no initiatives other than vague discussions with the pope concerning substitution of a mercenary force. And Victor Fialin Persigny's two missions to Germany in 1849 and 1850 had no significant results. And yet the influence of the prince-president is apparent in the conduct of foreign policy during these years. The insistence upon due recognition of French interests and prestige and upon the maintenance of good relations with Britain was his. Moreover, in the two great problems that, with Italy, were the chief concerns of European diplomacy from 1849 to 1852, another aspect of Louis Napoleon's ideas appears. He saw both the German and the Eastern questions as European problems in the solution of which the concert of Europe, often acting through conference diplomacy, had a major role to play.

From the first, this was true of the attitude taken by Paris in the vexatious question of the Elbe Duchies. Since March, 1848, Danish and German nationalism had caused disputes about the two territories of Schleswig and Holstein, rulership of which was vested by ancient right and the treaties of 1815 in the Danish crown. During the first armed clash between Denmark and Prussia in 1848, the government of the French Republic had clearly favored the Danish cause. That conflict having ended with the armistice of Malmö on July 2, 1848, Louis Napoleon inherited a suspended war in the north of Europe. Probably his feelings were mixed. Sympathy to nationalities would dictate a partition of the Duchies, but strictly French interest would be opposed to an extension of German power, which might whet the appetite for more and encourage Germany to look toward the German-speaking inhabitants of Alsace-Lorraine. And over all loomed the shadow of Russia and of a new anti-French Holy Alliance. Under other circumstances Louis Napoleon might have been tempted to combine a settlement along the lines of the principle of nationalities with a Prussian alliance from which France could obtain some compensation. But with Rome and French politics, the president's plate was already overfull. Nor is it easy to believe that he would have accepted a break with Britain. At any rate, French policy through 1849 would consistently stress three points: insistence that no definitive settlement could be made without France, counsel to Denmark to follow a moderate course, and espousal of a conference solution. "I can't repeat it too often," Drouyn de Lhuys wrote Cécille at London on February 22, "it is urgent to open the peace conference." The next day Denmark denounced the Malmö armistice, an act that the French foreign minister deplored, since, as he said, Denmark could have counted on the support of most of the great powers at the conference table.[15]

The war, which began on March 27, 1849, ended in another armistice on July 10. But Prussian troops remained in Holstein; and now another question emerged—that of succession to the present king of Denmark, who would leave no direct heirs and whose likely successor would be prevented by the Salic law from becoming ruler of the Duchies. In these complexities, Vicomte Jean Ernest Ducos de La

15. Charles de Montherot, chargé, to Drouyn de Lhuys, London, January 1, 1849, in AMAE, CP, Angleterre, 672:123–23v; Jennings, "French Diplomacy and the First Schleswig-Holstein Crisis," 223–24; Drouyn de Lhuys to Cécille, Paris, February 22, 1849, in AMAE, CP, Angleterre, 672:255; circular of Drouyn de Lhuys, Paris, March 20, 1849, in AMAE, MD, France, 740:21v.

Hitte, who had succeeded Drouyn de Lhuys as French foreign minister, held firmly to the view that the great powers must seek a solution in concert. On July 4, 1850, France, Britain, and Russia concurred that the Danish rule of succession should also apply in the Duchies. Two days before, by the treaty of Berlin, Prussia had agreed to withdraw its troops. Berlin had taken a long time, La Hitte observed, to end a situation "which put her in opposition with the unanimous sentiment of Europe." As difficulties persisted France rejected a Danish request for armed help, stressing, instead, support for any measure that tended "to bring the various powers together in a common entente concerning an affair which so closely touches the general interests of European policy." The London protocol of August 23 having failed to pacify the Duchies and restore the situation of 1847, Paris in October proposed joint intervention by France, Britain, and Russia. Both London and Saint Petersburg declined. But through 1851 and into 1852, French diplomacy continued to work for a "European solution" that would also be acceptable to Denmark. On May 8, 1852, a conference at London regulated the question of succession, restoring Schleswig-Holstein to the status of 1847 and declaring the integrity of the Danish monarchy to be a European necessity. The London convention was signed by the five great powers and by Sweden and Denmark. Subsequently the great powers agreed, when asked for clarifications by Copenhagen, that the integrity of Denmark and the order of succession to its throne were European questions that could only be settled collectively.[16]

In fact, the policy followed by France regarding Schleswig-Holstein between 1849 and 1852 coincided fully with the attitude taken by Louis Napoleon toward the broader question of German reorganization. It was, he maintained, a matter subject to European supervision and, at need, intervention. Probably the French president was himself sympathetic to Prussia in the quarrel with Austria and would have considered, under other circumstances, an alliance with the former that could have led to a reorganization of Germany and compensation for France. But there is no convincing evidence that he seriously contemplated this in the years 1849 to 1852 or that he would have attempted to impose such a settlement against the will of the other great powers. Persigny, whom the French president sent to tour

16. Circulars of Vicomte Jean Ernest Ducos de La Hitte, Paris, March 15, July 12, 1850, both in AMAE, MD, France, 740:48v, 64v; La Hitte to Drouyn de Lhuys, Paris, August 26, 1850, in AMAE, CP, Angleterre, 680:105.

Germany in 1849 and named minister to Prussia in 1850, had always been instructed to be strictly neutral.[17]

Moreover, Louis Napoleon's insistence that German reorganization must be considered a matter for European approval was hardly calculated to advance ambitious designs by France. As early as July and August, 1849, Tocqueville, then foreign minister, had maintained France's right as a signatory of the 1815 treaties to intervene in German affairs and had argued that any reorganization of Germany must be in line with those treaties. We cannot know what policy the French government would have followed had the Prussian scheme of German reorganization prevailed, for Berlin was forced by the opposition of Austria and of other German states to abandon its ambitions at the end of November, 1850. However, it is true that the French government had already invoked the treaties of 1815 against suspected Prussian designs in Posen, and that, as we have seen, Louis Napoleon had included in his general congress suggestion of March 5, 1849, "any change in the form of the relations of Germany with other states" as one of the questions requiring consideration.[18]

Concerning Schwarzenberg's intention, first suggested in March, 1849, and formally proclaimed on February 27, 1850, to include all of the Austrian Empire in a new German Confederation, there was never any doubt as to the attitude of Louis Napoleon and of his government. On July 22, 1850, in an interview with Normanby, the French president spelled out his misgivings over Austria's pretensions. He seemed especially concerned that Russia was supporting and encouraging Vienna and argued that while "it had been prudent as well as just on the part of France as well as the other Powers of Europe to keep aloof from interference with any internal arrangements which concerned Germany alone, she could not view with indifference the establishment of a central power which should act in concert upon alleged common interests from the frontiers of Russia to the centre of Italy, commanding alike the Baltic and the Adriatic." Louis Napoleon was clearly bidding for British support, and he later expressed his "great satisfaction" that Palmerston's views (requiring approval by the signatories of 1815

17. Victor Fialin Persigny to La Hitte, Berlin, March 18, 1850, in AMAE, CP, Prusse, 306:57v. For the rumors of Louis Napoleon's intentions, see Charles de Mazade, in *Revue des deux mondes*, December 14, 1850.

18. Tocqueville's instructions to Lamoricière at Saint Petersburg, July, 1849, Bapst, *Origines de la Guerre de Crimée*, 77. See also circular of Tocqueville, Paris, August 28, 1849, in AMAE, MD, France, 740:32, and La Hitte to Drouyn de Lhuys, Paris, February 16, 1850, in AMAE, CP, Angleterre, 676:206–206v.

of a reorganization of Germany) so completely coincided with his own "upon a point so materially affecting the balance of Power in Europe."[19]

From January, 1851, when a disapproving Austrian ambassador at Paris (Count Joseph Alexander von Hübner) was instructed to argue the virtues of including the entire Austrian Empire in the German Confederation, three successive French foreign ministers or acting foreign ministers maintained the strong objections of France not only to the effect of this particular agglomeration upon the balance of power but also to the principle that any change should be made in the composition of the confederation without Europe's consent. Under these circumstances, Louis Napoleon's allusions (to Hübner in February and March, 1851) to compensation that France would require if Austria's scheme succeeded can only be regarded as an additional warning against it. Even when Anglo-French opposition, difficulties within Germany, and wavering Russian support had persuaded Schwarzenberg to abandon his plan, Paris agreed with Palmerston's argument (Jules Baroche was then foreign minister) that the French and British representatives to the revived Frankfurt Diet should present their credentials simultaneously and also protest once more against any tampering with the composition of the confederation. The French president went further. He subsequently insisted that the theoretical arguments that the Diet persisted in advancing be countered. This final French protest was of an almost prophetic character. If the German Confederation were to be altered without European consent, the initial draft argued, then "*l'état de droit* would be ended for a considerable part of Europe whose organization would no longer repose on universally recognized foundations, and one would find oneself placed . . . purely and simply under the empire of material force."[20]

In view of what lay ahead, it is tempting to suspect that Louis Napoleon's appeal to the treaties of 1815 against Austrian ambitions

19. Mosse, *The European Powers and the German Question*, 41–42; Normanby to Palmerston, Paris, July 22, 1850, in PRO, FO, 27, 872; Normanby to Palmerston, Paris, October 3, 1850, in PRO, FO, 27, 875.

20. Drouyn de Lhuys to De la Cour, Paris, January 31, 1851, in PRO, FO, 27, 914; Mosse, *The European Powers and the German Question*, 41; Normanby to Palmerston, Paris, June 15, 1851, in PRO, FO, 27, 901; Normanby to Palmerston, Paris, July 21, 1851, in PRO, FO, 27, 902; Comte Alexandre Walewski to Palmerston, London, August 12, 1851, in PRO, FO, 27, 916; circular of Jules Baroche, August 14, 1851, in AMAE, MD, France, 740:108–111. The French protest was presented at Frankfurt on August 14.

in Germany represented the triumph, at a moment when his position was weak, of one aversion over another. And yet, it is also true that some two years later, after the proclamation of the Second Empire, and concerning matters in which there was opportunity to argue a vital French interest transcending collective responsibilities, Louis Napoleon would give further evidence of a penchant for involving the European concert when developments in central Europe threatened peace and the balance of power. These two problems, the Neufchâtel affair and the question of political refugees on Swiss soil, he had inherited with the presidency. Neither was of his own making, although, as a man of order, he certainly sympathized with the indignation of Berlin and Vienna at the unbridled press of certain "radical" Swiss cantons and at the failure of those governments to restrain the activities of the political refugees who were their guests after the collapse of the 1848 revolutions. As for Neufchâtel, a feudal possession of the Prussian king from 1707, the almost monomaniacal obsession of King Frederick William IV of Prussia with reasserting control of this canton, which had gradually slipped away after 1815, could become a serious problem for France if it led to Prussian military intervention. In fact, no amount of distaste for radical cantonal governments in Switzerland or for the weakness of the Swiss federal council could have reconciled Louis Napoleon to German intervention in that area. When in early 1850 it appeared that Prussia and Austria might take military action, the French government declined a proposed three-power conference and replied that "any armed attack upon the independence of Switzerland would be a very grave question, that the French Government would not consider it as merely involving the safety of the Frontier States, that it was a great European interest and ought, if necessary, rather to be treated by a general Congress of the States, Parties to the Treaty of Vienna, than in a conference between the three Governments." Persigny, who was convinced Frederick William wished to use the refugee question as a pretext for regaining control of Neufchâtel, took a high tone at Berlin, which the French president defended while himself moving troops to the frontier region. The crisis passed, only to revive at the end of 1851, this time as a result of French demands. Those demands, including supervision of refugees by the Swiss government and the expelling of such individuals as Paris should designate, had accumulated in the preceding years, and now the army, invigorated by the coup d'état of December 2, 1851, rattled its sabers. But for all the talk of coercion (a blockade was one favored method), two French notes in the first months of 1852 indicated a pattern of increasing moderation. By mid-March, Paris was hinting at an appeal to the other great powers if Switzerland proved intransigent. The French ambassador to Britain, Comte Alexandre Walewski, offered assurances "that he had induced his Government to promise that if their quarrel with Switzerland was not settled amicably they would refer the whole matter to the five powers."[21]

As it happened, Switzerland subsequently joined Belgium and Sardinia as a small liberal power prudently willing to control the excesses of the press and of the political refugees. But Louis Napoleon, still concerned that Prussia's king had designs on "radical" Neufchâtel, would have a conference, even if restricted in scope. He and Walewski, despite the opposition of the foreign minister Louis Félix, marquis de Turgot, but with the support of Edouard Thouvenel, director of political affairs at the Foreign Ministry, advanced the idea, and when Prussia, certain of French support, proposed a conference, Turgot had no choice but to go along. He had at least the satisfaction of seeing his *projet de protocole* accepted by the conference of the five great powers at London in May, the result of which was to inhibit any unilateral Prussian action against Neufchâtel. In effect, the powers recognized Frederick William's "rights" and then adjourned the question until the enforcement of those rights should be "opportune," stipulating at the same time that only diplomatic action was to be considered. And it was Turgot's opinion that this precluded Prussia's "taking the question into her own hands." Louis Napoleon himself assured the Swiss representative at Paris that "the affair would go no further." For the first but by no means for the last time, he had adroitly invoked conference diplomacy to defuse a potentially explosive situation. Moreover, within less than six months a French initiative resulted in the meeting at London (October 20, 1852) of a conference on the Greek throne, which laid the basis for revision of the treaty of 1832.[22]

21. Normanby to Palmerston, Paris, February 3, 1850, in PRO, FO, 27, 868; Normanby to Palmerston, Paris, confidential, February 24, 1850, in PRO, FO, 27, 869; Lord Henry Wellesley Cowley to Lord Granville, Paris, confidential, February 25, 1852, in PRO, FO, 27, 929 (Cowley had just replaced Normanby as Britain's ambassador to France); Cowley to Malmesbury, Paris, confidential, March 18, 1852, in PRO, FO, 27, 930; Cowley to Malmesbury, Paris, private, March 14, 1852, in PRO, FO, 519, 209.

22. Cowley to Malmesbury, Paris, private, March 14, April 27, 1852, both in PRO, FO, 519, 209; projet de protocole, May, 1852, in PRO, FO, 27, 947; Cowley to Malmesbury, Paris, private, June 21, 1852, PRO, FO, 519, 209; Cowley to Malmesbury, Paris,

But if it had proved possible in regard to the German (and related Greek) question to combine an insistence on French interests and prestige with a predilection for the concert of Europe, the Eastern question posed a much more difficult problem. For one thing, from 1849 to 1852, French prestige and interests could be served in central Europe by defending the status quo, while the opposite was true in at least one aspect of the Eastern question—that of the quarrel between Latin and Greek Orthodox Catholics over the Holy Places. As president, Louis Napoleon inherited a growing resentment within some French circles of the way in which ancient treaty rights accorded to Roman Catholics by successive Turkish rulers had been allowed to slip away. Persigny would later claim that French policy had been unduly influenced in this question by a *coterie cléricale* at the Quai d'Orsay, and there is some support for this assertion in the long memorandum written by the French chargé at Constantinople to the French minister there (General Jacques Aupick) on February 6, 1849, and in a meticulous note prepared at the end of 1850 by Eastern experts of the French Foreign Ministry. On the other hand, it probably required neither influences of this kind, nor even political considerations, to persuade the new president, with his sensitivity on all questions of French prestige and "honor," to raise the tone at Constantinople. On January 27, 1849, Drouyn de Lhuys instructed Aupick to act vigorously concerning a Latin star stolen from the grotto beneath the Church of the Nativity at Bethlehem, since the French "protectorat religieux," as established in the capitulation of 1740, was "déjà trop abaissée à Jérusalem."[23]

Yet, neither Louis Napoleon (however equivocal his personal opinion of the Turks) nor his foreign minister wished to reopen the Eastern question. The independence and integrity of the Ottoman Empire was, Drouyn de Lhuys argued in protesting Russia's occupation of the Danubian Principalities, a European matter, formally consecrated by the treaty of 1841; and Aupick assured his British colleague, Stratford Canning (later Stratford de Redcliffe), that Louis Napoleon's election would not change French policy, which remained devoted to defense of the Porte's interests. Almost four years later, when Louis Napoleon's

confidential, June 30, 1852, in PRO, FO, 519, 1:193; Cowley to Malmesbury, Paris, September 20, 1852, in PRO, FO, 27, 937.

23. Bapst, *Origines de la Guerre de Crimée*, 263 n.; memorandum and note, both in AMAE, MD, Turquie, 98; Drouyn de Lhuys to General Jacques Aupick, Paris, January 27, 1849, in AMAE, CP, Turquie, 300:263–63v.

reference in a speech at Marseilles to the Mediterranean as a French lake once more stirred British suspicions, Drouyn de Lhuys (who was again foreign minister) offered assurances, which the prince-president confirmed. By allowing the question of the Holy Places to be raised at the beginning of his presidency, Louis Napoleon certainly acted unwisely, as he himself later admitted. But were the French claims formulated and advanced in such a way as to indicate that there was more to this initiative than an ill-advised attempt to increase French prestige while winning some political support at home? The evidence does not suggest so.[24]

In one of his first instructions to Aupick concerning the question, La Hitte, who had become foreign minister on November 1, 1849, announced that he had advised the governments of all the Catholic powers of the initiatives that France intended to take in defense of Latin rights at Jerusalem, and sought their support in a question whose solution interested them all equally. Accordingly, before presenting on May 28 the French demand that the Latins be given possession of all the Holy Places guaranteed them by the 1740 capitulation, Aupick consulted the diplomatic corps at Constantinople, including Stratford Canning and Russia's representative, Vladimir Titov. This was not, he argued, a French question or even a political question, but merely a dispute concerning treaty rights. After his interview with the Turkish foreign minister, Reshid Pasha, on May 28, the French minister informed his Catholic colleagues of the results and urged them, also, to act as he had "dans l'intérêt de cette cause commune à la catholicité." If the support given France by other Catholic powers proved in the end to be merely nominal, it was not because of a lack of French effort, especially at Vienna. "In soliciting the help of the other Catholic powers in the negotiations," La Hitte argued, France had shown "that in her eyes this was not at all a question of exclusive influence."[25] Cer-

24. Drouyn de Lhuys to General Adolphe Emmanuel Charles Le Flô, Paris, January 4, 1849, in AMAE, CP, Russie, 202:179–80; Aupick to Drouyn de Lhuys, Péra, January 25, 1849, in AMAE, CP, Turquie, 300:250–59v; Cowley to Malmesbury, Paris, September 29, 1852, in PRO, FO, 27, 937; Cowley to Malmesbury, Paris, October 14, 1852, in PRO, FO, 519, 1:278–79. Of Louis Napoleon's role in the question of the Holy Places, Cowley later reported that "the Emperor also has on more than one occasion, while President, termed it 'une question mal engagée, et qu'il était bien content de la voir terminée'" (Cowley to Russell, Paris, confidential, December 30, 1852, in PRO, FO, 519, 1:349).

25. La Hitte to Aupick, in AMAE, MD, Turquie, 98:25; procès-verbal of the meeting of Aupick with Reshid Pasha and Ali Pasha, Constantinople, May 28, 1850, in AMAE, MD, Turquie, 98:31–37v; Aupick to La Hitte, Constantinople, June 3, 1850, in AMAE,

tainly Paris was in no hurry. Not until December, 1850, did the Porte announce that he would appoint a mixed commission to study in depth all capitulations, both before and after 1740. When Charles Jean, marquis de La Valette, replaced Aupick at Constantinople early in May of the following year, he was instructed by La Hitte to exercise moderation, and the foreign minister frankly admitted that Paris would be satisfied with very little, although it must have at least some satisfaction for the sake of certain circles in France. Nevertheless, the new minister (he was promoted to the rank of ambassador toward the end of April, 1852) took a high tone, especially after the czar's personal intervention, by autograph letter to the sultan, in October, 1850. Was the ambitious diplomat suiting his tone to the wishes of the French president, with whom he had good relations? Lord Henry Wellesley Cowley, the new British ambassador to France, thought so, but it is impossible to know. What we do know is that La Valette, who clearly wished to make the matter a struggle for prestige between France and Russia, was sharply and firmly called to order by Paris, and that, in the end, he achieved little.[26]

Taken together with La Valette's verbal concessions (about which Paris was to know nothing for several months), the Porte's firman of February 8, 1852, granted to the Latins some keys that they were pledged not to use and the right to hold services in the Tomb of the Virgin, balanced by an equivalent later concession to the Greeks. Even so, Turgot, who had succeeded La Hitte as French foreign minister, felt obliged to reassure the czar. When the sultan's letter to Nicholas of February 10 seemed to throw into question even these modest French gains, Louis Napoleon plaintively assured the Turkish representative at Paris that all he now wanted was "some little concession" that would enable him to withdraw from the affair with honor. In the end he agreed to forgo even that, although not without at least one ill-advised venting of bad humor that culminated in La Valette's returning to Constantinople in July, 1852, on board the French warship *Charlemagne*.[27] On July 29, 1852, Drouyn de Lhuys became foreign

MD, Turquie, 98:26–30v; Bapst, *Origines de la Guerre de Crimée*, 165; De la Cour to La Hitte, Vienna, June 10, 1850, in AMAE, CP, Autriche, 442:77–78v; La Hitte to De la Cour, Paris, June 20, 1850, in AMAE, CP, Autriche, 442:113v.

26. Bapst, *Origines de la Guerre de Crimée*, 208, 210–13; La Hitte to Charles Jean, marquis de La Valette, Paris, May 7, 1851, in AMAE, CP, Turquie, 305:198v; Cowley to Malmesbury, Paris, September 6, 1852, in PRO, FO, 27, 937. The French government wanted to keep the question out of the newspapers, and La Valette was reprimanded for "leaks" in his embassy (Bapst, *Origines de la Guerre de Crimée*, 240 n.).

27. Bapst, *Origines de la Guerre de Crimée*, 239, 242 n.; Cowley to Granville, Paris,

minister. Thereafter, three successive French ambassadors at Constantinople were instructed to settle the matter virtually at any price,[28] and when the first result of the mission to Constantinople at the beginning of 1853 of Czar Nicholas' special envoy, Prince Alexander Menshikov, was a firman (May 4) favorable to the Greek Orthodox community, Paris meekly accepted this inglorious end to the affair.

From 1849, then, into 1853, French foreign policy was characterized by its moderation and its sense of European concert. This period began with a bid by Louis Napoleon to resolve the Roman and other questions in a general European congress and ended, as we have seen, with a number of European conferences, each proposed or supported by France. In most instances, these fit easily within the pattern of the concert of Europe as it had existed since 1815. The Roman question in 1849, the question of Schleswig-Holstein, the dispute between Prussia and Austria in 1850, the problem of political refugees in Switzerland, the dispute concerning Neufchâtel, and the question of the Greek throne in 1852 were managed by the great powers in such a way as to do minimum damage to existing settlements and acquired rights. That is hardly surprising. Even after the coup d'état of December, 1851, Louis Napoleon had yet to consolidate his position in France and to win acceptance from the apprehensive governments of the other great powers. But already there had been indications that he and the conservative powers differed in their views of the European concert. His rejection of Schwarzenberg's attempt in early 1849 to reaffirm the 1815 treaties with regard to Italy, and his suggestion to Normanby in March of that year of a great European congress of revision, perhaps pointed to the path he would follow if ever the opportunity should present itself. In fact, events that would shape sweeping new opportunities for French policy were already at hand.

February 25, 1852, in PRO, FO, 519, 1:12–13. In the French version of the *Charlemagne* affair, the Porte had asked to have the warship sent up to Constantinople for examination, but was constrained by Britain and Russia to withdraw permission. Louis Napoleon, feeling that French honor had been offended, dug in his heels, but subsequently agreed to a compromise by which La Valette returned to Constantinople on the ship.

28. Drouyn de Lhuys told Cowley in December that he had written La Valette "to accept what he can get and let the matter drop" (Cowley to Granville, Compiègne, private, December 23, 1852, in PRO, FO, 519, 210). As for Alexandre Brenier, who replaced La Valette, "His instructions will prescribe to him to finish the question of the sacred places in the best way he can ('d'enterrer la question coute qui coute')" (Cowley to Russell, Paris, January 20, 1853, in PRO, FO, 519, 1:381, no. 42). Finally, of Brenier's successor, De la Cour: "If I am not mistaken the real feeling of the French Government is that M. de la Cour should take upon himself the responsibility of settling the question, *no matter how*" (Cowley to Lord Clarendon, Paris, April 29, 1853, in PRO, FO, 519, 1:501–504, no. 280).

CHAPTER 2

The Crimean War
1853–1855

The settlement of the dispute concerning the Holy Places did not avert a war in the East. Menshikov had other demands to make of the Porte, and in the end these proved unacceptable to France, to Britain, and to the Ottoman Empire. In July, 1854, Prince Albert told the Saxon envoy at London, Count Karl Friedrich Vitzthum von Eckstaedt, that he considered the main significance of the Crimean War to be that "of setting a precedent for the enforcement of her own will by Europe," a sentiment seemingly shared by Napoleon, who wrote in November to General François Certain Canrobert that "if Europe has without fear seen our long-banished eagles deployed with such great éclat, it is because she knows that we are fighting only for her independence." Certainly the Crimean War was a strange conflict. It required ten months to move from ultimatum to hostilities, and the war, once begun, was characterized almost as much by negotiations as by fighting. Obviously, in these years the concert of Europe remained a concept to be reckoned with; and so it was, by all the governments, whether sincerely or from expediency. But when we examine the degree to which Napoleon lent his influence to the concert, the question arises whether he did not go much further in this direction than might have been expected of a man who, after all, had a great deal to gain from the war and who was suspected of having caused it.[1]

---

1. Count Karl Friedrich Vitzthum von Eckstaedt to Count Friedrich Ferdinand von Beust, London, July 16, 1854, in Vitzthum, *St. Petersburg and London*, I, 108–109; Napoleon III to General François Certain Canrobert, Saint-Cloud, November 24, 1854, in *La politique impériale*, 205.

We have already seen that the manner in which Louis Napoleon raised the issue of the Holy Places, and the way in which he pursued it as emperor, gives little comfort to those who would see in him the chief architect of the first major war to follow the Congress of Vienna. Of course, there is the possibility that his willingness to settle a minor dispute came from his conviction that a more vital conflict was at hand. Such seems, in fact, to have been the attitude of Drouyn de Lhuys. But Cowley found the foreign minister much more bellicose than was his master, and Drouyn de Lhuys himself admitted the difference of opinion. In fact, by August, 1853, the British ambassador thought that he could detect a change in Drouyn de Lhuys' attitude under the influence of Napoleon, who was bored to death with the Eastern question and wanted to see it solved peacefully on any terms, even at the cost of abandoning the Turks.[2]

If Napoleon was leading Britain down the path to war, he was doing it with consummate artistry. "The history of all this is," wrote Cowley in January, 1854, "that there can be no doubt the idea of war is very unpopular in France, and the Emperor, if we would let him would back out of it." There were, of course, many reasons why Napoleon would not go to war with a light heart. War could threaten his position in France through the resulting economic dislocation (from the summer of 1853 there were serious food shortages following a poor harvest); it could, if he were seen to be the aggressor, reawaken old nightmares concerning Napoleonic France. Europe, insisted the minister of state, Achille Fould, had bestowed upon the emperor the title of adventurer, and that was what made him so prudent. "He has said more than once that he would rather err on that side and prove to Europe, if war is to break out that it is not his fault."[3] In February, 1853, Napoleon had, in fact, reduced the size of the French army.

To believe that Napoleon led the way to war in 1853–1854 while seeming to draw back is to assume that he knew the concert of Europe could no longer function and that appeals in its name would be merely *pro forma*—a difficult assumption to make, especially for the years preceding the Crimean War. The truth is that, from the begin-

2. Cowley to Clarendon, Paris, April 29, 1853, in PRO, FO, 519, 1:504, no. 280; Cowley to Clarendon, Chantilly, private, July 20, 1853, in PRO, FO, 519, 211:23–31; Cowley to Clarendon, Paris, private, August 11, October 3, 1853, both in PRO, FO, 519, 211:53, 124; Cowley to Stratford de Redcliffe, Paris, private, September 8, 1853, in PRO, FO, 519, 211:97–98.

3. Cowley to Clarendon, Paris, private, January 16, 1854, in PRO, FO, 519, 212:38; Cowley to Clarendon, Paris, private, September 26, 1853, in PRO, FO, 519, 211:114.

ning of 1853, France supported the idea of a European solution to the gathering crisis. Rightly or wrongly, Drouyn de Lhuys suspected the czar of intending to destroy the Ottoman Empire. Europe, the foreign minister insisted, could not permit this. France, for its part, had no pretension to act alone; France had no more at stake than did the other great powers. As early as March, Drouyn de Lhuys had begun to talk of a conference at Constantinople of Russian, Turkish, and French representatives; from this beginning, his penchant for a conference solution grew. If conflict came between Russia and Turkey, he instructed his agents in May, "the question would be, in a word, a European one." The following month it was in line with this theme, and in accordance with the instructions of the emperor, that he suggested to Count Paul Kisselev, the Russian ambassador at Paris, that there was an obvious method of dealing with the differences between Russia and Turkey—a conference of the five great powers involved in the Straits agreement of 1841. Since March, 1853, Drouyn de Lhuys had proposed converting the preamble of the 1841 Straits convention into a European guarantee of Turkey. As the site for the proposed conference, he preferred Vienna. "A conference on the Eastern affairs," Cowley wrote to Stratford de Redcliffe in June, "seems to be their principal desire at this moment."[4]

The conference would, of course, have as its immediate concern a solution of the existing differences between Russia and Turkey, which followed from the demand by the former for a virtual protectorate over Greek Orthodox subjects of the sultan. But Napoleon resisted the British proposal of a bilateral treaty between Turkey and Russia, favoring instead the so-called Bourqueney project, named for the French ambassador at Vienna, Baron François Adolphe de Bourqueney, by which the powers would approve in advance an agreement between the sultan and the czar. At any rate, it was Napoleon's idea "that these and any other projects which may be thought of, should be discussed at Vienna, and that which is most likely to succeed, chosen." Beyond this pragmatism, however, there was a wider view. As Drouyn de Lhuys explained it to some of Cowley's colleagues:

4. Cowley to Russell, Paris, February 4, 1853, in PRO, FO, 519, 1:404, no. 79; Cowley to Clarendon, May 17, 1853, in PRO, FO, 519, 1:404, no. 331; circular of Drouyn de Lhuys, Paris, May 17, 1853, in AMAE, MD, France, 740:160–63; Drouyn de Lhuys to De la Cour, Paris, June 13, 1853, in Guichen, La Guerre de Crimée, 44; Drouyn de Lhuys to Walewski, June 12, 1853, in Mange, Near Eastern Policy, 31; Cowley to Stratford de Redcliffe, Paris, June 29, 1853, in PRO, FO, 519, 210.

The position of Russia is such that she must either accept or refuse the right of the Five Powers to interfere under the treaty of 1841 for the defense and protection of the integrity and independence of Turkey.

If Russia accepts our interpretations of our rights under that treaty a valuable result will have been obtained. If she refuses it, a warning will be given to Europe of the necessity of insisting on some more obligatory act. This might consist of a treaty by which the Five Powers would bind themselves to respect and maintain the integrity of the Ottoman Empire and the independence of its Government, to refer all points of difference which may arise between them and Turkey to the arbitration of a conference, and in the event of a dissolution of the Turkish Empire from internal causes, to abjure all schemes of individual benefit.

Thus one of the results of the Crimean War, the admission of Turkey to the European concert, was anticipated by French diplomacy before the war began. What Bourqueney and Drouyn de Lhuys wanted in the summer of 1853 was a conference to meet at Vienna to impose a settlement on both sides.[5]

The first Vienna conference began on June 22. It was, in effect, a series of meetings of the French, British, and Prussian ambassadors under the chairmanship of Count Karl Ferdinand von Buol-Schauenstein, the Austrian foreign minister. The Russian ambassador, although invited, did not attend. The conference had been brought about by pressure from Paris, and its result, the Vienna Note (July 31), was written by Drouyn de Lhuys after consultation with Napoleon. Had this proposed solution, whose core was the statement that the Porte would not alter the condition of the Christians in his empire without previous understanding with the governments of France and Russia, been accepted, Napoleon would have secured for the Western powers an effective check on Russian ambitions without seeming to have imposed a European arbitration upon the czar. And yet at the same time he would have made France in this matter the official spokesman for "Europe." The note was, in this sense, a compromise between Buol's desire to avoid any appearance of coercion and Napoleon's growing preference for imposing a settlement on both Russia and Turkey through the European concert. Russia accepted the Vienna Note at the beginning of August. On the nineteenth the Turkish government, however, encouraged by Stratford de Redcliffe,

5. Cowley to Clarendon, Paris, private, July 7, 1853, in PRO, FO, 519, 211:10–12; Cowley to Clarendon, Paris, July 6, 1853, in PRO, FO, 519, 2:75, no. 510.

offered amendments that, under the circumstances, amounted to a rejection.[6]

Certainly that rejection angered the emperor and was the cause of the recall from Constantinople of Edouard De la Cour, whom Napoleon had called *un imbécile* for his part in the affair. It was on a French initiative that the conference, which Charles de Mazade in *Revue des deux mondes* (August 31) referred to as "une sorte de haute médiation de l'Europe," remained in session; and France showed a far greater willingness than Britain to cooperate with Buol in finding a formula for resuscitating the Vienna Note. Apparently Cowley was not unduly alarmist in his warnings that the French might join Austria in using the note to coerce Turkey. Such coercion had always been implicit in French policy, which had remained fairly consistent since the eruption of the crisis. The Eastern question was to be considered a European one, and "Europe" would make peace between the contending parties. Whatever the advantages to France of separating Austria from Russia or of organizing an anti-Russian coalition, Paris had made neither of these objectives its principal aim. While London regarded the concert with suspicion and Vienna saw it as a state of mind, French policy envisaged the concert of Europe as a mechanism, a conference system, through which could be found the formula that would restore peace and stability, if necessary by arbitration. But in September, 1853, a number of factors combined to limit the constraint that could be exerted upon the Porte. British and French public opinion would probably have rebelled against the appearance of coercion in view of Russian behavior. Moreover, it could be argued that Russian actions (Menshikov's ultimatum, the occupation of the Danubian Principalities in June) had already destroyed the concert as an atmosphere of mutual restraint and, to a certain extent, of trust, and that British opposition to Austrian efforts to turn the clock back was therefore neither vindictive nor ill-advised but, rather, clear-sighted and realistic. There was, besides, the matter of the "violent interpretation" of the Vienna Note offered in Russia's rejection of the Turkish amendments (September 7), although this was probably not decisive. In the new circumstances, coercion of Turkey could well have proved counterproductive. At any rate, Napoleon had no intention of breaking with his newly acquired British ally. He therefore abandoned

6. La Gorce, *Histoire du Second Empire*, I, 187; Spencer, "Drouyn de Lhuys," 46–47; Schroeder, *Austria, Great Britain, and the Crimean War*, 57.

the Vienna Note, at least for the time being, and on September 22, 1853, the Vienna conference was suspended. Several days later, however, Buol, who had persuaded Nicholas to disavow his foreign minister's interpretation of the note, proposed (the Buol project) that the czar's declaration be presented to the Vienna conference, guaranteed collectively by the four powers, and transmitted to the Porte, who would then accept the Vienna Note as containing nothing subversive of Turkey's sovereign rights. Napoleon was amenable to the proposal, despite Drouyn de Lhuys' lack of enthusiasm, but once again yielded in deference to London.[7]

But if the concert were not to coerce Turkey, then it must abdicate, become a coalition against Russia, or impose a settlement upon *both* the Russians and the Turks. It was that last policy for which the French emperor opted. The tightening entente with Britain and the moving of the fleets to Constantinople, which followed the suspension of the conference, could be seen as French moves to gain a position from which arbitration would be possible. But the arbitration was to be that of Europe and not of the sea powers alone. Napoleon, whose advice was that Britain and France should watch for any favorable opportunity to bring about a reconciliation between Russia and Turkey, even after the outbreak of war between those two powers in October, remained adamant that the Eastern question should be kept a European one.[8]

In November, Napoleon suddenly revealed his mind to Cowley. Matters had become so embroiled, he declared, that he was at his wits' end, but an idea *had* occurred to him, although he had not yet developed it. Britain and France should declare "that a state of things dangerous to the tranquillity and menacing the prosperity of Europe, could not be allowed to continue, and that they proclaimed their policy to be peace, and the integrity of the Turkish Empire and the independence of its Government." The other powers should then be invited to adhere to this declaration, thus "forcing them as it were to speak out." Then a note should be drawn up and offered to the bellig-

---

7. Cowley to Clarendon, Dieppe, private, August 28, September 2, 1853, both in PRO, FO, 519, 211:73–79, 87; Cowley to Stratford de Redcliffe, Compiègne, private, October 26, 1853, in PRO, FO, 519, 211:169–71; Schroeder, *Austria, Great Britain, and the Crimean War*, 41–42, 69–70, 72, 79–80; Cowley to Clarendon, Paris, October 4, 1853, in PRO, FO, 519, 2:207–211, no. 739; Spencer, "Drouyn de Lhuys," 50–51.

8. Cowley to Clarendon, Chantilly, private, October 16, 1853, in PRO, FO, 519, 211:146; Cowley to Clarendon, Paris, private, October 11, 1853, in PRO, FO, 519, 211:140–42.

crent parties "as a fair and honorable solution of their quarrel." Moreover, it should be made clear "that either party refusing it would find
the Powers arrayed against them." When Cowley argued for a "less
warlike" course, for example, a six-power conference at which the
belligerents would meet under the mediation of the four nonbelligerent great powers (in fact, would be constrained to meet), Napoleon replied that "such a course he thought would do as well."[9]

The idea of a six-power conference was in the air. Buol wanted to
revive the Vienna conference and invite Russian and Turkish plenipotentiaries to attend. Cowley and Clarendon were thinking in terms of
a meeting at London; Berlin was hinting at a conference to meet in
Germany; but Paris was also a possible site. It was therefore logical
that, in mid-November, Drouyn de Lhuys should bring together Napoleon's suggested declaration by Europe and the thought of a six-power
conference. At the end of October he had already suggested to Hübner
that the belligerents should send representatives to Vienna, there to
negotiate "au sein de la conférence." It was clear to him, he now told
Cowley, that little more could be achieved at Vienna and that the only
hope lay in a six-power conference. If it failed, however, the conference should be followed "by a declaration on the part of the four
Powers that they bound themselves whatever might be the result of
the contest now going on in the East, to prevent by every means at
their disposal the aggrandisement of either of the Belligerent Powers."
This was a faint echo of the plan that Napoleon had earlier proposed
to Cowley but was linked to the idea of a conference, as the ambassador had suggested at the time. Under Napoleon's orders Drouyn de
Lhuys continued to stress this theme: Europe must make clear to
both Turkey and Russia that it "will not permit either party to alter
permanently the status quo of Europe." And he urged a renewal of the
Vienna conference for the purpose of requesting the Turks to negotiate under mediation of the four nonbelligerent great powers. The result was the protocol of December 5, a collective note drafted by the
four powers meeting at Vienna and sent to Constantinople, requesting that the Porte let Russia know the conditions on which Turkey
would treat, that the Porte name a plenipotentiary and choose a neutral meeting place, and that the negotiations take place in the presence of the great powers. It was a far cry from the declaration by Eu-

9. Cowley to Clarendon, Paris, private, November 11, 1853, in PRO, FO, 519,
211:199.

rope to Russia and Turkey, which Napoleon had not yet abandoned.[10] But already, at Sinope on November 30, the irrevocable step toward a European war had been taken.

Russia's action in sinking a Turkish troop convoy almost under the guns of the Western maritime powers piqued British and French military honor at its most sensitive point and presumably ended any chance that the creaking concert machinery could avert a war. Yet, on January 29, 1854, in a letter to the czar, Napoleon made a final bid for peace. He had for some time been urging on the reluctant British a plan involving direct negotiations between Russia and Turkey. In his letter, the French emperor clearly posed the question of "national dignity" raised by the Sinope incident, and presented the alternative of a definite understanding or a decisive rupture. Hoping for the former, he suggested an armistice, withdrawal of belligerent forces, and a direct Russo-Turkish negotiation, the results of which would be submitted to a conference of the four nonbelligerent great powers. As Drouyn de Lhuys explained to Cowley, it would be shocking if war were to come over the *form* of negotiations. Russia had objected to mediation by a conference, so let Russian and Turkish plenipotentiaries meet to negotiate a peace treaty that would have force only when approved by the conference. Napoleon had never intended, Drouyn de Lhuys added, that Russian and Turk should meet secretly or privately. "H.M. had always maintained that the question at issue . . . was of European interest and could not be settled without the sanction of the Great Cabinets of Europe. The word direct had only been used to facilitate the commencement of negotiations."[11]

Was the letter sincere? Napoleon, aware of antiwar opinion in France, always sensitive to Europe's apprehensions concerning his name, might have hoped to wash his hands of responsibility by a last apparent peacemaking effort. Perhaps this explains his action in publishing the communication before the czar's answer was received. Cowley, however, who found the letter unpleasant in its "mixture of fanfaronade and begging for peace," was convinced that the emperor

---

10. Count Joseph Alexander von Hübner to Count Karl Ferdinand von Buol-Schauenstein, Paris, private, November 4, 1853, in Hübner, *Neuf ans*, I, 162–63; Cowley to Clarendon, Paris, private, November 13, 18, 30, 1853, all in PRO, FO, 519, 211: 204–205, 214, 216–17.

11. Napoleon III to Nicholas I, Tuileries, January 29, 1854, in *La politique impériale*, 183–88; Cowley to Clarendon, Paris, private, February 19, 1854, in PRO, FO, 519, 2:513–14, no. 182.

sincerely hoped for good results. And Count Maximilian Hatzfeldt, the Prussian minister to France, encountering Napoleon at a ball, gained the same impression. When he asked the emperor what he would do if Nicholas accepted and the Turks refused, the reply was "Let the Emperor make proposals that I think ought to be accepted and I will take care of the Turks." But what about Britain? "Ah! ba! L'Angleterre fera ce que je voudrai." Later, Queen Victoria was informed that the czar's rejection of the French proposal disappointed Napoleon extremely.[12]

At any rate, the overture failed. Russia, the czar replied, would be in 1854 what it had been in 1812. Thus, for Napoleon, the peace efforts of almost a year, which had begun with support for a conference of the 1841 signatories, ended with an appeal for yet another variety of conference solution. If after forty years the concert of Europe had been sufficiently disrupted to permit a major European war, the fault does not seem to have been his. With considerable consistency he had urged that Europe-in-conference impose a settlement, if necessary, upon Turkey and Russia. But Napoleon would not break with Britain, whose cooperation was, at any rate, necessary to a successful arbitration. In the end, British distrust of both Austria and Russia, Austrian determination to avoid confrontation, and Nicholas' imperious character left no alternative for France but a choice between Britain and Russia. On March 27 and 28, 1854, the maritime powers declared war on the Russian Empire. But the beginning of hostilities did not mean unemployment for the concert machinery. For this there were several reasons: the force of habit, perhaps, but, more important, the desire of France and Britain to mobilize Europe or, as Mazade in *Revue des deux mondes* (January 31) termed it, "le patriotisme européen" against Russia and in this way to involve Austria. The best way of limiting the war, Napoleon told Cowley, and of putting an end to it as quickly as possible "would be to let the Emperor of Russia understand that his aggressive policy would be resisted by all Europe."[13] In that sense, appeals to the concert from 1854 until 1856 were spurious. But there

12. Case, *French Opinion on War and Diplomacy*, 25; Cowley to Clarendon, Paris, private, January 26, 27, February 1, 1854, all in PRO, FO, 519, 212:74, 77, 83; Victoria to Leopold I, Buckingham Palace, February 21, 1854, in *Victoria Letters, 1837–1861*, III, 14. The official Russian diplomatic study of the war concluded: "It seems positive that he [Napoleon] expected great results from the letter, and that he was much hurt at the failure of this personal effort at conciliation" (Jomini, *Diplomatic Study on the Crimean War*, I, 283–84).

13. Cowley to Clarendon, Paris, private, March 17, 1854, in PRO, FO, 519, 212:206.

was another side to the question. Both Napoleon and the Austrian government had at one level of their plans the intention of achieving through the concert of Europe diametrically opposed schemes for Europe. Vienna would use the concert machinery to end the war without victors—in other words, to restore as closely as possible the old system, whose chief function had been preservation of the status quo. Napoleon would end the war in such a way as to give to the European concert a new vocation, that of anticipating by timely reforms the problems that might lead to future conflict. The difficulty is in disentangling this aspect of his thought from the other concerns that influenced him: the necessity to win the war quickly, the wish to preserve the British alliance, and the political imperative of satisfying French public opinion or, at the very least, of managing it.

At first, although Cowley had some doubts about him, fearing that he "would not be disinclined" to an armistice and a congress, Napoleon held fast against a return to the conference table. Drouyn de Lhuys made short shrift of a Prussian suggestion that the five-power conference be reconstituted at Berlin "to settle the guarantees which shall be given by the Porte for the amelioration of the state of its Christian subjects." He showed equal displeasure at the Austrian attempt to secure a congress in connection with the ultimatum that Vienna sent to Saint Petersburg on June 3, 1854, requiring a Russian withdrawal from the Danube. And when Buol, at the beginning of July, again requested the renewal of the Vienna conference, Drouyn de Lhuys replied that he was against a meeting of the conference at the present moment. Of course, negotiations continued. On August 8, 1854, an exchange of notes among the British, French, and Austrian governments enunciated the Four Points upon which a settlement could be based: the Russian protectorate of the Principalities to be replaced by a European guarantee; navigation of the Danube to be "freed"; the Straits convention of 1841 to be revised "in the interests of the Balance of Power in Europe"; a European protectorate of Ottoman Christians to replace that of Russia. But when Buol urged a congress of Britain, France, Prussia, and Austria, at which the Porte should also be represented, both London and Paris declined. "Both the Emperor and Drouyn," wrote Cowley on September 19, "are tired of the word conference and think that a sort of ridicule attaches to it, and this is one of the main reasons for their dislike of the new Austrian proposal." And yet, by October, Drouyn de Lhuys was prepared to accept a renewal of the Vienna conference to discuss problems related to the Danubian Principalities and to the third of the Four Points. This London rejected, but on French insistence a conference met at Vienna from November to deal with the Principalities.[14] And it was on the insistence of Napoleon that the British government with great reluctance accepted the alliance of December 2, 1854, with Austria and, consequently, a conference.[15]

In signing this treaty, Austria, France, and Britain agreed to enter into peace negotiations with Russia if the latter unconditionally accepted the Four Points as the basis of negotiations. And, as Napoleon knew before the signing, Russia would do so (and did, on November 29). Buol, almost immediately afterward, proposed the reopening of the Vienna conference. At first the French emperor seems to have seen the conference purely as a vestibule through which Austria might be led to war. He was willing, he wrote Francis Joseph, to give full powers to Bourqueney to negotiate, but he would rather send 200,000 soldiers to help in a common war against Russia. That he "had absolutely no hope of success for the peace negotiations" was something Hübner professed never to have doubted; and through January, 1855, there is no hint of any basis for a contrary opinion, in the reports of either Hübner or Cowley.[16] At any rate, the conference should have been as short and sharp as any soldier could have wished. While the third point had been left deliberately vague in the statement agreed with Austria, London and Paris had secretly negotiated a harsh interpretation. Sebastopol and, if possible, the other Russian fortresses on the eastern coast of the Black Sea were to be demolished, and Russia was to be bound by treaty not to reestablish them or to build new ones or to maintain more than four warships in the Black Sea—the same number that would be permitted to other powers, including

14. Cowley to Clarendon, Paris, private, June 12, 1854, in PRO, FO, 519, 213:85; Cowley to Clarendon, Paris, April 5, 1854, in PRO, FO, 519, 3:129–30, no. 443; Hübner, *Neuf ans*, I, 245, 246, journal entries of June 7, 8, 1854; Cowley to Clarendon, Paris, private, July 26, 1854, in PRO, FO, 519, 213:194; Cowley to Clarendon, Paris, September 19, 1854, in PRO, FO, 519, 214:45–46; Schroeder, *Austria, Great Britain, and the Crimean War*, 216–17.

15. "Nous allons maintenant signer un traité d'alliance," Palmerston told Hübner; "ce sera un enfant mort-né. Si nous nous y prêtons, c'est à notre corps défendant et en cédant aux instances de l'empereur Napoléon" (Hübner, *Neuf ans*, I, 282, journal entry of November 27, 1854). See also Cowley to Clarendon, Paris, private, November 19, 1854, in PRO, FO, 519, 214:216–20.

16. Hübner, *Neuf ans*, I, 278–79, 289, 307, journal entries of November 18, December 22, 1854, January 21, 1855; Napoleon III to Francis Joseph, December 20, 1854, in Puryear, *England, Russia, and the Straits Question*, 365 n.; Cowley to Clarendon, Paris, private, January 21, 1855, PRO, FO, 519, 215:77.

Turkey. This interpretation could hardly have been accepted by Russia while Sebastopol stood, and the Austrian government would never make such terms under such circumstances a casus belli.

And then, quite abruptly in February, a note of uncertainty appeared. Napoleon, wrote Hübner, "admits that it is not possible to demand that Russia demolish the Sebastopol fortifications or reduce the number of her warships in the Black Sea, so long as Sebastopol has not been taken." Again, on March 12, after their interview: "The Emperor Napoleon admits that the peace negotiations . . . can lead to peace. He is accustoming himself to the idea that *peace is possible without being preceded by the seizure of Sebastopol*." Cowley, beginning to think that peace might come out of the Vienna conference after all, blamed it on the "usual versatility" of the French, frustrated by the stalemate at Sebastopol.[17]

To what extent had Napoleon's attitude toward the conference changed, and why? When we consider Vienna's attitude, the state of French public opinion, the emperor's devotion to French military honor, and his commitment to the English alliance, it appears unlikely that Napoleon intended either a further trick in the game of catching Austria or an acceptance of whatever peace terms he could get from the conference. Probably the best explanation is to be found in the analysis by Gavin Henderson. For the French emperor, the taking of Sebastopol, under siege by the allies since September, 1854, had become an obsession; and yet, could it be done? Would French public opinion tolerate an indefinitely prolonged war? In mid-February it was an open secret that Napoleon intended to go in person to the Crimea to lead the allied forces and perhaps to organize a decisive attack. What more logical, then, than to keep the Vienna conference in session, either to salvage the best possible terms from failure or to achieve much better ones from victory?[18] All of this is speculation. The facts are that Napoleon's policy had led to the acceptance of the conference despite British opposition; that his decision to go to the Crimea greatly increased the possibility that peace might come from the meeting (if for no other reason than the panic it created in the ranks of the Bonapartists, fearing what might happen in the master's

17. Hübner, *Neuf ans*, I, 309, 315–16, journal entries of February 5, March 12, 1855; Cowley to John Hobart Caradoc Howden, Paris, March 17, 1855, in PRO, FO, 519, 215:217.

18. Henderson, *Crimean War Diplomacy*, 211; Case, *French Opinion on War and Diplomacy*, 32.

absence); and that, in the end, as we shall see, he proved willing to consider—and almost to accept—the proposed compromise settlement that eventually emerged from the negotiations at Vienna.

Russell, designated by the cabinet to represent Britain, arrived in Vienna on March 4. The conference had been in session since January 7, when Prince Alexander Gorchakov, Russian ambassador to Austria, had accepted the Four Points in principle, an act that Mazade in *Revue des deux mondes* (January 14) called "homage rendered by Russia to the ascendancy of Europe." Russell brought with him instructions that were seemingly ironclad (perhaps because he was more pacific than his cabinet colleagues): strict limitation of Russian naval strength in the Black Sea and acceptance by Russia of the allied interpretation of the third point without change—or negotiations were to be broken off. On March 7, at a preliminary meeting, Buol agreed to bring forward limitation of Russian naval power in the Black Sea as a solution of the third point, and the conference began in earnest on the fifteenth. Prussia, despite its own wishes and those of Saint Petersburg, was absent, since the Western powers insisted that "only those should participate in the peace who would take part in the war," and Berlin had not adhered to the treaty of December 2.[19] Thus the Vienna meetings were to be strictly limited in scope; their purpose was peacemaking within terms already sketched and in large part defined. But almost at once the negotiations assumed a wider range than had been intended, and for this, Paris was mostly responsible.

Aware by the third week of March that Austria would not make Russia's rejection of limitation a casus belli, and that his master would not go to the Crimea if peace were to result from the Vienna talks, Drouyn de Lhuys had become much more amenable to the idea that peace might after all emerge from the conference. He had persuaded Napoleon to accept as an alternative to limitation the idea of neutralization; that is, the exclusion of *all* vessels of war from the Black Sea. He then requested Hübner to suggest to the emperor that he, Drouyn de Lhuys, should go to Vienna; Napoleon, much to Cowley's disgust, agreed. The best that the British could obtain was that Drouyn de Lhuys should first visit London, which he did on March 30. There, if memorandums had been contracts, the French foreign minister would have been neatly bound. Russia must accept either

19. Puryear, *England, Russia, and the Straits Question*, 372–74; Drouyn de Lhuys to Baron François Adolphe de Bourqueney, Paris, January 20, 1855, in Harcourt, *Quatre ministères*, 104.

limitation or neutralization; otherwise the negotiations would be broken off. In the event, however, they were not. Buol having proved unwilling to make Russian rejection of either neutralization or limitation a casus belli, Russell and Drouyn de Lhuys declared their instructions exhausted. In a last effort to achieve a peace settlement, however, they worked out with Buol a compromise plan termed "counterpoise." Russian naval strength in the Black Sea would be limited to what then existed while Britain, France, and Austria could each have two frigates at Constantinople. If Russia moved to increase its strength, Britain and France could each send into the Black Sea a force half as large as the Russian, and if Russian naval strength should reach the level of 1853, that would be a casus belli for Austria as well as for the two maritime powers. Russell and Drouyn de Lhuys were not, of course, empowered to accept the counterpoise proposal but they agreed to recommend it to their governments.[20] And so, Napoleon had to decide. By his actions he had made the Vienna conference possible; he had tolerated there far more serious negotiation than his British allies liked. Would he now accept, as a result of those negotiations, a solution that in London was already anathema, a solution that would be far short of the professed aims of the war and very nearly an affront to the honor of the French army? That he did not, in the end, accept the counterpoise proposal is hardly surprising. That the issue was for some time in doubt is of obvious interest to any discussion of Napoleon's attitude toward the concert of Europe. Certainly other factors played their part; the French emperor's aversion to war, his concern for the political implications in France of a continuation of the conflict. But this was also the first of many times when Napoleon would show a willingness to accept from conference diplomacy settlements considerably inferior to those he had sought.

Napoleon had been one day in Britain, by invitation of a government eager to talk him out of his projected Crimean adventure, when word arrived on April 17 of the counterpoise plan. Until this moment he had left the negotiations in Drouyn de Lhuys' hands: "All that you have said and done is so good that I have no new instructions to give you." But now, if we are to believe Queen Victoria's words, the em-

---

20. Hübner, *Neuf ans*, I, 317, journal entry of March 25, 1855; Cowley to Clarendon, Paris, private, March 27, 1855, in PRO, FO, 519, 215:247; Henderson, *Crimean War Diplomacy*, 49–50; Drouyn de Lhuys to Napoleon III, April 1, 1855, in Harcourt, *Quatres ministères*, 113–22; L. Thouvenel (ed.), *Pages de l'histoire du Second Empire*, 66–69; Schroeder, *Austria, Great Britain, and the Crimean War*, 270–72.

peror condemned "the absurd notion of 'le chiffre de la flotte' remaining the same." Back in Paris, he continued adamant: "If Austria does not consent to limit the Russian naval power, break off negotiations. All the rest would be a delusion. Summon Austria to execute the treaty of 2 December and return immediately." Instead, Drouyn de Lhuys, claiming a change had been made in the Austrian proposal (it was Buol's agreeing that a casus belli would be attainment of, not the exceeding of, Russian Black Sea naval strength of 1853), persuaded his master to withhold final judgment until he, Drouyn de Lhuys, had returned from Vienna. Thouvenel, temporarily in charge of the Foreign Ministry, found the emperor resolved not to reach a definitive decision before the foreign minister's return, but clearly disposed to reject the Austrian offer. On May 1, after a two-and-one-half-hour conversation with Drouyn de Lhuys, Napoleon accepted a modified form of counterpoise, Drouyn de Lhuys being confident that Austria would agree to accept as a casus belli Russia's adding "excessively" to the immediate postwar strength of its Black Sea fleet.[21]

It lasted less than four days. The repugnance felt by London toward counterpoise, the influence at Paris of Cowley, and the opinion advanced by the minister of war, Marshal Jean Baptiste Vaillant, on behalf of the French army, which, he argued, would regard such a peace as dishonorable, proved decisive. At length Napoleon declared, in Cowley's words, "that he would accept nothing but limitation—an allied fleet equal to that of the Russians and Consuls—and he added that he must in his conscience declare that he should think such a peace bad enough." This time his decision was final. But it had been a very close thing. The easy explanation of the drama would be the fatuous one, that Napoleon's opinion was always that of the last person with whom he had spoken. In fact, however, his opinion tended to be singularly unaffected by others. A much simpler explanation is that, having been responsible for the meeting of a peace conference, Napoleon would have accepted any practicable solution coming out of it. He did not accept even a solution that he would have had every right

21. Napoleon III to Drouyn de Lhuys, Paris, telegram, April 15, 1855, in Harcourt, *Quatres ministères*, 141; Martin, *The Life of His Royal Highness, the Prince Consort,* III, 204; Napoleon III to Drouyn de Lhuys, Paris, telegram, April 23, 1855, in Spencer, "Drouyn de Lhuys," 106; Schroeder, *Austria, Great Britain, and the Crimean War,* 273; Thouvenel to Walewski, Paris, April 27, 1855, in L. Thouvenel (ed.), *Pages de l'histoire du Second Empire,* 90–96; Cowley to Clarendon, Paris, May 1, 1855, in Spencer, "Drouyn de Lhuys," 114.

to consider unreasonable, because marshaled against it were those two considerations that at this time he could not ignore—the wishes of his British ally and the feelings of the French army—and that weighed even more heavily, perhaps, in view of the small likelihood that Vienna could be persuaded to accept the proposed modification of counterpoise. And so, Drouyn de Lhuys resigned, and the French ambassador at London, Walewski, accepted appointment as his successor. In spite of considerable suspicion on Cowley's part that Napoleon, and especially Walewski, harbored a desire to resume conference negotiations, the Vienna conference was broken off at the meeting of June 4, much to the delight, if we are to believe the ambassador, of Napoleon. But exhilaration was hardly the imperial state of mind. "The Emperor . . . is dreadfully out of spirits about it all," Cowley reported some days later. "I never saw him so low, and the Empress told me the other day that since she had known him, she had never seen him so downhearted." The trouble, of course, was Sebastopol. If peace could not be made until French military honor had been assured, then the fall of the beleaguered port was the key to everything. "The fact is," the British ambassador assured his government, "his whole thoughts are concentrated on the Crimea and the necessity of taking Sebastopol."[22]

22. Cowley to Clarendon, Paris, private, May 4, 21, 1855, both in PRO, FO, 519, 216:66–67, 103; Cowley to Clarendon, Paris, June 6, 15, 1855, both in PRO, FO, 519, 216:151, 172; Cowley to Clarendon, Paris, private, August 5, 1855, in PRO, FO, 519, 216:277.

CHAPTER 3

Rêve Napoléonienne
1855

Not only the siege of Sebastopol occupied Napoleon's thoughts, however. In March, 1854, during a conversation with Ernest II, duke of Saxe-Coburg-Gotha, he had asserted that "when the war with Russia had resulted satisfactorily, a European Peace Congress would be absolutely necessary, to solve all the questions that had not been completely decided at the Vienna Congress, and to give the nations a permanent peace at last." In short, the opportunity afforded by the war must be used "pour régler la carte de l'Europe." And he even drafted a letter, intended for the Prussian king, Frederick William IV, promising that "Europe would soon see the monarchs united in congress, fixing the bases of the peace and forming among themselves an unbreakable bond." Hübner noted the same line of thought two months later in an interview with Napoleon, commenting: "These projects for remaking the map of Europe, which I often encounter at the back of the emperor's thoughts, can scarcely be pleasing to Vienna or Berlin or London." Perhaps, however, Napoleon thought he had reason to hope for British support in a wider war. In a memorandum of March 19, 1854, Palmerston had sketched his beau ideal for the results of the war that was to begin: the Åland Islands and Finland restored to Sweden; some Russian Baltic provinces given to Prussia; Wallachia and Moldavia to Austria; Lombardy and Venetia separated from the Austrian Empire; and a "substantive Kingdom of Poland reestablished as a barrier between Germany and Russia." The French emperor was not ignorant of Palmerston's attitude; in fact, he took pains at the end of 1854 to express to Cowley his agreement with it, adding a wish to see the Crimea restored to Turkey and Italy made independent.[1]

---

1. Ernest II, *Memoirs*, III, 66–69; Hübner, *Neuf ans*, I, 241, journal entry of May 21, 1854; Palmerston's memorandum is in Gooch (ed.), *The Later Correspondence of Lord*

Throughout 1854 and into 1855, Napoleon was tempted by the thought of a revolutionary war for which Turkey would foot the bill. Vitzthum was convinced that his aim was revision, and the emperor did nothing to discourage such an interpretation. He was eager, he told Cowley in early 1855, to enlist the support of as much of Europe as possible in the war against Russia. When the ambassador observed that the smaller states would hardly join the war without compensation, the result was "a fresh remaniement of the Map of Europe." Napoleon even suggested that Britain might take Sinope and make a new Gibraltar of it. Italy was another focus of Napoleon's musings on this theme. "You mention," Cowley wrote to Clarendon in November, 1853, "a plan of the Emperor's to give Moldavia and Wallachia to Austria. . . . His Majesty has more than once alluded to the idea . . . but I don't think that he has any fixed project in relation to it." Perhaps not, but in an earlier conversation with the British ambassador, Napoleon had certainly been explicit, arguing the advantages of giving Moldavia and Wallachia to Austria, which, in return, would grant independence to Lombardy. And later, in the March, 1854, interview with Ernest II, he reiterated the thought. Small wonder that Palmerston's partition speculations of that same month struck a responsive chord! By July, Cowley could report: "The Emperor from the beginning of this Eastern Question has always had what he calls 'his dream' viz. that Austria should give up her Italian provinces and receive the Principalities in exchange, the Turks being indemnified in Asia Minor."[2]

But, especially, there was the question of Poland. Napoleon had emphasized the problem in his conversation with Duke Ernest, and he returned to it frequently thereafter. On April 13, 1854, he had received Prince Adam Czartoryski, assuring the Polish leader of his sincere desire to restore Poland, beginning with a reconstitution of the Duchy of Warsaw. On several other occasions the emperor had conversations with Czartoryski in which he reaffirmed his sympathy for Poland, although clearly subordinating it to the exigencies of the war and the interests of France. Similarly, in conversations with Hübner, Prince Albert, and Cowley, he repeated the refrain of a restored Duchy

---

John Russell, II, 160–61; Cowley to Clarendon, Paris, private, December 12, 1854, in PRO, FO, 519, 214:278–79.

2. "Prospects and programme of the Second French Empire," November 22, 1854, in Vitzthum, St. Petersburg and London, I, 117–39; Cowley to Clarendon, Paris, private, February 2, 1855, in PRO, FO, 519, 215:109–110; Sencourt, Napoléon III, un précurseur, 141; Cowley to Clarendon, Paris, private, November 30, August 22, 1853, both in PRO, FO, 519, 211:218, 69; Cowley to Stratford de Redcliffe, Paris, July 23, 1854, in PRO, FO, 519, 213:183.

of Warsaw. "Another subject on which the Emperor spoke," wrote Cowley in October, 1854, "and which I have reason to think is now a favorite idea with him, is the restoration of the Kingdom of Poland." When Napoleon asked whether the British government would object, the ambassador replied that he was cerain that London would not make such a restoration an object of the war but would be glad if it resulted from the conflict. The emperor seemed satisfied and went on to say that he was trying to persuade Hübner "that the best thing that could happen to Austria and Germany would be to have a Kingdom of Poland established between them and Russia." When preparations for the second Vienna conference were under way in March, 1855, the French government suggested to London that one of the *conditions particulières* to be communicated to Russia should be the restoration in Poland of the regime of the 1815 treaties. Although London rejected the proposal as impolitic and impractical, Clarendon admitted that "it could become admissible and even very desirable in another circumstance," and as late as July, 1855, Napoleon mentioned the matter in a speech to the French Legislative Body. Walewski then persuaded him, presumably with some difficulty, to agree not to talk any more about it.[3]

Two months later, on September 8, 1855, the key defenses of Sebastopol fell, in an assault in which French divisions played the major role. Military honor was secured; French prestige was raised to new heights; and the earlier identification of the French army by Charles de Mazade in *Revue des deux mondes* (March 31) as the "heroic instrument of the defense of Europe" seemed justified. "Unless," wrote Walewski to Napoleon, "with the idea of remaking the map of Europe— and I do not think that such is the thought of Your Majesty—we have nothing to gain by prolonging the war." Apparently, however, the foreign minister was not particularly adept at reading his master's mind. "In case Your Majesty should persist," he wrote again a few days later, "in the idea of securing the inclusion of Poland in the negotiations whose object will be the re-establishment of peace I have had a dispatch prepared which argues with evidence our right to require at least the reconstitution of the Kingdom of Poland as established by

3. Henderson, *Crimean War Diplomacy*, 15–32; Kukiel, *Czartoryski and European Unity*, 285, 287–88, 294–98; Hallberg, *Franz Joseph and Napoleon III*, 81; Cowley to Clarendon, Paris, private, October 6, 1854, in PRO, FO, 519, 214:96–97; Drouyn de Lhuys to Walewski, Paris, March 26, 1855, in BFSP, XLVI, 809–811; Walewski to Drouyn de Lhuys, London, March 28, 1855, in BFSP, XLVI, 811–12; Bernardy, "Un fils de Napoléon," 393–94.

the treaty of Vienna." The evidence is, however, that Napoleon's ambitions went even further than this. So it seemed to Duke Ernest, who again talked with him in September. A peace concluded now, the emperor observed, "would have nothing but the character of a great truce."

> Greater satisfaction could only be felt, not merely by the two Powers of the West, who, after all, did not stand alone in the *Concert Européen*, but by all the other States, if the conclusion of peace were at the same time to bring about a solution of those questions which had either been badly settled at the conference of Vienna, or which had arisen since then.
>
> Poland, Italy, etc., said the Emperor, belong to these open questions.
>
> The Emperor observed that interest ought to be enlisted for the idea of a great Peace Congress: he told me straight out, that I might speak of this with the King of Prussia, as being an idea which he had communicated to me.
>
> The Emperor thinks of a congress, at which all the great and small sovereigns would have to appear in person. . . . The Emperor then expounded his general political views, saying that it was an impossibility, in our time, to carry on great wars, and make great political arrangements, which were opposed to the interests of the nations. The voice of the nations would always break through again, and undo everything that had been done contrary to their "interests."[4]

Cowley understood the evolution that was taking place in Napoleon's thinking. No one could doubt that, whatever the emperor's personal opinion, France was weary of the war, which had cost almost 100,000 French lives, and wanted peace. "It cannot be denied," Cowley wrote, "that there is a great change in the Emperor's mind respecting this war. . . . The results which we prescribed to ourselves . . . he looks upon as attained by the capture of Sebastopol, to be made binding and lasting by the conditions imposed whenever peace is signed." The tack that Napoleon had resolved to take was soon evident to the ambassador. "It is clear to me," he wrote, "both from what fell from the Emperor in my conversation with him the other day, as from what I glean from other persons who have seen him, that H.M. is fast coming to the conviction, that public opinion in France will not support him much longer in this war, and that if it is to go on its object, if not its seat must be changed." What Napoleon had told the ambassador was that the results of the war, as contemplated by Buol, would be

---

4. Walewski to Napoleon III, September 11, 14, 1855, in Bernardy, "Un fils de Napoléon," 394; Ernest II, *Memoirs*, III, 194–95.

small in comparison with the efforts made and that "among the dreams
which crossed his imagination, for he admitted they were but dreams,
was the possibility of saying to Europe that events had clearly proved
that the balance of the power of Europe was neither established nor
could it be maintained under the Treaties of 1815, and that it was necessary to call a congress in order to resettle the map." When Cowley
offered objections, the emperor said that he thought they could be
overcome by an agreement of France and Britain with Austria and
Prussia. The Englishman was convinced that the scheme was mad,
but concluded: "I only mention this to show what now occupies the
Emperor's thoughts, namely by what means he can satisfy France if
the war is to be prolonged. . . . Unfortunately when the Emperor once
gets an idea into his head, he broods upon it, until all the difficulties
disappear to his imagination."[5]

On November 22, Napoleon, who had already initiated informal direct talks with Russia and reached agreement with Austria concerning bases on which the war could be ended, presented a clear choice to
his ally. In a letter to Queen Victoria he listed three courses of action:
a limited defensive war of attrition, peace negotiations on the basis of
the Four Points with Austria as an ally, or "an appeal to all the nationalities, the re-establishment of Poland, the independence of Finland, of Hungary, of Circassia." Clearly his own preference was for the
second alternative, but he concluded: "If the government of Your Majesty should say that the conditions of the peace ought to be quite different, that our honor and our interests require a reshaping of the map
of Europe, that Europe will not be free so long as Poland has not been
restored, the Crimea given to Turkey, and Finland to Sweden, I would
understand a policy which would have something of grandeur and
which would put the results to be achieved at a level with the sacrifices to be made." Is it worth discussing whether this proposal was
sincere? Surely Napoleon had no real expectation that Britain would
follow him into such a war. The offer, then, could only lead to negotiations and peace. France wanted peace; therefore the Napoleonic
dream was no more than a ruse to achieve an end to an unpopular war.
And yet, it seems equally clear that, could London have shared his
dream, he would have led or would have tried to lead his country in
pursuit of it. After all, this ambition had, as we have seen, existed in

5. Case, *French Opinion on War and Diplomacy*, 38–42; Cowley to Clarendon, Paris,
private, October 22, 1855, in PRO, FO, 519, 217:130; Cowley to Clarendon, Chantilly,
private, October 24, 1855, in PRO, FO, 519, 217:135–39.

his mind from the beginning of the conflict. Later he would claim that it had been the very object of the war. In October, 1858, he would tell Cowley:

> My policy is very simple. When I came to my present position I saw that France wanted peace, and I determined to maintain peace with the Treaties of 1815, so long as France was respected and held her own in the Councils of Europe. But I was equally resolved, if I was forced into war, not to make peace until a better equilibrium was secured to Europe. . . . Well, when driven into war with Russia, I though that no peace would be satisfactory which did not resuscitate Poland, and I humored Austria in the hope that she would assist me in this great work. She failed me.

And in November of that year he startled Clarendon during a conversation at Compiègne by asserting: "Let us discuss general policy frankly. The object of our Eastern policy was two-fold—Poland and Italy." The following month, Napoleon told his council of ministers: "The Crimean War would have been the revolution everyone expects, and that's why I undertook it. Great territorial changes would have resulted from it if Austrian indecision and the slowness of military operations hadn't reduced a great political revolution to a simple tournament."[6]

Whether Napoleon really intended to give the British government a choice between peace and a broader conflict, it was obviously Walewski's intention to use the threat of revolutionary war to achieve peace.[7] Already, in an October interview with Lord Granville at Chantilly, the French foreign minister had opened his campaign. He assured the Englishman that his master had one fixed idea, Poland, and that if peace were not made "it would be impossible to prevent the Emperor from making the complete restoration of Poland a principle and the object of war." Fortunately, however, peace really depended on the allies, and if England were willing, he, Walewski, had an ingenious plan for putting the Polish question to rest without really doing anything about it. The approach to Cowley was similar. In mid-September, Walewski

6. Napoleon III to Victoria, Tuileries, November 22, 1855, in Martin, *The Life of His Royal Highness, the Prince Consort*, III, 428–29; Cowley to Malmesbury, October 31, 1858, in V. Wellesley and Sencourt (eds.), *Conversations with Napoleon III*, 154; Prince Albert to Leopold I, April 19, 1859, in Martin, *The Life of His Royal Highness, the Prince Consort*, IV, 353; memorandum of Napoleon III, December 20, 1858, in Ollivier, *L'empire libéral*, III, 538.

7. Both Simpson (*Louis Napoleon and the Recovery of France*, 337) and Ollivier (*L'empire libéral*, III, 327–29) recognize this aspect of French policy, but neither attempts to differentiate between the motives of Walewski and Napoleon.

had clearly stated France's wish to make the reestablishment of Congress Poland one of the aims of peace, and London had made it clear that British public opinion would not support a war for that purpose.[8]

In fact, French diplomacy was already actively seeking an end to the war, both through indirect soundings of Russia (begun in early November) and continued negotiations with Austria. Vienna, alarmed by what it knew of Franco-Russian contacts and uneasy at the projected state visit of King Victor Emmanuel II of Sardinia to Paris, at last agreed to an ultimatum to impose on Russia—the Buol-Bourqueney memorandum of November 14. This sketched the program that the peace congress would arrange: a European protectorate to replace that of Russia in the Principalities; free navigation of the mouths of the Danube; the Straits convention of 1841 to be revised in the sense of a neutralization of the Black Sea; Russia to abandon pretensions to a protectorate over Greek Orthodox Christians in the Ottoman Empire and to surrender a part of Bessarabia. Only a British conversion to the Napoleonic dream could now prolong the war. On December 5, London acquiesced to the memorandum, with the addition of a "fifth point," by which the allies reserved the right to put forward at the future peace conference further conditions "dans un intérêt européen." By December, 1855, Cowley's opinion was that Napoleon really cared for nothing but the third point: "If the neutralization of the Black Sea was fully granted, he would be ready to make peace immediately."[9]

What, then, remained of the rêve napoléonienne? Apparently only two things, a predilection for the conference table and a determination that the table should be installed at Paris. In effect, although Vienna had demanded a simple acceptance or rejection of the ultimatum that Valentin Esterhazy delivered at Saint Petersburg on December 28, the Russians attempted to negotiate. They offered three major objections to the ultimatum, arguing in particular that the fifth point "should belong . . . by its very nature, to the decision not of the parties engaged in the present conflict but that of a European congress, sole arbiter of existing arrangements." Several weeks later, Count Albin Leo

8. Granville to Clarendon, Chantilly, October 7, 1855, in Fitzmaurice, The Life of Granville, I, 120–21; Walewski to Persigny, Paris, September 15, 1855, in AMAE, CP, Angleterre, 702:115–17, no. 136; Clarendon to Cowley, London, September 22, 1855, in AMAE, CP, Angleterre, 702:122–25, no. 50.

9. Taylor, The Struggle for Mastery in Europe, 79–80; Renouvin, "La politique extérieure du Second Empire," unpaginated; Mosse, The Rise and Fall of the Crimean System, 19; Cowley to Clarendon, Paris, December 10, 1855, in F. A. Wellesley (ed.), Secrets of the Second Empire, 86.

Seebach reappeared in Paris as an intermediary and proposed, in the words of Comte Vincent Benedetti, then political director of the Quai d'Orsay, "to bring together at Paris plenipotentiaries who should discuss the preliminaries of peace and sign them at once."[10]

In November, when Napoleon was asked by Cowley what reply he would make if Austria asked the allies to consider Russian counter-proposals, he had replied: "Je l'enverrais promener." To Seebach, the following month, the emperor had said that the Russian government would be mad not to make peace and that peace could only be obtained by unconditional acceptance of the Austrian ultimatum. And yet, the mention of a conference seems to have had an immediate effect. "Last night," wrote Cowley on January 13, "I was told that the Emperor was all for making something of the Russian proposals and I was awoke this morning at 7 o'clock by a letter from him, which on opening, I found to contain one addressed to the Queen with a request, that I would forward it with as little delay as possible." This letter was followed closely by a long dispatch, the joint labor of Napoleon and Walewski, to Persigny, French ambassador at London, which concluded that the Russian proposal of a conference to set the peace preliminaries should be accepted, since it could make possible the achieving of allied terms without impeding their war effort. However (and this thought was Napoleon's), the conference should meet at Brussels, lest any power seem to be dominating the discussions. "It is impossible not to remark," wrote Cowley, "that this proposal of Russia has taken the Emperor's fancy; His Majesty considers it, of all those that have been brought forward, as the most likely to lead to peace." Such was emphatically *not* the opinion of London, as Napoleon was soon to discover. Fortunately, circumstances did not confront him with a choice between his conference proclivities and his desire to remain on good terms with Britain. On January 15, despite a last-minute telegraphic appeal by Gorchakov to put their case in the emperor's hands, the Russian imperial council decided upon unconditional acceptance of the Austrian ultimatum. Russia, proclaimed *Revue des deux mondes* (January 31), had been constrained by "la volonté européenne."[11]

---

10. Count Karl Robert Nesselrode to Prince Alexander Gorchakov, Saint Petersburg, January 5, 1856, in AMAE, CP, Autriche, 463:53; Comte Vincent Benedetti to Thouvenel, Paris, January 16, 1856, in L. Thouvenel (ed.), *Pages de l'histoire du Second Empire*, 210.

11. Cowley to Clarendon, Paris, private, November 26, 1855, in PRO, FO, 519, 217:233; Mosse, *The Rise and Fall of the Crimean System*, 21; Cowley to Clarendon,

Meanwhile, in all the evolution of attitude between September, 1855, and January, 1856, one aspect of Napoleon's thought remained unchanged: the peace congress should meet in Paris. As early as October, 1855, Walewski, in an unofficial talk with Granville, had stated the French preference. In proposing Brussels as the site of a possible preliminary conference, Napoleon had made it clear that he did not mean the peace congress itself. As it happened, support for Paris was immediately forthcoming; and the emperor's reaction left no doubt as to his wishes in the matter. "I was delighted," he wrote Cowley, "that Lord Clarendon consented to hold the conference in Paris and I am so grateful for this kindness, that I wrote yesterday to Savigny [secretary of the French embassy at London] to ask him to thank Lord Clarendon personally on my behalf." Of course, he explained, it "was not due to *amour propre* but solely for the advantage of the cause" that he had wanted Paris to be chosen. And having thus assured the good of the cause, Napoleon took no chances on a British change of mind. "The Emperor," wired Cowley, "wishes that the proposal to hold the conferences at Paris should come officially from H.M. Government; he thinks that the effect in France will be much greater, and that it will be more difficult for Austria to raise objections."[12] In fact, no effective objections were raised.

And now, as the convocation at Paris of the most important European conference to meet in a generation approached, did Napoleon harbor an *arrière-pensée*? Is there any evidence that he might attempt to achieve there a settlement broader than one restricted to the Eastern question, perhaps even the revision at which his rejected revolutionary war would have aimed? In November, several days before his letter to Victoria, the emperor had spoken at the official closing of the international exposition, which, despite the war, had been holding sway in Paris. As was fitting on such an occasion, he had taken peace as his theme. It ought, he said, to be both durable and prompt. To be durable, it must clearly resolve the questions which had led to the war. "To be prompt, Europe must pronounce. Because without the

---

Paris, January 13, 1856, in PRO, FO, 519, 218:83; Walewski to Persigny, Paris, draft of Walewski's modified by Napoleon, January 14, 1856, in AMAE, CP, Angleterre, 704:38 bis–39; Cowley to Clarendon, Paris, confidential, January 17, 1856, in PRO, FO, 27, 1122: no. 89.

12. Granville to Clarendon, Chantilly, October 7, 1855, in Fitzmaurice, *The Life of Granville*, I, 123; Napoleon III to Cowley, January 24, 1856, in V. Wellesley and Sencourt (eds.), *Conversations with Napoleon III*, 104; Cowley to Clarendon, Paris, telegram, [probably January 25], 1856, in PRO, FO, 27, 1122.

pressure of general opinion, conflicts between great powers threaten to prolong themselves, while, on the other hand, if Europe decides to declare who is in the right and who is in the wrong, that will be a great step toward a solution. At the period of civilization which we have now reached, military successes, however brilliant, are only ephemeral; it is public opinion which always carries off the final victory." The next month, on December 27, a pamphlet appeared in Paris under the title *D'une nécessité d'un congrès pour pacifier l'Europe par un homme d'état*. Although drafted by Charles Duveyrier, the pamphlet was said by some to have been inspired by Napoleon himself. Certainly the arguments advanced by Duveyrier were of the sort with which the emperor had toyed. The great powers were divided and unable to make peace, but the opinion of Europe was in favor of an end to the war, and the fall of Sebastopol had created the opportunity. Now let "Europe" intervene; let the rulers of *all* the states of Europe attend a congress that Russia would propose and that would consider all questions then pending. From such a meeting could come an honorable and stable peace and a reconciliation of interests. If the pamphlet was a trial balloon, it had little success. In Britain, especially, such a congress was vociferously and vehemently rejected.[13]

Cowley, in dissociating Napoleon from Duveyrier's pamphlet, was doubtless too dogmatic concerning Napoleon's ideas on congress diplomacy, as events would soon prove, but it does seem likely that by the beginning of 1856 the French emperor had abandoned his more ambitious plans for the peace congress, from the point of view both of agenda and of participation. Concerning the former, on January 18, 1856, Napoleon wrote Walewski a letter in which he clearly stated his thoughts: "In a word, I want peace, but I want to sell it as dearly as possible. I also want the English alliance to survive the peace. This said without offending you, let's see what there is to do! Couldn't we say to Austria: we require that the preliminaries of peace be the peace itself, that is, the preliminaries should contain the four points with certain modifications. This signed, we would open the conferences only for secondary questions."[14] In the end, that some role was left the peace congress in settling the reserved conditions and the Bessarabian

13. Speech of Napoleon III, November 16, 1855, in *La politique impériale*, 224; Isser, *The Second Empire and the Press*, 34–38, believes that Napoleon inspired the pamphlet.

14. Napoleon III to Walewski, January 18, 1856, in Bernardy, "Un fils de Napoléon," 812–13.

frontier was the work of Austria and of Walewski, not of the emperor. As for the composition of the congress, it is difficult, in view of the evidence available, to accept F. A. Simpson's judgment that Napoleon actively worked to increase the number of participants. In the case of Sardinia, an ally in the war against Russia since January, 1855, he appears merely to have accepted a strong British plea for its inclusion as a full participant in the congress; in the case of Prussia, he did nothing to combat the British veto of a similar participation. And nothing more was heard of a congress of sovereigns.

True, Persigny congratulated himself on having persuaded the British foreign secretary, Clarendon, to argue for the admission of Sardinia to the congress on a basis of equality, a proposition rejected by Walewski since June, 1855, when he had proposed a limited Sardinian role. And certainly Persigny's argument that the effective exclusion of the secondary states from the European concert benefited only the absolutist powers bears scrutiny as evidence of his friend Napoleon's strategy, but Persigny inclined to a rather inflated view of his own persuasiveness, and while he generally reflected the ideals of his master, he was often woefully off base in the matter of tactics. Whatever Napoleon's desire to "do something for Italy," the fact remains that he played a passive role in the matter of Sardinian admission. Clarendon's early reports from Paris (where he had gone as Britain's chief representative to the congress) reveal that the Englishman was not certain what attitude Napoleon would take and was, as he later told Cavour, "happy to find the emperor perfectly of his own opinion in this matter." All that can be said with certainty is that Napoleon accepted the inclusion of Sardinia in the congress, despite Walewski's opposition to the idea. We may guess, however, that he did so not unhappily.[15]

Would the French emperor have agreed to the admission of Prussia and even of a representative of the German Confederation to the peace congress if it had not been for London's attitude? Certainly Prussia did all it could to ingratiate itself with Napoleon, and Austria and Russia lent their support at least in appearance. Walewski's penchant was for admission; and perhaps Hübner was right in his suspicion that Napoleon, too, was sympathetic to Prussia. As for the German Confederation, Cowley reported on February 9 that the emperor

15. Persigny to Walewski, London, June 7, 1855, in AMAE, CP, Angleterre, 701: 21–23, no. 5; Cavour to Luigi Cibrario, Paris, February 19, 1856, in Cavour e l'Inghilterra, I, 188, no. 247.

seemed to think admitting the smaller German states to the peace conference would lead to a "third Germany," which, supported by France and Britain, could balance Prussia and Austria. And yet, London was opposed to this scheme as well as to the admission of Prussia, and Napoleon as readily shelved the one as he consistently opposed the other. "With respect to Prussia," Cowley could write, "the emperor is *dead* against having her in the conferences." Perhaps the fairest appraisal of Napoleon's role was offered by the Sardinian minister at Berlin. Paris had ended by deciding that "in the present state of affairs, the admission of Prussia would be of less value than the maintenance of good relations with England."[16]

The same could well have been said of the peace congress itself. With the rejection of his offer of a broader war, Napoleon had seemingly turned his attention to the practical problem of making peace. France, suffering from a poor harvest and rising prices, wanted peace, and Britain lacked sympathy with either a revolutionary war or a congress of revision. Mazade's reaction in *Revue des deux mondes* (December 31) to Duveyrier's idea of a general congress of sovereigns probably reflected the prevailing mood: "il faut revenir à la réalité." The reality of the moment was to contrive, if possible, a peace that would maintain the English alliance while at the same time reconciling France and Russia. Yet Napoleon had not abandoned his penchant either for grandiose plans or for seeking their implementation through European concert and conference diplomacy. Unsurprisingly, therefore, the Congress of Paris, under his aegis, was destined to prove, if less than a new Congress of Vienna, at least much more than a peace conference.

---

16. Cowley to Clarendon, Paris, January 19, 1856, in PRO, FO, 519, 218:102; Hübner, *Neuf ans*, I, 387–91; Cowley to Clarendon, Paris, February 9, 1856, in PRO, FO, 27, 1123: no. 229; Cowley to Clarendon, January 25, 1856, in PRO, FO, 519, 218:126; Count Edoardo di Launay to Cibrario, Berlin, February 6, 1856, in *Cavour e l'Inghilterra*, I, 169, no. 228.

CHAPTER 4

The Congress of Paris
1856

The peace conference opened at the Palais d'Orsay on the afternoon of February 25 under the presidency of France's foreign minister, Walewski. Englishmen and Russians agreed that Napoleon would play the major role in its deliberations, and each side hoped to profit from his support. That was why the British government had preferred Paris as the meeting place, while the Russian plenipotentiaries, for their part, were instructed on the necessity of ensuring the emperor's goodwill. Cowley had misgivings as to the outcome of this duel with the Russians for Napoleon's affections: "As H.M.'s weak point is being open to flattery, and as they can flatter and we cannot, they would have the pull upon us." Certainly Napoleon's position was both pivotal and difficult. To secure a satisfactory peace, maintain the English alliance, and establish good relations with Russia were goals that could be reconciled only by means of an agility approaching sleight of hand. Obviously, however, he did not consider the conference medium to be an added hardship. Napoleon had explained to Cowley in January, while declining to insist on Russian acceptance in advance of certain additional allied demands, "that from all he heard the Emperor of Russia was determined to make peace, but that there was still a strong feeling in Russia to continue the war . . . and that if the Western Powers insisted on the immediate acceptance of the particular conditions the Emperor would be unable to comply, but that there could be no doubt they would be obtained in conference." Probably he counted on the effect of his own prestige and persuasiveness, and perhaps the calculation was a good one. Later, Clarendon, the chief British representative, regretting that Britain had not achieved all it had hoped for, told Vitzthum: "We had reckoned without Napoleon. Not one of us can resist him when he tries to persuade us face to face in his own room."[1]

Even if we make the necessary allowances for Clarendon's susceptibility to those in high places, his reports from Paris provide both a good insight into the part played by Napoleon and an indication of the emperor's influence upon the more important members of the congress. From the beginning he indicated a desire to concert French and British policy, and Clarendon seemed convinced of his sincerity. "The Emperor," he reported of his initial private conversation with Napoleon, "appeared to be as much convinced as myself of the necessity of coming to an agreement upon every subject before negotiations begin, and to be as determined as we could desire to let it be known that the understanding between the two Governments was complete, and that the alliance was not to be shaken." And, in fact, Napoleon did prod his foreign ministers into preparing, for the benefit of London, a memorandum describing French views. Yet Cowley had early warned Clarendon that, on one matter at least, there would be difficulty with the emperor. Of all the points likely to arise, in the ambassador's opinion, "there are none on which he will not be amenable to reason except the Bessarabian frontier." Austria had insisted on Russian territorial sacrifices in this area, and Napoleon did not at all regard these as essential to the peace, while to lessen them for the Russians would be to advance the possibility of a Franco-Russian entente. Before the conference he had made clear to Walewski that what he wanted was to leave most of Bessarabia to Russia in return for the surrender of Kars to Turkey and Russian agreement not to refortify the Åland Islands. To this extent France would support Russia at the conference, but not to the point of breaking with Britain. Therefore the emperor lost little time in bringing his powers of persuasion to bear upon Clarendon. This matter of the Bessarabian frontier became the critical issue of the peacemaking, and Napoleon's role, decisive in its effect, well illustrates the method by which he was to dominate the conference.[2]

1. The terms *conference* and *congress* were used interchangeably. In fact, Napoleon does not seem to have been certain that the meeting could be termed a congress (Walewski to Napoleon III, January 31, 1856, in Bernardy, "Un fils de Napoléon," 413). Clarendon to Victoria, January 18, 1856, in Martin, *The Life of His Royal Highness, the Prince Consort*, III, 354–55; Boutenko, "Un projet d'alliance," 285; Cowley to Clarendon, Paris, January 19, 1856, in PRO, FO, 519, 218:101–104; Cowley to Clarendon, January 22, 1856, in V. Wellesley and Sencourt (eds.), *Conversations with Napoleon III*, 103–104; Vitzthum, *St. Petersburg and London*, I, 282.

2. Temperley, "The Treaty of Paris and Its Execution," 397; Clarendon to Palmer-

Clarendon feared that Count Alexis Orlov, the chief Russian delegate to the conference, would win concessions from the emperor, or at least the hope of some. And, indeed, French public opinion, at least in Paris, had become strikingly pro-Russian. Apparently Napoleon's efforts to reassure the Englishman were successful. But "the Emperor then proceeded to say that although he had given Count Orloff no reason to hope that a change in the Bessarabian Frontier could even be discussed, yet He must own that it was a subject which harrassed and perplexed His mind, and the more he considered it, the less important it seemed to Him, except so far as concerned keeping faith with Austria, and he feared that by taking our stand upon a point of little consequence we might lose the opportunity of making some arrangement of greater value." It was a subtle approach that was not lost upon Clarendon, who immediately wrote London of his fears that in the Bessarabian matter Britain faced a dangerous isolation. Orlov, who had threatened to break off negotiations, formally applied to Napoleon for an interview. This was firmly refused, but when Napoleon talked of the incident with Clarendon, the latter was not greatly encouraged. To Palmerston he confided: "I must not disguise from your Lordship that the Emperor appeared quite to have made up his mind that sooner or later we should have to give up the Bessarabian frontier in order to secure other objects of greater importance. His Majesty said that we must hold out as long as we could and give no encouragement to the Russians to hope for a change of the Frontier, but that it was not a matter to justify the renewal of the war." By now, Clarendon had no illusions. "I am almost certain that some underhand work on this subject is going on, and this is the state of things which I have all along wanted the Cabinet to consider. Not whether we should hold firm language to Russia, and thereby get all we want, but what course we should pursue if we were left in the lurch by the Emperor."[3]

The preparations thus made, before the third meeting of the con-

---

ston, Paris, confidential, February 17, 1856, in PRO, FO, 27, 1164: no. 1; Walewski to Persigny, Paris, confidential, February 11, 1856, in AMAE, CP, Angleterre, 704:190; Cowley to Clarendon, Paris, February 9, 1856, in PRO, FO, 519, 218:177.

3. Case, *French Opinion on War and Diplomacy*, 44–48; Clarendon to Palmerston, Paris, February 25, 1856, in Clarendon Papers, C-135, 303–306; Clarendon to Palmerston, Paris, confidential, February 25, 1856, in PRO, FO, 27, 1164: no. 15; Clarendon to Palmerston, Paris, February 26, 1856, in Clarendon Papers, C-135, 307–310; Clarendon to Palmerston, Paris, confidential, February 29, 1856, in PRO, FO, 27, 1164: no. 24; Clarendon to Palmerston, Paris, March 1, 1856, in Clarendon Papers, C-135, 328.

ference Napoleon took a decisive step. He drew up, in his own hand, a list of the conditions upon which France would insist, a list that conspicuously omitted many of the special British demands,[4] and instructed Walewski to present this to the British delegates. The next day Clarendon carried his opposition to the Tuileries. He argued that peace made on such terms would constitute a Russian victory. "The Emperor rather warmly expressed his entire dissent from this opinion and said that if Kars was surrendered, our wishes with respect to the Aaland Islands fulfilled, and the navigation of the Danube secured, he believed that France and England would consider that an honorable peace had been made." As for the Bessarabian frontier, Napoleon denied that he had held out any hopes to Orlov of a modification when the line came to be drawn, but he added that Clarendon knew his opinion about the frontier "and that he thought it would be well worth while to make some alteration in the line if important concessions . . . could be obtained for it, provided that the free navigation of the Danube was secured." Privately, to Palmerston, Clarendon revealed the full impact that this interview had had upon him:

I have never yet seen the Emperor so excited as last night and his manner was âpre when he said, Permettez moi de vous dire Milord que je suis complètement d'un avis contraire. . . . His irritation subsided before the talk was over, but nothing would be so easy as a quarrel at this moment . . . for the Emperor thinks, or has been made to think that we are in the wrong, and he fears a constant increase of our exigencies under the pressure of the war spirits in England. I feel sure that he has not intended to play us false, but his error has been want of firmness in dealing with Orloff, which led him to receive the Russian negative as conclusive, instead of imposing upon Orloff our affirmatives as the ultimatum of England and France.

Moreover, concluded Clarendon, Napoleon desperately wanted peace. "In his present yielding mood and extreme desire for peace (he even wants a preliminary treaty of peace signed now, leaving all details for future settlement), he is not to be relied upon."[5]

---

4. The British hoped to extend the neutralization of the Black Sea to the Sea of Azov and to Nicolaiev on the Bug. They wanted also to secure the demolition of Russian forts on the Circassian coast and to provide for the independence of certain areas east of the Black Sea. On these points Napoleon's note was silent. The British also demanded that Russia return the town of Kars to Turkey (it had fallen late in the war) without compensation.

5. Clarendon to Palmerston, Paris, confidential, March 3, 1856, in PRO, FO, 27, 1164: no. 29; Clarendon to Palmerston, Paris, March 3, 18, 23, 1856, all in Clarendon Papers, C-135, 338–45, 406, 450.

The next day, in one of those rare letters in which he seemed freely to express both his motives and his aims, the emperor confirmed Clarendon's judgment. The subject of this letter (to Walewski) was the dispute concerning the Bessarabian frontier.

> The more I think about today's session the more sorry I am that you weren't able to secure the line on which you agreed with Lord Clarendon: because just as I think we must hold firm on all the important questions, so I believe it unworthy of us to quibble (and that is the word) over a line that has an elbow rather than going straight on,—a difference which for us is completely indifferent but which would be for the emperor of Russia one less humiliation. . . . The straight line as indicated by Count Buol gives no advantage, either political or military, and since we are making peace it would be "gentleman like" not to cling to a bit of territory of great value to our enemy but without value for us. Besides, I can't help but recognize that the Russian plenipotentiaries have completely kept their word, that they have been very accommodating and conciliatory in all the important matters, and it would be very hard for me not to recognize this by a little generosity, especially since such generosity would in no way injure French or English interests.[6]

Obviously Walewski, who had quickly become the bête noir of British and Austrian delegates, was guided closely by his master in policy matters, however free he might have been to irritate France's allies on questions of procedure and detail. In the end, Napoleon largely had his way. On March 10, Cowley and Clarendon yielded. Only the Bessarabian frontier had been a subject of debate. Russia readily accepted neutralization of the Black Sea; freedom of navigation of the Danube posed no problem except of detail and on the condition of Christians in Turkey a face-saving compromise was easily worked out; the matter of the Danubian Principalities, autonomy assured, was deferred. The peace terms, signed on March 30, twelve days after the birth of Napoleon's son, and on the forty-second anniversary of the fall of Paris in 1814, were very nearly those for which he had worked from the beginning of the conference. He had insisted on neutralization of the Black Sea and removal of Russia from the Danube. He had promised London to support demilitarization of the Åland Islands and *to discuss* the Asian frontier between Turkey and Russia. The first two aims were achieved; the Åland Islands were demilitarized; and the frontier was discussed. But Russia ceded no territory in the east (al-

6. Napoleon III to Walewski, March 8, 1856, in Bernardy, "Un fils de Napoléon," 818.

though Kars was returned to Turkey); neutralization was not extended to the Sea of Azov nor was Nicolaiev on the Bug destroyed; and in Bessarabia the Russians retained two-thirds of what they had promised to cede, including the Bulgarian enclave at Bolgrad.

Well might Orlov conclude that Napoleon had "intervened actively, skillfully, and constantly to moderate now the exclusive views of England, now the interested calculations of Austria" and that he had exercised this intervention "not only in a way most favorable to the re-establishment of peace, but also with the object of giving fair satisfaction to Russia's direct interests." Cowley's appraisal was, understandably, less enthusiastic. "So ill do I think that both the Emperor and His Minister have behaved, that I begged to be relieved from the intolerable burden of carrying on business with those, in whom I can no longer have the slightest confidence." More surprising, Buol, the Austrian foreign minister, attributed the success of the conference primarily to Napoleon. And Clarendon's conclusion was judicious. The peace, he felt, was as good as could have been expected. "If it had been left to Cowley," he told Charles Greville, the memoirist, "there would have been no peace at all." As Greville had earlier pronounced: "Clarendon does not (like Cowley) complain of the Emperor Napoleon, but speaks with great satisfaction of His Majesty's conduct to him, and the renewed cordiality with which he has recently expressed himself towards England, and for the maintenance of his alliance with us. In short, he evidently thinks (and not without reason) that he will return, having obtained a sufficiently good peace, and having placed England in a very fine position." All in all, Napoleon had reason to be pleased on the afternoon of March 30 as cannon salvos proclaimed the peace, a great military review was organized, and he met the delegates come to congratulate him. In the first great European congress to meet in Paris since the eighteenth century he had played the decisive role.[7]

But the Congress of Paris, as history has generally agreed to call it, did not end with the signing of the peace treaty. From the point of view of the concert of Europe, some of its most interesting achievements—and lacunae—still lay ahead. Is it possible that Napoleon,

---

7. Orlov to Nesselrode, Paris, March 11, 1856, in Boutenko, "Un projet d'alliance," 290; Cowley to Stratford de Redcliffe, Paris, April 22, 1856, in PRO, FO, 519, 218: 179–80; Arthur Hercule Serre to Walewski, Vienna, April 22, 1856, in AMAE, CP, Autriche, 463:297–300, no. 40; Strachey and Fulford (eds.), *The Greville Memoirs*, VII, 219, entry of March 21, 1856.

once the representatives had convened and the concerted wooing of his influence had begun, adopted a grander view of the congress than he had previously allowed himself? Or could it be that he had never really given up the hope that this meeting might become a general congress? Of the latter possibility there was much suspicion at the time; for the former, there is some evidence.

Baron Christian Friedrich von Stockmar, adviser to Queen Victoria and to Prince Albert, had sources of information that made him believe that the French emperor was still hoping for a congress of revision, and Victoria cautioned Palmerston in the midst of the congress: "We have every interest not to bring about a European Congress *pour la Révision des Traités*, which many people suspect the Emperor wishes to turn the present Conference into." At that moment the queen was especially concerned that Napoleon might try to have removed from the treaty of Paris of 1815 the clause excluding the Bonapartes from the throne. "Such an absurdity," Clarendon had written, "ought not to remain; I know that the Emperor is very anxious, unnecessarily so perhaps, to have it annulled, and would like that a proposal to that effect should come from us." There is other evidence, too, that Napoleon had ambitious plans for the congress. At his first interview with Orlov he raised the questions of Italy and Poland, a fact of possibly great significance, especially after the congress, by admitting Prussia to its deliberations on March 18, made a broader scope of discussion more practicable. Even before that event, the French press had speculated that a general congress of all the powers might be needed.[8] And then, there was the emperor's initial attitude toward the Danubian Principalities of Moldavia and Wallachia (they would not be known as Rumania until 1862). A conference of ambassadors at Constantinople in mid-February, 1856, had advised that, following evacuation by Austria, the Principalities should remain separate but enjoy autonomy under Turkish sovereignty. Influenced by expressions of Moldavian and Wallachian public opinion, both Napoleon and Walewski had come to favor union, which the emperor warmly defended in a letter of March 5 to his foreign minister:

> It is impossible to let the commission be formed without having first decided, in conference, the principles of the reorganization of the Principali-

8. Baron Christian Friedrich von Stockmar to Albert, Coburg, February 21, 1856, in Martin, *The Life of His Royal Highness, the Prince Consort,* III, 375–77; Victoria to Palmerston, Buckingham Palace, March 6, 1856, in *Victoria Letters, 1837–1861,* III, 230; Clarendon to Palmerston, Paris, March 5, 1856, in Clarendon Papers, C-135, 352; Orlov to Nesselrode, Paris, March 2, 1856, in Boutenko, "Un project d'alliance," 287.

ties, because if we allow the commission to go off at random, it is clear that they will not do what I want.

As to the core of the question, it is essential for England and France not to commit the fault of the Congress of Vienna, which, in reconstituting Europe, failed to take into account the wishes and aspirations of the people. . . . I believe that in the interests of the people, in the interests of the independence of the Ottoman Empire, in the interests of the repose of Europe, it is necessary that the two Principalities be reunited and independent.

Thereafter he frequently reemphasized his argument that the Paris congress should profit from the example of Vienna and his insistence that the Principalities must be discussed. It seems that the suspicions were not without foundation. Buol would later suggest that Napoleon had hoped the war would offer the opportunity for revising the map of Europe and that at the peace congress "he had endeavoured to turn the negotiations in the same direction."[9]

And yet, the thesis is not entirely convincing. It is true, for example, that Napoleon suggested a revision of the 1815 treaty of Paris in regard to the Bonaparte exclusion clause, but it is also true that he tamely withdrew the suggestion, although he might reasonably have hoped for Russian support. It is true that Prussia was admitted to the congress, but Napoleon's responsibility for this is not very clear. Certainly there was little opposition to the idea that Prussia might be invited to the congress *after* the conclusion of peace. Hübner believed that the emperor personally wished to have Prussia at the congress; and Walewski intimated that his master had been won over by Prussian hints of support. But it seems likely that Cavour more accurately caught the nuance of Napoleon's attitude. First he would clear all the roadblocks to peace, and then "il ne sera pas contraire" to Prussian admission. Just three days earlier, the emperor had emphatically failed to put in a good word for the Prussians in one of his conversations with Clarendon. "His Majesty told me," Clarendon noted, "that he had received a despatch from Monsieur de Moustier [French representative at Berlin] which induced Him to think that the King of Prussia must be nearly, if not quite mad as His last proposition was that the Emperor should meet Him at Aix-la-Chapelle, and that they should come to Paris, not being aware, I suppose, added the Emperor, that I don't want to see Him and that His presence here would be unwelcome." It was, in fact, Walewski who seemed especially solicitous of

9. Napoleon III to Walewski, March 5, 1856, in Bernardy, "Un fils de Napoléon," 431–32; memorandum of Buol, "Mes idées sur la politique du Second Empire," in Hallberg, *Franz Joseph and Napoleon III*, 126; Case, *Edouard Thouvenel*, 105–111.

Prussian dignity, and when he attempted to impose a preamble to the treaty that would make it appear that Prussia had played a part in its formulation, Napoleon in effect disavowed him. The emperor told Clarendon a week after the admission of Prussia to the congress that "he cared nothing about Prussia, and that England had much more interest in pleasing the King of Prussia than France." Whatever the speculations, then, concerning Napoleon's own wishes in the matter, there is slight evidence to support Simpson's argument that it was to him that Prussia owed its admission to the congress.[10]

Nor is there convincing evidence of an ulterior motive on Napoleon's part to convert the peace conference into a general congress in the attitude taken by him toward three key questions, the Danubian Principalities, Poland, and Italy. There can be no doubt that he warmly supported unification of the Principalities, which he believed their population wanted. And yet, he did not press the issue to a conclusion in the congress. He had, it seems, the support of Britain, even if only lukewarm (and entirely opposed to a foreign prince as ruler), and he could also count on Russia, Prussia, and certainly Sardinia. On March 8, Walewski publicly proposed unification and even hinted that a majority vote should decide. But against Turkish and Austrian resistance, the French emperor contented himself with deferring the issue he had raised, one for which he would never again rally as much support. Even the decision by the congress to consult, through an international commission and elected assemblies, the wishes of the populations of Moldavia and Wallachia seems to have resulted from an inadvertence of Buol's, who rashly chose to question the true state of opinion in the Principalities. Clarendon was undoubtedly right. In this matter, Napoleon subordinated any ambitions he might have had for a decision by the congress to his desire for an immediate peace. "The settlement of the Principalities may take some time," Clarendon wrote, "and it was proposed by Walewski (in compliance with the earnest wishes of the Emperor) that the general Treaty of Peace should be signed as soon as possible."[11]

10. Clarendon to Palmerston, April 1, 1856, in Clarendon Papers, C-135, 489–90; Goriaïnow, Le Bosphore et les Dardanelles, 12; Hübner, Neuf ans, I, 388–91; Walewski to Lionel François René, marquis de Moustier, Paris, telegram, February 28, 1856, in AMAE, CP, Prusse, 327:156; Cavour to Launay, Paris, February 28, 1856, in Cavour e l'Inghilterra, I, 224, no. 285; Clarendon to Palmerston, Paris, confidential, February 25, March 24, 1856, both in PRO, FO, 27, 1164: no. 15, 1165: no. 72; Clarendon to Victoria, March 25, 1856, in Martin, The Life of His Royal Highness, the Prince Consort, III, 369.

11. Riker, The Making of Roumania, 42; East, The Union of Moldavia and Wal-

The Polish question offers an even more arresting illustration of the same attitude. Just six months after the rejection at London in September, 1855, of the French proposals regarding Poland, Clarendon wrote: "I have told Walewski that we must bring forward the question of Italy before the Congress closes, and that if the Emperor is prepared for it, the English Government will be ready to demand that at least the state of things provided by the Congress of Vienna shall be restored in Poland." Napoleon, however, had now become the relatively disinterested party. He would speak to Orlov, he said, if Clarendon really wanted him to and would tell him what to say. The result of his conversation with Orlov, and of subsequent ones between Clarendon and the Russians, was the French and British decision not to raise the Polish question at the congress but to trust the assurances of the czar that very shortly everything that would please the allies would be done for the Poles. Later, Napoleon would complain that he had been deceived, but it is obvious that, in view of his objectives of an immediate peace and conciliation of the Russians, little had been required to dissuade him from raising the Polish issue at the congress.[12]

In regard to Italy, Napoleon certainly brought to the congress a clear sympathy for the Italian cause. He had requested in December, 1855, that Cavour inform him of what might be done for Italy. The next month the emperor told General Alfonso La Marmora that he saw no solution for the Italian problem except a confederation with a Diet like that of Frankfurt, meeting at Rome, and he even went so far, between February 16 and 25, as to draft a plan for such a confederation. In February he revealed to Cavour a scheme by which the duke of Modena and the duchess of Parma would give up their states to Sardinia and would succeed, by way of compensation, to the thrones of Wallachia and Moldavia. Moreover, he told Cavour "that, the principal questions dealt with and the peace with Russia assured, he would bring up the Italian question and would propose . . . the cession of Parma to Piedmont." Several days earlier he had been even more unequivocal. "He talked with me," Cavour wrote, "about the affairs of Italy, of the difficulties that they present, and of his firm intention to deal with them [d'en traiter] at the congress."[13]

lachia, 49–51; Schroeder, *Austria, Great Britain, and the Crimean War*, 362–63; Clarendon to Palmerston, Paris, March 10, 1856, in Clarendon Papers, C-135, 369.

12. Clarendon to Palmerston, March 5, April 7, 1856, both in Clarendon Papers, C-135, 351, 517; Cowley to Clarendon, Paris, June 26, 1856, in PRO, FO, 519, 219: 60–66.

13. Mollat, *La question romaine*, 294–95, 297; Cavour to Victor Emmanuel, Febru-

Perhaps, had Austria proved more tractable, Napoleon would have seen the congress as a good place at which to "do something for Italy," especially since this would have given him the opportunity to do something for the Principalities as well. But Vienna would have nothing to do with the throne-swapping scheme, despite certain changes of detail.[14] At any rate, from the beginning, Napoleon was markedly cautious in his treatment of the Italian problem. The only two points in Cavour's modest program (of January 21) for which he was willing to make an effort were the repeal of Austrian sequestration of the goods of Lombard refugees and the introduction of municipal government into the Papal Legations. Moreover, in regard to the first, he was resolved to deal with Vienna, observing that he thought "a direct appeal of this kind would have more chance of success, than an appeal to the tender mercies of Buol in conference." As for the question of the government of the Legations, this could hardly be made a congress matter, unless Napoleon was willing to offend the pope. That he was not, quickly became apparent to both Cavour and Clarendon. "I am afraid we shall not be able to do much for Italy if anything," the British foreign minister informed Palmerston. "The Emperor is halting between two opinions. He wants to do what would be popular throughout the world and particularly in France, but he fears the effect upon his own clergy of anything that would appear hostile to the Pope." Napoleon told his cousin, Prince Napoleon, who relayed the information to Cavour, that "il ne croyait pas convenable toucher au pape pour le moment."[15]

In the end, Napoleon agreed to bringing up the Italian question at a closing session of the congress; he was by no means the chief advocate of the idea. Besieged by Clarendon and Cavour, he replied "that no change had taken place in His intentions, but that the more he reflected upon the subject the greater appeared to Him the difficulties with which it was beset." And he continued: "I don't like Austria . . . I detest her policy, but I don't wish to quarrel with her, and I desire not

ary 22, 1856, in *Cavour e l'Inghilterra*, I, 193–95, no. 251; Cavour to Count Francesco Arese, Paris, February 22, 1856, in Grabinski, *Un ami de Napoléon III*, 138.

14. An alternative proposal was that Parma should go to Sardinia; the duchess of Parma should receive Modena; and the archduke of Modena should become ruler of the united Principalities (Schroeder, *Austria, Great Britain, and the Crimean War*, 361).

15. Cowley to Clarendon, Paris, February 24, 1856 [two dispatches], both in PRO, FO, 519, 218:161, 162; Clarendon to Palmerston, Paris, March 13, 1856, in Clarendon Papers, C-135, 382–83; Cavour to Urbano Rattazzi, February 26, 1856, in *Cavour e l'Inghilterra*, I, 216, no. 276.

to injure the Pope, and yet without doing both I do not see what can be effected for Italy." But he yielded. As Cavour put it: "After a long discussion on March 19 the Emperor consented to order Walewski to submit the questions of Greece and of the Roman states to the congress. Clarendon was excellent; he encouraged and pushed [poussé] the Emperor."[16] And yet, at this same interview, Napoleon proved that if he could subordinate broader ambitions in order to achieve specific objectives, those ambitions were never far beneath the surface. "I have been for two hours with the Emperor this afternoon together with Cavour and Walewski talking about Italy," wrote Clarendon. "H.M. was rather wild, not in the revolutionary sense, but in his views about entrapping the other Powers to consent to discuss the question." Walewski, it appears, had raised numerous practical objections to the introduction of the Italian question and Napoleon, "en homme pratique," had proposed a thousand ways of overcoming them. Among these possible approaches, and the first to be suggested, was a general revision of the 1815 treaties. Clarendon reported on March 20:

> The Emperor said that the difficulty was how to get the question of Italy discussed at the Congress as the different Plenipotentiaries would affirm that they had neither Powers nor instructions to treat of matters which did not relate to the negotiations for Peace, but His Majesty thought that they might ask for instructions to discuss those portions of the Treaty of Vienna which had become obsolete or invalid and in that way the question of Italy might be introduced, moreover that as Austria, Prussia and Russia now distrusted each other they might be tempted by different means to come into the arrangement.

This was the "wild" scheme to which Clarendon objected and that he successfully turned (according to Cavour) by raising again the specter of a northern alliance.[17]

The twenty-second session of the congress, held on April 8, was justified to the delegates by Walewski as an opportunity to exchange

16. Clarendon to Palmerston, Paris, March 19, 1856, in PRO, FO, 27, 1165: no. 65; Cavour to Marquis Emanuele d'Azeglio, March 19, 1856, in Cavour e l'Inghilterra, I, 347, no. 416. This adds credence to the opinion of Benedetti, directeur politique of the Quai d'Orsay and secretary of the congress, that the session of April 8, at which Italy was discussed, was the idea of the British (L. Thouvenel [ed.], Pages de l'histoire du Second Empire, 287–88).

17. Clarendon to Palmerston, Paris, March 19, 1856, in Clarendon Papers, C-135, 412; Cavour to Cibrario, confidential, March 19, 1856, in Cavour e l'Inghilterra, I, 345, no. 414; Clarendon to Palmerston, Paris, confidential, March 20, 1856, in PRO, FO, 27, 1165: no. 66; Cavour to d'Azeglio, March 20, 1856, in Cavour e l'Inghilterra, I, 354, no. 427.

views on the existing military occupations and various problems of the hour that might disturb European peace. He himself commented on the situation in Greece (calling for reforms that would allow Britain and France to withdraw their troops), on the presence of French and Austrian troops in the Papal States, on the government of the kingdom of Naples, on the need for a discussion of maritime law, and, especially, on the "abuses" perpetrated by the Belgian press. Clarendon, with extraordinary vehemence, criticized the governments of both Naples and Rome and called for an end to the occupation of the Papal States. The Prussian representative even raised the matter of Neufchâtel. Short shrift was made of Buol's objection that the congress was not empowered to deal with matters other than the Eastern question, and on Walewski's initiative the discussion was embodied in a protocol.[18]

Nor was this session the only example of the way in which, particularly during its closing days, the congress passed beyond the strict bounds of a peace conference. It formally admitted the Ottoman Empire to the European concert and provided for collective mediation of disputes involving the Turks and a signatory or signatories of the treaty (Articles 7 and 8). It placed the Danubian Principalities and Serbia as well as the Ionian Islands under the protection of the signatory powers (Articles 28 and 29) and, in the former case, posited the principle of national self-determination and reserved to a future European conference the task of bringing about a definitive reorganization (Articles 22 through 27). The congress also extended to include the Danube the principle of the internationalization of certain great rivers, and gave that principle even further development by vesting control in a *European* rather than a riparian commission (Articles 15 through 17). Moreover, on the initiative of France, the congress adopted the Declaration of Paris, formalizing in a humanitarian and civilizing sense rules of naval warfare. "Perhaps," Cavour observed, "the Congress of Paris will owe it to this act that it will not occupy an entirely obscure page in the annals of history."[19]

18. Hagg, "The Congress of Paris of 1856," 142–46; Beyens, *Le Second Empire*, I, 128–30. Napoleon would have liked to include Poland in the list of topics, but Orlov again refused (Charles-Roux, *Alexandre II, Gorchakov et Napoléon III*, 104).

19. The declaration, proposed on April 8 and adopted on April 16, provided for the abolition of privateering, protection of enemy goods (other than contraband) even under an enemy flag, and abolition of paper blockade. There was, however, no adequate definition of contraband. Within two years, over forty nonsignatories of the 1856 treaty had adhered, but not the United States. Cavour to Cibrario, Paris, April 17, 1856, in *Cavour e l'Inghilterra*, I, 475, no. 555.

He had no such expectations for another declaration made by the congress in its closing days. Clarendon wished to have the signatories of the peace treaty engage themselves, before having recourse to war, to seek the mediation of a third power. At the session of April 14, however, "the general feeling was that the Congress should confine itself to the expression of an opinion favorable to the principle of mediation and not enter into any positive engagement upon the subject." This had certainly been the attitude of Napoleon from the beginning. The emperor was willing, Clarendon reported on April 7, to support the principle of mediation before a declaration of war, "but he was opposed to any engagement to that effect which might fetter the independent action of a Government where its honor or its interests might not brook delay." And so, as one of its final acts, the congress adopted a resolution consigned to the protocol of session that the "plenipotentiaries do not hesitate to express, in the name of their governments, the wish that states between which any serious misunderstanding may arise, should before appealing to arms, have recourse, so far as circumstances might allow, to the good offices of a friendly power." The congress also expressed the wish that other states should accede to the protocol, and over thirty did so within a year, but Walewski took care to point out to French diplomatic agents its limited and informal nature. Unimpressive as it seemed at the time, however, this mediation resolution was destined to become, in due course and after many vicissitudes, something more than Cavour's contemptuous dismissal of it as a "vague and insignificant wish having no practical value."[20]

That, however, lay in a future mercifully veiled from Napoleon as the congress that had raised him and his country to a pinnacle of power and influence held its last session on April 16. No one can know with certainty whether he had expected more or less from it than had been achieved. Clearly, however, his contemporaries did not expect an end to conference diplomacy. "Soon, perhaps," Palmerston remarked to Persigny shortly after the closing of the congress, "circumstances will present themselves which will be favorable for realising the elevated views of the French emperor by convoking certain

20. Clarendon to Palmerston, Paris, April 15, 1856, in PRO, FO, 27, 1166: no. 110; Clarendon to Palmerston, Paris, April 7, 1856, in Clarendon Papers, C-135, 517; circulars of Walewski to French diplomatic agents, Paris, May 14, 23, 1856, in AMAE, MD, 741:40–41; Cavour to Cibrario, Paris, April 17, 1856, in Cavour e l'Inghilterra, I, 475, no. 555.

conferences especially destined to resolve the difficult questions."
And Clarendon foresaw that Napoleon might wish to re-create his
success of 1856 on an even broader stage:

> I see that the idea of a European Congress is germinating in the Emperor's
> mind, and with it the *arrondissement* of the French frontier, the abolition
> of obsolete Treaties, and such other *remaniements* as may be necessary. I
> *improvised* a longish catalogue of dangers and difficulties that such a Con-
> gress would entail, unless its decisions were unanimous, which was not
> probable, or one or two of the strongest Powers were to go to war for what
> they wanted. He does not wish for such a Congress immediately, but he is
> looking ahead, and foresees that in a year or two, when the French people
> get tired of the arts of peace, he shall want something new and striking for
> their amusement.[21]

Indeed, throughout the crisis that had preceded the Crimean War, and
during the long and intricate diplomacy attending that conflict, Napoleon had shown clearly the guise in which he would have the concert
of Europe appear. It might, conceived as a conference system, preserve
peace by mediation or arbitration. In dire necessity it could, conceived
as a coalition, restore peace by restraining the aggressor. But above all,
the vocation of the concert of Europe was, for Napoleon, to solve
problems before they led to conflict and to solve them in accordance
with the ideas of the day. Thus both the limited conferences alluded
to by Palmerston and the general congress feared by Clarendon were
part of Napoleon's concept of the concert of Europe, and his personal
success at the Congress of Paris, the fact that France alone had reason
to be completely satisfied with the treaty of Paris, did nothing to diminish that predilection. In fact, largely because of the efforts of the
French emperor, the conference of Paris did not truly end in April,
1856, but might almost be said to have remained in session, interrupted by longish periods of adjournment, from 1856 into 1859. It was
largely, but not entirely, a matter of dealing with the Eastern question,
whose complexities and dangers had by no means been exhausted.

---

21. Persigny to Walewski, London, April 30, 1856, in AMAE, CP, Angleterre, 704:
282–83; Clarendon to Palmerston, Paris, April 13, 1856, in Martin, *The Life of His
Royal Highness, the Prince Consort*, III, 376 n.

CHAPTER 5

The "Conference of Paris"
1856–1859

The continued meeting of a European conference at Paris was assured by several provisions of the treaty of Paris. In the case of the Danubian Principalities, after a special European commission, in cooperation with the Porte, had ascertained the wishes of the people, a conference in Paris would organize those provinces. In the case of navigation of the Danube, the European commission charged with designating and carrying out certain necessary projects was to report in two years' time to a conference that would then dissolve it and establish a permanent riparian commission (as it turned out, the European commission became a permanent one). But the possibilities were much broader than those specifically provided by the treaty. In Binkley's words: "Almost every one of the peace terms agreed upon at Paris seemed to reaffirm the authority of Europe as against the independent action of any single power, and gave further precision and extension to the collective responsibility of the five great powers." This sense of "Europe" as tribunal, mediator, arbitrator, with an inherent right of intervention in disputes threatening peace, was in the air. Besides, putting a peace treaty into effect is often more difficult than negotiating one. The treaty of 1856 did not prove an exception.[1]

The British soon found a number of points on which complaint about the actions—or inaction—of Russia seemed justified, and Palmerston made clear his determination that the former enemy should not be allowed to depart one iota from the signed treaty, guaranteed since April 15, 1856, by an Anglo-French-Austrian alliance. Most irritating to London were the claim made by the new Russian foreign

1. Binkley, *Realism and Nationalism*, 177; *Revue des deux mondes*, October 14, December 14, 1856, April 14, 1857.

minister, Gorchakov, to Serpents Island and the question of the "new" versus the "old" Bolgrad. Serpents Island lay some ninety miles off the delta of the Danube. Its only asset was a lighthouse, formerly operated by Russia, but the British wished it to go to Turkey. As for Bolgrad, in adjusting the Bessarabian frontier between Russian territory and Moldavia, the peace conference had agreed to allow Russia to retain the town, which it claimed to be the *chef-lieu* of a Bulgarian colony in the area. However, the map used at Paris was outdated, and when the boundary commission came to the work of delineation it found that there were *two* Bolgrads. Russia lay claim to the new town, which was some miles south of the Bolgrad indicated on the congress maps. This, Saint Petersburg said, was really the *chef-lieu*. But the new Bolgrad also had a conspicuous advantage over the old; it was situated on the shore of Lake Yalpuck, and if, as Gorchakov insisted, the boundary ran south of the town, it would include part of the lake, by which (and its tributaries) the Danube could be reached. Since it had been one of the purposes of the treaty of Paris to deny Russia contact with the Danube, the spirit if not the letter of the document was against Russia, and it was hardly unexpected that Palmerston at once raised a hue and cry against these pretensions. For the moment, none of the evacuations proposed by the treaty seemed imminent. British forces remained in the Black Sea, Austrian in the Principalities, and Russian in Bessarabia.[2]

There need have been no problem. Had the allies stood together, Russia must certainly have yielded. But Napoleon, whether from sincere moderation or in line with his new pro-Russian policy, immediately suggested the way of transaction. As for Serpents Island, Paris thought the matter might be settled by assigning to the Danube commission the responsibility of maintaining the lighthouse there. In regard to Bolgrad, why not allow Russia to have the place, but insist that the lake remain Moldavian, separated from the town by a Moldavian road? Unfortunately, neither Gorchakov nor Palmerston would bend. Napoleon strove hard to set a tone of sweet reason. "If the new Bolgrad is really the *chef-lieu* of the Bulgarian colony, I believe myself committed to Russia to let the town remain in her territory. But if the new Bolgrad is not the *chef-lieu* of the colony, I regain all liberty of action, and then of course I stand for the line originally traced." Nevertheless, it was clear that a distasteful choice between wartime ally and

2. On the Bolgrad dispute, see Mosse, *The Rise and Fall of the Crimean System,* 69–104.

newfound friend could be avoided only if London or Saint Petersburg were to back down or if some transaction could be arranged, and either likelihood was diminished by the fact that Gorchakov would obviously do all that he could to drive a wedge between Britain and France.[3]

It was in these circumstances that Saint Petersburg in the first week of August had already raised, with regard to Serpents Island, the possibility of reconvening the conference at Paris. To this view the new French ambassador to Russia, Comte Auguste de Morny, had lent his support, making known to his British colleague before the end of August his opinion that "the only practical mode of coming to a conclusion would be to reassemble the Congress at Paris." Napoleon, not surprisingly, liked the idea. "I send you some of Morny's dispatches, which are quite interesting," he wrote Walewski. "I think it will be necessary, in order to put an end to the dispute [Serpents Island], to reconvene a commission at Paris." The further complication of the Bolgrad dispute only seemed to make a renewal of the conference more imperative, and at the beginning of September, Count Philip I. Brunnow, Russia's representative at Paris, proposed "that the Congress should be reconvened to decide all the contested points rather than conform [sic] its action to the simple question of Serpents Island," a proposal to which Alexander II added his personal weight, through Granville, who was then in Moscow for the czar's coronation. "It seems to me," Morny urged, "that nothing is more simple than to submit the points in dispute to the judgment of the conference of Paris."[4]

Of course, it was anything but simple. Asked by Walewski on September 20 to choose between a conference and a proposal just made by Gorchakov to give up Serpents Island if Russia could have the new Bolgrad (separated from the lake by a road), Palmerston refused both. Nevertheless, Paris on September 29 urged acceptance of a conference. Cavour and the Porte agreed on October 2, and Buol, who had

3. Walewski to Baron Joseph de Malaret, London, August 16, 1856, in AMAE, CP, Angleterre, 705:141–43v, no. 81; Napoleon III to Walewski, Biarritz, September 27, 1856, in Bernardy, "Un fils de Napoléon," 819–20.

4. Napoleon III to Walewski, August 27, 1856, in Bernardy, "Un fils de Napoléon," 459 n.; Cowley to Clarendon, Paris, confidential, September 7, 1856, in PRO, FO, 519, 6:203, no. 1033; Granville to Stratford de Redcliffe, Moscow, September 21, 1856, in Fitzmaurice, The Life of Granville, I, 212; Comte Auguste de Morny to Walewski, Moscow, September 25, 1856, in Morny, Une ambassade en Russie, 89. The episode illustrates Napoleon's habit of dealing over the head of his foreign minister. Of course, Morny was his half brother and had played a key role in the coup d'état.

suggested this expedient as early as July, followed suit on the ninth, as did Berlin (reluctantly) on the eighteenth. But Buol made his acceptance conditional on that of Britain; the Porte, on that of a majority of his allies. And even if the conference were to reassemble, there remained the question of its mechanics. Walewski made a strong bid at the end of September for decision by majority vote, while Napoleon, after stating that he would probably have agreed at the original peace conference to letting Russia have the new Bolgrad, even had he known its true location, appeared to Cowley "to take it for granted that London would withdraw its objections to reassembling the conference and agree to abide by the decision of the majority." In this, he had the enthusiastic support of Saint Petersburg, whose point of view had always been that "it would be necessary to resolve [the] matter by a common accord among the contracting powers . . . the work of the peace having been the result of their combined efforts, it would also require their common effort to assure the faithful execution of that peace." In other words, as Gorchakov added rather maliciously, Britain must not be allowed to substitute its will for that of its cosignatories. But that, in a sense, was just what the British proposed to do, with the consent of France. To Walewski's arguments in favor of a decision by majority vote, Cowley replied on September 24 "that that would not be putting us in the same place we occupied at the Congress." There, he argued, no majority could have forced the allies to make concessions. "We had but to take up our hats and walk out of the room and there was an end of the Negotiations, and now we were required to accept the decision of the Majority. It seemed to me to be impossible." Vienna, too, opposed the idea of decision by majority vote. In fact, neither the British nor the Austrian government made a secret of its intention to tolerate a conference only if there should be no doubt that the outcome would be a decision against Russia.[5]

The subsequent negotiations tell us a great deal about Napoleon's attitude toward conference diplomacy as an instrument of European concert. To begin with, his preference for the conference table would yield, as was true of most of his predilections, to pragmatic considerations. If Europe, functioning as a concert, preferred to solve the Bolgrad

5. Walewski to Persigny, Paris, September 29, October 6, 1856, both in AMAE, CP, Angleterre, 706:27v–28, no. 1081, 56, no. 113; Cowley to Clarendon, Paris, October 12, 1856, in PRO, FO, 519, 219:192–93; exposée de la marche adoptée par le cabinet de Russie pour mettre à exécution les articles 20 et 21 du traité du 18/30 mars 1856, [probably September], 1856, in Nesselrode, Lettres et papiers, XI, 116–31; Cowley to Clarendon, Paris, September 24, 1856, in PRO, FO, 519, 219:165–67.

dispute without conference diplomacy, he would not insist on it. He would have agreed, as we have seen, to an immediate solution by which Russia would have kept the new Bolgrad, separated from the lake by a Moldavian road. When this was rejected by London, the emperor next accepted Walewski's idea of arbitration by some disinterested party acceptable to Britain, perhaps the king of the Belgians. Again Palmerston interposed a veto. Well might Napoleon complain, "with some appearance of soreness," that the British "did nothing to help him out of his difficulty—that they had refused every proposal which he made." The French conclusion was probably inevitable: that only a reconvocation of the Congress of Paris (as Walewski put it) could deal with the problem. Soon, however, Saint Petersburg presented another alternative to a conference. On November 9, Morny wrote enthusiastically that, out of consideration for the French alliance and gratitude to Napoleon, the czar had decided to let the French emperor settle the matter; Russia would accept any compensation for Bolgrad that he might suggest. There was, however, a quid pro quo. In return for Russian tractability, Paris was to guarantee, in writing, the observation of the treaty of Paris and pledge itself to protest, along with Russia, British nonexecution of the convention of May 13, 1856, by which the allies had engaged to evacuate Turkish territory. Napoleon appears to have been tempted. But in the end, the difficulties were too great. Probably Cowley was right in suggesting that the emperor knew London would never agree to compensation for Bolgrad that Russia would consider adequate. Besides, there was the matter of Gorchakov's proposed convention. It was clearly designed to undermine the Franco-British alliance, and Napoleon could not accept this. On the evening of November 26, at Saint-Cloud, he sorted through the alternatives (Russian withdrawal, Gorchakov's convention, consultation through normal diplomatic channels to decide which Bolgrad the congress had intended to give Russia, a cabinet settlement including compensation) and decided for the conference.[6]

But, as his wavering views on the question of decision by majority vote had already indicated, it was the fact of the conference in which Napoleon put his faith, and not its mechanics, whatever those might

6. Cowley to Clarendon, Paris, confidential, October 15, 1856, in PRO, FO, 519, 6:318, no. 1269; Mosse, *The Rise and Fall of the Crimean System*, 86, 91–95; Walewski to Persigny, Compiègne, October 26, 1856, in AMAE, CP, Angleterre, 706:130–42v, no. 124; Morny to Walewski, November 9, 1856, in Morny, *Une ambassade en Russie*, 131–34; Cowley to Clarendon, Paris, November 27, 1856, in PRO, FO, 519, 220:126–28.

prove to be. At first he had supported Walewski in the argument that the conference should decide by vote. Then, at the end of October, there was a revealing interview with Cowley.

> The Emperor sent for me last night to his room where he still remains unwell. He said that he was most anxious to hit upon some plan, that would put an end to the present uncomfortable state of things between the two Governments and asked me what I thought of reassembling the Members of the Conference who took part in the discussion of the Bessarabian Frontier, not for the purpose of deciding by vote what the intention of the Congress had been, but to exchange opinions, in the hope that some result, which might be accepted by all parties, might come out of their discussions. . . . "Let us," says the Emperor, "put an end to this exchange of despatches, which can lead to no result, and see if we can do better by an exchange of verbal communications. If we cannot, no harm is done, we shall be just where we were."

Two days later, Napoleon told the ambassador that it had been a great mistake to propose that a majority vote should decide. "It would have been far better to have summoned the Congress in a friendly manner, and take the chance of some arrangement through discussion." Cowley frankly confessed to Clarendon that he could not see what the emperor hoped to gain by this approach. Given a few more years of observation, he would have realized that he was in the face of one of Napoleon's most stubbornly held convictions—that the most effective recourse of hard-pressed diplomacy was to bargaining over a conference table, bargaining among reasonable men that could conceivably lead to a solution attainable in no other way. For, as the emperor had admitted, "if this scheme was not brought to bear, he knew of no other and should despair of any termination of the Question at issue."[7]

Moreover, in order to assure that the conference would meet, Napoleon was capable of rather brutal manipulation. His honor was engaged toward Russia, he had told Cowley in mid-October, but his interest was in saving the appearance, not the substance. "H.M. assured me," wrote the ambassador, "that he had no wish that the decision of the reassembled Congress should be in favor of Russia; indeed he went so far as to say, that he should be glad if it was favorable to our views." Excluding Prussia, by limiting the participants to those pow-

7. Cowley to Clarendon, Compiègne, November 1, 3, 1856, both in PRO, FO, 519, 220:43–47, 58.

ers who had discussed the Bessarabian frontier at the congress, was the first step in this direction.

The second, as is well known, was Napoleon's agreement on November 4 to the proposition that Sardinia should secretly commit itself in advance to vote against Russia and France. Persuaded by Persigny (apparently, no great effort was required), the emperor had forgotten his earlier assurance to Cowley that "he would be no party to any arrangement in which he knew beforehand that he would be in the minority because it would be immediately said, if he did so, that it was a trick to enable him to escape from the word which he had given." But if London and Vienna thought they were now to have a "got-up comedy with a foregone conclusion," a conference that was neither to discuss nor debate but simply to vote yes or no, with the votes already counted, they were soon to be disillusioned. At the moment of informing Hübner of the arrangement with Sardinia, Napoleon raised again the matter of compensation. The British government assumed that, in opting for the conference, Paris had chosen between that meeting and compensation agreed by cabinet diplomacy. When Marquis Emanuele d'Azeglio, Sardinia's minister at London, asked Palmerston if he did not think that the French would end by trying to have both the conference and compensation for Russia, the latter smiled and replied that this was exactly what he expected, but the attempt would be opposed.[8]

It was not, however, quite that easy. When Cowley urged Napoleon to instruct Walewski not to permit discussion at the conference, the emperor replied: "But how can discussion be avoided? . . . I cannot prevent others raising a discussion . . . when once a Conference meets discussion is unavoidable." And to the ambassador's firm objections Napoleon countered: "But . . . your government had no objection to the system of a further concession of territory to Russia, and such a concession must have been discussed in conference." The emperor might have added what Cowley was to discover several days later, that Cavour, while he would not himself raise the question of compensation, would support such a proposal, if made by another at the conference—including Russia. Napoleon had returned then, in De-

8. Cowley to Clarendon, October 12, 1856, in PRO, FO, 519, 219:195; Mosse, *The Rise and Fall of the Crimean System*, 89; Cowley to Clarendon, Paris, October 31, 1856, in PRO, FO, 519, 220:38–39; Strachey and Fulford (eds.), *The Greville Memoirs*, VII, 251; Hübner, *Neuf ans*, I, 449–50; d'Azeglio to Cavour, London, December 1, 1856, in *Cavour e l'Inghilterra*, vol. II, pt. 1, p. 82.

cember, to the position that he had probably held since the beginning of the dispute, and certainly from the moment of his decision to reject a direct agreement with Saint Petersburg. If Russia were to give up Bolgrad, Russia must receive compensation sanctioned by a European conference. His maneuverings had brought Britain from opposition to compensation with or without a conference, to the idea of a choice between compensation or conference. The next logical step was to persuade Britain to accept both. But why did Napoleon insist that compensation be ratified by a conference (if not necessarily arranged there) rather than worked out through more conventional diplomatic channels? Partly the reason was pragmatic. In the first place, could Britain have been brought to agree to adequate compensation at all without the threat of a conference discussion and vote? Second, any direct arrangements containing guarantees that Russia would accept might prove dangerous to the Anglo-French-Russian entente that Paris desired. And there was another consideration as well, one to which the French emperor attached a great deal of importance—the moral authority of a decision sanctioned by Europe-in-conference.[9]

At any rate, to both Hübner and Cowley, Napoleon made clear that he now wanted an agreement as to the compensation to be given Russia, the conference then to meet, without a vote, in order to ratify the arrangement. If the British government looked on compensation in light of a further concession to Russia, Walewski told Cowley, then "in the name of the Emperor he asked them to make that concession." And the British, however much they might bluster, had little choice. On December 13, in a private letter, Clarendon accepted the principle of compensation: on the fourteenth, Palmerston concurred, adding his opinion that agreement on the details of compensation should be reached before the conference met. That, of course, is what happened. After an exchange of notes between Paris and London, the British government accepted a boundary line sketched by Napoleon himself. The Russians, while professing themselves unhappy over the stipulated compensation and preferring a solution to be worked out at

9. Cowley to Clarendon, Paris, December 7, 1856, in PRO, FO, 519, 220:147–48; Mosse, The Rise and Fall of the Crimean System, 99. In a note of Walewski's of November 8, the foreign minister had suggested that the single goal of the proposed conference should be "de lever des doutes et d'aplanir des difficultés qui ne sauraient être pleinement élucidées que par le concours direct des représentants de toutes les puissances." Napoleon substituted: "de provoquer une décision, dont l'autorité ne sera révoquée en doute par personne parce qu'elle aura été obtenue par le concours direct des représentants de toutes les puissances" (Walewski to Persigny, Paris, November 8, 1856, in AMAE, CP, Angleterre, 706:154–56, no. 128).

the conference, offered their acceptance in deference to the French emperor. And so, when the conference assembled at the Quai d'Orsay on December 31 under the presidency of Walewski, it had only to ratify an agreement already sealed. In this way, the Bolgrad dispute was finally resolved on January 6, 1857. The protocol signed at the second meeting of the conference provided that Serpents Island (occupied in August, 1856, by British marines) and the delta of the Danube would be recognized as Turkish territory. The lighthouse on Serpents Island was to be maintained by Turkey under supervision of the International Riverain Commission. The new Bolgrad remained Moldavian, and as compensation Russia received some two hundred square miles on the upper Yalpuck River, to be delineated within three months by a boundary commission. Finally, Britain agreed to withdraw from the Black Sea and Austria from the Principalities by the end of March.[10] Despite its aspect of contrivance, the "conference of Paris," in its first renewal, had served both Napoleon and Europe well. A complicated problem, capable of bringing about serious tensions if not war, had been solved without compromising French honor and prestige or the maintenance of good relations by France with both Britain and Russia. Perhaps no other device could have achieved all of these ends, and certainly neither this meeting nor its sequel, the conference on the Danubian Principalities of 1858, was calculated to diminish the French emperor's predilection for conference diplomacy.

Six months after the end of the Bolgrad affair, a new crisis broke in eastern Europe. On August 5–6, 1857, France, Russia, Prussia, and Sardinia broke off diplomatic relations with the Porte in protest against Turkish interference with the election of conventions or divans in the Danubian Principalities (Moldavia and Wallachia). France, as leader of those powers desiring union of the two Principalities, was especially concerned, since the divans' votes on the issue of organization were to be important guides to the European commission whose task was to prepare proposals for the conference at Paris. Under these circumstances, the falsification of electoral lists in Moldavia could indeed be considered an offense to what *Revue des deux mondes* (August 14) termed the "dignité européenne."

Concerning union of the Principalities, Napoleon had already made

10. Hübner, *Neuf ans*, I, 460–63; Cowley to Clarendon, Paris, December 14, 1856, in PRO, FO, 519, 220:177–81; Cowley to Clarendon, Paris, December 12, 1856, in Mosse, *The Rise and Fall of the Crimean System*, 99–100; copy of protocol, January 6, 1857, in AMAE, CP, Angleterre, 707:11–16.

his preference known. As early as the Vienna conference of March to
June, 1855, the French had presented an argument for unity, preferably
under a foreign prince. Even before the conclusion of the Congress of
Paris, Walewski had written to Thouvenel, French ambassador at
Constantinople, that "the emperor holds very much to this union of
the two Principalities. His Majesty wants you to make every effort to
arrive at this result, with or without the consent of the Porte. The emperor will not give up his ideas in this regard unless the Divans should
pronounce in a contrary sense." Thereafter, French influence was constantly exerted in the interest of union, and Cowley early guessed that
the impetus came primarily from Saint-Cloud and the Tuileries. He
was right. "Believe me," wrote Benedetti to Thouvenel concerning
the unity question, "we would have shown less persistence if we had
been able to. Just a few days ago the Minister tried again to bend the
will of the emperor, who has dictated all our conduct in the debate,
but he failed. The emperor wants us to hold firm, whatever the chances
and even the inconveniences." On February 5, 1857, a *Moniteur* article firmly supported union. Napoleon himself scrawled in the margin
of Thouvenel's April 2 request for instructions: "Press strongly to
obtain the support of Reschid Pasha for the union. Spare nothing to
achieve this."[11]

And yet, committed as he was to the cause of uniting the Principalities, Napoleon's first reaction to the crisis of 1857 was to seek
agreement with Britain, even at the price of concessions. On the eve
of his departure for Osborne, where the differences with Britain were
to be patched up and the way was to be prepared for the projected conference, the emperor revealed his attitude in a conversation with
Salmour: "I'm going to England because in talking it is possible to
reach agreement more easily and more quickly. I'll support my view
as well as I can, but if I can't have it accepted, I'll modify it, because in
politics amour-propre should have no place. I never run my head
against a wall; I go as far as I can toward my goal, but if I encounter an
obstacle, I stop." At Osborne, on August 7 and 8, Napoleon encountered an obstacle. The resulting compromise consisted of two precise
points and a major ill-defined area. On the one hand, the British gov-

11. Walewski to Thouvenel, April 5, 1856, in Mange, *Near Eastern Policy*, 56; Cowley to Clarendon, Paris, May 29, 1856, in PRO, FO, 519, 219:8–10; Benedetti to Thouvenel, Paris, November 25, 1856, in L. Thouvenel (ed.), *Trois années*, 63; Mange, *Near
Eastern policy*, 62. Another indication of Napoleon's personal interest in the problem is
that throughout this period most of Persigny's dispatches from London in the French
Foreign Office Archives are marked "envoyer à S.M."

ernment agreed to new elections in Moldavia; on the other, Napoleon abandoned the idea of real political union under a native or foreign prince, which London had opposed since August, 1856. But as to the extent of administrative union that was to be permitted, there was no agreement. This matter, Walewski implied, was for the conference of Paris to decide:

> Everything leads me to believe that we [Britain and France] are in agreement as to the course of conduct to pursue at the Congress of Paris with respect to the definitive organization. The framework for these transactions will be that of a broad administrative union which may be, in our eyes at least, the prelude to a complete union. Nothing definitive or precise has been determined, but we have told the British government . . . that it has always been our intention to seek an understanding and an agreement by means of mutual concessions, and that if complete union under a foreign prince—the combination we would find best—should meet with too great difficulties, we would be ready to modify our views in order to avoid discord with our allies. For the moment we are not prepared . . . for fear of false interpretations, to discuss the bases of any agreement; first it will be necessary that the commission finish its work and that the Divans make their statement. But when the Conference of Paris reassembles, we shall agree in a more precise manner with the English government regarding the combination to which we can give our support.

In other words, Britain and France would go to the conference with conflicting expectations. Clarendon, the British foreign secretary, was convinced that Napoleon had agreed, albeit secretly, to an absolute minimum of union for the Principalities. Walewski understood, however, that France would press as hard as possible for any attainable degree of union short of a single ruler. Of the two viewpoints, Clarendon's was certainly the less realistic, since Britain's concession— annulment of the Moldavian elections—was meaningless unless attention was to be paid to the wishes of the people, which the elections were meant to ascertain. Fair elections were subsequently held, in September, with the result that the divans declared overwhelmingly for autonomy, representative government, and union under a foreign prince. Meanwhile the European commission ineffectually pursued its task and at the end of March, 1858, presented a dry and factual report, leaving a clear field to the conference that assembled at Paris on May 22, its membership the French and Turkish foreign ministers (Walewski presiding) and the ambassadors at Paris of Britain, Russia, Prussia, Austria, and Sardinia. "C'est dans le congrès de nouveau rassemblé," Mazade had observed in *Revue des deux mondes* (September 30 and October 31, 1857), "et par les conseils de l'Europe que cette question se décidera."[12]

In the months between August, 1857, and May, 1858, Napoleon's actions appeared remarkably similar to those preceding the meeting on Bolgrad. Then as now, he had brought Britain to the conference table with a compromise; then as now, he appeared likely to do what he could, the conference having been secured, to gain from it what he had wanted in the first place. Thus Walewski expressed surprise that Clarendon should have left the Turkish ambassador at London under the impression that France had given up the idea of union in return for the annulment of the disputed elections. "We shall make every effort," he wrote to Thouvenel, "to find and secure the acceptance of a combination which would unite the *two* provinces as closely as possible and be the prelude to a complete and absolute union later." Cowley, after hearing Napoleon's scheme for a federal union of the Principalities modeled upon that of Switzerland or of the United States, suspected worse: "The emperor," he told Hübner, "will propose a *single* senate for the two Principalities; in other words, union—thus violating the engagement which he personally took last year at Osborne." Nevertheless, in his speech to the French Legislative Body at the beginning of the new year, Napoleon promised to bring to the conference "a spirit of conciliation of such sort as to attenuate the difficulties which are inseparable from a difference of opinions." Certainly he brought there, as he had in 1856 and 1857, a dominant influence. When Walewski spoke for union under a foreign prince at the first session of the conference, he was only, as he had told Cowley the day before, carrying out Napoleon's orders. When the conference in its second and third sessions evaded a discussion of the plan by which France hoped to achieve de facto union, a plan that was certainly, in Clarendon's judgment, of "Imperial, and not Walewskian origin," Napoleon put an end to the resistance by making it clear that he would break up the meeting if the project was not discussed at the next sitting.[13]

12. *Cavour-Salmour*, 217; Walewski to Bourqueney, Paris, August 9, 1857, in AMAE, CP, Angleterre, 708:155–56 (marked in red ink: "Cette lettre a été communiquée, avant d'être expédiée à Lord Palmerston et à Lord Clarendon, qui en ont approuvé tous les termes comme reproduisants fidèlement l'accord qui s'est établi à Osborne entre eux d'une part et M. le Cte Walewski de l'autre"); Clarendon to Stratford de Redcliffe, London, August 11, 1857, in Case, *Edouard Thouvenel*, 126–28.
13. Walewski to Persigny, Paris, August 31, 1857, in AMAE, CP, Angleterre, 708:

The French plan, as reluctantly taken up by the conference in its fourth session, had three major points: a name for the country ("The United Principalities of Moldavia and Wallachia"); a central commission for common affairs with such extensive powers as to virtually constitute legislative union, despite the existence of two separate provincial assemblies and two hospodars; and two militias, organized as separate corps of a single army under a single commander in chief and with a common flag. Each of these points was firmly opposed by Turkey, of course, but also by Austria, who now took the lead in threatening to dissolve the conference. Nevertheless, agreement was reached on at least one point. "The United Principalities of Moldavia and Wallachia" proved acceptable to all parties. As for the proposed central commission, Napoleon appeared conciliatory. His foreign minister had whispered to Cowley that the emperor, while resolved to have his way about the common flag, was prepared to accept considerable modification of the commission, and the Englishman, taking advantage of his bouton de Chasse de l'Empereur, went to Fontainebleau and received this same assurance, phrased in a rather truculent way, from a professedly disgruntled Napoleon. At the Osborne meeting, the emperor insisted, "all he had done, was to abandon the idea of uniting the Principalities under one Prince, but . . . he had expressly declared his intention of promoting the Union in every way he could short of that, and . . . as the only means of giving the Principalities what they wanted, was according them a common name, a common legislature and a common Army and Flag, he had proposed those things to H.M. Gov't and . . . if they were not granted, he should consider himself as released from all obligations and at liberty to promote Union under a Foreign Prince." Moreover, "however much he might consent to modification of the power of the Central Committee, if the community of the army and flag was not granted his [plenipotentiary] would retire from the conferences." The subsequent mediation of Cowley led to the adoption by the conference on July 3 of an emasculated central commission that was acceptable even to Austria.[14]

190v–93v; Walewski to Thouvenel, Paris, [perhaps late December], 1857, in L. Thouvenel (ed.), Trois années, 215–16; Hübner, Neuf ans, II, 141; speech of the emperor, January 19, 1858, in La politique impériale, 275; Cowley to Malmesbury, Paris, May 21, 1858, in PRO, FO, 519, 224:16; Clarendon to Malmesbury, Grosvenor Crescent, June 13, 1858, in Malmesbury, Memoirs, II, 302–303; Clarendon to Malmesbury, telegram, June 8, 1858, in East, The Union of Moldavia and Wallachia, 155.

14. Cowley to Malmesbury, Paris, June 14, 1858, in PRO, FO, 519, 224:57; Cowley to Malmesbury, Fontainebleau, June 15, 1858, in PRO, FO, 519, 224:50–55; Cowley to

But already, just three days after Napoleon's conversation at Fontainebleau with the British ambassador, Walewski had begun the campaign to win acceptance of a single army in two corps under one flag. Apparently Napoleon was more adamant on this point than was Walewski, who suggested on the eighteenth to Marshal Amable Jean Jacques Pélissier (duc de Malakov, France's ambassador to Britain) that France might agree to a common flag to be used only in the event of war. Hübner reported that Walewski was soundly dressed down by Napoleon at the ministerial conference of June 24. The foreign minister took so hard a line with Cowley the next day that the latter frankly advised his government to give way on the flag issue, as it had become sine qua non for Napoleon. Shortly afterward, the emperor departed for Plombières and his fateful interview with Cavour, but not before taking the Prussian ambassador, Hatzfeldt, aside and sourly upbraiding him for his country's "defection" at the conference.[15]

More defections were to follow. In the emperor's absence, successive compromise solutions to the flag issue were brought forward. Prussia proposed two separate flags to be combined in time of war to make a single standard. When this was rejected by Austria, Cowley suggested the attachment of a blue pennant to each separate standard in time of war. Now Napoleon discovered the difficulty of carrying on conference diplomacy by remote control. On July 9 he replied to Walewski's suggestion that he accept Cowley's proposal in response to a personal appeal from Francis Joseph.

> I have received your letter. I think we must hold firm because otherwise from concession to concession we'll end by having no opinion at all. Besides, just between the two of us I find it very desirable that Austria be isolated and that she refuse to agree to a proposition made by Prussia. Now that the conference is about to end at any rate, this isn't a great misfortune, and as everyone would be in accord [on the Prussian proposal] except Austria, I believe that the resolution of the conference ought to be executed.
>
> What I especially charge is that you avoid the combination which would have me yield as the result of a letter written to me by the emperor of Austria. Under no circumstances do I want that. We have yielded on enough points: we have abandoned the permanent common flag for one adopted

---

Malmesbury, Paris, secret and confidential, June 15, 1858, in PRO, FO, 519, 8:395, no. 669; Cowley to Alison, Paris, June 18, 1858, in PRO, FO, 519, 224:62–63.

15. Walewski to Marshal Amable Jean Jacques Pélissier, duc de Malakoff [sic], Fontainebleau, confidential, June 20, 1858, in AMAE, CP, Angleterre, 711:15–16, no. 88; Hübner, Neuf ans, II, 186; Cowley to Malmesbury, Paris, June 25, July 4, 1858, both in PRO, FO, 519, 224:73–75, 85.

only in the case of mobilization, as with the Swiss. We can't make any more concessions. Let this be well understood, and let happen then what will.

But Napoleon *did* yield, and to a letter written him by the Austrian emperor. Why? Before leaving for Plombières, he had expressed to his ministers the wish that the conference speed its work, and this might have been a factor. Also, as Britain, Austria, and Turkey had accepted Cowley's alternative to the Prussian proposal on the flag, no real chance of isolating Austria remained, even if Napoleon, after his interview with Cavour on July 21, had wished to break with Vienna on this relatively minor issue. Most likely, however, the French emperor was only playing true to his concept of conference diplomacy when he agreed to accept the best that he could obtain out of the give-and-take of negotiation. After all, Walewski had used his master's obstinacy to obtain agreement to a *permanent* common pennant. On July 19, Napoleon wrote in his own hand from Plombières: "If, in order to have done with the matter, it is necessary to accept a single pennant, then we must consent to that, in extremis."[16]

On August 16, after the French and Austrian emperors had graciously yielded one to the other, Napoleon on the issue of a common flag, Francis Joseph on the matter of a permanent common pennant, the conference completed its work of almost three months. Three days later the conventions were signed. "The United Principalities of Moldavia and Wallachia" were to be autonomous under Turkish sovereignty. Individual liberty and equality before the law were guaranteed. Each principality would be governed by its own hospodar elected for life by its own legislative assembly. A central commission of sixteen members (eight from each principality) could propose laws of general interest to the assemblies. There would be a single high court and, of course, a common blue pennant attached permanently to the separate flag of each province. Union of the Principalities had not been achieved, but the elements of eventual union, and, above all, the conviction that union was possible, had come out of the meeting. "If it is not immediate union," wrote Walewski, "it is certainly union assured for the future."[17] Once again it may be argued that only the conference

16. Napoleon III to Walewski, Plombières, July 9, 1858, in Bernardy, "Un fils de Napoléon," 827; Benedetti to Thouvenel, Paris, July 2, 1858, in L. Thouvenel (ed.), *Trois années*, 287; Napoleon III to Walewski, Plombières, July 19, 1858, in Bernardy, "Un fils de Napoléon," 522.

17. Case, *Edouard Thouvenel*, 134; Walewski to Thouvenel, Paris, August 14, 1858, in L. Thouvenel (ed.), *Trois années*, 293.

device could have so advanced the cause of Rumanian unity without at the same time unacceptably straining the relations of the great powers. And Napoleon could well be pleased with having achieved as much as he had in a conference where two powers (Austria and Turkey), supported by a third (Britain), were opposed to union while another (Russia) was decidedly lukewarm to the Rumanian cause although willing to support it for the sake of good relations with France.

But there is another aspect to this continuing "conference of Paris" that, in 1857 and 1858, made important contributions to European peace and concert. There is the fact that on more than one occasion Napoleon showed an inclination to view these meetings as a sort of standing "council of Europe" to which disputes could be referred as they arose. The earliest example of this occurred in regard to Neufchâtel, a long-simmering source of trouble that erupted once more at the end of 1856. In early September of that year a group of men calling themselves royalists had seized the castle of Neufchâtel in the name of the king of Prussia, whose claims to the principality had been, as we have seen, the subject of a conference in 1852. When the royalists were overwhelmed and imprisoned, Frederick William precipitated a more serious crisis by demanding, on November 29, their release and threatening the use of force. Napoleon, who had his own grievances against the Swiss, supported the demand for the release of the prisoners, but armed intervention was another matter. And so, his initial reaction was to think of a conference. He would, he said, do all in his power to save the lives and property of the conspirators and he was ready "to take part in Conferences with the other powers who signed the declaration of 1852 for the purpose of employing all means short of coercion to bring the Neufchâtel question to a settlement." Typically, when the Swiss minister at Paris argued that the federal constitution would not allow the government to proclaim an amnesty, Napoleon replied that Switzerland would certainly yield to the wishes of a European conference.[18] But the situation seemed dangerous. Frederick William talked of using force and mobilized the *Landwehr*. Diplomatic relations between Switzerland and Prussia were broken. Liberal opinion in France, expressed in *Revue des deux mondes* (December 14, 1856), called for Europe to exercise "quelque pacifique et salutaire médiation."

18. Cowley to Clarendon, Paris, September 25, October 8, 1856, both in PRO, FO, 519, 6:253–54, no. 1142, 300, no. 1230.

Under these circumstances, the conference on Bolgrad, which was approaching, seemed providential. Why not, the French emperor asked Cowley, bring the affair of Neufchâtel before that conference when it assembled? One thing had led to another, he said, until "in fact he was so involved in the affair, he did not know which way to turn." As it happened, however, Napoleon's perplexity did not prove a sufficient argument to broaden the scope of the Bolgrad conference, and so, even after French mediation had brought about the release of the prisoners by the Swiss Confederation on January 15, 1857, he insisted on a separate convocation, preferring, in Cowley's words, to fight the king of Prussia in conference rather than single-handedly. The conference, it was early made clear, should meet in Paris. The British government, which had accepted the idea of a conference before the end of December, had no enthusiasm for this French propensity for "trying to get everything to Paris," and the Austrians very much hoped to insinuate Vienna as an alternative site, but in the end Napoleon had his way. "It will perhaps be better to yield the point with a good grace," Cowley advised, "in consideration of the extent to which the Emperor is personally engaged." This London did, but only after insisting, as a condition, that Britain and France should agree in advance on every point likely to be discussed.[19]

The conference convened in Paris on March 5, 1857. At the second session Prussia was admitted, but in reality the four other great powers served the function of mediators, preparing a treaty, whose acceptance at Berlin was urged by Napoleon's personal emissary, Prince Napoleon. The treaty, signed at the final session of the conference on May 25, assured to Frederick William his title Prince of Neufchâtel, provided he did not exercise it, and a compensation of 100 million francs (which he subsequently renounced). A complete amnesty was secured. Thus, through the conference device, or, as *Revue des deux mondes* (April 14) termed it, "l'arbitrage d'une conférence européenne," Napoleon ended, without alienating either Switzerland or Prussia, a situation that, in the judgment of contemporary observers, might otherwise have led to war.[20]

19. Cowley to Clarendon, Paris, December 20, 1856, in PRO, FO, 519, 6:208–209; Cowley to Clarendon, Paris, January 16, 1857, in PRO, FO, 519, 220:214; Cowley to Clarendon, Paris, December 20, 1856, in PRO, FO, 519, 6:209–210; Hübner, *Neuf ans*, I, 468; Cowley to Clarendon, Paris, January 8, 23, 1857, both in PRO, FO, 519, 220:266, 273.

20. Loftus, *Diplomatic Reminiscenses*, Vol. I, pt. 1, pp. 280–83; Walewski to Persigny, Paris, May 27, 1857, in AMAE, CP, Angleterre, 707:308–309, no. 55.

Strikingly similar was the instance of an outbreak of trouble in Montenegro preceding the 1858 conference on the Danubian Principalities. The Turkish-Montenegrin frontier was in question; and in the spring of 1858 a clash appeared imminent as Turkish troops, operating in the disputed area against Bosnian, Herzegovinian, and Albanian rebels, prepared to seize Grahovo. Prince Danilo appealed to the czar, who in turn requested the aid of Napoleon. On March 27, Hübner noted: "Several days ago Walewski hinted at the idea of confronting the Paris conference with the problem of Montenegro, Savoy, Bosnia, etc. I told him that we would hardly accept this idea, that the conference was intended only to *terminate* the matters left unfinished by the Congress of Paris and not to bring up new ones." Francis Joseph took the matter seriously enough to interpose his personal objections. The evidence, then, is that Napoleon's first impulse had been, as in the case of Neufchâtel, to refer the new problem to a conference about to meet. However, on this occasion he did not take the initiative in proposing a separate conference, as Russia had suggested. Cowley later doubted that either Russia or France really wanted to bring the matter of Montenegro before the Principalities conference, but in this he was probably mistaken. At any rate, he felt called upon to speak out strongly against the possibility when it was hinted by Walewski and advocated in the French press, and Buol took the matter seriously enough to instruct Hübner quite emphatically against it. As it happened, the Montenegrin affair was settled by European action, but not by a conference. After considerable maneuvering and delay, during which France and Russia made use of a naval demonstration in the Adriatic and threats to recognize the independence of Montenegro, the Turks agreed to a five-power commission, plus representatives of Turkey and Montenegro, which met in Constantinople from October 14 to November 8, 1858, and drew a frontier line that was destined to cause more trouble. "We thought," wrote Walewski in support of the idea of a five-power commission, which France had initiated, "that there was the opportunity of applying in a broad and liberal manner the terms of the Treaty of 30 March by allowing all the great powers to unite in the East to solve all questions of general interest."[21]

21. Charles-Roux, *Alexandre II, Gorchakov et Napoléon III*, 232–33; Hübner, *Neuf ans*, II, 132, 139–140; interview of Lord Augustus Loftus with Francis Joseph, April 11, 1858, in Loftus, *Diplomatic Reminiscenses*, vol. I, pt. 1, pp. 324–25; Goriaïnow, "Les étapes de l'alliance franco-russe," 25; Cowley to Malmesbury, Paris, May 16, 1858, in

Even without Montenegro, the conference on the Principalities had had a number of items to consider. There had been, for example, the regulation of the navigation of the Danube, in the interests of Europe as a whole, and the delineation of the Russo-Turkish frontier in Asia in accordance with the proposals of the Asiatic Boundary Commission. But the suspicion had persisted in Vienna that Napoleon hoped to go beyond this agenda. In a conversation with the British ambassador, Buol was almost brutally explicit:

> He said that he did not wish to cause unnecessary delay. On the contrary, he wished the Conference to commence and finish its labours as speedily as possible; but there were certain indications that France was desirous of submitting other questions which did not devolve from the Treaty of Paris, and to this he must give his decided opposition. . . . He did not object to questions of political interest being treated by the five great Powers, but he had an insuperable objection to the establishment of a permanent Conference at Paris, and to acknowledge a position to which France appeared to lay claim—of constituting herself the "arbiter or great tribunal of Europe."[22]

What Vienna feared, of course, was that the Italian question might once more be brought to the conference table. For it is at this point, even as the "conference of Paris" prepared in early 1859 to meet yet again on the issue of the Danubian Principalities, that the attention of European diplomacy was changing focus from the Eastern question, in the course of which Napoleon had raised both France and the concert of Europe to new eminence, to the problem of Italy, in whose complexities both the concert and the Second Empire were eventually to founder.

PRO, FO, 519, 224:8; *Revue des deux mondes*, June 30, 1858; Hallberg, *Franz Joseph and Napoleon III*, 132; Walewski to Malakoff [*sic*], Paris, May 15, 1858, in AMAE, CP, Angleterre, 710:174v, no. 67.

22. Loftus, *Diplomatic Reminiscenses*, vol. I, pt. 1, pp. 329, 357.

CHAPTER 6

Crisis in Italy
The Congress Proposal
of 1859

In September, 1857, the emperors of France and Russia met at Stuttgart. That meeting, although leading to no concrete results, symbolized the changes brought about in Europe by the Crimean War. The Holy Alliance was dead. Russia, embittered by the Black Sea clauses of the treaty of Paris, had become a revisionist power. But the peace brought neither stability nor security to Europe. Rather, the mood was one of malaise, uncertainty, and fear. And for this, Napoleon was at least partly to blame. He had chosen to interpret the results of the war as favorable to change. This policy of revision was, of course, consistent with his earlier ideas and policies, but it also served the requirements of the moment. Within France, the elections of 1857 had revealed an irreducible core of opposition at the same moment that the economic surge that had distracted the country for almost ten years began to falter. Political life showed unmistakable signs of revival. Then, on January 14, 1858, a group of Italian patriots, led by Felice Orsini, attempted to kill the emperor. Within six months, Napoleon seized upon the problem of a fragmented, Austrian-dominated Italy, demanding that it be resolved. But had his policy changed in any respect other than urgency? Ten years earlier he had attempted to involve Europe in the Italian question. The conservative concert of Europe of 1849 was no more. Could a new one be forged, this time for change rather than for conservation? And was it Napoleon's purpose, following the successes of the "conference of Paris," to use such a concert to resolve this most difficult and dangerous of Europe's problems? At the end of March, 1858, Walewski had hinted that the question of Savoy, among others, should be referred to the then-pending conference on the Danubian Principalities. Was he acting on instructions of the emperor? Or was this a premonition, a reflection of his fears that Napoleon would next turn toward an Italian adventure? During the conference the French emperor and Cavour met secretly at Plombières, where, on July 21, they plotted how to provoke a war with Austria that would drive that state from the peninsula, reorganize Italy into a confederation, and gain Lombardy-Venetia for Sardinia, and Nice and Savoy for France. The Austrian ambassador at Paris had his suspicions, but they differed from the apparent reality. Cavour, he told the French foreign minister, was seeking to stir up dissension among the powers; he would accomplish this by bringing the Italian matter before the conference, but "if the name of Italy were pronounced in the conference," he (Hübner) would follow his instructions and withdraw at once.[1] Cavour had no intention of bothering the Paris meeting. But can the same be said of Napoleon?

On New Year's Day, 1859, the emperor startled Europe by remarking to Hübner, a remark easily overheard, that he was sorry that relations between France and Austria were not as good as he would wish them to be. No one can know with certainty the motivation of this incident. The easiest to formulate is that Napoleon had taken the first step toward preparing France and Europe for war. And yet, in an 1862 interview with the Spanish ambassador, Napoleon asserted: "I was a thousand miles from expecting my words to have the effect they had, and I had even wished to be heard only by M. de Hübner." This explanation would ring true if it could be allowed that the French emperor, who had nothing to gain, after all, by frightening Europe or France, might well have wished to frighten Austria, perhaps to the extent of shaking its determination to withdraw at once from any conference that ventured to discuss the Italian question. For the fact is that a new conference on the Principalities was about to meet at Paris, and Napoleon showed, immediately after his ominous remark to Hübner, a great interest in convoking it. Hübner noted on January 8: "Rothschild has seen the emperor today. He [Napoleon] wants the conferences and he wants them at Paris. This explains the zeal, so strange and sudden, which Cowley has displayed for several days now in favor of the convening of the Paris conference." Vienna vetoed an early meeting, but the election of Prince Alexander Couza as hospodar of both Moldavia and Wallachia (January 17 and February 5, 1859) changed the situation. Although the "double election" was a clear violation of the convention of 1858, Couza immediately placed him-

---

1. Hübner, *Neuf ans*, II, 201.

self under Napoleon's protection and called on him to convene a conference at Paris as soon as possible. Moreover, the Turks themselves, anxious to denounce the election, made the same request. Austria had no choice but to accept.[2]

Cavour clearly saw, in these developments, the advantages and disadvantages to his own policy. The Principalities could prove a useful diversion. "The only bad side is the possible meeting of a conference, and the efforts of England to bring the Italian question before it," he wrote to Prince Napoleon. Cavour suggested that if there must be a conference it should meet in Constantinople so that Napoleon could easily maintain his reserve. Did this mean that Cavour feared English intentions? Or was it Napoleon about whom he had reservations? He knew of French willingness to enlarge the agendas of the two preceding conferences. He knew, also, that the emperor was already alarmed at the possibility of a war in which France would not clearly be seen to have the right on its side. Just four days after Cavour's expression of concern, Walewski had assured Charles Rogier, the Belgian minister at Paris, of Napoleon's peaceful intentions and added: "I have another hope. This is that the powers who were represented at the Congress of Paris will agree on the speedy opening of a new conference, made necessary by recent events in the Danubian Principalities. When these difficulties will be, as I like to believe, regulated by the cordial entente of the powers, there will be an opportunity perhaps to make use of this diplomatic gathering in order to deal with Italian affairs and bring them to a satisfactory conclusion." Certainly Napoleon made no attempt to prevent the conference on Couza's double election from convening at Paris. He did act to delay the meeting, but the reason he gave to Cavour's personal representative in Paris, Count Costantino Nigra, was simply that he wished to allow Couza time to consolidate his government. And in this same interview of March 4 the emperor urged a policy of caution, arguing that Europe had divined Franco-Sardinian intentions, that public opinion was aroused in Britain and Germany, that under these circumstances it was impossible to prepare for war before early 1860, and that a respite was needed, a period of getting more firmly in the saddle, during which it would be necessary to pursue "la campagna diplomatica."[3]

2. Beyens, Le Second Empire, I, 146; Riker, The Making of Roumania, 175, 189; Hübner, Neuf ans, II, 251, journal entry of January 8, 1859.

3. Cavour to Prince Napoleon, Turin, February 10, 1859, in Cavour-Nigra, II, 8, no. 248; Charles Rogier to Baron Adolphe Pierre de Vrière, Paris, February 14, 1859, in Discailles, Un diplomate belge à Paris, 502; Count Costantino Nigra to Cavour, Paris, March 4, 1859, in Cavour-Nigra, II, 51–54, no. 282.

As it turned out, the diplomatic campaign was not to be developed in relation to the conference on the Principalities,[4] because, on March 16, Russia proposed a five-power congress to deal with the crisis in Italy. Observers at the time were convinced that Russia acted in this instance at Napoleon's instigation, which may indeed have been the case. Certainly in his concern with public opinion, in his desire to appear in the right and, if possible, to "act vigorously and skillfully to detach England and Prussia from Austria," the emperor might well have seen advantages in a congress. Besides, the thought of such a meeting was not a novelty with him. Palmerston later commented, "I have heard him suggest it in almost every conversation I have had with him on European affairs at any time for several years past." At the end of January, Walewski had talked with Hübner of the possibility of a congress, and the Austrian had had no doubt that the idea was Napoleon's. He also attributed to the French emperor London's "insinuation" to Buol in February of the idea "de soumettre à un congrès européen le règlement des affaires d'Italie." On the other hand, the idea was very much in the air. Berlin, in late January, was beating the drum on its behalf both at Saint Petersburg and at Paris, and the negotiations, which culminated on March 3, 1859, in a secret Franco-Russian alliance, might have inspired the Russian proposal without need of direct French intervention. After all, Napoleon had written to the czar during those negotiations: "Chance puts us today in the same position. Your Majesty would like to change, in part, the treaty of Paris [of 1856]; I would like to change, in part, the treaties of 1815. Nevertheless, both of us are forced to respect the existing treaties so long as war has not given existence to a new congress. Soon a happy circumstance will present itself. The more we make common cause, the stronger we will be at the peace to dictate to the other powers." Well enough, but why *after* a war? From Napoleon's point of view, the alliance, which pledged Russia to benevolent neutrality in the event of a Franco-Austrian war, would be just as useful at a congress (where prudent participants would have lined up their supporters in advance) as during a conflict. Once the congress had been proposed, Gorchakov talked freely of using it to secure revision of the 1856 treaty.[5]

4. The conference met only twice before being interrupted by the outbreak of hostilities in northern Italy. Following the war, it reconvened at Paris (September 6) and accomplished its work in one session. In effect, the protocol of September permitted Couza to accept both elections but upheld the principle of separation of the Principalities (Riker, *The Making of Roumania*, 226–49).

5. Napoleon III to Victor Emmanuel, Tuileries, January 12, 1859, in *Cavour-Nigra*, I, 299, no. 228; Palmerston to Clarendon, 94 Piccadilly, April 24, 1859, in Maxwell, *The*

In the end, the most telling argument against Napoleon's having directly instigated the congress proposal is the curious fact that Saint
Petersburg attempted to yield the initiative to Paris and was only dissuaded by an exchange of telegrams. After all, Napoleon could always
have proposed a congress had he wished to do so. If he had asked for
any assistance from Russia, it would have certainly been in the form
of a Russian *initiative*. No misunderstanding would have been possible on that point. Nor does it really matter who proposed the congress. The promptness of French acceptance (which came on March
17), and Napoleon's own appraisal of the Russian action, clearly indi-
cates that if he had not suggested it to Saint Petersburg it was only
because he had not had to do so. He wrote to Cavour: "Russia, who
makes common cause with me in this situation, has understood the
falsity, even the danger, of my position. She has proposed the only
means now existing of my putting myself in the right without abandoning the cause I want to serve, and that is the convocation of a congress."[6] There can be no doubt, then, that Napoleon welcomed the
congress proposal. But to what end?

Among the possibilities, two immediately present themselves. Perhaps Napoleon accepted the congress merely as a means of buying
time in which better to prepare public opinion and complete his military preparations. Perhaps, at the other extreme, he now desperately
wanted a way out of his commitment to Cavour and saw the congress
as a device to serve that purpose. Observers (sometimes the *same* observers) saw reason to accept each of these explanations in turn. Certainly public opinion in France and in Europe was clearly opposed to
the war, and for that very reason military preparations had been allowed to lag. La Gorce would later find evidence in the archives of the
War Department that Marshal Vaillant, the minister of war, regarded

---

Life and Letters of Clarendon, II, 182; Hübner, *Neuf ans*, II, 270–71, 276–77; Baron
Alexander G. A. von Schleinitz to Prince Heinrich VII von Reuss, Berlin, January 22,
1859, in *APP*, I, 184–85; Napoleon III to Alexander II, Paris, December 22, 1858, in
Hauterive, "Mission du Prince Napoléon à Varsovie," 850; Count Emerich von Szechenyi
von Sarvar und Felso-Videk to Buol, Saint Petersburg, private, March 28, 1859, in
HHSA, PA IX, Russland, Varia, Box 48 (reference supplied by John Jensen).
    6. Walewski to the French chargé at Saint Petersburg, Paris, and the chargé to Walew-
ski, telegrams, March 20, 1859, both in AMAE, CP, Russie, 218:200, 202; Walewski to
Count Paul Kisselev, Paris, March 17, 1859, in AMAE, CP, Russie, 218:198–99. Napoleon himself lent such speedy support to the idea in a conversation with Cowley that
for a while London was to assume that the congress proposal had come from him
(Malmesbury, *Memoirs*, III, 21–22). Napoleon III to Cavour, Tuileries, March 23, 1859,
in *Cavour-Nigra*, II, 136, no. 352.

the congress as a chance to complete military preparations. That, of course, was his job. Cowley, who had come into possession of a letter that he believed genuine (it was) and in which, on the emperor's orders, the prefects were urged to prepare a war opinion in France, could not simply dismiss the rumors that abounded. Was it not said that Napoleon had told Cavour that he must be patient until July, that the French army would then have 700,000 men ready to take the field, and that Turin "must pay no attention to anything which H.M. might do or say in the interim"? And yet, the British ambassador could also write:

> The Emperor has no wish to treat separately with Austria, because he is equally convinced that nothing which he, or even Europe, can do will satisfy the Italian Revolutionists, which is his fear, and he prefers treating in a Congress, because he can then tell Italy that the work which may be accomplished is the work of the Congress, who will bear the responsibility, and not he. His object is the expulsion of the Austrians from Italy and nothing else will really satisfy him, but this he knows he cannot obtain in a Congress, therefore he wishes the Congress to bear all the onus of the shortcomings which must result from negotiations.

In fact, according to Cowley, Napoleon had asked him to persuade London to accept the congress "because it would open a door of retreat for him, and would enable him to tell Sardinia that he must be satisfied with that which satisfied Europe."[7]

One thing is certain; the French emperor would not accept a settlement achieved through normal diplomatic channels. When the British government sent Cowley on a special mission to Vienna (February 27 to March 13), charged with seeking such a solution, Napoleon told Nigra in detail how he would frustrate any possible fruitful outcome by simply raising the stakes. More than that, Cowley strongly suspected that Paris and Saint Petersburg had concocted the congress when his mission seemed likely to succeed, a rather ungracious point of view, since the British ambassador did not find at Vienna any willingness to make meaningful concessions. But would Napoleon accept a settlement from a congress, and did he really want one? In view of his strong penchant for conference diplomacy, his earlier efforts (and many subsequent ones) to bring the Italian question before a con-

7. Case, *French Opinion on War and Diplomacy*, 51–68; La Gorce, *Histoire du Second Empire*, III, 5; Cowley to Malmesbury, Paris, private, February 14, April 25, 1859, both in PRO, FO, 519, 225:60–61, 185; Cowley to Malmesbury, Paris, confidential, April 5, 1859, in PRO, FO, 519, 9:251, no. 377.

gress, and his ultimate acceptance of this one, despite, as we shall see, the strong objections of Cavour and several opportunities to sabotage it without great blame, the explanations that he himself gave of his policies in a long letter to Walewski (March 25) are worth considering.

> As Count Cavour will arrive tomorrow it would be a good idea for us to understand each other in advance in order to use the same language.
>
> 1. What is it that I want? That Austria leave the congress isolated.
>
> 2. How to arrive at this result? By pushing our demands as far as possible. M. Pourtalès [Count Albrecht von Pourtalès, the minister of Prussia at Paris] told me again the other day that Italy must be given a real satisfaction. But it can be real only if equivalent to the famous "nonintervention" system of Louis Philippe; because you understand that if the congress does not lead to a result at least equal to that proclaimed by the last government it would be shameful for me.
>
> So, the thing that has to be done (and here is the whole point) is to find a terrain which will isolate Austria—not satisfy her. You will have to grasp this idea fully in advance so that once the congress has gathered, the result will not be a rejection of all our proposals.
>
> This said, here is what I intend to tell Cavour.
>
> "The question of Italy has been badly presented; the congress will replace it on a good footing. Today I cannot make war without great danger. Wait for the solution of the questions brought forward at the congress and help me find and advance them.
>
> "If, as I hope, the congress takes a decision contrary to Austria, the war will come in good circumstances. If, on the contrary, Austria yields on all points, it will be necessary to console ourselves and to postpone the game until another day."[8]

Now, in one hypothesis, this policy is unequivocal. If Austria were to refuse the congress or, having come to the conference table, were to reject a program for Italy acceptable to the other powers, then the congress would have served the useful purpose of putting Vienna in the wrong and of giving an aura of respectability to the quarrel that Cavour had picked. Understandably, it was this possibility that Napoleon stressed to the Sardinians, even going so far as to leave Nigra under the impression that he had accepted the congress only because he knew that Austria would not do so. Nevertheless, the policy clearly had a corollary: if Austria came to the congress and negotiated seri-

8. Nigra to Cavour, Paris, March 12, 1859, in *Cavour-Nigra*, II, 136, no. 352; Cowley to Malmesbury, Paris, confidential, April 5, 1859, in PRO, FO, 519, 9:251–53, no. 377; Cowley to Walewski, Vienna, private, March 2, 1859, in PRO, FO, 519, 225:65–68; Napoleon III to Walewski, March 25, 1859, in Bernardy, "Un fils de Napoléon," 578–79.

ously, then Napoleon must accept a compromise, even if it achieved less for Italy than he had hoped to accomplish. In fact, it requires no reading between the lines to see that the emperor understood this very well. "If Austria . . . yields on all points, it will be necessary to console ourselves and to postpone the game until another day." Earlier he had advised Turin "that one ought to have the air of believing in the possibility of a diplomatic solution outside any infraction of the existing treaties—a solution which would certainly not be definitive, but which would make patience possible." In his first interview with Nigra following the Russian proposal of a congress, Napoleon stated his reason for accepting as being the hope either of obtaining something good for Italy (*qualche cose di buono*) if the congress met or of modifying the dispositions of Berlin and London in his favor if it failed to meet because of an Austrian refusal. Several days later he encouraged Cavour not to lose courage; think, he urged him, "of what must be done at the Congress." And the letter that he wrote at about this time to the prince regent of Prussia, requesting support for the congress, concludes with the thought that "if the congress results in giving a legitimate satisfaction to the griefs of Italy all will be calmed [*apaisé*] and we will be able, as in the past, to concentrate without fear on the works of peace."[9]

As to what Napoleon would consider a "legitimate satisfaction" for Italy, Cowley came to hold a very moderate view:

From the conversations which I have had, both with the Emperor and with Count Walewski, I infer that they are under no illusion as to the difficulties with which they will have to contend in obtaining any great amelioration in the internal administration of the affairs of the different States of Italy. If the Pope can be persuaded to appoint a separate Government for the Legations under a Roman Prince; if an Assembly of some sort, even if named by the Sovereign, was to be instituted in each separate State, without the consent of which no taxes could be voted; and if something like a Confederation was to be formed among all the States, for their mutual internal and external safety—Austria abandoning her separate Treaties; I should hope that the Emperor would declare himself satisfied.

Count Walewski assures me that the confidential reports received by the French Government from Italy tend to prove that the Moderate party nei-

9. Nigra to Cavour, Paris, telegram, March 17, 1859, in *Cavour-Nigra*, II, 103, no. 323; Nigra to Cavour, Paris, February 28, 1859, in *Cavour-Nigra*, II, 42, no. 274; Marquis Salvatore Pes de Villamarina to Cavour, Paris, March 22, 1859, in *Cavour-Nigra*, II, 128, no. 346; Napoleon III to Prince Regent William, Tuileries, in *APP*, I, 348, no. 213.

ther expect nor desire more than I have stated; and the realization of so moderate a scheme ought not to be impossible.

Cowley even thought that "all . . . the French really care about is rescinding the separate treaties" and that, in the face of British opposition, Napoleon would not press for what he really wanted—expulsion of the Austrians from Lombardy. On March 26, the day after his long letter to Walewski, Napoleon stated in notes to his foreign minister and to Cowley what he would consider an acceptable solution to the Italian problem: an Italian confederation, some reforms, and the abolition of the Austrian treaties with individual Italian states. A month earlier, Walewski had sketched these same points in an interview with the British ambassador and had indicated that they were by no means sine qua non and would be subject to negotiation at the conference table. His tone was very moderate. Of course, at this point the foreign minister and his master probably had rather different views, at least to the extent that Walewski wanted to avoid a war, while Napoleon would accept one if he could not begin the realization of his program in any other way.[10]

Certainly the idea of an Italian confederation was at the heart of the French emperor's plans for the congress. It was, as we have seen, an old idea, dating at least to 1849. In April, 1851, he had told Normanby that he was considering a project to establish at Rome "a sort of confederation of the Italian powers"; to General La Marmora he had expressed the opinion in January, 1856, that only a confederation could bring an end to Italy's troubles; and several months later, after the opening of the congress, he had sketched, in a note dictated to his private secretary, Jean François Mocquard, a brief plan of organization, featuring the pope as nominal head, a Diet (based on population) meeting at Rome and having sovereignty in matters of general interest. Austria would, for its Italian possessions, have the same relation to the confederation as the king of Holland had to the Frankfurt Diet for his possession of Luxemburg. Now, on the presumed eve of another congress, he returned to the idea. But sincerely? On March 4, he told Nigra that a sort of "confédération restreinte" should be proposed

10. Cowley to Malmesbury, Paris, private, March 18, 1859, in PRO, FO, 519, 19:252, no. 377 (see also, for Napoleon's account to Cowley of what he would consider an acceptable minimum settlement, Ollivier, L'empire libéral, III, 551); Cowley to Malmesbury, Paris, private, March 20, April 8, 1859, both in PRO, FO, 519, 225:86, 140; Walewski to Napoleon III, March 26, 1859, in Raindre, "Les papiers inédits du Comte Walewski," 299; La Gorce, Histoire du Second Empire, I, 402–403.

(a league of Rome, the duchies, Tuscany, and Sardinia), even if unrealizable, because Austria would not accept it, and it would therefore make an excellent ultimatum. Yet, before receiving Napoleon's instructions to find an issue on which Austria would be isolated at the congress, Walewski assured Cowley "that if the league of the small states is obtained, never mind how restricted in its application, the Emperor will be quite satisfied," because such a league was "the dream of his life." And as for Austria not accepting such a proposal under any circumstances, had not a Foreign Office memorandum of June 4, 1856, argued against an Italian confederation, because, among other reasons, it would serve to reinforce Austria's position in Italy? Would not Britain be a powerful advocate at Vienna of the *principle* of a confederation, if war could be avoided only through such a device? And could not Walewski be expected to work diligently toward devising an acceptable formula, for the same reason?[11] If the congress were to meet, it is obvious that no one could guarantee that it would fail, and certainly no one could promise the isolation of Austria. Clearly the touchstone of Napoleon's policy lay, therefore, not in anything that he might say as to what he would or would not do at the conference table, but rather in whether he would do everything in his power to assure that the congress did not meet or, more exactly, that Austria should reject it. Cavour well understood this, and his attitude toward the emperor as the negotiations unfolded is another indication that should not be ignored.

Cavour must have been pleased with Napoleon's first move. On February 4, there had appeared at Paris a pamphlet titled *L'Empereur Napoléon III et l'Italie*. Signed by Louis Etienne, vicomte de La Guéronnière, but inspired, as everyone knew, by the emperor, the pamphlet sketched a program that was certainly calculated to frighten Austria away from the conference table: an Italian federation with Rome as capital and the pope as president; reformed lay government in the Papal States; an Italian army under Sardinian leadership; the withdrawal of Austria from the peninsula. Now Cavour urged Napoleon to take any of the decisive actions that would have forestalled

11. Simpson, *Louis Napoleon and the Recovery of France*, 51 n.; Pingaud, "Napoléon III et ses projets de confédération italienne," 333–36; Cowley to Malmesbury, Paris, private, March 21, 1859, in PRO, FO, 519, 225:94–95. By March 19, Walewski had approved the draft of a detailed constitution for an Italian confederation (Blumberg, "The Demise of Italian Federalism," 65–66). Cowley did not reject the principle, but discouraged any plan of discussing these details at the congress (Cowley to Malmesbury, Paris, confidential, April 5, 1859, in PRO, FO, 519, 9:252–53, no. 377).

the congress without doing too much damage to appearances. One of these would have been to insist on the inclusion of Sardinia on the same footing as the great powers; another, to establish an agenda in advance. At the very least, Cavour wanted an agreement, in writing, to a list of minimum concessions to be demanded of Austria by France and Sardinia. What would happen, after all, if at the congress Vienna accepted the terms worked out by Cowley during his mission, asking in return only a guarantee of Austria's Italian possessions? Napoleon's reply was hardly reassuring: "The response to make to England would in that case be more difficult; but I don't think Austria will go that far."[12]

In the end, Napoleon rejected all of Cavour's proposals. Obviously he did not, as did the Sardinian, want simply to dispose of the congress in order to get on with a war. He even permitted Walewski to give French support to the Russian hint that, if Austria proved balky, a *four*-power conference would be in order, and he attempted (unsuccessfully) to bring Cowley to this point of view. When Cavour arrived in Paris on March 26, he learned, at his first interview with the emperor, that Napoleon had already agreed that Sardinia and the other Italian states should be invited to attend the congress in a consultative role only. As for the rest of Cavour's objectives, Walewski's appraisal that he failed to obtain them is supported by the many accounts of the supreme discouragement that now prevailed at Turin. The French representative there reported, several days after Cavour's return: "Before his trip to Paris, Cavour, at the mere mention of the reunion of a congress, remarked that Italy was sacrificed, that outside of war there was no solution possible for her. . . . Today,—I state it with pleasure and the same observation has been made by those of my colleagues who have had occasion to see Cavour since his return—he admits the possibility of a more or less lengthy adjournment of the realization of his hopes." Perhaps so. But according to Cowley, Cavour had been furious during his meeting with the emperor at Paris and had told Napoleon to his face that it was a *lâcheté* to abandon Sardinia.[13]

12. Cavour to Napoleon III, March 19, 1859, in *Cavour-Nigra*, II, 117–20, no. 336; memorandum of Cavour, March 30, 1859, in *Cavour-Nigra*, II, 146–50, no. 364; Nigra to Cavour, March 12, 1859, in *Cavour-Nigra*, II, 85, no. 304.

13. Pierre F. F. d'Aymard, marquis de Chateaurenard, to Walewski, Saint Petersburg, April 3, 1859, in AMAE, CP, Russie, 218:241–44, no. 32; Walewski to Napoléon Auguste Lannes, duc de Montebello, Paris, April 4, 1859, in AMAE, CP, Russie, 218:248–51, no. 21; Cowley to Malmesbury, Paris, private, April 8, 1859, in PRO, FO, 519,

In fact, Napoleon had made hardly any effort to gain a special place for Sardinia at the congress. By his own admission he agreed that "when it is a matter of discussing a question of European interest with the great powers alone, it is impossible to admit, as an exception, another power to that discussion." His proposal was that the Italian states be invited to the congress for consultation. Since Buol, at almost exactly this time, had suggested the consultative participation of all Italian states except Sardinia, and since Russia and Britain soon joined France in arguing for the inclusion of Sardinia on the same terms, and since Cavour's determination not to attend the congress under such circumstances (but to supply necessary information by letter) freed the Austrians from rubbing elbows at the conference table with a Sardinian representative, Vienna would have found it very difficult to reject the arrangement. To this point, Napoleon's actions had certainly not been those of a man determined to scuttle the congress on any reasonable pretext.[14]

However, if such was really his intent after all, one more opportunity now presented itself. Unable (in all probability) to prevent at least the limited participation of Sardinia, Vienna turned to a demand clearly stated from the beginning—preliminary Sardinian disarmament, without which Austria would not attend the congress. Buol's subsequent proposal of general disarmament, which all the great powers quickly accepted in principle, France among the first, did not alter the critical issue. If Paris did not order the recalcitrant Sardinians to disarm, there would be no congress. It was, as Hübner foresaw, the final test of Napoleon's intentions. And at first he was obstinate, arguing that the Austrian proposal of general disarmament could apply only to the five great powers, since they alone would be full participants in the congress. To Walewski, on April 14, he marked out a clear position. "Here is what I want you to phrase in a note that could be published: 'The French government has accepted the proposition of a congress. It has not refused to admit the principle of a general disarmament. If the cabinet of St. James will be willing to admit Sar-

225:142; Cavour to Victor Emmanuel, Paris, March 28, 1859, in *Cavour-Nigra*, II, 140–42, no. 358; Hübner to Buol, April 1, 1859, in V. Wellesley and Sencourt (eds.), *Conversations with Napoleon III*, 162; Henri Godefroi, prince de La Tour d'Auvergne, to Walewski, Turin, April 5, 1859, in AMAE, CP, Sardaigne, 345:254–55, no. 41; Cowley to Malmesbury, Paris, private, April 1, 1859, in PRO, FO, 519, 225:124.
    14. Napoleon III to Prince Napoleon, March 19, 22, 1859, both in Hauterive (ed.), *Napoléon III et le Prince Napoléon*, 150–51, 156.

dinia to the congress as the most interested party, but *au même titre* as the great powers, then France will officially invite Sardinia to accept the principle of disarmament.'" It was a reasonable stand, which could have been maintained and yet was not. Why? The strong advice from London and Saint Petersburg as well as from Walewski to yield to Austrian demands was certainly a factor, as was the popularity of the congress in France. Napoleon could not be indifferent to Cowley's clear intimation that England could not even promise neutrality if he persisted in backing Sardinian aggression. Probably there was more. Cowley had said that the French emperor had now to choose between the congress and Cavour. In the end, it was Cavour's misfortune that one of Napoleon's most obstinate ideas—to help Italy—had collided with an equally obstinate one—to work, if at all possible, within the context of the European concert. For whatever reason, the requisite pressure was brought to bear; on the evening of April 18, Turin accepted the principle of disarmament, as France had done ten days before.[15]

Napoleon's role in this final scene is not clear. We know that Walewski, at noon, had advised Turin, in his own name, to yield on the understanding that Sardinia would be fully represented at the congress in all matters relating to the disarmament. Apparently Cavour remained unmoved, because at 3:45 P.M. the French foreign minister sent a telegram of quite different import: "The emperor charges you to engage Sardinia to accept the principle of disarmament and to make it known at London by the telegraph. Add that we will accept the congress only if Sardinia and the other Italian states are invited to take a part in it." Had Walewski deliberately acted against the orders of his master? Nothing would have been more out of character. Had Napoleon chosen to give the impression that his foreign minister, and not he himself, had coerced Cavour? Such an explanation would be more in line with the characters of the two men as we know them. But it really does not matter, because Napoleon not only accepted the result; he plainly showed his relief. "Cavour has already officially replied that he would accept the principle of disarmament if he were

---

15. Buol to Victor Petrovich Balabine, Vienna, March 23, 1859, in AMAE, CP, Autriche, 474:26v; Prince Napoleon to Cavour, Paris, telegram, April 13, 1859, in *Cavour-Nigra*, II, 158–59, no. 380; Napoleon III to Walewski, April 14, 1859, in Raindre, "Les papiers inédits du Comte Walewski," 300–301; Case, *French Opinion on War and Diplomacy*, 66–67; Cowley to Malmesbury, Paris, private, April 10, 14, 1859, both in PRO, FO, 519, 225:145, 163.

admitted to the congress," the emperor wrote to Prince Napoleon. "England accepting, the chances of war diminish for the present."[16]

London did accept, but on condition that Sardinia and the other Italian states not attend the congress on the same footing as the great powers. In its final form the arrangement was that the disarmament should be carried out by a commission of six, including Sardinia, and that when this task was completed the congress would convene, subsequently inviting the Italian states to attend on the same basis as at Laibach. Paris concurred. "The emperor," Cavour exploded, "has been deceived or is a traitor."[17] Or was he, rather, the strong-nerved Sphinx of the Seine, confident that Vienna would never sit at the same conference table with representatives of Sardinia and that the concession was therefore meaningless? No evidence supports such an interpretation, and much circumstantial evidence argues against it. Only two facts are incontestable. Napoleon had accepted the congress and Austria, by its ultimatum delivered at Turin on April 19, rejected and wrecked it. The simplest explanation of French policy, the one that accords best not only with the facts but also with what had preceded and with what was to follow, is that Napoleon had decided, after years of hesitation, that the time had come to do something for Italy, by diplomacy if possible, by war if necessary. It was neither safe nor right that the Italian sense of nationality should continue indefinitely to be frustrated. Nor could Austria be allowed forever to rule Italians under treaties that took no account of the wishes of the peoples. In 1849 and again in 1856, Napoleon had tried unsuccessfully to win Europe to this point of view. Now he would cut the knot by war, and in such a case France, too, would have claims to make. But if by the threat of war Austria could be brought to the conference table, he would be willing to trust to his skill—and luck—in a congress from which might come at least a first step toward a solution of the Italian prob-

16. Walewski to La Tour d'Auvergne, Paris, telegrams [sent at noon and 3:45 P.M.], April 18, 1859, both in AMAE, CP, Sardaigne, 345:301, 302. The day after Cavour's surrender, the emperor told Prince Napoleon: "I have had an explanation of Cavour's dispatch; La Tour d'Auvergne took a personal reflection of Walewski's for an official dispatch" (Napoleon III to Prince Napoleon, April 19, 1859, in Hauterive [ed.], *Napoléon III et le Prince Napoléon*, 158; the editorial comment attached to this document, as it appears in *Cavour-Nigra*, II, 172, no. 400, suggests Walewski was subjected to a dressing down by the emperor). Napoleon III to Prince Napoleon, April 19, 1859, in Hauterive (ed.), *Napoléon III et le Prince Napoléon*, 158–59.

17. Memorandum, April, 1859, in AMAE, CP, Angleterre, 713:35–36; Cavour to Giacinto Corio, April 19, 1859, in Matter, *Cavour et l'unité italienne*, III, 182 n.

lem under the aegis of the concert of Europe. Contemporaries recognized Napoleon's intent. "It would have been enough," wrote Eugène Forcade in *Revue des deux mondes* (June 30, 1859), "to obtain *something* for Italy, no matter how little, under European sanction." In the sense of a coalition of the great powers to preserve the status quo, the concert had been weakened by the Crimean War and had been dealt a fatal blow at Plombières; in the sense of an instrument to effect necessary changes and reforms, even if slowly and cautiously, it would certainly find a champion in the French emperor. Some three years before, Napoleon had foreseen the pitfalls of the Italian question: "The aim of all statesmen should be to provide against the ferments of discord still existing in Europe. But one only needs to open one's eyes to see that Italy is the country most menacing to European repose, because it is constituted in such a way as not to satisfy any legitimate interest. To reconstitute it would necessitate a revolution or a war, two extreme fatalities; and even in such a case, what man would be strong enough to impose his will on a country so divided?" The mood with which he now prepared for war is perhaps best reflected in a sentence that he had himself added to La Guéronnière's pamphlet: "We ardently hope that diplomacy may accomplish before a conflict what it will certainly do after a victory."[18] Soon, in his search for a durable resolution of the Italian question, Napoleon would turn again to diplomacy—and to the concert of Europe as he would have it be.

18. Pingaud, "Napoléon III et ses projets de confédération italienne," 333; Case, *French Opinion on War and Diplomacy*, 59.

CHAPTER 7

The Italian Question
1859–1860

Almost from the beginning of hostilities between France and Austria in May, 1859, it was assumed that Europe would be called upon to sanction, perhaps even to help shape, the settlement that would emerge from the war. An article prepared for *Moniteur* that month praised Napoleon and Victor Emmanuel for having taken care to reserve until the conclusion of peace the solution of questions involving the organization of certain Italian states, since it was their intention to resolve them "only in concert with the powers of Europe." Gorchakov had predicted a congress as early as May 24, while the Russian ambassador at London spoke soothingly in the first week of June of his conviction that there was no cause for worry, the war would end sooner than people might expect and in a transaction to which Europe would be called upon to give its consent. For his part, Victor Emmanuel expressed his regret at the revolution that had broken out in the Papal States on June 11, since it might cause Italy, in a congress, to lose the fruits of the war. On June 25, three weeks after the victory at Magenta, which had opened Lombardy to him, and the day following the great French victory at Solferino, Napoleon spoke through his ambassador, Antoine Alfred Agénor, duc de Gramont, to the people of Rome: "Even if God should give me the victory, I would not have the presumption to suppose that I alone could regulate the destinies of Italy. Europe would want to resolve the questions which attach to the European balance."[1]

1. Project of an article for *Moniteur*, May, 1859, in AMAE, MD, France, 2119: no. 9; notice on a conversation of Gorchakov with Sir J. T. Crampton, confidential, May 24, 1859, in AMAE, CP, Russie, 219:46; Persigny to Walewski, London, June 5, 1859, in AMAE, CP, Angleterre, 713:266, no. 65; Victor Emmanuel to Prince de Carignano, June 24, 1859, in *Cavour-Nigra*, II, 229, no. 471; Napoleon III to Antoine Alfred Agénor, duc de Gramont, Cavriana, June 25, 1859, in AMAE, MD, France, 2119: no. 13.

Certainly Napoleon was under pressure to turn again to diplomacy. Persigny, who had replaced Pélissier in May as French ambassador at London, repeatedly urged that France announce for a congress. And Walewski, an opponent of the war and of Cavour's ambitions, was un-equivocal: "It is indispensable [he wired on the eve of armistice dis-cussions between Napoleon and Francis Joseph] that Your Majesty pose as an absolute condition that a European congress will be called to regulate the peace on the bases decided between you and the em-peror of Austria, bases which ought to be only preliminaries." The revolutions in Italy (especially in the Papal States), the inconclusive nature of the French victories, the growing desire in France for peace, the hostility of Prussia—all factors that led Napoleon on July 11 to conclude an unexpected armistice with the Austrians at Villafranca— were also reasons for his wanting to involve Europe in the reorganiza-tion of Italy. Can they be said to have caused the subsequent congress proposal? Only, perhaps, in the sense that, had all gone well, Napo-leon might have been tempted to turn from the path he had followed with regard to Italy since 1849. "Unless the Emperor changed his mind completely," Cowley had written at the beginning of June, "he would make no separate terms with Austria, but would ask for a Con-gress of all the Powers." Things did not go well; and the emperor did not exactly change his mind. Still, there was a distinction to be drawn between making peace in a congress and seeking sanction by a con-gress of peace terms already agreed upon. Whether from preference, or—which was more likely—because he knew of Francis Joseph's un-willingness to participate in a congress, Napoleon chose to argue that France and Austria should agree together before Europe imposed terms on them. Perhaps Walewski was uneasy as to how far his mas-ter would push that argument. "I have told the three powers," he tele-graphed Napoleon on the day following Villafranca, "that Your Maj-esty had wanted a congress and that you are ready to give support to any sort of conference or analogous arrangement which seems suit-able." In Paris a week later, Napoleon offered no resistance to his for-eign minister's thesis. The emperor, Walewski assured Cowley, "was very anxious that a Congress should take place." The foreign minister even suggested that Britain propose the congress and, on the follow-ing day, reassured French representatives that Napoleon continued to "hope that the powers will be able to come together . . . to concert on the questions raised by the present state of things in Italy—questions which touch the general interest." In fact, Napoleon was not long in dispatching to Francis Joseph a personal plea: "I wish with all my heart that those questions may be settled between us as soon as possible. The great powers, in effect, cannot prevent us from personally concluding the peace, but they seem to demand the right to sanction all arrangements which have a European character and which do not interest us directly. I come, then, to inquire of Your Majesty if you would offer opposition to this—that after the signature of the peace treaty there be some conferences to examine and sanction the consequences of this treaty."[2]

Napoleon did not necessarily want a congress for its own sake. What he did want was a settlement he could accept and a ratification of that settlement by the other great powers. Evidently he held out to the new Austrian envoy, Prince Richard Metternich, the possibility of a direct understanding that would end the matter without a congress. Walewski had hinted at this in the first week of August. A month later, Napoleon told Metternich that if Francis Joseph accepted an Italian confederation including Venetia, a simple Austro-French declaration could arrange everything. If Italy then resisted, a congress would be needed, but Austria and France, being agreed, could be almost certain of having their proposals accepted. At any rate, however, the suspicions of London and Saint Petersburg, the unwillingness of the Italians to take back their deposed rulers (including the pope), the preference of many Italian leaders for union rather than confederation, the intractability of Vienna, and the personal quandary in which Napoleon found himself concerning the temporal power of the pope (which he did not support, but which he could not too openly condemn without alienating the Catholic party in France) all conspired to make a settlement "out of court" unlikely if not impossible. Besides, as Russell pointed out, a congress on Italian affairs was "a favourite project of the Emperor Napoleon."[3]

2. Walewski to Napoleon III, Paris, telegram, July 10, 1859, in AMAE, MD, France, 2119: no. 69; Cowley to Malmesbury, Paris, private, June 3, 1859, in PRO, FO, 519, 225:232–33; Walewski to Napoleon III, Paris, July 12, 1859, in Raindre, "Les papiers inédits du Comte Walewski," 313; Cowley, to Russell, Paris, private, July 18, 1859, in Russell Papers, 30/22, 53; Walewski to French representatives at the major capitals, July 18, 1859, in AMAE, CP, Angleterre, 714:56; Napoleon III to Francis Joseph, July [24], 1859, in AMAE, CP, Autriche, 474:250 bis.

3. Prince Richard Metternich to Count Johann Bernhard von Rechberg, Paris, August 7, 1859, in HHSA, PA IX, Fr. Ber., 1859, VIII–XII, Box 63, no. 1A-B, fols. 9–19; Metternich to Rechberg, Paris, September 5, 1859, in HHSA, PA IX, Fr. Ber., 1859, VIII–XII, Box 63, no. 8A-C, fols. 178–96 (although Napoleon and Metternich had had several conversations since the beginning of August, this was apparently the first occa-

Walewski had already suggested that France would attend a congress without Austria if necessary, and even while Napoleon dangled the possibility of a direct understanding before Vienna he was writing to Victor Emmanuel that, although he wanted nothing more than that Italy should be able definitively to constitute itself, "unfortunately, the Villafranca preliminaries bind me, and if Austria does not show herself more conciliatory it will be necessary to put all our efforts [*esprit*] into a European congress." On September 14, despite an earlier personal appeal to the French emperor, Francis Joseph agreed to go from the peace talks at Zurich to a European congress. Did Napoleon want a congress? That was the question that Metternich put to him in November, and the answer was clear: "Certainement et j'en suis bien aisé. Je serai plus tranquille quand il sera convoqué et réunie." It was a response that he could have made at almost any point during the preceding ten years.[4]

But what results could be expected from a European discussion of so difficult a problem on which the views of the great powers diverged so widely? At the very least, of course, there was Cowley's cynical prognosis; having gained a preponderant influence in Italy and new military prestige, Napoleon would now "throw upon a congress all responsibility for an unpopular arrangement," or, as Queen Victoria put it, France would use Britain (and the other great powers) "for the purpose of solving the complications which she has brought about, or to serve as a scapegoat for their being left unsolved." Metternich, too, suspected that Napoleon would be pleased to have the congress enforce the Villafranca terms. But on the whole this view seems both unrealistic and ungenerous. After all, Italy was not only France's problem, and Napoleon, in his perplexity, seems genuinely to have hoped that something, anything might emerge from a congress discussion. He thought, reported Cowley, that "great good would arise from sifting and examining into the whole question and that perhaps the discussions would lead to some new combination which had not yet been thought of, and upon which all parties would agree, and recommend to Italy."[5]

sion on which the emperor mentioned the word *congress*); Russell to Palmerston, October 16, 1859, in Gooch (ed.), *The Later Correspondence of Lord John Russell*, II, 24.

4. Napoleon III to Victor Emmanuel, Saint-Sauveur, September 1, 1859, in *Cavour-Nigra*, II, 254, no. 485; Metternich to Rechberg, Paris, November 16, 1859, in HHSA, PA IX, Fr. Ber., 1859, VIII–XII, Box 63, no. 16A-B, fol. 462.

5. D'Azeglio to Cavour, London, June 29, 1859, in *Cavour e l'Inghilterra*, vol. II,

France would come to the congress with a minimum program, but that program altered according to circumstances. In May, Napoleon could still talk of the separation of Lombardy and Venetia from Austria. In June his *minimum des minima* was Lombardy, Parma, Piacenza, and Modena for Sardinia. Two weeks later he wrote to Walewski: "It will be better to ask nothing for France but it is necessary to make one state of the Romagna, Parma, and Modena, since these areas will never be pacified otherwise." At Villafranca it was agreed that Lombardy should be ceded to France (who would transfer it to Sardinia); that the Austrian rulers should be allowed to return to Modena and Tuscany if they could do so without the armed aid of Austria or France and if they would agree to grant a general amnesty; that Venetia should be retained by Austria but included in an Italian confederation whose honorary president would be the pope; and that the pope should institute reforms in the Papal States.[6]

By the end of August, Napoleon had had time to make his interpretation of the Villafranca terms known. Of special concern was the Italian confederation. No state would be forced to enter; if any irrevocably refused, the idea would fail. Each state would have votes according to population. The seat would be at Rome, and the pope would be honorary president, but the real head would be "the Italian Sovereign having the largest possessions," represented, as was Austria at Frankfurt, by a minister. The states in the confederation would help each other in resisting aggression and in putting down internal discontent, but only federal troops could be employed and only by order of the confederation. Venetia would be a part of the confederation, the Austrian emperor ruling there by a purely Italian administration and with only Italian troops, while the Venetian fortresses would be "federalized." More than once Napoleon told Cowley that in this confederation scheme he saw "the only possible remedy for the evils to which Italy had been so long subjected."[7]

---

pt. 1, p. 342, no. 1032; Victoria to Albert, July 20, 1859, in Martin, *The Life of His Royal Highness, the Prince Consort*, IV, 392; Hallberg, *Franz Joseph and Napoleon III*, 203; Cowley to Russell, Chantilly, private, November 10, 1859, in Russell Papers, 30/22, 53.

6. Cowley to Malmesbury, Paris, private, May 12, 1859, in PRO, FO, 519, 225:208–209; Napoleon III to Walewski, June 23, July 4, 1859, both in Raindre, "Les papiers inédits du Comte Walewski," 93, 96; Case, *French Opinion on War and Diplomacy*, 90.

7. For Napoleon's interpretation of Villafranca, see Prince Napoleon to Victor Emmanuel, August 2, 1859, in *Cavour-Nigra*, II, 237–52, no. 481; Cowley to Russell,

As an item for action by the congress, an Italian confederation was certainly feasible. It was, after all, an old idea with a fairly reputable precedent in the German Confederation, and the great powers might well have found it to be the least troublesome of possible arrangements. Venetia would pose a problem, but more immediately there was the difficulty of reorganizing the states of central Italy—Parma, Modena, Tuscany, the Romagna—all of which were in revolt against their rulers. In fact, Napoleon tried to the end of August to relate the problems of Venetia and of central Italy. In a letter to Francis Joseph he proposed that, in return for the recall of the grand duke of Tuscany, Austria should give Venetia a separate administration and army, make Mantua and Peschiera federal fortresses, and agree that Parma and Piacenza should be annexed to Sardinia, the duchess of Parma receiving Modena.[8]

In late September, Metternich was invited by Napoleon to Biarritz, and there, on the twenty-seventh, a memorandum was agreed. Veneita, although remaining under the Hapsburg crown, would be a part of the Italian confederation and would have an Italian administration, consisting of provincial assemblies and a central legislature. Moreover, if the Italian federal assembly should decide to create federal fortresses, Venetia would participate in their creation, and only Italian regiments would garrison the fortresses that lay outside Austria. As for the duchies of central Italy, sincere efforts were to be made to clear the way for the annexation of Parma and Piacenza to Sardinia, but this would depend on the restoration of the grand duke of Tuscany. A congress of the great powers signatory to the treaty of Vienna of 1815, and of Rome, Sardinia, and Naples would follow at once "to deliberate upon the use of the most suitable means of pacifying Italy." Except that the French might pronounce in favor of the duchess of Parma, the Austrian and French plenipotentiaries at the congress would act in harmony. Later (November), Napoleon agreed to add to the memorandum a statement that France and Austria would oppose the annexation of the states of central Italy to Sardinia.[9]

Paris, July 18, 1859, in Russell Papers, 30/22, 53; Napoleon III to Francis Joseph, July [24], 1859, in AMAE, CP, Autriche, 474:250 bis; Napoleon III to Francis Joseph, August 26, 1859, in Mallarmé, "Napoléon III et Villafranca," 41–42; Cowley to Russell, Chantilly, private, August 7, 1859, in Russell Papers, 30/22, 53.

8. Metternich to Rechberg, Paris, telegram, no. 16, August 30, 1859, in HHSA, PA IX, Fr. Ber., 1859, VIII–XII, Box 63, fol. 168.

9. Metternich to Rechberg, Biarritz, confidential, annex: project of memorandum, September 27, 1859, in HHSA, PA IX, Fr. Ber., 1859, VIII–XII, Box 63, fols. 264–65;

Undoubtedly the Biarritz memorandum fell far short of what Napoleon had hoped for. He would have preferred Venetia to stand in the same relation to Austria as Luxemburg to Germany, to have an Italian army, to be, in effect, "quasi-independent." And he dreamed of a confederation having one law, one flag, and similar constitutions for all the constituent states, including those of the pope. Nevertheless, in a letter of October 20, he urged Victor Emmanuel to accept the program agreed with Austria, promising to advance at the congress the idea of an Italian army for Venetia and the "federalizing" of Mantua and Peschiera. And to Metternich he offered the additional solace of an assurance that, while France must propose an Italian army so that the Italian states would accept the confederation, Austria could easily persuade the congress to reject such a proposal, especially if Austria were willing to carry out some reforms in Venetia. "Have confidence," he told the ambassador in mid-November, "we will get through the Congress more easily than you think, especially if the Austrian Emperor gives me good arguments vis-à-vis England's pretensions."[10]

In summary, then, Napoleon's minimum program for Italy may be stated as follows. He wanted something more for Sardinia, at least Parma and Piacenza; he very much wanted an Italian confederation, which would include Venetia; he wanted reforms in Italy (especially the Papal States) and the "pacification" of central Italy without annexation to Sardinia or the imposition of unpopular governments upon the Italians. Were these beyond the power of a congress to secure? Certainly there were great difficulties. Cavour's agents would work incessantly for annexation of central Italy to Sardinia; the pope would be intransigent in matters of reform and would resist despoliation; Britain would support nothing that might mean involvement in commitments, open Italy to French control, or seem to frustrate legitimate Italian aspirations; and Austria would hold doggedly to Venetia in hopes of continuing to dominate the peninsula. Napoleon was doubtless aware of all this. In a moment of extreme frankness he admitted to Cowley that, if the Austrians withdrew their garrisons from

---

Metternich to Rechberg, Paris, telegram, no. 73, November 27, 1859, in HHSA, PA IX, Fr. Ber., 1859, VIII–XII, Box 63, fol. 515. Duchess Louise of Parma was a Bourbon, the sister of the comte de Chambord. She had powerful allies in France (Eugénie, Walewski), and Napoleon could not, therefore, promise to ignore her interests.

10. Napoleon III to Victor Emmanuel, Saint-Cloud, October 20, 1859, in AMAE, CP, Sardaigne, 347:275–76; Metternich to Rechberg, Paris, November 16, 1859, in HHSA, PA IX, Fr. Ber., 1859, VIII–XII, Box 63, no. 16B, fols. 470–75.

Venetia, they would lose the province; if their troops remained, Austria would constitute a continual menace to Italy. And to Metternich he bluntly summed up the situation: "There are only two ways to finish the Italian question quickly. Either France and Austria must insist, if necessary by force, upon the restoration of the deposed princes and the submission of the Legations, and that I am pledged not to do. Or you must establish an Archduke in Venetia with an Italian administration and an Italian army finding your compensation elsewhere, and seek in Central Italy the material for a Kingdom of the Center— and this means neither you nor the Holy Father would care to employ." The ambassador observed that it appeared the situation was impossible to resolve. "For the moment," replied Napoleon, "I consider it indeed very difficult."[11]

And yet, the French emperor continued to desire the congress and to oppose any change in the status quo before the representatives assembled. Nor would a European meeting be entirely without devices or resources. Russia was friendly toward France; the British government was favorably inclined toward Italy. To Cowley, Napoleon suggested that Britain could help him greatly by pointing out the impossibility of implementing the Villafranca agreement, thus posing the need for new combinations. What he really wanted, as he made clear on a number of occasions, was that Britain (or Russia) should propose a kingdom of central Italy that would include the Romagna, the whole to be under the rule of the grand duke of Tuscany. Walewski had grave misgivings regarding the Romagna, but by the end of the month Cowley could report that Paris was ready to adopt any plan, "including the separation of the Legations from the Pope, if possible, that may meet with the general sanction of the Congress." And certainly, as Napoleon told Cowley, the congress could "appoint commissions to ascertain the real wishes of the populations, which at all events had not been fairly taken yet," despite the August elections in Tuscany, Parma, Modena, and the Romagna. This, and the moral authority of the European concert, might well have buttressed the particularist sentiments of Italy against the cajoling of Cavour's agents. Perhaps this same authority would have had an effect at Rome and Vienna. Napoleon even suggested "that he felt certain that Austria would if pressed in Congress, herself abandon the idea of participating in an

11. Cowley to Russell, October 5, 1859, in V. Wellesley and Sencourt (eds.), *Conversations with Napoleon III*, 173; Metternich to Rechberg, Paris, very secret, November 26, 1859, in HHSA, PA IX, Fr. Ber., 1859, VIII–XII, Box 63, no. 18A-B, fols. 495–508.

Italian confederation." In fact, Napoleon may already have more than
hinted to Metternich what he really had in mind. "If the Emperor so
wished," he had announced in early September, "I would join with
Him to help Him take His revenge [for granting autonomy to Venetia
within an Italian confederation] in the Orient." And he continued:
"The name Ost-Reich seems to indicate that Austria is predestined to
grow in the East! Would the Emperor hesitate to place an Archduke
over the Danubian Principalities? . . . Well! . . . I should not oppose it,
and besides an Archduke could be summoned by the Rumanian people, if the matter were handled well." The ambassador's objections
seemed to make little impression. "You'll see that you shall come to
it," Napoleon insisted, "as you consider your true interests." Turkey
was going to collapse, and Austria had best prepare for the eventuality.[12] Clearly transactions of this magnitude would require the active cooperation of the great European powers in concert.

And so through the fall of 1859 the mechanism of the congress was
worked out. It would meet in the French capital and would consist of
the eight signatories of the Vienna treaties of 1815 and the three principal Italian states. "The task of the future congress," argued Walewski, "embraces interests at once so considerable and so numerous that
it also seems to the government of the emperor that the gathering of
the powers cannot take on a character too extended or too solemn."
The British, as usual, disagreed, but when all other powers assented to
sending their foreign ministers to Paris, and French handling of the
British grew rather rough, Cowley's protests brought from Walewski
the statement that "the fact was, the Emperor had been so much ému
at the idea of the first Ministers not coming, and the Congress thereby
degenerating into a Conference that H.M. had desired him to write a
circular to all the Powers interested to request them to send their Foreign Ministers to Paris." Another theoretical difference between a
congress and a conference was that the former would not be restricted
to one topic. Here, Paris and Vienna clashed. The French argued that
the powers should concert on all questions raised by the state of Italy
that concerned the general interest. Walewski even thought of including the matter of navigation of the Danube, while Napoleon toyed
with the idea of introducing other non-Italian questions. Austrian

12. Cowley to Russell, Chantilly, private, November 29, 10, 1859, both in Russell
Papers, 30/22, 53; Cowley to Russell, Paris, private, October 26, 1859, in Russell Pa-
pers, 30/22, 53; Metternich to Rechberg, Paris, September 5, 1859, in HHSA, PA IX, Fr.
Ber., 1859, VIII–XII, Box 63, no. 8A-C, fols. 188–91.

protests seemed to have their effect. On September 27, at Biarritz, Napoleon agreed not to introduce any question at the congress without prior accord between France and Austria, and said that he had given up any thought of having the meeting accomplish more than the pacification of central Italy. But Metternich was not at all sure. The French government, he reported, "had always started with the principle that, the deliberations of the Congress being subordinated to the desires that the Powers will express, there will be full freedom for them to speak according to their convictions." Napoleon obviously hoped that in such expressions of conviction a solution could be found. But whatever might be agreed at the congress, it must be acceptable to all parties; for, in the face of British intransigence, Napoleon had ended by denying any thought that the congress could use force to carry out its decisions. On the other hand, Walewski threatened that, if Britain continued to insist that the congress blindly respect "les voeux des populations," it might be necessary to meet without the British representatives.[13]

On November 10 the treaty of Zurich was signed, formally ending the state of war between France and Austria. Shortly afterward, Paris and Vienna issued invitations to a congress to convene January 19. In *Revue des deux mondes*, Eugène Forcade hailed "this relief, this sense of peace and quiet that follows from the certainty that the congress will soon meet." While recognizing that congresses ratified rather than innovated, Forcade hoped that the "Congress of Paris," guided by European opinion, would provide a "natural way of restoring the European concert." And then, on December 22, the pamphlet *Le pape et le congrès* was published anonymously at Paris and became an instant sensation. Understood by all to have been written by La Guéronnière under the direct inspiration of Napoleon, the pamphlet argued that France would not permit restoration of the deposed rulers by force, that the congress could provide a legitimate solution, that it should agree to the separation of the Romagna (and, by implication and in

13. Walewski to French representatives at the major capitals, Paris, October 14, 1859, in AMAE, CP, Angleterre, 714:232–34; Cowley to Russell, Paris, private, December 16, 1859, in Russell Papers, 30/22, 53; Walewski to French representatives at the major capitals, Paris, July 18, 1859, in AMAE, CP, Angleterre, 714:56; Metternich to Rechberg, Biarritz, September 27, 1859, in HHSA, PA IX, Fr. Ber., 1859, VIII–XII, Box 63, no. 11, fol. 261; Metternich to Rechberg, Paris, November 6, 1859, in HHSA, PA IX, Fr. Ber., 1859, VIII–XII, Box 63, no. 11, fol. 405v; Cowley to Russell, Chantilly, private, November 10, 1859, in Russell Papers, 30/22, 53; Metternich to Rechberg, Biarritz, telegram, no. 37, October 4, 1859, in HHSA, PA IX, Fr. Ber., 1859, VIII–XII, Box 63, fol. 277.

due course, the other Legations) from the Papal States, and that the pope ought himself to see the wisdom of such an action. The assumption was made at the time and has been continued since that Napoleon published the pamphlet to sabotage the congress. This is regrettable, not only because it may be wrong, but because its acceptance hides important perceptions of French policy. From Napoleon's point of view, *Le pape et le congrès* was not a repudiation of Villafranca, because for him the essence of the Villafranca agreement had surely been that no settlement should be imposed by force on the Italians and that Venetia should be part of an Italian confederation. All else was negotiable as circumstances developed, preferably by a congress. The arguments of the pamphlet were, in fact, reasonable ones with which a reasonable man might well hope to persuade other reasonable men. The pope's spiritual and moral authority *would* be increased by his withdrawal from the snares of temporal power; and as for the legal difficulties, it *was* true that the Congress of Vienna had given the Romagna to the pope in the first place and that another could take it away, and that popes had agreed to a loss of territory in the past, *e.g.*, Avignon. Moreover, there was to be a major gain for the papacy, to counterbalance its loss of territory, for the pamphlet ended by proposing (and Napoleon's December 31 letter to Pius IX confirmed this intention) that the congress guarantee the pope's possession of the city of Rome. At any rate, no informed person could have doubted, even before the appearance of the pamphlet, that Napoleon favored the separation of the Romagna. As early as July 4, he had wired Walewski to the effect, as we have seen, that it would be necessary to make a separate state of the Romagna, Parma, and Modena. Cavour also knew of this; and at Biarritz in September, Napoleon urged upon Metternich the wisdom of Austria's agreeing to the annexation of the Legations by Tuscany. To Cowley he made clear his preference for a kingdom of central Italy that would include the Romagna, the whole to be under the rule of the grand duke of Tuscany. "The Emperor," Metternich admitted on the day following the appearance of *Le pape et le congrès*, "has many times repeated in his conversations that the Legations would never submit to the pontifical authority and he has not hidden his repugnance toward what he calls the worst government of Europe."[14]

14. *Revue des deux mondes*, August 14, September 14, December 14, 1859; Isser, *The Second Empire and the Press*, 97–122, discusses the pamphlet; Cowley to Russell, October 5, 1859, in Russell Papers, 30/22, 53; Metternich to Rechberg, Paris, December 23, 1859, in HHSA, PA IX, Fr. Ber., 1859, VIII–XII, Box 63, no. 23A-B, fols. 569v–70.

Moreover, if Napoleon intended by the pamphlet to sabotage the congress, he was ahead of some of the most astute diplomatic observers of the day in his estimation of cause and effect. Cowley initially saw the pamphlet as merely a "feeler of public opinion," and ended by concluding that it would not (unfortunately) prevent the congress from meeting. Leopold, the shrewd Belgian king, gave no evidence of suspecting that Napoleon had intended to prevent the congress. Pourtalès regarded the pamphlet as a *faute*, but reasoned that Austria would not seize on it as a pretext for frustrating the congress. And Rogier, Belgium's minister at Paris, not only continued to regard the congress as a thing agreed upon but ended an account of Napoleon's New Year's greeting to the diplomatic corps with the judgment that the emperor's remarks had made a favorable impression on his listeners, indicating that the congress would be able to commence its work sooner than hoped.[15]

Napoleon, for his part, continued to insist that the congress should meet. His December 31 letter to Pius IX revolved around the idea of a congress guarantee. To Metternich at Fontainebleau during the same period he repeatedly demonstrated "the necessity for a Congress." Walewski firmly opposed such a line, declaring that the congress was impossible if Napoleon would not change his policy, and addressing to French representatives a telegram announcing that the congress would not meet on January 19 as planned. But it was Metternich's opinion that Walewski's resignation, on January 4, was the consequence of this telegram. Palmerston remained convinced that Napoleon wanted the congress; Jules Baroche, the interim French foreign minister, repeatedly informed his agents that imperial policy had not changed; Fould, the minister of state, professed himself persuaded that Napoleon "would be disposed to receive favorably any sort of transaction facilitating a preliminary understanding and which would permit Austria to take part in the congress." Well into January, in fact, the emperor continued his efforts to persuade the pope, Cowley, and Metternich that the congress should meet. He was unsuccessful. Rome demanded that the temporal rights of the papacy be guaranteed in advance; and Count Johann Bernhard von Rechberg, the new Aus-

15. Cowley to Russell, Chantilly, private, December 23, 25, 1859, both in Russell Papers, 30/22, 53; Martin, *The Life of His Royal Highness, the Prince Consort*, IV, 422–23; Count Albrecht von Pourtalès to Schleinitz, Paris, confidential, December 31, 1859, in *APP*, I, 845–46, no. 559; Rogier to de Vrière, Paris, December 30, 1859, January 1, 1860, both in Discailles, *Un diplomate belge à Paris*, 568.

trian foreign minister, bluntly informed Paris that if the Romagna were not to be restored, a congress could serve no useful purpose. On January 15 the British government rejected the congress as hopelessly divided.[16]

The evidence suggests, then, that *Le pape et le congrès* was the pretext rather than the reason for Austria's decision. In fact, there is a logical inconsistency in arguing that Napoleon published his pamphlet to sabotage the congress and that Austria rejected the congress because of it. If Napoleon wanted to escape the congress, it could only be because he feared an unacceptable settlement. But a congress that seemed likely to impose such a settlement ought certainly to have been acceptable to Austria. The emperor told Metternich that he had intended, through *Le pape et le congrès*, simply to express his opinion in an anonymous form "in order to make a decision in accordance with the effect produced" and to allow public opinion to declare itself on a combination he considered inevitable. The explanation seems reasonable. Two opposing and irreconcilable views of the concert of Europe had for some time existed, and the notorious pamphlet merely made explicit what must already have been clear to an astute observer. Napoleon would not accept a return to the concert of 1815– 1853, monopolized by the great powers and dedicated to preserving the status quo. He meant to launch a new concert, broader in its membership, sensitive to public opinion, and willing to embrace change. Austria would not submit the Italian question to such a "tribunal" and therefore rejected the congress. The French emperor might be faulted for having provided Austria with a useful pretext, but it could be argued that he had domestic political situations that also required his attention, and that French public opinion proved favorable to the arguments advanced in the pamphlet.[17]

Ironically, if Napoleon would not accept a congress designed to maintain or to impose the status quo, he would nevertheless have attended a congress whose free discussion might have ended in a deci-

---

16. Metternich to Rechberg, Paris, telegram, no. 90, December 31, 1859, in HHSA, PA IX, Fr. Ber., 1859, VIII–XII, Box 63, fol. 600; Salomon, *Ambassade de Richard Metternich*, 57; memorandum of Palmerston, January 5, 1860, in Craven (ed.), *Lord Palmerston*, II, 579; Pourtalès to Schleinitz, Paris, confidential, January 13, 1860, in *APP*, vol. II, pt. 1, pp. 27–29, no. 12.1; Rechberg to Metternich, Vienna, January [10], 1860, in AMAE, CP, Autriche, 476:72–75; Russell to Cowley, London, January 15, 1860, in AMAE, CP, Angleterre, 715:23–26.

17. Metternich to Rechberg, Paris, January 3, 1860, in HHSA, PA IX, Fr. Ber., 1860, I–V, Box 65, no. 1A-D; Case, *French Opinion on War and Diplomacy*, 115–16.

sion much closer to the status quo than he wished. Free discussion there must be. As Walewski told Metternich, in answering the ambassador's charge that France had broken its engagement in the memorandum of September 27 to maintain a complete accord with Vienna and to give full moral support, the French plenipotentiaries would abide by the memorandum but "rather than allow the congress to adjourn without result [they] will not refuse to examine other combinations." Still, Napoleon asked the Austrian on January 20, what did Vienna have to fear? "He did not understand how we would think it to our advantage to renounce participation when everything proves to Him that our ideas and our principles would meet with the greatest sympathy from the majority. . . . The Emperor wished to prove to me that nothing in our understanding had changed—and that on the Roman question he had but expressed an opinion which he would not force anyone to share." In this light, Persigny's reassurance to Metternich that if Austrian rights and interests had to yield, at least they would have "the honor of yielding only before the decision of the whole of Europe," takes on a new significance. Obviously the same argument could hold for France, or even for France and Britain (Cowley feared that, concerning the questions raised by *Le pape et le congrès*, Austria would be sure of having all the powers on its side except Britain and France). In the last analysis, all that Napoleon wished for the congress was that it be allowed to remain "a lottery from which a winning number might be drawn."[18]

Unable to bring the other powers to share his gambling instinct, the French emperor made one final effort to persuade them at least to join him in holding the stakes. His new foreign minister, Thouvenel, had arrived in Paris on January 20, determined that there should be no congress and that Italy would be allowed to find its own way. On January 24, Thouvenel adjourned the congress indefinitely, arguing that the clash of two irreconcilable principles—legitimacy and popular sovereignty—made it unworkable. A week earlier, Cavour, convinced that the congress and the Austrian interpretation of Villafranca were dead, had returned to office in Sardinia. But Thouvenel was pledged to

18. Metternich to Rechberg, Paris, telegram, no. 88, December 28, 1859, in HHSA, PA IX, Fr. Ber., 1859, VIII–XII, Box 63, no. 24, fol. 593 (this statement followed a special meeting of the French council of ministers); Metternich to Rechberg, Paris, January 20, 12, 1860, both in HHSA, PA IX, Fr. Ber., 1860, I–V, Box 65, no. 4A-G, no. 3; Cowley to Russell, Chantilly, private, December 25, 1859, in Russell Papers, 30/22, 53; Cowley to Russell, Paris, private, January 18, 1860, in Russell Papers, 30/22, 54.

execute the policy of his master and to have none of his own. We may assume, therefore, that when on February 3 the French foreign minister suddenly called for a five-power conference to settle the Italian question using recent British proposals as the basis of discussion, he spoke for Napoleon. Brought back from London by Cowley on January 17, the British proposals consisted of four points: France and Austria should agree not to intervene in Italy by force unless called upon to do so by the five great powers; with due precautions for the safety of the pope, French troops should evacuate Rome (and arrangements should be made as well for the evacuation of northern Italy); the internal government of Venetia should not be a matter of negotiation among the powers; and Italian troops should not enter central Italy unless as the result of a plebiscite favoring annexation.[19] In addition, Napoleon had three points of his own that he hoped to have accepted by Turin and ratified by the conference: the annexation of Parma and Modena to Sardinia, restoration of the grand duke of Tuscany (for whom, if necessary, a Sardinian prince could be substituted), and establishment of a vicariate exercised by Victor Emmanuel in the name of the pope for the Romagna, Ferrara, and Bologna. Perhaps on this occasion the emperor thought he had British support. When Thouvenel later claimed that the conference was Cowley's idea, the latter retorted that, in order to turn Napoleon from his idea of a congress, he had merely stated "that of the two a conference was the least liable to objection and that I thought H.M. had committed a great fault in proposing a congress." But London tied all possibility of a conference to the decision of Sardinia, and Cavour in effect made the French proposals unworkable by insisting on their approval by plebiscites. Vienna, too, rejected them. And Thouvenel, reassured concerning the pacific intentions of the great powers, had little enthusiasm for an international gathering. The conference had met the same fate as the congress. Cavour would have his annexations in central Italy without interference from Europe.[20]

19. For Thouvenel's attitude toward the congress, see Case, *Edouard Thouvenel*, 143–52.

20. Thouvenel to Charles Angélique, baron de Talleyrand-Périgord, Paris, confidential, February 21, 1860, in AMAE, CP, Sardaigne, 348:162v–66v, no. 14; Cowley to Russell, Paris, private, February 28, 1860, in Russell Papers, 30/22, 54; Persigny to Thouvenel, London, February 25, 1860, in AMAE, CP, Angleterre, 715:188–91, no. 18; Cavour to Nigra, February 29, 1860, in *Cavour-Nigra*, III, 122–30, no. 608; Baron Karl von Werther to Schleinitz, Vienna, telegram, March 8, 1860, in *APP*, vol. II, pt. 1, p. 209, no. 90.

But if Europe would not accept responsibility for Italy, had Europe any right to meddle in the pretension that France now advanced to have Nice and Savoy as compensation for the unforeseen enlargement of Sardinia?[21] It was a fair question, and French irritation at the challenge immediately raised by Britain is easy to understand. Nevertheless, Napoleon's first reaction was to assure Cowley that France would not act without consulting Europe and gaining the consent of the populations involved. Of course, he did not say that France would be bound by what Europe might advise; but, as he told the British ambassador following a rather heated exchange of views in early March, "he had pledged himself to consult the Great Powers, and . . . he need hardly add that if their opinion should be unfavorable to his wishes, it would have a great weight with him." After all, it was not likely that he would act "against the advice of all Europe." Thus when the promised French "explanation" went out on March 13 it contained, in its first paragraph, the pledge "to submit to the wisdom and justice of Europe a question which was not raised by the ambition of France." The treaty of cession (March 24) contained in Article 2 the suggestion that France consult the powers. Already Switzerland had appealed to the signatories of the 1815 treaties and called for a conference. Britain took the side of Switzerland, and Napoleon indicated to Cowley that he did, indeed, intend a conference, although one that would be strictly and carefully limited. But Thouvenel knew a better way, and in the end the consent of Europe was obtained and the particular problem of Chablais-Faucigny (neutralized in 1815) was solved not by conference but through ordinary diplomatic channels. On July 20, 1860, the Swiss federal council accepted the inevitable. For the Italian problem as a whole, however, Napoleon seems not to have wavered in his belief that only a European congress could solve it. Early in March, Thouvenel sketched French policy for Metternich's benefit: to hold Sardinia in check, to prevent it from absorbing all of Italy, to annex Nice and Savoy if Sardinia obtained Parma and Modena, but to submit all questions pertaining to Italy to a congress.[22] Recriminations now were

21. Talleyrand, at Turin, was formally instructed on February 24 to make the French claim, but the intention dated from mid-January at least (Case, *Edouard Thouvenel*, 153). French public opinion clearly demanded the annexations.

22. Cowley to Russell, Paris, confidential, February 10, 1860, in PRO, FO, 519, 10: no. 102; Cowley to Russell, Paris, March 7, 1860, in *Victoria Letters, 1837–1861*, III, 498–501; circular of Thouvenel to French representatives in the major European capitals, March 13, 1860, in AMAE, MD, Circulaires 742:151–63; Cowley to Russell, Paris, private, March 23, 1860, in Russell Papers, 30/22, 54. On this question of

as easy as they were sterile. For many, the concert of Europe and the maintenance of the treaties were synonymous; and both had been struck down in a spirit of pure (or not-so-pure) adventurism. For Napoleon, on the other hand, Europe, and especially the great powers, had a responsibility to revise and supervise, not merely to maintain. His actions from Plombières on, which have generally been criticized as an irresponsible releasing of forces beyond his control, could also be defended as the initiative necesary to bring to solution questions that had for too long been ignored or suppressed. But rightly or wrongly, France of the Second Empire would advance no pretension to solve these questions itself. And, wisely or tragically, Europe would show little inclination to involve itself as long as there remained an option of noninvolvement. So it was with the Italian question in the remaining months of 1860.

During the spring of that year Paris had watched Garibaldi's preparations with growing disquiet. On May 11, the Red Shirts landed in western Sicily. At Paris, almost the first thought was of a congress. Revolution in Italy, Thouvenel told the Austrian ambassador, was becoming a menace to all of Europe. Only by acting together in either a congress or a conference could the powers put an end to this danger. The powers, however, had little prospect of acting together. French annexation of Nice and Savoy, formalized on June 14, had sharpened an already acute mistrust of Napoleon in London, while at Paris equally strong suspicions existed as to the possibility of the Continental great powers creating a new Holy Alliance, directed against France. Thouvenel might argue, as he did, the virtues of an Italian confederation recognized and guaranteed by Europe, and press Sardinia and the Two Sicilies to negotiate an alliance. And he might warn Turin against the "great and fatal error" of supposing that Europe would view "with indifference the violation of the principles of international law." But Cavour well understood that it was only France he had to fear and that Napoleon, by his own admission, would never intervene alone, for that would be to risk undoing the work for which Frenchmen had died. Napoleon's perplexity is revealed not only by the hints that he redoubled throughout June and July of the necessity for Europe to meet in general congress but also by the extraordinary letter that he wrote and dispatched to Persigny at the end

Chablais-Faucigny, see Case, *Edouard Thouvenel*, 170–77. Metternich to Rechberg, March 9, 1860, in Hallberg, *Franz Joseph and Napoleon III*, 226.

ot July without consulting Thouvenel. Earlier in the month London had rejected a French proposal that, as a first step to having the great powers guarantee a six-month truce in southern Italy, Garibaldi should be prevented by an Anglo-French fleet from crossing to the mainland. The new commercial treaty between the two countries, signed on January 22, had not disarmed British hostility, and a measure to increase military expenditures was before the House of Commons. He desired nothing better, wrote the emperor after a general defense of his foreign policy, than to reach an agreement with Britain regarding southern Italy and all other questions, but, in the name of God, why would the English not put aside their distrust and sit down to talk as among honest men? And to Cowley a month later he complained that "whatever he did was misunderstood, and selfish motives were attributed to every action of his. There was evidently a set of people at work to sow distrust everywhere. . . . He was so annoyed and vexed that he was all but resolved to withdraw France from all participation in the affairs of Europe. No one could then throw any responsibility upon him."[23]

But the French emperor did not withdraw from European affairs. Five days after Garibaldi crossed the Strait of Messina on his way to Naples, Napoleon was at Chambéry, on a visit to Savoy. There, on August 28 he met with Luigi Farini and General Enrico Cialdini, sent by Cavour to clear the way for a Sardinian expedition through the Papal States to intercept Garibaldi on his march north. On August 30 the emperor wired Thouvenel: "M. Farini talked to me with great frankness. Here is his objective and that of M. de Cavour. To take control of the movement; to conserve for the Pope the Patrimony of St. Peter; to prevent any attack against Venetia; *to invoke the aid of Europe in order to regulate the affairs of Italy, once Naples and the Marches are in their control.*" Was Napoleon sincere in this congress promise that he claimed to have obtained? The Sardinians professed to believe that he was not. According to Nigra, Napoleon's advice, as late as September 26, was to "appeal to a congress which will not meet; this will help to put us in a more tenable position." And yet, there is some evidence to the contrary. Reports from Gramont at Rome through July had indicated that some of the papal court now saw the only hope in a con-

23. Metternich to Rechberg, Paris, May 16, 1860, in HHSA, PA IX, Fr. Ber., 1860, I–V, Box 65, no. 34B, fols. 565–67; Thouvenel to Talleyrand, Paris, June 18, 1860, in AMAE, CP, Sardaigne, 349:416v; Metternich to Rechberg, July 9, 1860, in Salomon, *Ambassade de Richard Metternich*, 67; Napoleon III to Persigny, Saint-Cloud, July 29, 1860, in *Archives diplomatiques*, I, 98–100; Cowley to Russell, Paris, private, August 21, 1860, in Russell Papers, 30/22, 55.

gress. Perhaps Napoleon did in fact believe that the pope, facing the loss of everything, would agree to a European settlement that would at least leave him something.[24]

Gorchakov was longing for a conference stage. Did the French emperor also hope that Vienna might be receptive? On July 26 he had rather wistfully asked Metternich if, in view of the distrust in which he himself was held, Austria would not take the initiative of a general congress proposal. Some weeks later Rechberg remarked to the Prussian ambassador, Baron Karl von Werther, that he could not see on what grounds Napoleon had felt able to remark to Cowley "that he thought Austria would propose the meeting of a European congress to regulate the affairs of Italy and that he would not oppose it." Under these circumstances, had Turin made an appeal to a congress that would not meet, Napoleon might well have tried to assure that it *did* meet. After all, bringing Sardinia to the conference table was half the battle and might well end British objections to the congress. Cavour, however, was not to be caught so easily. "If France or any other power should put forward the idea of a congress," he wrote to d'Azeglio at London, "I hope that England will prevent its meeting." Perhaps when the emperor wrote to Victor Emmanuel on September 9 to complain that Farini had misrepresented Sardinian policy to him, he had Turin's attitude toward the congress in mind as much as or more than the fact that Cavour had not waited for rebellion in Umbria and the Marches before launching his invasion of the Papal States the previous day. Pressed by Thouvenel, Napoleon, who was still in southern France en route to Algeria, reluctantly ordered the recall of Charles Angélique, baron de Talleyrand-Périgord, France's representative at Turin (September 12). Later, in his official circular to French diplomatic representatives, Thouvenel again stressed that one of the emperor's Chambéry conditions had been that the right to establish a definitive organization of Italy be assigned to Europe.[25]

24. Napoleon III to Thouvenel, Annecy, telegram, August 30, 1860, in AMAE, CP, Sardaigne, 350:173 (emphasis added); Cavour to Nigra, Turin, August 29, 1860, in *Cavour-Nigra*, IV, 187, no. 1079; Nigra to Cavour, Paris, September 26, 1860, in *Cavour-Nigra*, IV, 233–34, no. 1145. There is even a report that the pope, about August 25, proposed to Napoleon through Carlo Sacconi, the apostolic nuncio, a congress for the settlement of the Italian question and "altri importanti affari internazionali" (see Carlo Sacconi to Giacomo Antonelli, Paris, August 26, 1860, in Pirri [ed.], *Pio IX e Vittorio Emanuèle II*, I, 282–83, no. 1591.

25. Metternich to Rechberg, Paris, private, July 26, 1860, in HHSA, PA IX, Varia, 1860, Box 68, fols. 138–41; Werther to Schleinitz, Vienna, September 11, 1860, in *APP*, vol. II, pt. 1, p. 630, no. 250. Perhaps Cowley had misinterpreted Napoleon's remark to

On his return to Paris, Napoleon immediately informed Thouvenel that he was thinking of calling for a great-power congress. The next day (September 24) the council of ministers rejected an Austro-Spanish proposal of intervention on behalf of the pope by the Catholic states, in favor of a congress of all the powers. As the rulers of Austria, Prussia, and Russia prepared to meet at Warsaw (October 22–23) the French position was clearly stated. France would insist that the treaty of Zurich be carried out unless modified by a congress. If Sardinia initiated and lost a war with Austria over Venetia, Sardinia would still keep Lombardy and France would keep Nice and Savoy, but a congress would determine new boundaries, designate new rulers, and establish an Italian confederation.[26]

The problem, of course, is to gauge Napoleon's sincerity. With French opinion evenly divided between Garibaldi and the pope, Paris found caution advisable, and talk of a congress had a soothing effect. But could it be taken seriously? In the autumn of 1860 the concert of Europe clearly meant very different things to different governments. For Berlin, Vienna, and Saint Petersburg, it remained an instrument for enforcing rights and treaties; for London, if it existed at all, it was as a last resort in crises that were already at hand and could be resolved in no other way. Napoleon would not agree to make France part of a *gendarmerie* to call the Italians to order. Britain could see no reason at all for European action, whether in support of Cavour or in opposition to him. And the other great powers were unwilling to sanction at a congress principles of which they disapproved. Under these circumstances Thouvenel transparently paid lip service to a future congress in order to head off eventualities that would be unpalatable for France—an intervention by Catholic powers to restore the pope's lost provinces, for example, or even a decision by the pope to leave Rome. The congress would come, he repeated over and over, but only when the Italians, made wise by the difficulties that lay ahead, should ask for it. Thouvenel, most assuredly, did not want a congress, however often he invoked its name, fearing that France would find itself isolated there by the conservative powers.[27]

---

him, on August 21, that if Austria were attacked and proved victorious Vienna would propose such a congress (Cowley to Russell, Paris, private, August 21, 1860, in Russell Papers, 30/22, 55). Cavour to d'Azeglio, September 22, 1860, in *Cavour e l'Inghilterra*, vol. II, pt. 2, p. 127, no. 1218; circular of Thouvenel to French diplomatic agents, Paris, October 18, 1860, in AMAE, CP, Russie, 222:152.

26. Case, *Edouard Thouvenel*, 221–28.

27. *Ibid.*, 196, 242.

Nevertheless, French opinion above all wanted a solution, any solution, to the Italian imbroglio, and on occasion the foreign minister was disarmingly frank: "The emperor wants a congress," he told Metternich toward the end of October. "As for me, I see neither the opportunity nor the possibility." At the beginning of the month Napoleon had concluded the first of two letters to the czar with the assertion that only a congress could resolve the great questions of the day, whether in eastern or southern Europe. In mid-October he had the opportunity, during a farewell interview with the papal nuncio, to advance his personal views. "His Majesty expressed the thought that in his view the only way to remedy the present state of affairs was to bring about an agreement among all the Powers, and that a Congress was the only means of halting Sardinia's encroachment and of settling the Italian question as a whole." When the nuncio continued his recriminations, especially regarding the principle of nonintervention, Napoleon replied (in the words of the Austrian diplomat, Count Rudolf von Mülinen): "What do you want? It is England, supported to a certain extent by Prussia, who deserves the honor of introducing the principle of nonintervention, and who, as it were, imposed it upon us. France alone cannot act; she cannot, on the other hand, allow a return to the starting point of 1859. The only route open therefore is the Congress, without it there can be no safety. The essential thing is to reach an agreement and I am convinced that faced with Europe's decree Sardinia will bow its head. If not we will take the necessary steps." A week later, at the end of an interview with Cowley, Napoleon suddenly asked the Englishman's advice as to whether a congress on Italian affairs was practicable. When Cowley replied that he did not think so, the emperor concluded with the thought "that even if the Congress did not meet at present, he conceived that the alarm and excitement which persisted concerning Italy would be calmed, if the principle of a Congress were to be proclaimed and accepted by the Great Powers." And he went further, proposing to Metternich at the beginning of November that Austria and France should negotiate an agreement so that there could be a congress that would take as a basis for discussion the terms of the treaty of Zurich.[28]

---

28. *Ibid.*, 229, 233; Metternich to Rechberg, Paris, private, October 26, 1860, in HHSA, PA IX, Varia, 1860, Box 68, fols. 159–62; Count Rudolf von Mülinen to Rechberg, Paris, secret, October 18, 1860, in HHSA, PA IX, Fr. Ber., 1860, VI–IX, Box 66, no. 78B, fols. 95–97v; Cowley to Russell, Paris, private, October 25, 1860, in Russell Papers, 30/22, 55. Napoleon also raised the question of the congress in an interview with

The problem was that Vienna had no confidence in congress discus sions, and with some reason. Had not Thouvenel, just a few days be fore Napoleon's overture, assured the Austrian chargé that there was no need for a *base* for the congress, that the parties should get to gether without any preliminary agreement (*sans rien fixer*) and try to agree like honest men? Here, indeed, was Napoleon's concept of the concert of Europe, and Rechberg's response epitomized the resistance it had met and would continue to meet:

> To count on the assistance of France in order to re-establish today a state of affairs in Italy based upon former treaties and upon the principles which we profess, will be to surrender ourselves to a dangerous illusion. In seeking this method it would not be long before we would be engaged in a course of transactions difficult to reject and impossible to accept. We would inevita bly find ourselves facing the same danger if today we were to try to effect with the aid of a congress of the great powers that which we do not believe ourselves able to realize with the aid of France alone. We do not then desire the meeting of a congress.

It was a dialogue of the deaf. On November 15 the Belgian minister at Paris reported that there was no more talk of a congress. For the mo ment, at least, Europe would have nothing more to do with the Italian question.[29]

---

the former Austrian ambassador, Hübner, then in Paris (résumé attached to Mülinen to Rechberg, Paris, October 29, 1860, in HHSA, PA IX, Fr. Ber., 1860, VI–IX, Box 66, no. 82A, fols. 169v–73v).

29. Mülinen to Rechberg, Paris, October 18, 1860, in HHSA, PA IX, Fr. Ber., 1860, VI–IX, Box 66, fols. 130–30v; Rechberg to Metternich, November 12, 1860, in Hall berg, *Franz Joseph and Napoleon III*, 254 (Metternich had favored entering into nego tiations with France); Rogier to de Vrière, Paris, November 15, 1860, in Discailles, *Un diplomate belge à Paris*, 614.

CHAPTER 8

European Intervention in Syria
1860–1861

When Napoleon wrote to Persigny at the end of July, 1860, to complain of the distrust with which the British government regarded him, he had in mind not only the crisis in southern Italy but also a more distant affair. In Syria, or, rather, that part of Syria called the Lebanon, Roman Catholic Maronites had been attacked since the end of May by their neighbors, the more warlike Muslim Druses. On July 9, 10, and 11, disorder became general when Muslims, unrestrained and even aided by the Turkish authorities, attacked the Christian quarter of Damascus. Toward the middle of June it was known in Paris that thousands of Christians had lost their lives and many more had been made homeless. Here was a problem that the European powers could not as easily leave to its own devices as they had done in the case of Italy after Villafranca. The administrative arrangement in the Lebanon was the collective work of the great powers, who had possessed since 1842 the right of intervention to protect the Maronites. The threatened extermination of the Christians constituted an affront to the conscience of Europe and to the specific susceptibilites of the French, who had long prided themselves on their traditional role as champion of the Roman Catholic peoples of the Near East, and to whom the Maronites looked for protection. And yet, this was an area so jealously watched over by all the great powers that any unilateral intervention would be a dangerous undertaking.[1]

In fact, the issue had already arisen at the beginning of May, when Gorchakov had proposed joint Franco-Russian action in response to alleged ill-treatment of Christians in Turkey. Napoléon Auguste Lannes, duc de Montebello, the French ambassador, countered with a sug-

---

1. See Mange, *Near Eastern Policy*, 76–82; Monicault, *La question d'Orient*, 205.

gestion that Europe as a whole should be involved. Gorchakov concurred, proposing a European inquiry into troubles arising in the Christian parts of the Ottoman Empire. Thouvenel found this term of reference too broad to be acceptable to certain other powers, although Paris had no objection to it; and, in fact, the British quickly gave their support to a Turkish counterproposal that the Porte establish his own inquiry. The French government foresaw that this would not be sufficient. Thouvenel told Pourtalès, the Prussian ambassador, on May 14: "We want to maintain this [Ottoman] empire, but to maintain it in conditions which can be reconciled with the rights of humanity and of civilization. . . . Well, then, it is necessary that the great powers restore order there. The major difficulty will be to establish and to make function a tutelage that has become necessary. . . . We must not withdraw from what is now a duty and we must maintain that collective character which is the basis of those treaties of 1856 that we intend to respect." Thouvenel's specific proposal amounted to the substitution of a collective *démarche* for the proposed European inquiry, but even this had proved impracticable by the beginning of June.[2] At this point, the Syrian disorders began.

Thouvenel, whose first thought had been of Anglo-French cooperation, proposed on July 6 that a European-Turkish commission be established to assess blame, punish the guilty, secure reparations, and make proposals for the future. Gorchakov, of course, was willing; let the conference of the great-power representatives at Constantinople constitute such a commission, he suggested, and proceed to decide on the measures to be taken. Matters stood at this point when news reached Paris of the massacres that had ravaged the Christian quarter of Damascus beginning on July 9. The violence at Damascus marked for Napoleon the turning point of the Syrian crisis. Having already followed the lead of Britain in sending several warships to Syria, he decided on July 17, after a conference with Thouvenel, to propose armed intervention. What were the motives of this French initiative? It would be difficult to argue that public opinion was a determining factor, although Napoleon may have hoped to regain some lost ground with the clerical party, alienated by his Italian policy. Perhaps, too, he

2. Montebello to Thouvenel, Saint Petersburg, May 2, 1860, in AMAE, CP, Russie, 221:52–53, no. 31; Gorchakov to Kisselev, Saint Petersburg, May 5, 1860, in AMAE, CP, Russie, 221:13–19; Pourtalès to Schleinitz, Paris, confidential, May 14, 1860, in APP, vol. II, pt. 1, pp. 398–99, no. 168.2; Thouvenel to Montebello, Paris, May 16, June 6, 1860, both in AMAE, CP, Russie, 221:109–112, no. 63, 159–67, no. 69.

wished to distract French opinion from Italy, where, as we have seen, the summer of 1860 was a particularly frustrating time for Paris. Certainly there was a sincere humanitarian concern, on the part of both the emperor and his foreign minister. Probably Napoleon was also following his determination that France should be heard and respected everywhere in the world and should have a foreign policy that could never be criticized, as that of the July Monarchy had been, for its weakness. Might there also have been an *arrière-pensée* relating to designs on Turkey? One thing only is certain. What Napoleon wanted was not a French but a European intervention. On the same day that intervention had been decided upon, Persigny was instructed to obtain British cooperation. France had no intention of acting alone and would intervene only in accord with the treaties and as the agent of Europe. Moreover, it would be preferable that each of the powers contribute to the expeditionary force. As it turned out, the price of British approval was acceptance by France of several conditions, the most important being the conclusion of a formal convention. On July 19, Thouvenel proposed a conference at Paris to discuss a draft of convention that he had prepared.[3]

Although Article 9 of the treaty of Paris of 1856 had in effect placed the Ottoman Empire under the collective supervision of Europe, and although Thouvenel had emphasized this treaty in his earliest conversations on the Syrian crisis, when Cavour demanded that Sardinia be admitted to an action falling within the scope of the treaty of Paris, the French foreign minister replied that it was not this treaty but the special convention of 1845 that applied. In other words, the task was one for the great powers alone. And of those powers, it was Britain that most concerned Napoleon. Palmerston, ever suspicious of France, opposed the conference, and it required a combination of Thouvenel's threats (to isolate Britain on the issue) and Napoleon's blandishments to overcome British resistance. Through Persigny the emperor pleaded for understanding:

> When La Valette left for Constantinople the instructions which I gave him amounted to this: "Bend every effort to maintain the *status quo*; it is to the interest of France that Turkey live as long as possible."
>
> Now come the massacres in Syria and they say that I am quite happy to have found an occasion for making a small war or for playing a new role.

3. Montebello to Thouvenel, Saint Petersburg, telegram, July 16, 1860, in AMAE, CP, Russie, 221:238; Thouvenel to French diplomatic representatives, telegram, July 19, 1860, in AMAE, CP, Russie, 221:248.

The truth is that this credits me with precious little common sense. If I immediately proposed an expedition it was because my feelings are those of the people who have placed me at its head and because the news from Syria filled me with indignation. Nevertheless my first thought was to reach an understanding with England.

What interest other than that of humanity would prompt me to send troops into this country? . . . I said it in 1852 at Bordeaux and it remains my opinion today—I have great conquests to make, but in France. . . .

I would very much prefer not to be obliged to make a Syrian expedition, and in any case not to make it alone, first because it will constitute a great expense, and second because I am afraid that this intervention will precipitate the Eastern Question, but, on the other hand, I cannot see how to resist the public opinion of my country, which will never understand the failure to punish not only the murder of Christians but also the burning of our consulates, the mutilation of our flag, and the pillaging of monasteries entrusted to our protection.

Certainly Napoleon convinced the Austrian ambassador of his reluctance to intervene. It was Metternich's opinion that the intervention was primarily Thouvenel's idea. In an earlier conversation with the emperor at Saint-Cloud, Metternich had found him to have "a manifest repugnance . . . to become involved in so adventurous an expedition." Thouvenel, on the other hand, had a detailed plan for European action: a European garrison on Rhodes, a European fleet in the Bosporus, a five-power commission at Constantinople to advise the Porte (each delegate having a special function), and an Austrian force "pour faire la police" in European Turkey. However that may be, on July 26, Thouvenel was able to convene the first meeting of a conference on Syrian affairs, bringing together the representatives at Paris of Russia, Austria, Britain, Prussia, and Turkey.[4]

Immediately the familiar pattern was repeated, France attempting to broaden and Britain to restrict the scope of action of the European concert. Saint Petersburg had early envisaged European intervention in sweeping terms. The original Russian proposal had called for an inquiry into conditions in all the Christian provinces; and in adhering to Thouvenel's proposal of a European commission to investigate the disorders in Syria, the czar had made it clear "that he sees there a pre-

4. Pourtalès to Schleinitz, Paris, confidential, May 14, 1860, in APP, vol. II, pt. 1, p. 399, no. 168.2; Nigra to Cavour, Paris, confidential, July 24, 1860, in Cavour-Nigra, IV, 103–104, no. 1001; Napoleon III to Persigny, Saint-Cloud, July 29, 1860, in Archives diplomatiques, I, 98–100; Metternich to Rechberg, Paris, July 26, 1860, in HHSA, PA IX, Fr. Ber., 1860, VI–IX, Box 66, no. 48C, fols. 236–44.

cedent which can be invoked elsewhere—if there should be occasion—and a justification of the proposition which the cabinet of St. Petersburg has made relative to the Christian provinces of Turkey-in-Europe." Several days later, Gorchakov decided to insist on an article in the convention, secret if desired, that would commit the Porte to improve the condition of the Christians in the entire Ottoman Empire and that would engage the powers to act as they had in Syria wherever similar trouble occurred. In the words of Nigra, Sardinia's minister at Paris, the effect of the Russian proposal would have been to establish "une espèce de tutelle des Grandes Puissances envers le Sultan." Gorchakov won the support of Prussia and of Austria, but the British government immediately joined the Porte in an opposition that made rejection of the Russian proposal a sine qua non for participation in the convention. The positions taken by Russia and Austria on the one hand and by Britain and Turkey on the other in this question were fairly predictable. Much more interesting is the French stand. Ollivier states, although without direct evidence, that Napoleon lent his support to Gorchakov's proposal. Certainly Thouvenel did not object in principle to the Russian plan. "No doubt," he wrote to Montebello, "a general entente on the situation of the Christians will soon become necessary." And he continued: "At base, as I have several times told the Russian ambassador, there is no divergence between the cabinet of St. Petersburg and us. We envisage in the same way as they the state of affairs in Turkey." The central question for both Russia and France remained the improvement of the condition of the Ottoman Christians and their protection against Muslim fanaticism. "My conviction is that the powers will be led before long to occupy themselves in common with this great interest which touches at the same time considerations of civilization and of policy."[5]

And yet, as in the past, Paris proved willing to work the compromises that alone would allow the rickety European apparatus to function.[6] Thouvenel from the first recognized the danger involved in

5. Montebello to Thouvenel, Saint Petersburg, telegrams, July 16, 20, 1860, both in AMAE, CP, Russie, 221:238, 258; Nigra to Cavour, Paris, confidential, July 29, 1860, in *Cavour-Nigra*, IV, 114, no. 1013; Thouvenel to Montebello, Paris, telegram, July 26, 1860, in AMAE, CP, Russie, 221:268; Ollivier, *L'empire libéral*, IV, 461; Thouvenel to Montebello, Paris, telegram, July 26, 1860, in AMAE, CP, Russie, 221:268; Thouvenel to Montebello, Paris, August 1, 1860, in AMAE, CP, Russie, 221:282, no. 93.

6. "J'ai demain une seconde conférence pour les affaires de Syrie," Thouvenel wrote to Gramont at Rome in the midst of the major conference crisis. "Les hésitations diplomatiques devant ces épouvantables menaces sont jugées sévèrement par l'opinion pub-

Gorchakov's proposal. The principle was excellent, he maintained, but it would only interfere with the work immediately at hand. That work Thouvenel proposed to accomplish by dispatching an expeditionary force that would be all-French at the outset and reinforced later, if necessary, by other national contingents. The commander would concert in Syria with the sultan's agent, Fuad Pasha. A multinational naval force would support the expedition, the duration of which would be decided later. Turkey would pay the costs. It would be best to act in Syria, and thus set a precedent to which later appeal could be made. From the first, too, the French foreign minister searched for a practical compromise, and found one at last in the device of two protocols, one stipulating the agreed conditions upon which intervention could proceed pending official ratification of a convention, the other stating the desire of the powers that there be effective reforms in the Christian provinces of Turkey. With the acceptance of these protocols at its second meeting on July 30, the conference completed its task, and the great powers of Europe had, for the first time since the Congress of Verona, clearly delegated to one of their number the role of executor of the European will. That the lot had fallen again to France, after the passage of twenty-seven years, was probably a goal and most certainly an achievement of the conference diplomacy of Napoleon III and of his commitment to a certain ideal of the concert of Europe.[7]

At any rate, having achieved a European mandate, the French government took pains to stress the international aspect of the venture and the limited liability of France. Under the terms of the convention, occupation was to be for a period of no more than six months by a force of six thousand French troops; the number could be increased if necessary to twelve thousand by the addition of contingents from either France or other countries.[8]

On August 22, four thousand French troops, under the command of

---

lique. Si une cause d'humanité est impuissante à réunir les cabinets, on peut juger des déchirements auxquels donnera lieu la question d'Orient. Je vous quitte pour continuer, à la sueur de mon front, une rédaction que l'Angleterre et la Russie consentent à accepter" (Thouvenel to Gramont, Paris, July 29, 1860, in L. Thouvenel (ed.), *Le secret de l'Empereur*, I, 160–62).

7. Thouvenel to Montebello, Paris, telegrams, July 21, 26, 1860, both in AMAE, CP, Russie, 221:259, 268; Thouvenel to Montebello, Paris, August 1, 1860, in AMAE, CP, Russie, 221:281–84, no. 93. Thouvenel to Montebello, Paris, telegram, August 1, 1860, in AMAE, CP, Russie, 221:279v. See Case, *Edouard Thouvenel*, 340–42. The convention was signed on August 16 by all but Britain and Russia and by those two powers on September 5.

8. The powers were to agree with the sultan as to which of them should provide

General Charles Marie Napoléon Beaufort d' Hautpoul, disembarked at Beirut; on October 5 the European commission met at Beirut; and on October 29, Thouvenel dispatched instructions stipulating the limits of responsibility that Paris intended to assume:

> As for us, invested by the conference with a mission which involves so many difficulties, we intend to establish firmly the fact that we are not *responsable*. We cannot accept the responsibility of what remains to be done beyond the extent actually promised by us. We have engaged ourselves to furnish six thousand men; we will maintain our force at exactly that number. But if, as we are beginning to fear, this should prove insufficient, we could only maintain the stipulated arrangements; and, from the moment when it should become necessary to increase the number of troops, I reserve the right to bring about an agreement of the powers to the effect of deciding, in conformity with the terms of Article 2 of the convention, which of them should make the necessary provisions.

There was in this circular no explicit mention of a prolongation of the intervention, but London was quick to sense what it was predisposed to fear, and perhaps not without reason. In France the song "Parting for Syria" had long been a sort of unofficial anthem of the Second Empire. At the end of November, Napoleon told Cowley that, while he was "most anxious" to bring his troops away from Syria, "it would be impossible to do so until matters assumed there a more settled shape." By the first week of January, 1861, it was clear that Paris was quite near the conviction that matters would *not* have assumed a sufficiently settled shape before the expiration of the occupation period on February 5, since the European commission had not yet had time to consider long-range reform proposals. The French motivation poses an interesting problem. Thouvenel's official position was that the question had become more one of humanity than of politics; to London it was obviously a matter of *arrière-pensée*, the desire to extend French influence yet a bit more in the world; while to Cowley it appeared likely that Napoleon was motivated primarily by the necessities of French politics.[9]

---

whatever further troops were required. The five powers were to contribute any naval force that might be needed. At the end of July, Thouvenel had told Metternich that he thought Austria, having the same interest in the region as had France, should provide the additional six thousand men. But he added: "Si cette combinaison était tout-à-fait impossible il serait alors plus simple de désigner la France comme devant fournir *à elle seule* le contingent entier" (Metternich to Rechberg, Paris, July 26, 1860, in HHSA, PA IX, Fr. Ber., 1860, VI–IX, Box 66, no. 48D, fols. 245–52).

9. Thouvenel to French agents in London, Vienna, Berlin, Saint Petersburg, October 29, 1860, in AMAE, CP, Angleterre, 718:149, no. 147; Cowley to Russell, Paris, private,

More interesting than the motivation, however, is the degree to which French policy remained within the compass imposed by conference diplomacy and the concert of Europe. "In carrying out the special mission which we have accepted," Thouvenel wrote to Joseph, comte de Flahaut, who had replaced Persigny as French ambassador at London, "we are acting in the name of the convention of September 5, 1860, and we intend loyally to execute all the stipulations." And the foreign minister concluded: "If it is not possible to achieve the desired goal in the agreed upon time, it is not for us to propose other arrangements. We must leave to the powers the responsibility of bringing about new dispositions, if there should be occasion, and of initiating the agreement that they consider necessary." Nevertheless, just five days later, he wrote to inform Flahaut of his resolve to address himself to "the powers from whom we hold our mandate, as to a sort of jury, and to give them the opportunity of telling us what they, in their heart and soul [âme et conscience], think." It was phraseology that would have sounded more natural coming from Napoleon himself, and one wonders if, in fact, the reversal of position was not the result of the emperor's intervention. At any rate, on January 18, one week after Cowley had officially requested the withdrawal of French troops by the agreed date, Thouvenel issued the call for a new conference, as "the most natural way" of reaching accord on a situation in which France had to choose between the strict adherence to the convention that Paris intended and the new disorders that were likely to follow French withdrawal from Syria.[10]

To the British, with memories of the Holy Alliance and of the "Congress system" that had followed the Napoleonic Wars, European conferences held few charms. Indeed, at the end of 1860, in response to a pamphlet inspired quite probably by Napoleon and ending with an appeal for a "congrès universel permanent," Russell had made the British viewpoint abundantly clear. "It is not difficult," he wrote to Cowley, "to discover under the veiled phrases of this proposition an old enemy of European independence. . . . A council which would

November 25, 1860, in Russell Papers, 30/22, 55; Thouvenel to Joseph, comte de Flahaut, Paris, December 17, 1860, January 9, 1861, both in L. Thouvenel (ed.) Le secret de l'Empereur, I, 328–31, 344; Cowley to Russell, Paris, private, January 28, 1861, in Russell Papers, 30/22, 56.

10. Thouvenel to Flahaut, Paris, private, January 4, 1861, in AMAE, CP, Angleterre, 719:10, no. 4; Thouvenel to Flahaut, Paris, January 9, 1861, in L. Thouvenel (ed.), Le secret de l'Empereur, I, 344; Thouvenel to French representatives at London, Saint Petersburg, Berlin, Vienna, Constantinople, January 18, 1861, in AMAE, CP, Angleterre, 719:40–42.

pretend to represent all the nations and to embrace all the interests would soon become a center of intrigues and the organ of the boldest and least scrupulous of the great powers." Of course, no such proposal was intended with regard to Syria, but the fact remained that, in summoning a conference to consider an extension of the date of the Syrian intervention, Paris could anticipate the support of all the great powers save Britain, and Thouvenel as well as the British ministers knew it. The Frenchman therefore pressed his advantage. To Russell's argument that the Turks must decide whether they needed aid, he obligingly replied through Flahaut on January 29: "What is important is to know if the Turkish government is prepared at the moment to preserve order in Syria and if with the will to do so it has the means. In our opinion it is only in conference that the explanations which the Porte will be called upon to present in regard to these two points can be appreciated, and we therefore consider the language of the Principal Secretary of State to be an assent to the proposal to convoke the plenipotentiaries."[11] Under the circumstances, there was no effective reply possible. On February 19 the conference reassembled.

Initially all went well for the French. Metternich remained silent throughout the first meeting and frankly admitted afterward to Cowley that, while his government agreed with London in principle, "such was their necessity to keep on good terms with France that they could not offend her on a question of so little importance to Austria as Syria." The Prussian representative proved even more obsequious, so much so that Cowley scented a "considerable deal of intrigue." Yet, Britain could not be ignored entirely, nor, for that matter, could a Bonaparte be trusted without reservation. Thouvenel wanted an extension of the occupation without date, its termination to depend upon the state of affairs in Syria; the conference was willing to grant an extension, but only to a specified date, perhaps May 1, as proposed by Turkey. This the French foreign minister would have accepted, but Napoleon, "grievously wounded by English suspicions and resistance," professed himself ready, instead, to withdraw as soon as possible and leave the consequences to Turkey. Thouvenel informed the powers of this decision on February 21, but he also urged that the expeditionary force be expanded to make it truly European, as France had wished from the first.[12]

11. Russell to Cowley, December 24, 1860, in Pingaud, "Un projet de désarmement," 3; Thouvenel to Flahaut, Paris, January 29, 1861, in AMAE, CP, Angleterre, 719:86, no. 20.
12. Cowley to Russell, Paris, private, February 19, 22, 1861, both in Russell Papers,

It soon became obvious, however, that what the French really
wanted was agreement and that their only insistence would be upon a
wording duly considerate of imperial prestige. Let the conference extend the intervention by three months, Thouvenel argued on March
2, but let there be no stipulation that this limit should not in any case
be surpassed. Thus each power would retain the right to summon another conference. It was a play on words, which, as the foreign minister admitted, became almost metaphysical. But after the words were
sufficiently weighed (ought the evacuation of troops by June 5 be stipulated "devra s'effectuer" or "devra être effectuée" or "sera effectuée"?),
agreement was at last reached. On March 15, at the second and last
session of the conference, an additional convention was accepted, setting June 5 as the date when the evacuation would have been completed ("aura été effectuée"!). The British had had their way, and
Napoleon pronounced himself disgusted at the manifest distrust of
France by the other European powers. In fact, said Thouvenel, he was
so disgusted that he was decided to withdraw entirely from European
politics: "Nous laisserons faire, voilà tout!" Through his foreign minister, Napoleon urged Austria forward, perhaps to take over the French
role in Syria.[13]

In spite of the wording of March 15, however, Thouvenel continued
to assert the right of France to call for a third conference (and another
prolongation) if Paris considered it necessary. In the weeks that followed, rumor persisted that he in fact intended to request a further
prolongation, and the idea of allowing fifteen hundred French troops

---

30/22, 56; Metternich to Rechberg, Paris, telegrams, nos. 22, 23, February 19, 21, 1861,
both in HHSA, PA IX, Fr. Ber., 1861, I–VI, Box 69, fols. 245, 247. "Nous considérerions
comme essentiellement désirable que la réunion d'autres troupes aux nôtres vint donner au corps d'occupation un caractère réellement Européen et lui permettra d'achever
avec promptitude et dans des conditions assurées de succès l'oeuvre qu'il a com-
mencée" (Thouvenel to French representatives at London, Vienna, Berlin, Saint Petersburg, February 25, 1861, in AMAE, CP, Angleterre, 719:135v–36). The dispatch was
read by Napoleon and "Approuvé" is in his hand.
    13. Thouvenel to Flahaut, Paris, March 2, 1861, in AMAE, CP, Angleterre, 719:154,
no. 32; Thouvenel to Flahaut, Paris, March 11, 1861, in L. Thouvenel (ed.), Le secret de
l'Empereur, I, 485–88. The text finally agreed upon was Lord Russell's: "La durée de
l'occupation Européenne en Syrie sera prolongée jusqu'au 5 juin de la présente année,
époque à laquelle il est entendu, entre les hautes parties contractantes, qu'elle aura at-
teint son terme définitif et que l'évacuation aura été effectuée" (Flahaut to Thouvenel,
London, telegram, March 13, 1861, in AMAE, CP, Angleterre, 719:188). The French
managed to have the word définitif omitted, but that, of course, changed nothing. Metternich to Rechberg, Paris, March 12, February 21, 1861, both in HHSA, PA IX, Fr. Ber.,
1861, I–VI, Box 69, no. 21D, fol. 360v, no. 16A-B, fols. 253–53v.

to remain after June 5 was broached. But on May 23, despite the introduction in the French Senate of a petition calling for the maintenance of French forces in Syria, Thouvenel announced the approaching end of the intervention: "Delegated by Europe, charged with carrying out a common mission, we would be in a position to prolong its duration only should this have the unanimous consent of the cabinets from whom we have received it. They have not found themselves in accord on the necessity of a new prolongation and therefore the armed intervention which we have exercised in the Lebanon in the name of the powers, draws to its end." Already, in the Senate, where a majority favored a continuing French intervention, Adolphe Billault had stated Napoleon's position: "Our soldiers were the delegated agents of Europe; it is not France that evacuates this unfortunate country but Europe. Nevertheless, the Emperor, while remaining faithful to his pledged word, regains his freedom of action. He is forgetful of none of his duties toward humanity, civilization, and Christianity. He will sweep the coasts of Syria with a fleet whose forces will be ready for disembarkation, and even at this distance, our flag will yet be the terror of murderers."[14]

Billault's speech not only marked the end of the Syrian episode; it also epitomized that incident from the French viewpoint. The policy of collective action had not proved completely to the advantage of Paris. But the prestige of acting in the name of Europe was something. It was something, too, to have contained by conference diplomacy events that might have had serious consequences for the peace of Europe. And, perhaps above all else, the two conferences on Syria had provided Napoleon with the means of placating opinion at home and of maintaining French prestige, at a time made difficult by complications in Italy, while avoiding both an involvement of too great an extent and a collision of too rough a nature with any of the great powers whose friendship he wished to retain. In certain areas of the world, at least, the concert of Europe was a reality, and conference diplomacy had its uses and its successes.[15]

14. Thouvenel to Flahaut, Paris, March 18, 1861, in AMAE, CP, Angleterre, 719:200, no. 40; Thouvenel to Flahaut, Paris, May 7, 1861, in L. Thouvenel (ed.), *Le secret de l'Empereur*, II, 98–100; Metternich to Rechberg, Paris, May 14, 1861, in HHSA, PA IX, Fr. Ber., 1861, I–VI, Box 69, no. 36D, fols. 598–600; circular of Thouvenel to French representatives in the major European capitals, Paris, May 23, 1861, in AMAE, MD, 742:281.

15. The meetings of a European commission that began at Beirut on October 5, 1860, continued for months. Three major objectives were sought: surveillance of the

La Gorce regretted, in retrospect, that France had been willing to limit its action in Syria to a scope that could win assent from the great powers. In another European intervention that took shape several months after the withdrawal from Syria, and a year after the successful Anglo-French intervention in China, Napoleon chose not to so limit himself. It would be useless, therefore, to reflect at length on whether he ever truly intended to involve Europe in the Mexican affair. Certainly he would have liked British support. Thouvenel sounded Cowley on the issue in early September and, on the ninth, proposed a common action by France, Britain, Spain, and the United States (with no real expectation that the last would cooperate) to collect from Mexico's new government debts due Europeans. In a letter to Flahaut of October 11, 1861, written, once again, without his foreign minister's knowledge, Napoleon argued that he preferred a monarchy in Mexico in order to keep that country out of American hands and to open it to the commerce (and influence) of Europe. However, when the mere presence of French, British, and Spanish forces, sent under the London tripartite convention of October 31, 1861, to supervise the payment of Mexico's foreign debts, did not result in a spontaneous uprising and the overthrow of the republican government, and when London maintained its refusal to interfere in Mexico's internal affairs, Napoleon began his own ill-fated adventure. In Syria, hedged about by the requirements and limitations of conference diplomacy, he had achieved less glory, perhaps, than he had hoped for. But in Mexico, there proved to be no glory at all and tragedy in the end for everyone who involved himself in the affairs of that unhappy country.[16]

---

administration of justice and the reestablishment of order; assurance that indemnities would be paid; and revision of the administrative organization of the Lebanon. None was attained with complete satisfaction to all, but a conference at Constantinople finally adopted (June 9, 1861) the French plan for autonomous government in the Maronite area ("the Mountain"), including a Christian governor and elected councils. French troops left Beirut on June 5. The new governor was installed at the beginning of July.

16. La Gorce, Histoire du Second Empire, III, 352; Cowley to Russell, Paris, September 5, 1861, in PRO, FO, 519, 229:54; Cowley to Russell, Paris, confidential, October 16, 1861, in PRO, FO, 519, 11:297–98, no. 1243.

CHAPTER 9

The Italian, Roman, and
Polish Questions
1861–1863

Only in Mexico, after 1859, did Napoleon permit himself the luxury—and the risk—of a major unilateral initiative in foreign policy. In Italy, and later in Poland, throughout 1861, 1862, and 1863, he continued his efforts to involve Europe in the solution of problems that he perhaps sensed were beyond the strength and will of France. On the other hand, it should be recalled, he had argued for Europe's responsibility in these areas long before the conspiracy of Plombiéres. At the beginning of 1861, Napoleon professed himself resigned to a policy of nonintervention in Italy. And yet, that was obviously not the direction in which his thoughts were moving. In fact, his basic convictions had remained unchanged from the beginning. The experiment with unity would fail; Europe would be called upon to intervene; only in confederation could the Italians find stability and hope of eventual success. "Be patient," he had advised the Russian ambassador toward the end of 1860. "Anarchy will lame them and we will intervene." If war broke out in Italy as a result of Garibaldi's and Cavour's adventures, he explained a few days later to Pourtalès, "there are only two things that I can do: either send a powerful army over the Alps . . . or convoke a European congress and thus regulate, with the assistance of all the great powers and definitively, the Italian question. I very much prefer the second mode of action, as it seems to me to be the most equitable and the most conformable to my own interests as well as those of Europe." By early 1861, Palmerston was convinced that Italian unity had become a fact; in October even Thouvenel, once as adamant as his master concerning the ill fate that lay in store for the Italians, admitted that Italian unity was a reality. Not so Napoleon. By all evidence his words to Metternich in January, 1861, continued to reflect his judgment of events long after less obstinate men

had bowed to the facts: "In principle I cannot materially oppose Italian unification, but I am deeply convinced that it will never succeed.
. . . It is because I know Italy and the municipal spirit animating its
great cities, the passion for individuality and independence of its
main provinces, that I've advanced the only lasting arrangement—
confederation."[1]

Of course, Napoleon may have been right in his advice to Victor
Emmanuel that a united Italy ought to be, for its own good, the result
of the slow working of time.[2] At any rate, the emperor held more
firmly to his illusions as the alternatives grew ever more bleak: a state
of 22 million on France's southern flank, alienated from its liberator
by the question of Rome; two *irredentas*—Rome and Venetia—that
might become at any moment the source of a new European war; and
an interminable French occupation of Rome that could not be continued without embarrassment or ended without risk. From Napoleon's wishful thinking, there came, however, a least one concrete result. Since the corollary of the expectation of imminent disaster for
Italy was the certainty that sooner or later Europe would have to intervene, thought had to be given to an acceptable program to be placed
before a future congress. Such a program would have to take into account the specific problems of Venetia and of Rome within the context of an overall reorganization of the peninsula. If Italian unity were
to fail, if chaos in the peninsula should force the Italians to come, cap
in hand, to Europe, the scope of the resulting congress might be very
broad indeed. Under such circumstances, Napoleon might press for
the return of Umbria and the Marches to the pope, for an independent
Romagna with its capital at Bologna, for a Lombardo-Venetian state
under an Austrian archduke, for an independent Neapolitan government, and, above all, for a confederation that would bind these various states together. Meanwhile, however, attention would have to
focus on the immediately unresolved problems.

To begin, there was Venetia. Until that province was united with
the Italian kingdom proclaimed in March, 1861 (or became part of an

1. Discours de l'Empereur à l'ouverture de la session législative, February 4, 1861, in
La politique impériale, I, 339–45; Giulio Figarolo, Count Gropello, to Cavour, Paris,
telegram, November 22, 1860, in *Cavour: Mezzogiorno*, III, 358, no. 2555; Pourtalès to
Schleinitz, Paris, November 26, 1860, in *APP*, vol. II, pt. 2, p. 33 n.; Case, *Edouard
Thouvenel*, 289; Metternich to Rechberg, Paris, January 22, 1861, in HHSA, PA IX, Fr.
Ber., 1861, I–VI, Box 69, no. 5B, fols. 118–18v.
2. Napoleon III to Victor Emmanuel, Vichy, July 12, 1861, in AMAE, CP, Italie,
351:453.

Italian confederation), the objectives Napoleon had proclaimed for the 1859 war, objectives for which Frenchmen had died, would not have been attained. But unless Austria were to display a spirit of self-sacrifice unheard of in the Hapsburg annals, no solution to this problem was possible without the consent and most probably the active participation of the other great powers. As we have seen, Napoleon in September and again in November, 1859, had hinted to Metternich that in return for giving Venetia autonomy within an Italian confederation, Austria might find compensation in the Danubian Principalities, the Adriatic coast, or Egypt. Cavour, with his usual shrewdness, perceived the game: "The question of Italy is going to receive a temporary solution. The Emperor is in a hurry to be finished with it. With or without consent the annexation of the Romagna and even of Tuscany will take place. The result will be not a durable peace but a truce; and the Emperor wants just that. Because more than ever he is dreaming of remaking the map of Europe. . . . And only the solution of the question of the East can furnish the means of reaching this goal." Walewski, who had remained in the confidence of Napoleon after his resignation as foreign minister, later confirmed Cavour's appraisal. He told Cowley in July, 1860, that the emperor was thoroughly tired of the whole Italian question and did not much care how it ended, so long as it ended. Eventually Europe would arrange things. As for the East, according to Walewski, Napoleon had for months been intent on bringing up that question with a view to arriving at a territorial revision in Europe. In fact, he had long been brooding on an exchange of the Danubian provinces for Venetia and had "only abandoned it lately in consequence of Russia having got wind of it and declared in the most positive manner to the French Government that nothing should ever induce her to consent to the Danubian provinces going to Austria."[3]

Napoleon, however, was not the man to be found wanting in expedients. While it seems unlikely that he was naïve enough to place any stock in the idea then current that Italy should buy Venetia from Austria,[4] he soon found a way of combining this with his predilection for

3. Cavour to Giacomo Durando, Turin, March 5, 1860, in *Cavour-Nigra*, III, 142, no. 629; Cowley to Russell, private, July 13, 1860, in Russell Papers, 30/22, 55.

4. On the scheme and its development, see Barker, "Austria, France, and the Venetian Question," 145. According to Metternich, Napoleon's opinion was that "a great Power could not undertake such a transaction." He would never, he said, make such a suggestion to Austria (Metternich to Rechberg, Paris, December 15, 1860, in HHSA, PA IX, Fr. Ber., 1860, XI–XII, Box 67, no. 90G, fols. 378–78v).

a redistribution of territory. "What would be more natural," he asked Cowley in early 1861, "than to arrange a transaction of this nature—let Italy purchase Venetia of Austria and let Austria purchase Bosnia or Herzegovina of the Porte. Austria wants territory and the Porte wants money. Let Austria keep the half of what she obtains for Venetia and give the other half to the Porte. But you probably will not consent to this arrangement and I know that Russia will not, for I mentioned the idea to Kisseleff, who told me plainly that his Government would never consent." Nevertheless, Persigny continued to argue for an exchange of Venetia for Herzegovina, an idea that Cavour understandably liked, although he rejected the suggestion of a Sardinian initiative. And Napoleon himself took up the matter again in the summer of 1861 during a conversation with Metternich. He still thought that Austria would be wise to cede Venetia, and he talked of territorial compensation in the East, even a "fine secret alliance" to arrange it, but he promised that he would never wage a war to take the province from Austria nor make it a matter of diplomatic pressure. Perhaps. But as the year ended, Thouvenel flatly asserted that "the Emperor's very firm intention, when circumstances permit, is *to settle the Italian question in the East.*"[5]

This line of thought at Paris apparently influenced the attitude taken by France toward troubles in the Balkans during 1860 to 1862. Thouvenel's predilection in early 1860 was for a European inquest into the relations between the Porte and his Bosnian and Herzegovinian subjects ("in accepting the proposal, the matter enters the domaine of European control; in refusing it, we leave the field clear for Prince Gorchakov"). A mixed European commission was sent into Herzegovina in May, 1861, following an uprising by Christians there against the Turks, but earlier Thouvenel had hinted broadly that Austria should take advantage of the disturbances in Herzegovina, Bosnia, Serbia, and Montenegro. "You ought to send another Leiningen," Napoleon told Metternich, adding that he would be pleased to see Austria impose its veto and put an end to a regrettable conflict. There was a problem, however. While Napoleon's goal was a resettlement that might give these areas to Austria as compensation, the method

5. Cowley to Russell, Paris, private, January 11, 1861, in Russell Papers, 30/22, 56; Charles Lafitte to Cavour, Paris, January 16, 1861, in *Cavour: Romana*, I, 201, no. 143; Cavour to Lafitte, Turin, January 29, 1861, in *Cavour: Romana*, I, 244–46, no. 179; Metternich to Rechberg, Paris, private, June 30, 1861, in HHSA, PA IX, Varia, 1861, Box 70, fols. 139v–40; Metternich to Rechberg, Paris, July 1, 1861, in HHSA, PA IX, Fr. Ber., 1861, VII–XII, Box 70, fol. 8; Thouvenel to Gramont, Paris, December 24, 1861, in L. Thouvenel (ed.), *Le secret de l'Empereur*, II, 211.

he preferred was collective action rather than unilateral intervention. Consequently, when Vienna made known its willingness to intervene, Thouvenel replied that France, taking Article 29 of the treaty of 1856 as a guide, could not consent to any intervention "which would not be the result of a preliminary accord among the powers convoked in conference." A conference held in Constantinople from mid-August to mid-September, 1862, proved inconclusive. But Napoleon's goal remained unchanged, as he indicated to Metternich in January, 1863. He still wished to turn Austrian attention to the possibility of accepting compensation in the East for sacrifices elsewhere, particularly in Italy. And that, if it were feasible at all, would only be so with the consent and cooperation of the concert of Europe.[6]

The Roman question was even more complicated. As in the case of Venetia, Napoleon could not conceive a truly satisfactory solution except within the context of a general reorganization of Italy, that is, an Italian confederation in which the role of the Papal States (however constituted and however governed) would be to divide Italy into at least three parts. At the beginning of 1861, Cowley sketched for his Austrian colleague what he understood Napoleon's policy to be: restoration of the Kingdom of the Two Sicilies; maintenance of the pope as sovereign of Rome and its immediate environs; establishment of a vicariate for the rest of the papal territory; and a confederation. But there were partial measures that might prove more immediately realizable. Any arrangement, for example, that permitted the withdrawal of French troops from Rome would be welcome. In seeking this, Napoleon did not neglect bilateral approaches. Until the unexpected death of Cavour in June, 1861, the French government was laboriously negotiating with Turin the sort of guarantees that would allow their forces to leave Rome. When Cavour's death made adequate guarantees unobtainable for the moment, Napoleon even turned to Vienna. But so long as the pope remained intransigent and Italian patriotism continued to demand Rome as the national capital, no such negotiations could succeed. And a settlement imposed upon Italy by France and Austria alone, even if it could have been achieved in the face of British opposition, would have required Napoleon to put his past be-

6. Metternich to Rechberg, Paris, May 16, 1860, in HHSA, PA IX, Fr. Ber., 1860, I–V, Box 65, no. 34A-E, fols. 551–60; Metternich to Rechberg, Paris, secret, August 17, 1861, in HHSA, PA IX, Fr. Ber., 1861, VII–XII, Box 70, no. 50C, fols. 137–40 (Count Leiningen was the Austrian envoy who dissuaded the Porte from waging war against Montenegro in early 1853); Thouvenel to Gramont, Paris, telegram, June 23, 1862, in AMAE, CP, Autriche, 482:32; Metternich to Rechberg, Paris, January 24, 1863, in HHSA, PA IX, Fr. Ber., 1863, I–IX, Box 75, no. 6C, fols. 119v–20.

hind him, abandon the foreign policy he had followed since 1849, and bind himself to a conservative alliance. No wonder, then, that the French emperor, in his perplexity, held fast to his conviction, professed ever since 1849, that Rome was a European problem, to be solved by the powers in concert. And not just the Catholic powers, as Thouvenel made clear in rejecting an Austro-Spanish bid for such an intervention in the spring of 1861. Clearly it was no coincidence when Napoleon, at about this time, coupled a confession of his frustration over Rome with a return "to his old plan of a Congress for the '*remaniement de la carte de l'Europe*.'"[7] In June, 1861, following Cavour's death, Napoleon recognized the new Italian kingdom and entered a period of watchful waiting.

As 1862 began, even Thouvenel seemed to waver and to look once more to a European solution. "He is inclined to think," Metternich wrote, "that in the last analysis Italy will be established *without Rome*, and with Europe's agreement the ancient city of the Popes will be made a free town like Frankfurt with Catholic garrisons, the Holy Father receiving private possessions, considerable lands either in Italy or elsewhere."[8] In March the foreign minister told Gramont, then ambassador to Austria, that if Russia and Prussia would recognize Italy, then "the idea of a congress to decide the temporal position of the Pope and to asure Italy's respect of this, would perhaps be less tenuous today," and that "it would be quite hard for Austria and Spain to decline to participate." Vienna, however, showed no enthusiasm for the idea. As Rechberg pointed out, 1862 was not 1815, and a congress would do more to compromise peace than to preserve it. Neverthe-

7. Metternich to Rechberg, Paris, January 2, 1861 [two dispatches], both in HHSA, PA IX, Fr. Ber., 1861, I–VI, Box 69, no. 1C, fols. 12–15, no. 1G, fols. 31–31v. For a discussion of Napoleon's approach to Austria, from the summer of 1861, see Barker, "Austria, France, and the Venetian Question," 146–48. On the difficulties of the Roman question at this time, see Case, *Franco-Italian Relations*, and Case, *Edouard Thouvenel*, 251–331. Thouvenel to Moustier, Paris, June 7, 1861, in AMAE, CP, Autriche, 479:377–78; Cowley to Russell, Paris, private, January 9, 1861, in Russell Papers, 30/22, 56.

8. "Le Ministre m'a dit ce matin qu'il ne pouvait plus espérer d'arriver à une entente directe avec Rome et que lorsque le moment serait venu de procéder à des arrangements définitifs en Italie, l'Europe ne sera certainement pas disposée à rendre au Saint Père toutes ses anciennes provinces. . . . Ces paroles sont remarquables en ce qu'elles témoignent de l'intention d'en revenir à des idées de congrès, tout-à-fait abandonnées dans les derniers temps" (Metternich to Rechberg, Paris, confidential, January 30, 1862, in HHSA, PA IX, Fr. Ber., 1862, I–VI, Box 72, no. 5A-G, fols. 54–54v). See also Metternich to Rechberg, Paris, February 3, 1862, in HHSA, PA IX, Fr. Ber., 1862, I–VI, Box 72, no. 7B, fols. 85v–86. Thus Thouvenel returned after more than a year to a plan he had discussed with the Belgian minister to Paris in November, 1860 (Rogier to de Vrière, Paris, November 10, 1860, in Discailles, *Un diplomate belge à Paris*, 611–12).

less, within two months Napoleon brought forward a proposal that Europe guarantee the pope's possession of Rome and make the other arrangements necessary to put the Roman question to rest. The idea was certainly the emperor's. Thouvenel, who had come to favor the withdrawal of French troops from Rome independently of any final resolution of the Roman question, more or less dissociated himself from it: "M. Thouvenel doesn't believe in the possibility of such an understanding in present circumstances," Metternich reported, "and he affects to regret that the Emperor does not once and for all cease to nourish this sort of hope." Walewski stated flatly that "Napoleon was alone responsible for the initiative of the proposed definitive guarantee," a judgment apparently confirmed by Eugénie in her comments to the Austrian ambassador.[9]

Politics were at the root of it. With elections due in 1863, the economy suffering from civil war in the United States, and France abandoned by Britain and Spain to its own devices in Mexico, Napoleon probably felt he had to be seen as having made an effort at doing something for the pope. And yet his very real agony over the problem, as well as his sincere hope for a solution, seems to be reflected in the long letter he addressed to Thouvenel on May 20. "Since I have been at the head of Government in France," he began, "my Italian policy has always been the same: to support Italian national aspirations, to persuade the Pope to become the champion rather than the adversary of these aspirations, in a word to consecrate the alliance of religion and liberty." True, this policy had met with little success in the face of "two parties diametrically opposed, absolute in their hatreds as in their convictions, deaf to counsels inspired only by the wish to accomplish some good." But this was no reason to abandon so important a cause:

It is urgent that the Roman question receive a final solution, because it is not only in Italy that it troubles spirits; everywhere it produces moral disorder because it involves what man has most at heart—religious and political faith. . . .

It is the duty of statesmen to study ways of reconciling two causes that only the passions present as irreconcilable. If we should fail, the effort

9. Thouvenel to Gramont, Paris, March 22, 1862, in L. Thouvenel (ed.), *Le secret de l'Empereur*, II, 263; Rechberg to Metternich, Vienna, March 20, 1862, in Hallberg, *Franz Joseph and Napoleon III*, 271; Metternich to Rechberg, Paris, reserved, May 16, 1862, in HHSA, PA IX, Fr. Ber, 1862, I–VI, Box 72, no. 32C, fols. 141–44; Metternich to Rechberg, Paris, June 13, 9, 1862, both in HHSA, PA IX, Fr. Ber., 1862, I–VI, Box 72, no. 38A-B, fol. 248v, no. 36A-E, fols. 226v–28.

would not be without some glory, and, at any rate, there is an advantage to declaring clearly the goal toward which we aspire.

This goal is to arrive at a combination by which the Pope would adopt what is great in the thought of a people and would recognize what is salutary in a power whose influence is universal.

At first glance, taking into account the prejudices and the resentments, equally bitter on both sides, one despairs of a good result. But if, after examining the heart of the matter, we consult reason and good sense, then we would like to persuade ourselves that truth, the divine light, will eventually penetrate all minds and illustrate in its full clarity the supreme and vital interest which engages, which obliges the partisans of the opposed causes to agree and to conciliate.

Italy, Napoleon argued, had everything to gain, in its exposed position, from a reconcilation with the pope. And the church, by accepting this reconciliation, would in effect have accepted the modern world and would thus have given "to religion a new luster, by revealing faith seconding human progress." The difficulty lay in the question of means. But if Italy would recognize the independence of what remained to the pope, and he in turn would grant self-government to his subjects (once more, the vicariate plan), then the thing could be done. This, Napoleon concluded, was a policy that "I believe I should attempt to make prevail by our legitimate influence and our disinterested counsels." Dutifully, Thouvenel sent the emperor's letter to La Valette at Rome. The French position, he explained, was to let Italy keep what it had taken. France and Europe would guarantee what was left. In its entirety the French plan embraced a European guarantee of the remaining papal territory, transfer to Italy of a large part of the papal debt, a civil list for the pope provided by the Catholic powers, and reforms in the pope's government. Metternich called the scheme "utopian," and, indeed, papal rejection was never in doubt, despite the threat from Paris to take the measures necessary to escape an intolerable situation. On June 24, La Valette wrote that he had received from Cardinal Giacomo Antonelli a definitive refusal. The pope could not and would not surrender any of his territory; and to accept the guarantee of a part would be in effect to abandon the rest. Why should France "impose sacrifices on the victim rather than on the despoiler?"[10]

10. Napoleon III, Paris, draft dated May 28 and then corrected in pencil to May 20, 1862, in AMAE, CP, Autriche, 480:250–54 (the letter, as Thouvenel later stated, was addressed to the foreign minister); Thouvenel to La Valette, Paris, May 31, 1862, in

Despite this papal intransigence, however, despite the determination of Vienna to hear no more of "congresses,"[11] Nigra could still write at the end of August, 1862, as a freebooting expedition against Rome led by Garibaldi was preparing to cross from Sicily to the mainland, that Napoleon wanted to bring about an understanding among the powers in regard to the future position of the pope. And Metternich learned from a confidant of the emperor's that, if Garibaldi succeeded in defying Turin, he, Napoleon, would make Sardinia give up southern Italy and would "launch negotiations with the powers on the basis of a confederation or the formation of three Italian kingdoms." Even after an Italian army defeated Garibaldi at Aspromonte, when Thouvenel turned his hand for one last time to the project of a direct agreement with Turin concerning Rome, his *projet de solution* of October, 1862, contained an Article 5 that incorporated Italy's promise to attend a congress on Rome. At the same time Eugénie assured Metternich that, if Austria would give up Venetia, "the Emperor would accept all the conditions, even the most harsh, which you would lay down, were this in regard to the Pope and Naples, or to obtain compensations in Germany, in the East, where you would wish." Vienna refused.[12]

That Napoleon sincerely desired a European solution to the Italian and Roman questions seems more than probable. Talk of a congress in the difficult autumn of 1860 might well have been a tactic to discourage intervention by the conservative powers, but no such explanation suffices for the following years. In part this persistent appeal to Europe resulted from perplexity. Napoleon could not permit the undoing of the work of 1859 in Italy, nor could he believe that the devel-

---

AMAE, CP, Autriche, 481:281–89; extract from a private letter (Metternich to Mülinen, undated) attached to Metternich to Rechberg, June 9, 1862, in HHSA, PA IX, Fr. Ber., 1862, I–VI, Box 72, no. 36A, fol. 230; La Valette to Thouvenel, Rome, June 24, 1862, in AMAE, CP, Rome, 1020:238v.

11. "If you see the Emperor Napoleon," Rechberg instructed Metternich, "make every effort if the word 'congress' is pronounced, to dissuade your interlocutor from such an idea" (Rechberg to Metternich, Vienna, August 5, 1862, in Hallberg, *Franz Joseph and Napoleon III*, 283–84). Yet even Rechberg expected in Italy "une effroyable anarchie, à laquelle un Congrès européen pourra seul mettre fin, en tenant compte, avec un juste mesure, des droits et des circonstances" (Gramont to Thouvenel, Vienna, confidential, August 30, 1862, in AMAE, CP, Autriche, 482:167, no. 53 bis).

12. Entry of August 23, 1862, in Durando's diary (in Colombo *et al.* (eds.), *Carteggi di Nigra*, 290); Metternich to Rechberg, Paris, August 24, 1862, in HHSA, PA IX, Fr. Ber., 1862, VII–XII, Box 73, no. 49, fols. 86v–87; Metternich to Rechberg, Paris, secret, September 1, 1862, in HHSA, PA IX, Fr. Ber., 1862, VII–XII, Box, 73, fols. 110–10v.

opments of 1860 were permanent. In regard to Rome he could not, for political reasons, withdraw his troops so long as there remained a possibility that the sequel would be an attack on the pope. On the other hand, he could not defend indefinitely a situation that separated him from Italy and that he believed contrary to the interests and principles of the modern world. The death of Cavour, the clumsiness and weakness of his immediate successors, and the absolute intransigence of Pius IX made forlorn any hope of bilateral negotiation. Convinced, as well, that both Italy and Rome were European problems, Napoleon wanted a congress at which he would have tried hard to achieve an Italian confederation and a vicariate solution to the Roman question. But Europe could not be persuaded. When, following Aspromonte, the Italian government demanded anew the possession of Rome as capital (Durando circular, September 10), Napoleon, unwilling to follow Thouvenel and the other *Italianissimes*[13] to the extent of a withdrawal of French forces from Rome, dismissed his foreign minister, replaced him with the pro-Austrian Drouyn de Lhuys (October 16), and continued to wait patiently upon events.

But if the European concert would not or could not accept responsibility for Italy, and especially for the Roman question, could or should Europe involve itself in the revolt of the Poles against their Russian masters that erupted at the end of January, 1863? The insurrection of January 22 certainly brought with it a period of soul-searching at the Tuileries. French public opinion was from the first overwhelmingly sympathetic toward the Poles but equally insistent upon peace. This factor, the desire to avoid a rupture with Saint Petersburg, his sense of Napoleonic destiny, and his determination to avoid the "mistakes" of Louis Philippe combined to torment Napoleon to such an extent that for nights in succession he could not sleep. Still, all in all, he would rather have done nothing, and his most ardent wish was probably that Russia would quickly put down the insurrection and that the problem would simply go away. If Drouyn de Lhuys had not been too clever by half—if he had not, in protesting the Alvensleben convention, by which Otto von Bismarck, newly appointed president of council at Berlin, had arranged on February 8 for Russo-Prussian cooperation

13. These included Eugène Rouher, Fould, Morny, Persigny, Baroche, La Valette, Prince Napoleon, Princess Mathilde, Jacques Alexandre Bixio, and Benedetti. Economic difficulties resulting from the Civil War in the United States, and the imminence of an election in the Corps législatif, made it imperative that Napoleon not appear to have abandoned the pope.

against the rebels, attempted to substitute Berlin for Saint Petersburg as the target of a European censure—would Napoleon have remained clear of the affair? The enthusiasm with which he entered at once upon personal negotiations with Metternich certainly gives reason to doubt it.[14]

Drouyn de Lhuys' objectives, in proposing on February 21 that France, Britain, and Austria protest the Alvensleben convention, emerge clearly: to detach Austria from Prussia and from Russia and to cement an entente *à trois* of Austria, France, and Britain. He gave some lip service to restoring the 1815 treaties in Poland, even vaguely hypothesizing an independent Polish kingdom, appropriate compensation being offered to Austria. But his real objective was a conservative alliance that would put an end to the "revolutionary" policies of his master. Napoleon, however, had other ideas. Whether Eugénie, in her remarkable *vol d'oiseau* of February 21 in which she blithely remapped Europe, spoke for the emperor, the outline of his thoughts regarding an Austrian alliance, as they appear between February 24 and the end of March, are sufficiently suggestive. This was, wrote Metternich, the Napoleon of earlier and happier days. "His language recalls the great periods of his reign, periods which preceded the wars of the Orient and of Italy. His words breathe political passion and their effect is all the greater inasmuch as they offer a complete contrast with his usual attitude. In these moments one glimpses the unbounded ambition and indomitable energy of this extraordinary man." What he wanted was hinted at rather than stipulated, but the implication is clear. First of all, Austria would help in "doing something" for Poland. This something would involve the loss of Galicia; but more than that, Napoleon also intended that Vienna should give up Venetia. In return, there would be compensation "in the east and in Germany" and an end to Italian unity.[15] So sweeping a program could be realized only by

---

14. Case, *French Opinion on War and Diplomacy*, 179–81; Cowley to Russell, Paris, private, April 14, 1863, in Russell Papers, 30/22, 59; Count Ludwig von der Goltz to William I, Paris, February 20, 1863, in *APP*, III, 277, no. 206. (Goltz was the new Prussian ambassador at Paris); Cowley to Russell, Paris, confidential, February 17, 1863, in PRO, FO, 519, 12:204.

15. Drouyn de Lhuys to Baron Jean Baptiste Gros, Paris, confidential, February 21, 1863, in AMAE, CP, Angleterre, 723:150–51, no. 22; Drouyn de Lhuys to Gramont, February 21, 1863, in AMAE, CP, Autriche, 483:161–62, no. 17; Metternich to Rechberg, Paris, February 22, 1863, in HHSA, PA IX, Fr. Ber., 1863, I–IX, Box 75, no. 8C, fols. 217v–18. See Henry, *Napoléon III et les peuples*, 88–89, and Hallberg, *Franz Joseph and Napoleon III*, 318–19; Salomon, *Ambassade de Richard Metternich*, 88–89; Ollivier, *L'empire libéral*, VI, 184–85; Metternich to Rechberg, Paris, February 26,

war or with the consent and cooperation of Europe. Although the method by which these changes would be arranged and sanctioned does not appear to have been discussed, there are a number of objections to the thesis that Napoleon was plotting war. Not since 1859 had the French emperor resorted to war as an instrument of policy, and even then, as we have seen, he would have accepted a conference solution. After 1863 he would reject war on several occasions, notably during the crises of 1866 and of 1867. There is every reason to believe, in fact, that only in an extraordinarily favorable circumstance would Napoleon have adopted a war policy, and circumstances in the first half of 1863 were decidedly not favorable. Elections were scheduled for May, a plebiscite of sorts on the reforms of 1860 and on the consequences of Napoleon's Italian and Roman policies, and they would take place in the midst of a major economic and financial crisis resulting from the Civil War in America. French opinion was strongly for peace, however much it might sympathize with the Poles. The bourgeoisie, shaken by the economic crisis, partly disaffected from the regime by the Roman question and the 1860 commercial treaty with Britain, would be horrified by the prospect of war. Moreover, the army, which had revealed many of its defects in 1859, was deeply committed abroad: in Mexico (thirty thousand men), where the siege of Puebla was about to begin; in Senegal and Indochina, where revolts had recently broken out; in China against the Taiping rebels; at Rome (twelve thousand men); and in Algeria, where Napoleon was attempting to impose on the unhappy *colons* a new property organization more favorable to the Arabs. War with the United States was a possibility that could not be ruled out. In January, Secretary of State Seward had brutally rejected a French mediation proposal. In addition to these general objections to a war in Europe, there were particular ones to war on the side of Austria. It would mean a betrayal of almost the entirety of Napoleonic diplomacy and foreign policy objectives, an irremediable break with Britain and Russia, the two great powers whose friendship Napoleon had most consistently courted, a choice in Germany against the power at that time considered most likely to favor French interests, and within France it would mean adding to the disaffection of the Catholic Right a deeper alienation of the Left. But alliances are made for other purposes than war, and the most reason-

---

1863, in HHSA, PA IX, Fr. Ber., 1863, I–IX, Box 75, no. 9, fols. 241–41v; Barker, "Austria, France, and the Venetian Question," 147–48. Napoleon had earlier hinted at this thought of substituting a tripartite for a unified Italy (Metternich to Rechberg, Paris, private, June 30, 1861, in HHSA, PA IX, Varia, 1861, Box 70, fols. 139v–40).

able interpretation of Napoleon's motives in seeking an alliance with Austria at the beginning of 1863 is that he hoped to use it to bring Europe to the conference table and, once there, to secure an acceptable result, if necessary by the threat of war. We shall see that alliances were always a part of Napoleon's plans for the concert of Europe. And in early 1863 the idea of a congress was once more in the air.[16] In mid-March, Metternich took the French proposals to Vienna.

Obviously Napoleon had not tied his personal diplomacy to Drouyn de Lhuys' proposal of a protest at Berlin against the Alvensleben convention, for London had rejected this bid on March 1 and the next day the French foreign minister announced that France reclaimed its entire liberty of action. On March 6, Cowley presented to Drouyn de Lhuys the proposal that a collective note be delivered at Saint Petersburg by the signatories of the 1815 treaties, recalling Russia to the terms of these treaties in regard to Poland. Although Paris approved the principle that Europe had a right of intervention in Poland, the foreign minister was not pleased with this proposal of a collective note. In the words of La Gorce: "The interview was not long. 'There will be a Council tomorrow,' Drouyn de Lhuys replied, rather coldly and without further explanation, 'and I shall take the orders of the Emperor.'" In fact, Drouyn de Lhuys had already instructed Montebello that, Britain having rejected the French proposal of a collective note to Berlin, "we do not think that we can give our counsels to St. Petersburg the form of a common and simultaneous *démarche*." It can only be assumed, therefore, that the "orders of the Emperor" were duly received. On the day following the council, Drouyn de Lhuys abruptly reversed his position:

As for the form to give to the *démarche* which Lord Russell proposes, the initiative that we have taken ever since first hearing of the Alvensleben Convention proves the importance that we attach to an entente with the other courts. The Polish affair is a question of public European order which interests, therefore, all the cabinets, and we would be only too happy to see them associate themselves with the views which direct our policy. The English proposition raises, then, no objection on our part and if the powers

16. "We are used to getting startling news from Paris," King Leopold wrote to Russell in March, "but the proposition for a Congress which is to unsettle all the old international arrangements and to give us quite a new political code came very unexpectedly upon us" (Leopold I to Russell, March 13, 1863, in Gooch (ed.), *The Later Correspondence of Lord John Russell*, II, 286). On March 29, Bismarck discussed the possibility of a conference or congress at some length with the new Russian ambassador (Paul Petrovich Oubril to Gorchakov, Berlin, very confidential, March 29, 1863, in *APP*, III, 437, no. 374).

should adhere to these overtures we would be ready to give our assent to a collective manifestation.[17]

Under these circumstances, the French attempt of early March to persuade Saint Petersburg to make concessions in Poland that would head off a European intervention (Baron Eugène Beyens states that Napoleon wrote directly to the czar) must be considered a maneuver rather than a serious effort, especially since the French admonition was published at Paris on the sixteenth and since even it seemed to envisage a European "transaction" that would guarantee to Russia (an independent Poland having been reestablished through Russian magnanimity) the possession of the old Polish provinces. Moreover, on March 20, Billault, one of the three "speaking ministers," rising in the Senate to reply to a harangue of Prince Napoleon's calling for French intervention in Poland, had firmly committed the government to collective action. The constant concern of the emperor, Billault asserted, had been never to act alone. Even the Mexican affair had been at first a collective enterprise. As for Poland, "the Polish question is European and it is with the aid of Europe that the imperial government intends to resolve it," for the czar would never resist the moral pressure of Europe. "Your words," Napoleon wrote to his spokesman the next day, "conform with my thought on every point and I reject any other interpretation of my sentiments."[18]

At this moment Napoleon appears still to have hoped that Vienna would accept the proposals he had made to Metternich, proposals that would lead to a major revision by Europe of the treaties of 1815. Several days later, at the end of March, these hopes were crushed. At almost the same moment Gorchakov's intransigence had vitiated in advance the proposed appeal to the 1815 treaties in the case of Poland. The sole remaining possibility of united action lay in a collective note of protest by France, Britain, and Austria. At this possibility the French government now grasped. To Ollivier, writing in later years, it was a fatal decision.[19] But Napoleon must have made it with hope. Not only was the path of collective action a familiar one for him; not only did it offer, in the case of Poland, the only reasonable hope of

17. Drouyn de Lhuys to Montebello, Paris, March 4, 1863, in AMAE, CP, Russie, 230:157, no. 23; La Gorce, Histoire du Second Empire, IV, 437; Drouyn de Lhuys to Gros, Paris, March 7, 1863, in AMAE, CP, Angleterre, 723:200v–201v.

18. Beyens, Le Second Empire, I, 331–32; Drouyn de Lhuys to Montebello, Paris, March 10, 1863, in AMAE, CP, Russie, 230:175–76, no. 25; Ollivier, L'empire libéral, VI, 172–74.

19. Ollivier, L'empire libéral, VI, 167.

skirting the gulfs on either side; but the path might be contrived to lead where few but himself had any wish to go.

It led, in fact, to the proposal of a European congress. The dispatch of a collective note proved impracticable. Austria demurred because of its Galician possessions, and the French were reluctant to accept an appeal to the 1815 treaties as the basis of such a *démarche*. Consequently, on April 17 the ambassadors of France, Britain, and Austria delivered simultaneous but separate notes at Saint Petersburg. The British note stressed the treaties of 1815 and spoke of the "deep interest which in common with the rest of Europe [the British government] take in the welfare of the Kingdom of Poland." It emphasized the international obligations accruing to Russia as "a member of the community of European states." Drouyn de Lhuys' note closed with the thought that "it is a common interest of all the powers to see these constantly recurring perils banished once and for all." In none of the notes was a conference proposed. Nor did the replies sent by Gorchakov on April 26 contain any suggestion of a conference. Nevertheless, at the beginning of May, Cowley found both Napoleon and Eugénie convinced that Russia was prepared to accept the proposal of a congress. Of course, Gorchakov had always shown a predilection for such gatherings, and his dispatches to Berlin at this time appear to have been more explicit. "Please say to Prince Gorchakov," Bismarck told the Russian ambassador on April 30, "that . . . I completely agree with the idea of a congress and especially with the thought of basing it on an understanding among the three courts, as indicated in your dispatch." At any rate, by the first days of May the French government had decided to propose a congress on the affairs of Poland. Apparently the initiative came again from Napoleon. It was a matter, wrote Metternich, "of coming back (and that is the Emperor's favorite thought) to the idea of a European Congress." Drouyn de Lhuys showed no enthusiasm at the time for such an approach, and later he would explicitly deny any inclination in that direction. But he put his diplomatic finesse at the service of his master. In several skillfully worded dispatches of May 3 and 4, Drouyn de Lhuys argued that, as Russia had recognized the jurisdiction of Europe and had sought its advice, it was necessary to find the best means of reaching agreement, and in the view of the French government the most convenient and effective method was a conference.[20]

20. Rechberg to Metternich, Vienna, March 31, 1863, in AMAE, CP, Autriche, 483:278–80; Drouyn de Lhuys to Montebello, Paris, April 2, 1863, in AMAE, CP, Rus-

But was Drouyn de Lhuys, the professional diplomat, really happy
with the scope of French ideas concerning this projected meeting? In
effect, what Paris proposed was a congress of almost *all* of the European states, that is, the addition of Holland, Denmark, Turkey, Italy,
and the German Confederation to the signatories of the 1815 treaties.
Belgium and Switzerland would be excluded by their neutrality, and
the pope would have to decide whether he wished to be represented.
Paris offered no absolute objection to a conference of 1815 signatories
but noted that Russia had rejected an appeal to these treaties and had
itself indicated "the opportunity to appeal to all interested parties,
that is, everybody, to establish in Poland a new order, offering guarantees not to be found in the present arrangements." And Drouyn de
Lhuys concluded: "An appeal to the entirety of Europe would seem to
us to respond much better to ideas that we have ourselves suggested
by placing the question in the realm of the general interest." In fact,
France had called during the earlier protest stage for "a unanimous
manifestation of Europe," and in response several smaller European
states had addressed notes to Saint Petersburg. As to the agenda of a
conference, it would not, in the French view, be restricted to the Polish question. Metternich reported on May 7: "The idea of this congress again holds sway at the Tuileries and it seems almost to be
counted upon. This is why it has already been suggested to Spain that
she bring up *the question of Naples*, declare in conference that the
principle of universal suffrage has been distorted [*faussé*] and ask for a
new vote *after the removal* of Sardinian troops." After all, the possibilities inherent in Saint Petersburg's hint that Russia would only
agree to a congress that "was not limited to the Polish question" but
embraced "the totality of the political situation of Europe" could not
have been missed at the Tuileries, and, in fact, the passage of Montebello's dispatch that contains this assertion is underlined in the
Quai d'Orsay copy. When the Russian ambassador came to suggest it
officially, Drouyn de Lhuys replied that, while he did not think France

---

sie, 230:244–46, no. 30; Russell to Francis, Baron Napier, London, April 10, 1863, in
AMAE, CP, Angleterre, 724:31–37; Cowley to Russell, Paris, private, May 8, 1863, in
Russell Papers, 30/22, 59; Oubril to Gorchakov, Berlin, April 30, 1863, in *APP*, III, 533,
no. 470; Cowley to Russell, Paris, private, May 3, 1863, in Russell Papers, 30/22, 59;
Metternich to Rechberg, Paris, May 7, 1863, in HHSA, PA IX, Fr. Ber., 1863, I–IX, Box
75, no. 18A-D, fol. 361v; Cowley to Russell, Paris, private, August 21, 1863, in Russell
Papers, 30/22, 59; Drouyn de Lhuys to Montebello, Paris, confidential, May 3, 1863, in
AMAE, CP, Russie, 231:15–16, no. 37; Drouyn de Lhuys to French agents at London
and Vienna, May 4, 1863, in AMAE, CP, Angleterre, 724:110–12.

should take the initiative, "with reference to the broadening of the object of this meeting he, for his part, saw no objection to it."[21]

Other governments, however, saw major objections. Vienna, which opposed a conference, regarded Gorchakov's penchant for widening its scope as an effort to divert attention from Poland and feared it would set a dangerous precedent. London balked, as always, at the thought of a meeting whose scope and purpose would not be strictly defined in advance. And while Bismarck had no intention of rejecting a congress invitation should it be offered, he saw in the proposal of an all-European meeting a French attempt to create dissension "between the Powers of Europe, or at all events between the Governments of Germany." Besides, there was the evident fact that if only the great powers discussed the Polish question, France and Britain would be outvoted by the three partitioning powers.[22]

Faced with this opposition, the French fell into line at once. About May 6, Russell had stated Britain's program: an immediate suspension of hostilities in Poland and thereafter a conference of the eight Vienna signatories restricted to a six-point basis of negotiation. Gorchakov having declared his willingness to accept the treaties of 1815 as a basis for discussion, Drouyn de Lhuys announced that if necessary France would accept a conference of the Vienna signatories, provided its decisions were submitted for approval to the other European governments; and he agreed as well that the conference could be limited in advance to the Polish question. Thus Paris had again, as on several occasions in the past, sacrificed the grand for the achievable. A general discussion was desirable, but it was necessary before all else to find a solution to the Polish problem. When Cowley talked with Napoleon on May 26 he found him enthusiastic for the immediate assembling of a conference, resigned to restricting its scope, and convinced that it constituted the only alternative to a rupture. On June

21. Drouyn de Lhuys to Gros, Paris, confidential, May 4, 1863, in AMAE, CP, Angleterre, 724:113v–14, no. 48; Ollivier, L'empire libéral, VI, 190; La Gorce, Histoire du Second Empire, IV, 449; Metternich to Rechberg, Paris, private, May 7, 1863, in HHSA, PA IX, Varia, 1863, Box 77, fols. 86–89; Montebello to Drouyn de Lhuys, Saint Petersburg, confidential, May 9, 1863, in AMAE, CP, Russie, 231:44v–45; Drouyn de Lhuys to Montebello, Paris, confidential, May 26, 1863, in AMAE, CP, Russie, 231:75–76, no. 43.

22. Gramont to Drouyn de Lhuys, Vienna, May 12, 1863, in AMAE, CP, Autriche, 484:37–40, no. 44; Gros to Drouyn de Lhuys, London, confidential, May 6, 1863, in AMAE, CP, Angleterre, 724:123, no. 62; Sir Andrew Buchanan to Russell, Berlin, May 16, 1863, in APP, III, 574–75, no. 507.

17, similar notes went out again from Paris, London, and Vienna, calling upon the Russian government to accept a conference on Poland, at which the bases of discussion would be a general amnesty, national representation, national administration, liberty of conscience and of worship, recognition of Polish as the official language, and the establishment of a regular and legal system of recruiting. In the weeks of negotiation, however, the Russians had massed their forces for repression and Gorchakov had convinced himself that neither Britain nor Austria would intervene with force. Since the conference would not be a general one, and since the velvet glove was no longer needed, Saint Petersburg replied to the allied notes with a blunt rejection. The proposed conference, wrote Gorchakov, "would constitute a direct interference which a great power could all the less admit in that it has justification in neither the spirit nor the letter of existing treaties." And he added insult to injury by proposing a restricted conference of Prussia, Russia, and Austria to consider administrative arrangements for Poland![23]

Napoleon was probably neither surprised nor unduly disappointed at this reply. His thoughts had followed a pattern remarkably similar to that of the recent past. He would have welcomed a *general* congress; but when that was rejected, conference diplomacy ceased to be for him the means to an end and became the end of the means, still important, but secondary to whatever direct action might be undertaken that would do something for Poland. He told Metternich:

> I admit I know nothing of diplomacy and the tortuous wording of dispatches but I know perfectly well that if we continue as we are doing we will be a long time before reaching a solution. As I see it, the question is this: France and England cannot be satisfied with illusory concessions. We will ask for real guarantees of independence for Russian Poland. Will you go with us, draw back, or turn against us? *I like to tackle things head-on* and I wonder if the moment hasn't now arrived which you yourselves said could force you to take a definite decision.

If France and Austria stood together and meant business, Russia would yield. Such, Napoleon told Hübner, then visiting in Paris, was his

23. Russell to Napier, London, May [6], 1863, draft, in AMAE, CP, Angleterre, 724:127–36; Drouyn de Lhuys to Gramont, Paris, May 13, 1863, in AMAE, CP, Autriche, 484:47, no. 41; Drouyn de Lhuys to Gramont, Paris, confidential, May 14, 1863, in AMAE, CP, Autriche, 484:50–53, no. 42; Cowley to Russell, Paris, private, May 26, 1863, in Russell Papers, 30/22, 59; Gorchakov to Baron Andrei de Budberg, Saint Petersburg, July 1, 1863, in AMAE, CP, Russie, 231:153.

conviction. If Russia did not, the conference, meeting perhaps in Brussels or Frankfurt, could still serve a useful purpose, provided France, Austria, and Britain had a firm understanding beforehand. At least one week before receipt of Gorchakov's reply to the second round of notes, however, Paris knew that this bid for a triple entente had failed. Since the conference would not meet, and since Britain, Austria, and France would not consider the use of force (in the first days of August, Napoleon consulted a number of advisers in conferences at Saint-Cloud and decided against war), there remained for Paris only the dubious satisfaction of castigating others for their weakness and declining all responsibility for the fiasco. The French government, according to Drouyn de Lhuys, had sacrificed its original preference for an all-European congress in order to make a three-power entente possible, and the rejection of the logical consequences of this entente at the crucial moment was nothing less than a betrayal. Now France could only await events, its opinion still unchanged "on the European character of the Polish question and on the rights which the general interest and the treaties confer on us."[24]

Certainly Napoleon had not changed his opinion on the European character of either the Polish or the Italian question. And it is significant that from the beginning of the Polish crisis the two were linked in his thoughts. "What you propose," he wrote, on the very day that the Polish insurrection broke out, to Prince Napoleon, who had suggested an exchange by Austria of Venetia and Galicia for various compensations, "is, as you say, a dream; but it is a dream which can one day be realized." The emperor's negotiations with Austria in the spring did not, as we have seen, advance him any further toward that realization. Even had they proved more successful, the breadth of the proposed combinations, the linking of Italy and Poland,[25] would surely have required active participation of the European concert. As 1863 neared its end it seems probable that Napoleon was truly unable to

24. Metternich to Rechberg, Paris, May 20, 1863, in HHSA, PA IX, Fr. Ber., 1863, I–IX, Box 75, no. 21A-B, fols. 384–85; Hübner to Rechberg, Paris, May 28, 1863, annex to Metternich's no. 22B, in HHSA, PA IX, Fr. Ber., 1863, I–IX, Box 75, fol. 402; Case, *French Opinion on War and Diplomacy*, 183; Drouyn de Lhuys to marquis de Cadore, Paris, September 22, 1863, in AMAE, CP, Angleterre, 726:143–53, no. 101.

25. Hallberg, *Franz Joseph and Napoleon III*, 316; Napoleon III to Prince Napoleon, January 22, 1863, in Hauterive (ed.), *Napoléon III et le Prince Napoléon*, 238. Metternich wrote: "Walewski est furieux de ce que l'Empereur ait mêlé la question italienne qu'il abhore à la question polonaise qu'il protège" (Metternich to Rechberg, Paris, March 29, 1863, in HHSA, PA IX, Fr. Ber., 1863, I–IX, Box 75, no. 12B, fol. 300v).

conceive of a solution to the Italian and Polish questions that would not involve a European congress. Yet, these specific problems were only part of the motivation of the general congress proposal that he was to advance in November, 1863.

CHAPTER 10

"Idées Napoléoniennes," 1849–1863
The Ottoman Empire and the Reorganization
of Europe

By 1863, only seven years after he had raised France to a height of power and influence that it had not known for more than a generation, Napoleon could find little in Europe to regard with satisfaction. Two victorious wars and a decade of autocratic rule had seemingly produced little more than sharpened mistrust and a foreign policy in growing disarray. How could this be so? Victory over Russia in 1856 had opened the way for France to several foreign policies, each of which might have succeeded. If Napoleon had wished to reach for a moderate amount of hegemony and of territorial gain on his side of the Rhine, Russia, eager to undo the consequences of its defeat, could have provided the needed support and Sardinia's and Prussia's ambitions the catalyst. If, on the contrary, he had chosen to freeze, as it were, the moment of French ascendancy by adopting a conservative (some would say traditional) policy, what better ally could he have found than Austria? And if, finally, he had preferred to preside over a Europe that continued, untrammeled and unguided, the development abnormally cramped by Metternich's system, the British alliance, so dear to his heart, would probably have been adequate, seconded perhaps by that of Prussia. But Napoleon chose none of these. True to the ideas that he had developed before he came to power, his actions to 1863 confirmed the aims that during those years he was perfectly willing to explain to anyone who would listen. Paul W. Schroeder has called attention to the tragic consequences of Napoleon's failure to reestablish the concert of Europe after the Crimean War.[1] But that concert, restricted to the great powers and committed to conservation, he had never intended to restore. Rather, his foreign policy con-

---

1. Schroeder, *Austria, Great Britain, and the Crimean War*, 423.

sisted of the reorganization of Europe roughly in accord with the principle of nationalities, a reorganization for which the Ottoman Empire would largely foot the bill, and which would be arranged and thereafter supervised by a new concert of Europe. He conceived of this concert as a congress system, dominated by but not restricted to the great powers, brought about by a system of alliances, and willing not only to accept necessary change but, in fact, to supervise its development.

No one could doubt that Napoleon intended, if ever he had the opportunity, to redraw the map of Europe. As early as 1849 he had prefaced an interview with Malmesbury by remarking that "the danger to Europe lay in the absolute necessity of modifying the treaties of 1815, which should be done before a war broke out." During the Crimean War and the subsequent peace congress this idea remained very much in his mind, and he himself later told his ministers that the chief purpose of the Crimean War had been to revise the treaties of 1815 and to reorganize the Continent, and that the war he was then preparing against Austria in Italy would make it possible to regain a lost opportunity. Once again the crisis passed without the hoped-for results. But Napoleon was no more deterred from his ultimate goal than he had been in 1849 or 1856. "More than ever," Cavour speculated in March, 1860, "he is dreaming of remaking the map of Europe." And Cowley warned his government: "Ever since he [Napoleon] has been upon the throne, he has had before his eyes the idea of a pacific revision of the map of Europe, and we must now expect constant efforts in that direction."[2]

The evidence of Napoleon's intent to reorganize Europe could be multiplied, but it is no more necessary to do so than to elaborate on the accepted fact that, in his mind, this reorganization should be in general accord with the wishes of the people. For him, in F. A. Simpson's words, "the troubling of the waters would be for the healing of nations," since only a Europe reorganized in accordance with the principle of nationalities could be a peaceful Europe. His concern for Italy, Poland, and the Danubian Principalities in 1856; his efforts on behalf of the Principalities from 1856 to 1866 and subsequently; the Italian war of 1859; and the attempt to do something for Poland in 1863 are

2. Malmesbury, *Memoirs*, I, 256, diary entry of March 30, 1849; note de la main de l'Empereur Napoléon III: considérations politiques sur une guerre avec l'Autriche, December 20, 1858, in Ollivier, *L'empire libéral*, III, 538; Cavour to Durando [at Constantinople], Turin, March 5, 1860, in *Cavour-Nigra*, III, 142; Cowley to Russell, May 2, 1860, in PRO, FO, 519, 227:122.

perhaps sufficient examples of the sincerity of this *politique des nationalités*. Several qualifications are required, however. The first is that Napoleon did not himself elaborate a consistent explanation of the policy of nationalities. That work was done by a minister of the last years of the Second Empire, Emile Ollivier. For Ollivier, the theory of nationalities was an amalgam of the "visions" of Saint Helena and principles of the Revolution, worked upon by democratic thinkers. It was nourished by a natural impulse of the French to champion the oppressed, but its foundation was juridical. This theory had nothing to do with ideas of agglomeration or natural frontiers or race. As to the first, the will of the people might be to agglomerate or not—the principle of nationalities would accommodate itself to either decision. As to the second, "the true frontiers are those constituted by the will of the people; all other boundaries are but walls of a prison which one has always the right to destroy." And as for race, that idea was barbarous, exclusive, and atavistic, while the idea of nationality "is able to expand and to develop without end; it could even come to encompass all humanity, as under the Roman Empire."[3]

Napoleon, moreover, was far from immune to the attractions of philosophizing, and his musings on the theme of nationalities, especially on the possibilities of agglomeration that it contained, could easily take wing. "The agglomeration of people of the same race under one rule," Cowley wrote in 1856, "is a theme so consonant to the Emperor's ears, that His Majesty would be likely to listen with complacency to any scheme the basis of which is the restoration of nationality." And listen he did (when he was not himself the instigator), to schemes of a Slavonic principality consisting of Serbia, Montenegro, Herzegovina, and part of Bosnia; to dreams of a vast Danubian confederation of Hungarian and Slavic peoples; to talk of a Greek kingdom, extending to the Dardanelles and including the European side of that strait, or of an Iberian confederation; and to plans for a Scandinavian union. There was also an element of realism in this passion for confederation, since it posed less of a threat to France than unitary movements might have and was also a useful transitional stage from particularism to full union. In 1861, Gorchakov showed Bismarck a "future map of Europe" from a French source in which the Continent

3. Simpson, *Louis Napoleon and the Recovery of France*, 11; Ollivier, *L'empire libéral*, I, 162–78. This "French" view of nationalities was not, of course, unique to Ollivier.

was divided into Iberian, Gallic, Italian, Greek, and German confederations![4]

Although Napoleon's hope of reorganizing Europe cannot be understood in isolation from the principle of nationalities, it is clear that, for him, this principle was more suggestive than binding. In his application of the theory he had always to bear in mind the realities of the moment, the need, at times, to sacrifice a lesser object in order to gain a greater. Nor could he ignore the requirements of France. In the case of the Danubian Principalities, for example, the thought of sacrificing them in the interest of a greater cause (at least to the extent of consigning their rule to an Austrian archduke) was, as we have seen, neither a hasty nor a fleeting one. Concerning Hungary in 1860,[5] Poland before 1863, and Schleswig after 1866, Napoleon showed an unwillingness to endanger his relations with this or that great power by arguing the principle of nationalities too vigorously.

Did the policy of nationalities veil a Napoleonic design to regain by deceit and cunning the territories that France had lost through war? Historians having failed to corroborate the dark suspicions of his contemporaries, perhaps the time has come to weigh Napoleon's own explanation to Cowley in October, 1858:

> I am told that my policy is tortuous, but I am not understood. I am blamed for coquetting with Austria one day and with Russia the next, and it is inferred therefore that I am not to be depended upon. But my policy is very simple. When I came to my present position I saw that France wanted peace, and I determined to maintain peace with the Treaties of 1815, so long as France was respected and held her own in the Councils of Europe. But I was equally resolved, if I was forced into war, not to make peace until a better equilibrium was secured to Europe. I have no ambitious views like the first Emperor, but if other countries gain anything France must gain also.

The question was, however, gain what? That same year, during the negotiations with Russia preparatory to the 1859 war, Napoleon indicated to Kisselev what France would want as its share of a general revision of the treaties of 1815 and of 1856: "For my part, it would not be a question of the Rhine frontier, desirable as that might be for

4. Cowley to Clarendon, Paris, May 11, 1857, in PRO, FO, 519, 7:300; Binkley, *Realism and Nationalism*, 182.

5. He was willing to suppress a pamphlet published in Paris in early 1860 that called for the independence of Hungary (Metternich to Rechberg, Paris, May 22, 1860, in HHSA, PA IX, Fr. Ber., 1860, I–V, Box 65, no. 35, fols. 574–81).

France. The resulting complications would be too great. . . . It would be a matter, then, for France not of a Rhenish frontier but of a better boundary line in the direction of Metz, for example, since the present line was obviously drawn with hostile intent toward France." A year later, it was still the same theme. The treaties of 1815, he told Metternich, forced France to keep 600,000 men under arms:

> Europe well understood that to avoid a new expansion of France it was necessary to facilitate a future invasion by rolling back her frontiers far enough to allow the crossing of the Alps and of the Rhine without danger; that one had to be able to enter by way of Savoy and Luxemburg. It is therefore my duty to think of changing what is dangerous for France in these treaties. By dispelling the fears of Europe which led to these arrangements, I think I can also dispel the fears of France and thus relieve her of the burden of maintaining an immense army. The day when I shall have Savoy and Nice in the South and sufficient fortresses in the North *my mission will be accomplished.*

In fact, Napoleon even speculated to the Belgian minister, Beyens, that the burden of armaments accounted for the discrepancy between the economic strengths of Britain and France: "Therefore it is necessary that France have a system of frontiers which will defend themselves. The acquisition of Nice and of Savoy now covers her on the Italian side; the neutrality of Belgium guarantees her against an aggression coming from the North. It is, then, only from Mayence to Cologne that rectifications are indispensable." But *not* Mayence or Cologne. "If France were to go to Mayence," a colleague of Lord Augustus Loftus' was assured by the emperor, "she would require also to go to Coblence, and from thence to Cologne, and if once at Cologne she would be further obliged to go to the Zuyder Zee, which would be committing over again the faults of the First Empire." What Napoleon had in mind were the fortress of Landau and the Prussian districts of Saarbrücken and Saarlouis. He had hinted as much to Pourtalès a month earlier:

> It is absurd to conclude [from the name Bonaparte] that I wish to make conquests, that I dream, for example, of the Rhine and of Belgium. I wouldn't be able to bring it off at any rate. Oh, if there should be a general reworking of the map out of which the other great powers would gain, then I don't say that I wouldn't seek, with the full consent of the contiguous states (a consent with which I would not pretend to dispense, as you now see in the case of Sardinia), I don't say that I wouldn't seek a small rectification of frontiers. But this would require free consent and it would be a matter of sev-

eral bits [*pouces*] of land only. When I say "bits" I mean several square miles. But this would suppose circumstances quite different from those of the moment and, especially, an understanding with which I have no wish to dispense.

In this instance, the common sense of the situation lends weight to Napoleon's own version of his ambitions. That version accords with his almost complacent assumption (before 1866) that French resources were ample in their present limits and that France remained, without aggrandizement, the dominant power of Europe, whose destiny was to exercise a moral hegemony over the continent. Besides, how could he ever have hoped to reconcile his stubborn adherence to the British alliance or his general commitment to the policy of nationalities with major territorial ambitions? It seems likely, then, that if he could have achieved a reorganization within which French security, prestige, and moral ascendancy would have been assured, Napoleon could have contented himself with a very small territorial gain. Perhaps, in fact, he was sincere when he told Cowley in 1853 that he could not help thinking sometimes "of what a noble and disinterested game England and France might play in resetting to a certain degree the boundaries of some of the States of Europe, while renouncing an aggrandizement for themselves."[6]

Here, then, was a foreign policy whose major purpose was to reorganize Europe, guided by the principle of nationalities but taking into account, as well, the realities of the moment, including the demands of French security and of public opinion. But such a revision would require sacrifice and compensations, and where could the latter be found? The answer reveals a thread of Napoleon's foreign policy that has received little attention, although it was vital to the whole fabric—his attitude toward Turkey and his plans for its empire. On the attitude, at least, there can be no doubt; it was one of contempt. Al-

6. Cowley to Malmesbury, October 31, 1858, in V. Wellesley and Sencourt (eds.), *Conversations with Napoleon III*, 154; Kisselev to Gorchakov, Paris, December 7, 1858, in Goriaïnow, "Les étapes de l'alliance franco-russe," 531–32; Metternich to Rechberg, Paris, very secret, November 26, 1859, in HHSA, PA IX, Fr. Ber., 1859, VIII–XII, Box 63, no. 18A-B, fols. 497–98; Beyens to the Belgian foreign minister, April 13, 1860, in Beyens, *Le Second Empire*, I, 313 (in this version of Napoleon's remarks that Beyens had from Jules Devaux, who probably had it from Jean Baptiste Nothomb, the Belgian minister at Berlin, Beyens speculated that Napoleon coveted "the Palatinate and the left bank of the Rhine"); Pourtalès to Schleinitz, Paris, reserved, March 11, 1860, in *APP*, vol. III, pt. 1, p. 221, no. 96; Cowley to Clarendon, Paris, August 22, 1853, in PRO, FO, 519, 211:69.

ready in 1853 he could refer to the Turks as "stupid—friends as stupid as that!" The Ottoman Empire, he declared four years later, was "a disgrace to our times." The Turks were "a sorry set," a people "as stupid as they are weak." Their government was "an anomaly." He could not, the emperor told Metternich at the end of 1862, find any enthusiasm "for an impossible, anti-Christian government in the midst of European civilization." In fact, concluded the Austrian, Napoleon's antipathy for the Turk was "inveterate."[7]

Still, it was not easy for Napoleon to abandon the traditional rhetoric of defense of Ottoman territorial integrity. Britain wanted to preserve Turkey, and the emperor wanted to be on good terms with London. Besides, with his dislike for conservative Austria and his suspicion of the Russian colossus, Napoleon could not himself regard the dissolution of the Ottoman Empire as something to be taken lightly. The professional French diplomats, Drouyn de Lhuys and Thouvenel, for example, saw the necessity of preserving Turkey, and usually their master ended by agreeing, if with an ill grace. Although his sympathies preceding the outbreak of the Crimean War were probably with Russia, Napoleon came down on the side of a European defense of Turkish territorial integrity and sovereignty. Nevertheless, he insisted upon making a distinction. The Turks, he told Cowley, were to understand "that France and England were not protecting her, as Turkey, but as a parcel of territory the integrity of which was necessary to the balance of power in Europe." Later, he went even further, exclaiming to Hübner: "I did not make war for her [Turkey], I made it against Russia but not for Turkey. They told me that the integrity of the Porte was a European necessity. So! It is a very sad necessity." More than a year later, he repeated the same theme to Metternich. But if Napoleon would not allow either Austria or Russia to profit exclusively or excessively from the collapse of Turkey, he could not, apparently, escape the conclusion that this collapse was inevitable. Even in the midst of the Crimean War he would not believe in the possibility of "regenerat-

7. Simpson, *Louis Napoleon and the Recovery of France*, 363; Cowley to Clarendon, Paris, March 29, 1857, in PRO, FO, 519, 221:138; first memorandum of Albert, on the visit of Napoleon and Eugénie to Osborne, August 6, 1857, in Martin, *The Life of His Royal Highness, the Prince Consort*, IV, 91; Hübner, *Neuf ans*, II, 162, journal entry of May 15, 1858; Metternich to Rechberg, Paris, September 5, 1859, in HHSA, PA IX, Fr. Ber., 1859, VIII–XII, Box 63, no. 8A-C, fol. 191; Metternich to Rechberg, Paris, September 1, 1862, in HHSA, PA IX, Fr. Ber., 1862, VIII–XII, Box 73, no. 50B, fol. 117v; Metternich to Rechberg, Paris, January 8, 1863, in HHSA, PA IX, Fr. Ber., 1863, I–IX, Box 75, no. 1A-C, fols. 6v–7.

ing" Turkey. The czar, he told Bourqueney, was right—"Turkey was dying a lingering death"—and it was not possible "to galvanise a dead man to life." "The Sultan's Empire in Europe is going to collapse," he told Metternich at the end of 1859, "and I'll certainly not prevent it from doing so, because I consider it an anomaly."[8]

During the Crimean War, as we have seen, Napoleon showed a willingness more than once to play fast and loose with Turkish territorial integrity, agreeing in March, 1854, with Palmerston's beau ideal of a redistribution of Turkish territory, speaking repeatedly of expanding the conflict into a revolutionary war whose settlement would be made possible by partitioning the Ottoman Empire. He even suggested that Turkish territory could be used to enlist further European aid in the war against Russia. And the French emperor was not alone in his conviction that the days of the Ottoman Empire were numbered.[9]

It is difficult to believe, therefore, that Napoleon, at least before the late 1860s, placed much faith in an alternative to dissolution that was often raised at Paris (sometimes by the emperor himself)—a European supervision of the Ottoman Empire that would save it through reform. Certainly Napoleon told Cowley in 1854 that the only way he saw of saving Turkey was to take its whole administration into his own hands. And in 1860, after the Congress of Paris had internationalized the Eastern question to a certain extent, Thouvenel returned to the theme, imagining a European garrison stationed on Rhodes, a European fleet in the Bosporus, and a five-power commission established at Constantinople to advise the Porte. Probably Napoleon was predisposed to a skeptical view of this "reformism" not only by his cynicism as to the viability of Turkey but also by his doubt that the effort was even worth making. "I will be frank with you," he told Bourqueney in 1853 as the latter prepared to leave for his post in Constantinople. "The idea of establishing Christianity where infidelity

---

8. Cowley to Clarendon, Fontainebleau, private, November 23, 1853, in PRO, FO, 519, 211:223; Hübner, *Neuf ans*, II, 162, journal entry of May 15, 1858); Cowley to Clarendon, Paris, private, October 30, 1855, in PRO, FO, 519, 217:161; Cowley to Clarendon, Paris, February 3, 1856, in PRO, FO, 519, 218:153.

9. Thouvenel concluded, for example, that while an effort should be made to preserve Turkey, this should not prevent the powers from thinking of the day "when the last spark of life will leave the corpse" (Metternich to Rechberg, Paris, confidential, May 10, 1860, in HHSA, PA IX, Fr. Ber., 1860, I–V, Box 65, no. 33B, fols. 539–39v. See also Cowley to Clarendon, Paris, private, March 16, 6, 1854, both in PRO, FO, 519, 212:202, 172–73.

now exists has always had a charm for me—I could not regret such a change." And Cowley concluded four years later: "His Majesty's conviction that the Turkish Empire cannot last, that Mohammedanism and civilization cannot coexist and that it would be a blessing for the world in general were the Crescent everywhere replaced by the Cross, leads him too easily to dispose, by anticipation, of the component parts of an Empire, the dissolution of which he pre-conceives." In January, 1863, Metternich reported: "I can only state the constant confirmation of his [Napoleon's] profound repugnance for anything which would resemble an encouragement or a support given to Ottoman power in Europe."[10]

But one aspect, at least, of the idea that Europe should take Turkey's administration in hand appealed to Napoleon. To Stratford de Redcliffe, he had remarked enigmatically in 1853 that he was "in favour of Turkish independence and the progress of civilization." If the two were to prove incompatible, Europe, and not any of its constituent powers, must so decide. And if it should ever come to the point of Eugénie's 1863 tour of the map as reported by Metternich— "*Turkey*: Abolished from motives of public utility and Christian morality"—Europe would need to determine the utility, impose the morality, and supervise the abolition. In awaiting that result, Napoleon mused on the theme of Turkey, his thoughts taking almost invariably a significant direction. In March, 1856, for example, Cowley reported a conversation that he had recently had with the emperor:

Keeping France very much out of view, he said, that it was difficult not to admit that the present territorial arrangements were bad and incomplete and he said he could not see why some peaceful arrangement should not be made which would better suit all parties than the present distribution of territory. He had no wish for anything particular for France he said, tho' of course, she would profit in the general readjustment. . . . Having thus disposed of Europe H.M. went off to the Mediterranean, the shores of which he again partitioned, as I have had occasion to tell you before.

Then, to Cowley's usual objections, Napoleon replied that Turkey could not last long, that "the subject was constantly in his thoughts,"

10. Cowley to Clarendon, Chantilly, private, July 9, 1854, in PRO, FO, 519, 213:142; Metternich to Rechberg, Paris, July 26, 1860, in HHSA, PA IX, Fr. Ber., 1860, VI–IX, Box 66, no. 48C, fols. 240–41v; Cowley to Clarendon, Paris, private, March 9, 1853, in PRO, FO, 519, 210; Cowley to Clarendon, Paris, May 11, 1857, in PRO, FO, 519, 7:300; Metternich to Rechberg, Paris, January 8, 1863, in HHSA, PA IX, Fr. Ber., 1863, I–IX, Box 75, no. 1A-C, fol. 6.

that from time to time he had put his ideas on the matter in writing but had not yet completed the work.[11]

The ambassador did not, apparently, notice the connection between European revision and a partition of Turkey, although three years earlier Ernest II had already convinced himself that Napoleon "considered the Eastern Question a matter which was suitable for territorial compensations." A few months after his conversation with Cowley, however, the emperor explained himself more explicitly to Prince Albert. The prince had delivered his usual lecture on the difficulty of revision. "If everybody were to get great advantages, where were they to come from?" Certainly not from within Europe. " 'That is,' replied the Emperor, 'why I always thought better means, "*pour rendre de grands bienfaits au monde*" could be found out of Europe than within.' There was Africa, for instance. He would not make of the Mediterranean as Napoleon I had wished, 'un lac Français,' but 'un lac Européen.' . . . These were all magnificent countries rendered useless to humanity and civilization by their abominable governments." The idea was both deeply rooted and persistent. In March, 1853, Napoleon had expressed himself in exactly the same way to Stratford de Redcliffe. He told Cowley in 1856 that he wished "to see the coast of the Mediterranean in the hands of Christians alone." Some four years later, Metternich reported that the emperor had again advanced "his favorite thought of civilizing the coasts of the Mediterranean and making it a European lake." Almost at that moment Walewski was telling Cowley that Napoleon had for months been intent on bringing up the Eastern question, with a view to arriving at a territorial revision in Europe. And in the spring of 1862, Hübner discovered the same pattern of thought during conversations with Napoleon and with Thouvenel.[12]

And it was not only theoretical. In wrestling with the Italian and Polish problems, Napoleon had had recourse on many occasions be-

11. Memorandum of Stratford de Redcliffe, March 10, 1853, in Lane-Poole, *Life of Stratford Canning*, II, 238; Cowley to Clarendon, Paris, March 29, 1857, in PRO, FO, 519, 221:133–38.

12. Ernest II, *Memoirs*, III, 67; second memorandum of Albert, on the visit of Napoleon and Eugénie to Osborne, August 11, 1857, in Martin, *The Life of His Royal Highness, the Prince Consort*, IV, 97–98; memorandum of Stratford de Redcliffe, March 10, 1853, in Lane-Poole, *Life of Stratford Canning*, II, 237; Cowley to Clarendon, Paris, December 28, 1856, in PRO, FO, 519, 6:490; Metternich to Rechberg, Paris, July 9, 1860, in HHSA, PA IX, Fr. Ber., 1860, VI–IX, Box 66, no. 45B, fols. 189v–90; Cowley to Russell, Paris, private, July 13, 1860, in Russell Papers, 30/22, 55; Hübner to Rechberg, Paris, April 18, May 9, 1862, both in HHSA, PA IX, Fr. Ber., 1862, I–VI, Box 72, fols. 35–46, 122–25.

tween 1853 and 1863 to an imaginary piecemeal partition of the Ottoman Empire. In 1853–1854 he had often raised the possibility of an
exchange of the Danubian Principalities for Lombardy; in 1856 he
had suggested a scheme by which the duke of Modena and the duchess of Parma would give up their states to Sardinia and succeed to the
thrones of Wallachia and Moldavia; and at the end of 1859, Lombardy
having been secured to Sardinia by war, Napoleon had begun urging
Austria to take the Danubian Principalities or Egypt or the Adriatic
coast as compensation for granting Venetia autonomy within an Italian confederation. Throughout 1860 the French emperor had seemed
determined to "settle the Italian question in the East"; he had thought
of an arrangement by which Sardinia would buy Venetia from Austria
and Austria would use part of this money to purchase Bosnia-
Herzegovina from the Porte. Through 1861 he had hinted often at
Franco-Austrian alliance on the basis of compensation for Austria in
the East, a viewpoint reflected by the French attitude toward the conflict in 1861–1862 of the Turks with their Bosnian and Herzegovinian subjects. In January, 1863, Napoleon returned to this theme, and
in February he told Metternich that if Austria gave up Venetia and
Galicia it could expect compensation in Germany and in the East. In
fact, three years after the Crimean War the French emperor had flatly
asserted to Clarendon: "Let us discuss general policy frankly. The object of our Eastern policy was two-fold—Poland and Italy." And in
1861 he had told an Italian observer that he was sympathetic to the
Polish cause, but since the Poles had not risen during the Crimean
War, "now it was necessary . . . that they delay their uprising until the
territorial revisions that will be brought about by the Eastern Question." That such projects were neither devices of desperation nor mere
flights of fancy is strongly indicated by the more detailed and sys-
tematic partition schemes that found their way out of the Tuileries in
these years, particularly after 1856.[13]

   Three serve as representative. Robert Sencourt, in his biography of
Napoleon III, outlines one such scheme based on a map by Edward
Stanford in F. Fernández de Córdoba's *Mis memorias intimas*. Sardinia would have Venetia, Parma, Modena, and the Romagna; the
pope would acquire the Abruzzes from Naples, the king of Naples to
be rewarded with the regency of Tunis, and the duchess of Parma
would receive Sicily. Prussia would absorb Hanover, Mecklenburg,

13. Prince Albert to Leopold I, April 19, 1859, in Martin, *The Life of His Royal Highness, the Prince Consort*, IV, 353; Vimercati to Cavour, Paris, May 7, 1861, in *Cavour:
Romana*, II, 180, no. 430.

Hesse, Waldeck, Anhalt, and Lippe; Prussia would cede the left bank of the Rhine to Belgium or Holland. Austria would give up Venetia (to Sardinia) and Galicia (to Russia), receiving Serbia, Bosnia, and Egypt. The king of Hanover would acquire Rumelia and the title King of Constantinople. The duke of Mecklenburg would have Bulgaria, Moldavia, and Wallachia. And Britain would receive Cyprus and the valley of the Euphrates. In May, 1861, Metternich received a confidence from an informant who had daily contact with Napoleon and who had just taken, in the ambassador's words, "un de ces voyages entrepris au crayon rouge à travers la carte de l'Europe, dont Sa Majesté est si prodigue." If, argued this informant, Napoleon was to be turned from his revolutionary course, it would first be necessary for the rulers of Europe to set free the oppressed nationalities.

> For that, it would be necessary before all else that Russia, Prussia, and Austria reconstitute an independent Poland, by putting the Saxon dynasty again on the Polish throne; Prussia would be compensated by extending its boundaries up to the frontiers of Bohemia; Russia would gain renewed strength, claiming sovereignty over the shores of the Black Sea and assuming an unassailable position on the Dardanelles, and Austria would more than compensate for the transfer of Galicia by annexing the Eastern shores of the Adriatic.
>
> The Emperor Francis Joseph would, further, have to yield up Venetia, the policing of which paralyzes all his movements and empties the coffers of the State. [He would do this] in his own interest first, and then in the interest of the Holy Father and of the King of Naples, whom it would then be easy to [reestablish] in their states, following an honest understanding with France. There would be no objection to Austria's keeping her secular influence in Germany and gradually extending herself toward the West.

Finally, less than two years later, Metternich himself was conducted on one of these famous tours of the map, although this time the red pencil was in the hand of the empress. Probably Eugénie flew higher and further in this *vol d'oiseau* than the emperor would have ventured, but the outline of the flight, as submitted to Vienna by Metternich, is at least suggestive:

> *Russia*: Repulsed in the East and meagerly compensated for the loss of Poland and the provinces which are a part of it by gains in Asiatic Turkey.
>
> *Poland*: Reconstituted with an archduke as King, if you wish, but even better with the King of Saxony assuming the throne as compensation for ceding his Kingdom to Prussia.
>
> *Prussia*: Would give up Posnan to Poland, Silesia to Austria, and the left

bank of the Rhine to France, but would obtain Saxony, Hanover, and the duchies north of the Main.

Austria: Would cede Venetia to Sardinia, a part of Galicia (Lemberg and Cracow) to Poland and would take in return a new line of frontier across Serbia along the Adriatic, Silesia, and whatever she would like south of the Main.

France: Would cede nothing! But would acquire the left bank of the Rhine, except Belgium out of deference for England—unless this power should let her have Brussels and Ostend, etc., etc. in return for Antwerp.

Italy: Sardinia would have Lombardy, Venetia, Tuscany, Parma, Piacenza, Bologna, and Ferrara; but she would restore the Kingdom of the Two-Sicilies to the King of Naples, who would compensate the pope.

Turkey: Abolished from motives of public utility and Christian morality. She would be partitioned, her Asiatic possessions going to Russia, the line of the Adriatic to Austria. Thessaly, Albania, and Constantinople would fall to Greece, the Principalities remaining an independent enclave under a local prince.

The dispossessed kings and princes of Europe would go to civilize and monarchize the American republics, which would all follow the example of Mexico.[14]

Of course these schemes, relayed at second or third hand, fantastic in scope, differing and even contradictory in detail, are of no great importance in themselves. But with other evidence they complete a pattern. To reorganize Europe in general accord with the principle of nationalities, and to achieve this reorganization by means of a redistribution of Ottoman territory, these were the objectives of Napoleon's foreign policy. What, however, were to be the methods?

Certainly not military conquest. Even if the aversion to war that appears in his earlier writings had not been sincere, the experience of two wars by the end of 1859 and a growing awareness of French reluctance to embark on new adventures must have cured the third Napoleon of any temptation to achieve his ends by force. The 1859 war would be the last that France would seek in Europe, before the debacle of 1870, and it should be recalled that one of the arguments Napoleon

14. Sencourt, *Napoléon III, un precurseur*, 237 (internal evidence suggests August, 1859–August, 1860, as the date); Metternich to Rechberg, Paris, May 14, 1861, in HHSA, PA IX, Fr. Ber., 1861, I–VI, Box 69, no. 36C, fols. 591–95v; Metternich to Rechberg, Paris, February 22, 1863, in Oncken (ed.), *Rheinpolitik*, I, 4–5. Metternich concluded his summary of Eugénie's *vol d'oiseau* with these words: "Voilà le plan de l'Impératrice, et je Vous prie M. le Comte, de vouloir bien ne pas le considérer comme une plaisanterie; je crois l'Impératrice et même l'Empereur très convaincus de la possibilité et de *la nécessité* de la réaliser une fois."

had used to justify the conflict with Austria in 1859 was that it could end the need of further wars:

> A great success in Italy will tremendously shake European public opinion, which will no longer see in the government of France only the bugbear of anarchists but rather the power that wishes to be strong at home in order to break its own chains and thus deliver and civilize the peoples. Once the house of Austria is weakened our own influence will increase immensely in Europe. The people who are our neighbors on the Rhine, in Switzerland, in Belgium will beg for our alliance—either through fear or sympathy. . . . Then France, without again firing a single cannon, will be able to obtain whatever is just and to abolish the treaties of 1815 forever.

"I am not thinking of conquests," the emperor was supposed to have told Lionel François René, marquis de Moustier in April, 1860. "I want to act peacefully and progressively; I want to arrive at my goal by a friendly exchange of explanations and by agreements." Cowley, for whom skepticism and suspicion were professional requirements, reached, after ten years at Paris, a judgment that is difficult to challenge in retrospect:

> It would be more than puerile to attempt to argue that the Emperor must not be desirous of associating his name with the restitution of what the French are pleased to call the natural limits of France, but it is a curious fact that I have never heard the Emperor or any Frenchman with whom I am acquainted allude to that restitution by means of war. I have heard of the peaceful *remaniement* of the map of Europe by which the Treaties of 1815 might be modified, but war undertaken for the express purpose of recovering the frontier of the Rhine does not seem to me to have been ever seriously contemplated. . . .
>
> When I . . . look at the Emperor's time of life and his somewhat impaired health, when I think it must be his desire to leave to his son an Empire, that Europe would not be inclined to dispute, when I know his avowed horror of war since he has seen it in detail, I cannot bring myself to believe that he will lightly and without provocation risk the stability of his Dynasty, and the prosperity of France, by commencing a war of aggression, the end of which, although it might be successful for France in the commencement, no man can foresee.[15]

Yet, the foreign policy of Napoleon was an active one. He had objectives and he believed that he could attain them. He had also a method.

15. Considérations politique, autographe de l'Empereur, December 20, 1858, in AMAE, MD, France, 2119: no. 3; Beyens to the Belgian foreign minister, April 13, 1860, in Beyens, *Le Second Empire*, I, 313; memorandum of Cowley to Russell, Chan-

What he would not seek through war, he hoped to accomplish through negotiation and, where possible, at the conference table.

That this was so is indicated first by the common sense of the situation. Sweeping territorial exchanges, of the sort envisaged by Napoleon, could not be carried out by French policies or actions alone, or even by France and one or two allies, and certainly not by a France unwilling (and probably unable) to impose its will by force. This Napoleon recognized, particularly where it was a question of Turkish territory. In 1853, to the opinion that no peaceable solution to the Eastern question would be possible once the Ottoman Empire was dissolved, he replied, "Why could not a Congress settle it?" When Prince Napoleon in 1857 sent his cousin a partition scheme ("Les Turcs en Europe"), the emperor returned it with the comment: "The plan is a good one, but let's not forget to make it entirely a question of religion and of civilization, and not at all one that is English, French, or Russian." Only the concert of Europe could realize these projects; only a congress could initiate the changes; and only a congress system could supervise the settlement thereafter. Besides, it is impossible to doubt Napoleon's predilection for, one might almost say his addiction to, conference diplomacy. As we have already seen, it is attested to by the array of congresses and conferences held, contemplated, or proposed between 1849 and 1863, as well as by the French willingness to expand the scope and competence of such meetings as were held. He had great faith, Napoleon once told Cowley, in the effectiveness of a general *causerie* in which matters could be broached that, in writing, would become "stiff and formal." This faith he reaffirmed many times in the years before 1863. Conceivably the gambler's instinct lent fascination to a diplomatic method that Napoleon sometimes seemed to regard as a lottery, one that he might win. It is more likely, however, that he sincerely believed, as he told Cowley at the end of 1859, that out of discussion might come new combinations that no one had thought of and upon which everyone might agree. The French emperor, after his personal success at the Congress of Paris of 1856, had faith in his star, aided by his charm and persuasiveness, so much so that Pourtalès' judgment in 1860 does not seem exaggerated:

> It has reached me from a good source that Emperor Napoleon . . . is thinking of convoking a meeting of sovereigns, relying in such an event, on his

---

tilly, January 10, 1862, in Russell Papers, 30/22, 57 (the ambassador was replying to a query as to whether he thought Napoleon contemplated a policy of aggression).

eloquence and on the justice of his views to win from these rulers the ac
ceptance of a general revision of the treaties—a revision in which the principle of nationalities would be called upon to play a major role. The Emperor of the French is so convinced of the utility of such a revision and of
the advantages that all the great powers would reap from it, that he flatters
himself with the hope of convincing the sovereigns as well by addressing
himself directly to them with the intention of realizing, through their aid,
the projects he has nurtured for a long while. . . . Undoubtedly Emperor
Napoleon counts heavily on the infallibility of his political doctrines and
hopes that the reasonableness of the other rulers will bring them gradually
to adopt these ideas.[16]

16. Cowley to Clarendon, Paris, private, March 9, 1853, in PRO, FO, 519, 210;
Napoleon III to Prince Napoleon, Compiègne, November 11, 1857, in Hauterive (ed.),
Napoléon III et le Prince Napoléon, 97; Cowley to Clarendon, Paris, February 25, 1857,
in RA, J 77/18; Pourtalès to Schleinitz, Paris, January 17, 1860, in *APP*, vol. II, pt. 1,
p. 42 n.

CHAPTER II

"Idées Napoléoniennes," 1849–1863
The Congress Idea and the Alliance Policy
of the Second Empire

From his first allusion, in 1844, to Henry IV's dream of a "European Areopagus," Napoleon was strongly drawn to what might be called his congress idea, the thought of a great European gathering where the hated treaties of 1815 could be revised and Europe reorganized and set on the road to peace and stability. As we have seen, in 1849, at the very beginning of his rise to power, he had proposed such a congress to the British government, and it soon became evident that this initiative was no passing fancy. In early November, 1853, Hübner wrote: "The talk is of a new congress. You know that this is a predilection of Emperor Napoleon." Obviously it was, for he subsequently attempted to ensure that the Crimean War would end in a great general congress of revision, and although that failed, there were moments during the Congress of Paris when the emperor's preference for a broader congress was revealed. In the end, the meeting fell short of that goal, although it became something more than a mere peace conference. It was, in fact, as Paul Henry has suggested, the first of those meetings that in Napoleon's thought, at least, were meant to confront the great problems likely to lead to conflict and put them on the road to a peaceful resolution. Clarendon, for his part, had no doubt that the idea of a general congress of revision was continuing to germinate in Napoleon's mind, for the emperor had raised the question in many interviews with him. The Englishman's prediction was that France needed two years of rest, but that the specter of the congress had not been laid to rest. Certainly there was nothing in the success of Napoleon's personal role at the Congress of Paris to discourage him from the congress idea.[1]

1. Hübner, *Neuf ans*, I, 162, journal entry of November 2, 1853; Henry, *Napoléon III et les peuples*, 47; Martin, *The Life of His Royal Highness, the Prince Consort*, III,

From 1856 to 1859 a sort of standing conference of Paris dealt, as
we have seen, with various problems as they arose; and often Paris
showed its inclination to view these meetings as omnicompetent. If
Napoleon had had his way, it is reasonable to assume that Italy would
have been discussed in congress long before the crisis of 1859. And
whatever his motives at Plombières, it is certainly arguable that he
would have accepted the beginning of a European solution to the Italian problem in preference to a Franco-Austrian war. Moreover, there
is reason to believe that either of the two conference proposals of 1859
concerning Italy would, if accepted, have led to a general congress. At
Berlin in January, 1859, the Prussian foreign minister, Baron Alexander G. A. von Schleinitz, spoke to Britain's ambassador of his understanding that "Louis Napoleon is desirous that a Conference of
Sovereigns should be held and that Berlin should be the place of meeting. He thinks this would be a means of averting war and that it is
dictated by Louis Napoleon's feeling that he scarcely yet belongs to
the family of kings and wishes to become the better acquainted with
his brothers and sisters." Unlikely as it is that Napoleon would choose
Berlin as the site of his congress, or worry unduly about getting to
know his "brothers and sisters" better, the fact is that he had held out
to Russia in 1858 the hope that the peace conference following a
Franco-Austrian war could result in revision of both the 1815 and
1856 treaties. In the fall of 1859, Gorchakov gave an indication of
hoping, with Prussian and French support, to broaden the authority of
the proposed conference on the Italian problem.[2] Such support might
well have been offered by Paris, since at this same time Napoleon was
attempting to interest Austria in finding compensation in the East
for its sacrifices in Italy. Walewski even suggested to Metternich at

---

376 n., 388–89; Prince Albert to Stockmar, Buckingham Palace, April 13, 1856, in Martin, *The Life of His Royal Highness, the Prince Consort*, III, 392.

2. John Arthur Douglas, Baron Bloomfield, to Malmesbury, Berlin, January 15, 1859,
in *APP*, I, 166, no. 79. Pourtalès reported: "Très secret: la Russie désire ne point limiter
l'action du congrès et veut avoir faculté d'y discuter des questions en dehors de celle de
l'Italie" (Pourtalès to Schleinitz, Paris, telegram, September 5, 1859, in *APP*, I, 819 n.);
Reuss wrote that "Russland, im Interesse der Festigung des allgemeinen Friedens nur
auf einen Kongress eingehen zu Können, an dem alle Machte, auch England, teilneh-
men wurden und fur den von Keiner Seite irgendein bindendes Programm aufgestellt
wurde" (Reuss to Schleinitz, Paris, November 5, 1859, in *APP*, I, 819 n.). When Reuss at
Compiègne told Walewski of Prussia's support of the Russian proposition, the Frenchman approved and expressed the hope that the attitude of Prussia and Russia would
have an effect in London (Reuss to Schleinitz, Compiègne, confidential, November 9,
1859, in *APP*, I, 818–19, no. 539).

the end of November that the whole matter might be concluded if the Austrian foreign minister would visit Paris a few days before the opening of the proposed conference and confer directly with Napoleon and Gorchakov. Cowley concluded that Napoleon, while not himself planning to bring additional questions before the conference, would not have been sorry had others done that service for him. At the end of August, 1859, he had written to Walewski: "As I see that it will be almost impossible to reach an understanding with Austria, don't you think that it would be possible to put forward the idea of a congress that would regulate not only the Italian question but all the great questions that still disturb Europe?" Still, at the end of 1859, Napoleon was primarily interested in finding some solution to the problem of Italy, and it was on this ground that the conference proposal foundered.[3]

Nevertheless, the thought of a general congress persisted. In January, 1860, Pourtalès reported that Napoleon wanted such a meeting, adding that this was "characteristic of the adventurous sweep which Emperor Napoleon too often allows to his imagination." Apparently that imagination was given relatively free rein throughout 1860. "Word has reached me from many sources," wrote Metternich in February, "that the Emperor clearly spoke in the presence of several of my colleagues about a congress of sovereigns." Two months later, the Austrian detected in a pamphlet by Edmond About (*La nouvelle carte d'Europe*) Napoleon's "favorite idea of a Congress of Sovereigns summoned to rework the Map of Europe." And in June, Napoleon "spoke again earnestly about a congress of all the Sovereigns to rework the map of Europe." At the end of July, a terrible storm having kept the emperor and the ambassador closeted together for two hours at Saint-Cloud, Napoleon returned to the theme. "I must mention," Metternich wrote, "a question put to me by the Emperor and which seems like an official overture; His Majesty, à propos of his favorite idea of a congress of sovereigns, asked me if I thought the Austrian Emperor would take a certain initiative in this matter." Metternich replied that he did not think so. "The Emperor responded that he knew our August Sovereign had looked favorably on this idea and that he hoped His Majesty would understand all its advantages in the present state

3. Metternich to Rechberg, Paris, November 26, 1859, in Hallberg, *Franz Joseph and Napoleon III*, 296; Cowley to Russell, December 15, 1859, in Russell Papers, 30/22, 53; Napoleon III to Walewski, Saint-Sauveur, August 29, 1859, in Raindre, "Les papiers inédits du Comte Walewski," 319.

of Europe. 'Everyone mistrusts me,' added the Emperor, 'and consequently I cannot take the initative.'" And then, to further his argument for such a meeting, Napoleon threatened that if, instead, an
anti-French coalition were to take shape, he would be forced to "embrace the revolution."[4]

It was in the midst of speculation that a general congress was being
prepared to regulate the problems of Italy, the East, and Switzerland[5]
that a pamphlet appeared in December at Paris entitled L'Empereur
François-Joseph I et l'Europe. Written by Duveyrier and published
after having been revised by Napoleon, it was primarily concerned
with a peaceful solution to the Venetian question (through purchase
of the province by Italy), but it concluded: "Europe calls for the institution of a permanent general congress, where all the powers without exception will come to renew their engagement to respect established frontiers, and whose arbitrament, recognized and respected,
will henceforth impose a peaceful solution to all disputes. The re-
wards would be immense: solidarity of interests, friendly relations,
the inviolability of all borders, the conciliation of all conflicts." Four
months later the Polish question led, in Cowley's words, "to an exposition of the Emperor's general ideas of passing events, particularly
with regard to Poland and Hungary, and they were in the sense of old
treaties having done their duty and new ones having become indispensable. He reverted to his old plan of a Congress for the 'remaniement de la Carte de l'Europe' but as there is no novelty in this, I will
not dwell on it any longer." Napoleon, however, dwelt on it, so much
so that Paul Henry has concluded that by 1861 the French emperor
"had vaguely foreseen the radical transformation of international relations by the institution, in the form of a Congress, of regular European
assizes which would consider the great problems of the moment."[6]

In the summer of 1861, Napoleon approached Prince Heinrich VII
von Reuss, the Prussian chargé, at Fontainebleau, and, recalling the

---

4. Pourtalès to Schleinitz, Paris, January 17, 1860, in APP, vol. II, pt. 1, p. 42 n.;
Metternich to Rechberg, Paris, February 8, April 29, 1860, both in HHSA, PA IX, Fr.
Ber., 1860, I–V, Box 65, no. 7D, fols. 142–42v, no. 31B, fols. 493–94; Metternich to
Rechberg, Fontainebleau, June 19, 1860, in HHSA, PA IX, Fr. Ber., 1860, VI–IX, Box 66,
no. 41, fol. 71v; Metternich to Rechberg, Paris, private, July 26, 1860, in HHSA, PA IX,
Varia, 1860, Box 68, fols. 138–41.
5. Bixio to Cavour, Paris, October 6, 1860, in Cavour-Nigra, IV, 243, no. 1157.
6. Pingaud, "Un projet de désarmement," 2; Isser, The Second Empire and the Press,
123–29; Cowley to Russell, Paris, April 1, 1861, in Russell Papers, 30/22, 56; Henry,
Napoléon III et les peuples, 72.

late king of Prussia's 1856 suggestion of a general congress, mused: "I don't know if it would be possible to come back to this project, which was certainly a very good one. It would be the only way of dealing with many of the questions that continually threaten the repose of Europe. If the sovereigns were to meet together, each saying whatever he has at heart, then the cards would be laid on the table, and we could agree. But as it is now, we are reduced to living from day to day; we hardly dare examine a question seriously for fear of having it burst into a general conflagration." Throughout 1862 the emperor continued to argue the virtues of a general congress. In January he told the Swedish king that he considered the prickly Schleswig-Holstein question "as being within the province of a European congress." And in March he again urged his "favorite idea" upon Metternich.

> After the hundred and one indirections which I have just quoted to Your Excellency the Emperor arrived at what I think was the purpose of his talk with me.
>
> His Majesty noted that a thousand questions awaited radical and total solutions, and,—a rather curious thing,—came around to praising the treaties of 1815 and their salutary result during forty years of peace.
>
> The Emperor spoke again of an idea which he admitted he had broached to me a hundred times, an idea which according to him would be almost unrealisable were not everyone to accord it their good will. This old idea is the one of a congress of sovereigns in which each monarch would be allowed to deliver himself freely of his wishes, his refusals, his complaints, in short of everything which he *would have on his mind*. According to the Emperor, such an assembly must surely lead to a result like that of the Congress of 1815, and to have taken the initiative of it would redound, according to Him, to the honor of the Sovereign or of the man whose courage would equal his abilities.

Metternich replied that the 1860s were not 1815, that there were too many conflicting interests. "A Congress of Sovereigns would lay bare all the incompatibilities from which we all suffer." Napoleon did not deny the difficulties, but "in the embarrassment in which all, and perhaps he more than others, found themselves, if he again brought up this question it was to satisfy a real need for clearing the air." He did not discuss the means by which he hoped to realize "son rêve." "We shall speak of it again," he told the ambassador as they parted. According to the Belgian minister at Paris, Napoleon discussed the matter with his foreign minister. In April the French emperor returned once more to the theme, this time with Hübner, who was visiting

Paris. "A long time ago [he told the Austrian] I spoke to you of the idea of bringing Europe together in a congress. While I dislike the Congress of Vienna for having humbled France, yet I have to admit that it had the merit of giving Europe forty years of peace. A new congress could produce like results and this idea occurs to me once again as the only means of getting out of the difficulties which weigh on Europe." What matters should be discussed? The emperor was vague. There was, he said, the question of compensation "to offer the powers which might be invited by the Congress to make sacrifices in the interest of world peace"; there was Italy and the need to establish an Italian confederation including Venetia; and there was Germany. "The King of Prussia is in a difficult situation; this again would be a topic for a congress." Some days before this conversation Napoleon had remarked to the British ambassador that, if there was need of a common object for which all of the powers might strive, why not say that the object should be to oppose revolution?[7] Undoubtedly the thought was too enigmatic to be taken seriously, but it was nevertheless timely. Revolution came that winter to Poland and led, as we have seen, to yet another vain effort by Napoleon to bring about a general European congress.

Thus the congress idea. No serious historian of the Second Empire has failed to mention it in passing; most have seen it as a device for reorganizing Europe to the territorial advantage of France; a few have credited Napoleon with a certain gift of prophecy in foreseeing, if only vaguely and imperfectly, the League of Nations and with having tried to realize this idea before its time. But none has traced the congress idea from its inception in Napoleon's writings before he came to power; none has analyzed it or sought the reasons for its failure; none has attempted to study it within the context of that predilection for conference diplomacy and adherence to an idea of European concert that were so inseparable from the development of French foreign policy between 1849 and 1863; none has explored the relation between the congress idea and the attitude taken by Napoleon toward the Ot-

7. Reuss to Schleinitz, Fontainebleau, private, June 14, 1861, in *APP*, vol. II, pt. 2, p. 381, no. 391.2; Metternich to Rechberg, Paris, secret, January 15, 1862, in HHSA, PA IX, Fr. Ber., 1862, I–VI, Box 72, no. 3C, fol. 32v; Metternich to Rechberg, Paris, March 14, 1862, in HHSA, PA IX, Fr. Ber., 1862, I–VI, Box 72, no. 17C, fols. 207–212v; Beyens to Rogier, Paris, confidential, March 16, 1862, in Belgian Foreign Ministry Archives, Légation de Paris (reference supplied by Lynn M. Case); Hübner to Rechberg, Paris, April 18, 1862, in HHSA, PA IX, Fr. Ber., 1862, I–VI, Box 72, fols. 35–46; Cowley to Russell, Paris, March 25, 1862, in PRO, FO, 27, 1436: no. 402.

toman Empire. Most surprising of all, in searching for an explanation of the alliance policies of the Second Empire, historians have perpetuated a curious dichotomy. Yes, Napoleon's purpose was to arrange a general European congress of revision; no, it is not possible to find a common or even a meaningful purpose to the alliances he sought.

In his pioneer study (1927), Albert Pingaud was able to discover some pattern to Napoleon's search for alliances in terms of the powers to whom he directed his attention at various periods, Britain from 1852 to 1857, Britain and Russia from 1857 to 1863, Austria in 1863, and Prussia from 1864 to 1866. But alliances are sought for a purpose, and, in focusing on the assumed specific objectives of French foreign policy, Pingaud was unable to find any explanation for the pattern he had discerned, other than the French emperor's inability to choose. More recently Pierre Renouvin concluded that the mere fact of having sought so many alliances disqualified Napoleon from having had a "precise program," because each attempt required new proposals and new solutions. And yet, more than seventy years ago Emile Ollivier suggested that the key to Louis Napoleon's foreign policy lay not in any specific territorial ambitions, for example, but in his congress idea. And Ollivier concluded: "La sincérité de ses intentions est confirmée par le choix de ses alliances." It is at least possible that Napoleon's general alliance policies have seemed to us so enigmatic because, while we have attempted to interpret them in terms of the ends sought, they were in fact developed in terms of the *means* by which those ends were to be achieved. The consistent purpose of the alliances and ententes entered into or sought by Napoleon between 1849 and 1863, then, would have been to make the concert of Europe function as he wished it to function, that is, to bring the powers together in general congresses that would reorganize Europe, solve its most urgent problems, and thereafter regulate the new arrangements. What Napoleon really hoped to gain for France or even what he hoped to achieve for Europe we shall probably never know with any certainty. But it is probable that such a congress system not only was at the heart of his foreign policy but also illuminates his view of the concert of Europe and of French alliances.[8]

Napoleon himself understood that if the congress idea were to be realized it would have to be preceded by carefully prepared agree-

8. Pingaud, "La politique extérieure du Second Empire," 41–68; Renouvin, "La politique extérieure du Second Empire," n.p.; Ollivier, "Napoléon III," 54.

ments and alliances. In 1855, replying to Cowley's usual objections to a general congress, the emperor argued "that he was quite aware of all the difficulties which must be encountered and that they could only be overcome by a previous understanding, first between France and England, and then between these two and Austria and Prussia." It would be unwise, he told Clarendon the following year, to think of assembling a congress until three or four of the major powers were in general agreement. In fact, Napoleon had referred to this type of entente as early as 1832, in his *Rêveries politiques*. "The great obstacle," the French emperor told Prince Albert in 1856, "to any real improvement in Europe were the miserable jealousies of the different governments [and] that was why he thought a mutual understanding so essential." The same theme was repeated to the Russian ambassador at the end of 1858. The treaties of Vienna weighed upon France, he said, as did that of 1856 upon Russia. "He much preferred not to have recourse to violent means and he thought that if Russia, France, Prussia, and England were to reach an agreement, the common goal could be attained without provoking a general war. What could Austria do against the concert of these four powers? Finally, in March, 1862, the pattern was completed when Napoleon took the Austrian ambassador aside to speak to him of "an entente of two or three by which one would be able to prepare a future congress."[9]

He began with Britain. Louis Napoleon admired the English (he had, of course, lived in England during several years of exile); moreover, he regarded his uncle's policy toward Britain as one of the major mistakes of the First Empire. But he had, as well, a very definite use to make of a good understanding with Britain. One of the prince-president's earliest acts was, as we have seen, to propose a general congress to the British ambassador in March, 1849. "France and England together," he assured his old friend Malmesbury shortly afterward, "could remodel everything," a thought he repeated to Cowley in 1853. And this would be especially true if Prussia were included, a "liberal" Prussia to serve as counterweight to conservative Austria. Hence Persigny's two missions to Berlin in 1849 and in 1850, which

9. Cowley to Clarendon, October 24, 1855, in V. Wellesley and Sencourt (eds.), *Conversations with Napoleon III*, 95; Martin, *The Life of His Royal Highness, the Prince Consort*, III, 389; Corley, *Democratic Despot*, 79; second memorandum of Albert, on the visit of Napoleon and Eugénie to Osborne, August 11, 1857, in Martin, *The Life of His Royal Highness, the Prince Consort*, IV, 100; Kisselev to Gorchakov, Paris, December 7, 1858, in Goriaïnow, *Le Bosphore et les Dardanelles*, 531; Metternich to [Rechberg], Paris, March 19, 1862, in Salomon, *Ambassade de Richard Metternich*, 87.

Tocqueville, who was foreign minister from June to November, 1849, understood to have been soundings for an alliance through which the map of 1815 might be redrawn. The difficulty was that this sort of alliance required a certain amount of agreement in advance on problems likely to arise. By February, 1857, Cowley could refer to Napoleon's "favorite theme . . . the necessity of both Governments being prepared for events which may arise, so as not to thwart each other's interests." That year the French emperor developed the same thought in conversations with Granville and with Prince Albert. There were, he told Granville, questions in existence that might lead to serious consequences. "He would like such questions to be discussed beforehand and general principles laid down between the two Governments." Many little improvements were possible in the state of Europe, he told Albert. "He wished to do nothing to create disturbance; all he wished was *de bien s'entendre avec le Gouvernement Anglais, sur toutes les éventualités,* so that, when they arose, they should not find us unprepared and disagreeing." But always the answer stressed by Cowley was the same. It was against the policy and principles of any British government to bind itself in advance. To discuss problems before they had become crises would be the best way to assure that the crises would develop. For Prince Albert, there was not the slightest doubt as to the correctness of the British position. As he explained to Vitzthum in early 1859:

> The game stands simply thus. Every time I have seen the Emperor Napoleon, he has endeavoured to persuade me that there was only one means of preventing the complications he foresaw, namely that England and France should come to a previous understanding as to the reconstruction of the map of Europe. A last attempt of this kind was made at Cherbourg. To this I invariably replied: We in England maintained that there are no better means of bringing about the complications feared, than to tie one's hands against eventualities of the future, since by so doing the party who has an interest in change can morally compel the other to co-operate. To play such a part no British statesman would either now or at any future time consent, and least of all would I. The Emperor regretted what he called these mistaken English theories. I cut short the discussion by remarking that he would find himself convinced to his cost of the correctness of our principle.[10]

10. Malmesbury, *Memoirs,* I, 257, journal entry of March 30, 1849; Cowley to Clarendon, Paris, private, August 22, 1853, in PRO, FO, 519, 211:69; Tocqueville, *Souvenirs,* 238; Cowley to Clarendon, Paris, February 25, 1857, in PRO, FO, 519, 221:81; Granville to Clarendon, Paris, April 10, 1857, in RA, J77/22; first memorandum of Albert, on the visit of Napoleon and Eugénie to Osborne, August 6, 1857, in Martin, *The*

Despite such obvious distrust toward him, Napoleon persisted. At the end of 1859 he was still maintaining, in Cowley's words, "his usual desire that the two Governments should interchange opinions as to what should be done in the event of the dissolution of the Ottoman Empire." And, in fact, from 1849 through the Crimean War the catalog of Anglo-French cooperation is impressive: the questions of Sicily and of northern Italy in 1848–1849, the extradition crisis of 1849, Austrian pretensions in Germany in 1851, the question of the Greek throne in 1852, Haiti, Cuba, the Schleswig-Holstein question, the Eastern question culminating in war with Russia. And running through these years was a strand of cajolery that one might almost consider an outright attempt at bribery. What would Britain do, Napoleon asked Malmesbury in 1849, in the same conversation in which he spoke of a general congress, if there should be a revision of the map of Europe? France would not be jealous if the British were to gain more power in Egypt. Then on the eve of reestablishing the empire had come the speech at Marseilles, in which Louis Napoleon spoke of the Mediterranean as a French lake. Cowley was alarmed; Napoleon, reassuring. In fact, he later told Stratford de Redcliffe, he had no wish to make the Mediterranean a *French* lake, but rather a *European* one. Several months later, Drouyn de Lhuys again brought forward the idea that Britain would do well to possess itself of Egypt, and in 1855 the emperor sketched with an even freer hand. It was a question at that time of a restoration of Poland. Would Britain accept Sinope as its prize? "Asia," Napoleon told Cowley, "interests you more directly than it does us." Again in 1856 and in 1857, Napoleon returned to the theme, talking to both Cowley and Prince Albert of Britain's having Egypt.[11]

Of course these efforts merely served to deepen British suspicions. Cowley reported rumors that France would seek aggrandizement in

---

Life of His Royal Highness, the Prince Consort, IV, 94; Vitzthum to Beust, London, March 3, 1859, in Vitzthum, *St. Petersburg and London,* I, 320–21.

11. Cowley to Russell, Chantilly, private, December 4, 1859, in Russell Papers, 30/22, 53; Malmesbury, *Memoirs,* I, 256–57, journal entry of March 30, 1849; memorandum of Stratford de Redcliffe, March 10, 1853, in Lane-Poole, *Life of Stratford Canning,* II, 237; Zamoyski to Prince Adam Czartoryski, June 29, 1853, in Handelsman, "La Guerre de Crimée," 271; Cowley to Clarendon, March 8, 1855, in Sencourt, *Napoléon III un précurseur,* 141; Cowley to Clarendon, Paris, December 28, 1856, in PRO, FO, 519, 6:488–90; second memorandum of Albert, on the visit of Napoleon and Eugénie to Osborne, August 11, 1857, in Martin, *The Life of His Royal Highness, the Prince Consort,* IV, 97–98.

the Mediterranean, and Clarendon concluded that the French wanted to bring about the collapse of Turkey in order that they might benefit. This was a rather oversimplified view. France had its hands full in Algeria, and Napoleon was hardly an ardent colonialist. In his earlier writings he had criticized French colonialism, and apparently he did not find it easy to resolve his doubts on this score. In October, 1858, Cowley wrote: "I doubt if we shall hear much more of the colonization scheme. The Emperor spoke to me very much in that sense yesterday, saying that he regretted that France had colonies, that it was so difficult to maintain them in a prosperous state, that they were a weakness to the Mother Country." If Napoleon talked of the necessity of having Morocco, as he did in December, 1856, it is probable that he meant just that—a possible military necessity arising from the Algerian situation. In due course he would, as we shall see, dangle Egypt before Austrian eyes, and Austria could be of no use to French ambitions in Africa. In fact, it is difficult to see what territorial conquests Napoleon could have hoped to advance through the British alliance. Certainly not in Italy or on the Rhine or in Belgium. But the congress idea, a reorganization of Europe in general accordance with the wishes of the peoples, these aims he might well have hoped to persuade the British government to share.[12]

Yet, as Napoleon must himself have begun to recognize by 1856, it was a vain hope. Prince Albert had done his best to dispel any illusions that might have lingered. Several years after the Osborne meeting of 1857, Albert presumably told Vitzthum that Napoleon had at the time freely admitted his "fixed idea" to revise the map of Europe and proposed an offensive and defensive alliance. "I told him very quietly but firmly, that it was against all the traditions of this country to bind our hands for future eventualities, especially with a neighbour powerful enough to create such eventualities at any moment. He liked the hint, and tried then to obtain from Russia what he failed to obtain from us." Certainly Napoleon had his moments of frustration with "this touchy and egotistical country" that would not listen to reason (as he described Britain to Metternich in 1859), and he did turn, immediately following the Crimean War, to the cultivation of Russia. But there were other reasons for this than his lack of success with Britain. Russia's defeat had ended the moral hegemony that

12. Clarendon to Queen Victoria, February 26, 1857, in RA, J77/17; Cowley to Malmesbury, October 31, 1858, in V. Wellesley and Sencourt (eds.), *Conversations with Napoleon III*, 153.

Nicholas I had exercised over much of Europe in the name of a concept of European concert greatly different from that of Napoleon III. For Nicholas, the concert existed to maintain the status quo. But now Russia was itself a revisionist power. For if France regretted the treaty of Vienna, the Russians were even more eager to escape the treaty of Paris of 1856. Already there were portents. A worried Baron Stockmar relayed to Prince Albert a thought received from a French source: "Is it then so probable that the *idées Napoléoniennes* have been abandoned? I do not believe it. Could not some of them be realised through a Congress, now that experience has shown that it is not easy to bring them to pass by prolongation of the war? . . . Why should not a Tilsit scene be performed before long as it was in 1807? How would England stand then?"[13]

Napoleon did use the Congress of Paris and its immediate aftermath to effect a rapprochement with Russia. To Saint Petersburg as French ambassador went the emperor's half brother, Morny, enthused with the speculator's vision of an inexhaustible Russian market, but inspired also with the insider's knowledge of what arguments would most effectively bring Napoleon to his views. Was it not, he asked, the emperor's wish "to bring together the three great powers of Europe [France, Russia, and Britain] in order to see if it would be possible, by a sincere and intelligent entente, to resolve the questions great and small which divide the world, to regularize the true nationalities, and to remake the map." Morny was also capable of more direct arguments. "May you and the Emperor carefully consider what this entente could hold for the future," he wrote to Walewski, then foreign minister. "God alone knows; but I am certain of one thing, that only Russia will agree to the aggrandizement of France." Had French aggrandizement been Napoleon's major aim, he would certainly have found Morny's argument compelling. But, as we have seen, he refused to sacrifice the British alliance. Instead, throughout 1857 and 1858, his theme was a triple entente by which Europe could be reorganized. "He [Napoleon] has a vague wish to resettle Europe," wrote Granville following a dinner conversation with the emperor in April, 1857, "and he thinks it might be done by a cordial understanding between Russia, England, and France." These three were the most powerful states

13. Vitzthum, *St. Petersburg and London*, I, 215; Metternich to Rechberg, Paris, November 16, 1859, in HHSA, PA IX, Fr. Ber., 1859, VIII–XII, Box 63, no. 16A-B, fols. 464–65; Stockmar to Albert, Coburg, February 21, 1856, in Martin, *The Life of His Royal Highness, the Prince Consort*, III, 376.

in Europe, Napoleon argued, and together they could settle all of the great questions, since Germany would always be on the winning side. In May, Persigny, then the French ambassador at London, urged upon Clarendon his master's conviction "that England, France, and Russia ought between them to régler les affaires de l'Europe." And in September, 1857, Napoleon presented the same argument to the czar during their interview at Stuttgart. Why, he asked, "should not these three Governments endeavour to come to some understanding beforehand on all political questions which might arise—Turkey, the Mediterranean, etc." One of the projects of a joint statement drawn up at the Stuttgart meeting included a sentence to the effect that if it should prove necessary to revise the 1815 treaties in the interest of peace, the rulers of France and Russia would agree in advance on the principles to be followed. "With regard to politics," Cowley reported at the beginning of 1858, "H.M. said, that he still entertained the same opinion, which he had adopted at the peace, that a close alliance between England, France and Russia was the safest for themselves and the World, and that they ought to endeavour to come to an understanding on all questions which might present themselves." And the year ended with Napoleon's suggestion to Russia that, if France, Prussia, England, and Russia were to agree, "le but commun could be obtained without a general war." It is true that the Franco-Russian alliance of December, 1858, made possible Napoleon's war with Austria in the following year. But, as we have seen, the major incentive held out to Russia was of a peace congress in which the treaties of 1815 and 1856 would be discussed; and it was Russia who, to Napoleon's obvious pleasure, proposed in the spring of 1859 that a congress should precede and prevent the war. The congress proposal failed because of Austria's intransigence; but once again war brought about a new tack in French alliance policy, without changing its general direction.[14]

Before 1859, there had seemed to be no chance that Napoleon would or could include Austria in his alliance plans. "He has a long-cherished

14. Morny to Napoleon III, December 9, 1856, in Morny, *Une ambassade en Russie*, 171; Morny to Walewski, November [9–24], 1856, in Morny, *Une ambassade en Russie*, 137; Granville to Lord Canning [sic], Paris, April 8, 1857, in Fitzmaurice, *The Life of Granville*, I, 230; Granville to Clarendon, Paris, April 10, 1857, in RA, J77/22; Clarendon to Albert, May 20, 1857, in *Victoria Letters, 1837–1861*, III, 294; Cowley to Clarendon, Chantilly, October 18, 1857, in PRO, FO, 519, 222:161–62; Goriaïnow, "Les étapes de l'alliance franco-russe," 21; Cowley to Malmesbury, Paris, April 2, 1858, in PRO, FO, 519, 223:208; Kisselev to Gorchakov, Paris, December 7, 1858, in Goriaïnow, "Les étapes de l'alliance franco-russe," 531.

hatred of Austria," Clarendon wrote in 1857, "and he proposed to me
at Paris [in 1856] that a closer alliance should be formed between
France, England, and Russia, from which Austria should be excluded."
Cavour's analysis probably represented the conventional wisdom of
even the shrewdest of observers when, as late as 1860, he suggested
that Napoleon wanted revision, preferred to arrange it in accord with
Britain, would turn to Saint Petersburg if he failed at London, "but in
any event he will not enter an arrangement with Austria." In fact, the
French emperor was already seeking just such an arrangement. There
were a number of reasons for this. The new Austrian ambassador,
Prince Richard Metternich, and his wife had quickly ingratiated themselves with the imperial couple. More important was the need for
Napoleon to replace (or at least supplement) an uncooperative Britain
in his scheme of things. This was a bad time in Anglo-French relations. French annexation of Nice and Savoy aroused a storm of anger
and suspicion in Britain that the Cobden-Chevalier commercial treaty
of early 1860 did not dispel. The British alliance, Thouvenel flatly asserted to Metternich, was impossible. Besides, the experience of 1859
must have persuaded the French emperor that Austria could ruin his
hopes by the weight of its veto alone, while that same experience may
have encouraged him to believe that Vienna, having lost half its Italian possessions, would be more flexible about the rest. Whatever the
reason, from 1860 to 1863, French wooing of Austria followed the
usual line of cajolery interspersed with enticement. Walewski began
the process before his resignation, calling for an understanding in advance concerning the collapse and dismemberment of Turkey. "If
Austria, Russia and France come to an agreement," he insisted, "this
question, so delicate, long foreseen but justly feared, will be solved
the day it presents itself and no one, not even England, will be able to
resist the immense force of our action." In November, 1859, and again
in July, 1860, Napoleon suggested that Austria might take Egypt; in
1860–1861 the lure, as we have seen, was Bosnia and Herzegovina.
Finally, in early 1863 the Polish crisis led to Napoleon's proposal of a
formal Franco-Austrian alliance. "Between ourselves," he admitted to
Metternich, "we are widely separated in our ideas as to what constitutes Austria's real interest." But he continued:

> I think you have everything to gain by advancing with France and England,
> and with France alone in the event that England should not wish to follow
> us. Between us we would control the whole of Europe—Germany *would
> be split in two*—some would go with you and others with Prussia—but

this much is certain, that we would make of Europe what we willed. . . . Well, I say it again . . . I think that our agreement can be kept on the most pacific terms . . . but let us remain united so that if events should surprise us we could impose our will upon Europe.[15]

Did Napoleon really intend an offensive alliance of France and Austria against Russia? Was his Polish policy geared toward war? The reasons for doubting it have already been stated, and, in fact, the cajoling of Austria, like that of Russia and of Britain before, had as its constant accompaniment the refrain of congress. From January to July, 1860, Napoleon talked frequently with Metternich about the possibility of a general congress, even proposing that Austria might take the initiative. At the same time, Thouvenel made clear the French goal of a wide-ranging entente. France, he wrote to Moustier at Vienna, hoped to agree on Italy and the East with both Russia and Austria. "If we should succeed," he added, "in posing the principles of an entente among the three Empires and thus giving back to Europe the firm seating that she had lost, then it seems useful to try to extend this understanding to the other great powers and in that way to avoid the chance of a long and serious war in regard to the East."[16] So far as Italy was concerned, in November, 1860, and again a year later, Napoleon made clear that he still hoped for an entente with Austria that would precede a congress at which compensation could be arranged—in the East. In 1862 the emperor continued his efforts to bring Austria to support the idea of a general congress, even going so far as to offer some guarded praise for the Congress of Vienna and admitting that the Franco-Austrian alliance was linked in his mind with a future congress. And finally, the thrust of Napoleon's policy during the Polish crisis itself was toward a congress solution rather than a war.

15. Clarendon to Albert, May 18, 1857, in Martin, *The Life of His Royal Highness, the Prince Consort*, IV, 49; Cavour to Durando, Turin, March 5, 1860, in *Cavour-Nigra*, III, 142–43, no. 629; Metternich to Rechberg, Paris, secret, October 28, 1859, in HHSA, PA IX, Fr. Ber., 1859, VIII–XII, Box 63, no. 13A-E, fols. 352–58; Metternich to Rechberg, Paris, secret, October 29, 1859, in Hallberg, *Franz Joseph and Napoleon III*, 292; Metternich to Rechberg, Paris, November 16, 1859, in HHSA, PA IX, Fr. Ber., 1859, VIII–XII, Box 63, no. 16A-B, fols. 464–65; Metternich to Rechberg, Paris, July 9, 1860, in HHSA, PA IX, Fr. Ber., 1860, VI–IX, Box 66, no. 45B, fols. 189v–90; Metternich to Rechberg, Paris, June 12, 1863, in HHSA, PA IX, Varia, 1863, Box 77, fols. 107ff.

16. Thouvenel to Moustier, private, Paris, April 23, 1860, in AMAE, MD, Papiers Thouvenel, 14:53–54; Metternich to Rechberg, Paris, telegram, no. 132, November 3, 1860, in HHSA, PA IX, Fr. Ber., 1860, XI–XII, box 67, fols. 190–97; Mülinen to Rechberg, Paris, telegram, no. 78, November 6, 1861, in HHSA, PA IX, Fr. Ber., 1861, VII–XII, Box 70, fols. 495–96; Metternich to Rechberg, Paris, March 19, 1862, in Salomon, *Ambassade de Richard Metternich*, 86–87.

Here, then, is a theory of Napoleon III's alliance policies from 1849 to 1863 that is no more susceptible of proof than any other but is certainly in keeping with his own words, the general tenor of his action, and the persistent themes of Second Empire diplomacy. He sought through alliance with one or two great powers, not a series of concrete goals, but rather to shake the status quo, to "unblock" the evolution of Europe as he interpreted it, and through the concert of Europe (whose chief instrument would be the general congress) to reorganize Europe and, subsequently, to regulate its affairs. From 1849 to 1856 he thought such a task within the capability of an enlightened Anglo-French entente. From 1856 to 1863 he sought to add Russia, as buttress, perhaps, to a Britain whose traditional policies and ingrained distrust of Napoleonic France were obstacles to achieving these ends. After 1859, Napoleon attempted to bring into the "system," perhaps as a replacement for Britain, more likely as a supplement, that very Austria whose resistance had chiefly prevented submitting the Italian question to the jurisdiction of Europe and whose active support could help to remove the obstacles blocking a similar disposition of the Polish problem. By the end of 1863 this alliance policy had failed. The Italian and Polish questions had not drawn Britain closer to France, but had estranged the two. The recent Polish crisis had destroyed the Franco-Russian entente without substituting an Austro-French one. Nevertheless, at the beginning of November, 1863, Napoleon at last proposed the general European congress to which he had aspired for so long. How are we to explain this seemingly perverse timing?

CHAPTER 12

The Congress Proposal of 1863
and Its Aftermath
1864–1866

The congress proposal of November 4, 1863, was Napoleon's idea alone, and it was meant to succeed. The speech to the Corps législatif on November 5, in which he announced that invitations had been issued, was prepared without formally consulting his ministers. Drouyn de Lhuys, then foreign minister, had already shown during the Polish crisis his aversion to congresses, which were, in his opinion, "as bad as a council of war" when decisions had to be made. After the emperor's speech Fould, the finance minister, told Cowley that he had tried to dissuade Napoleon from the idea; the ambassador, for his part, could not find anyone who believed the proposal to have any chance of success. After the invitation had been rejected, Drouyn de Lhuys admitted that he had never thought the idea practicable. He had not discouraged the proposal, hoping it would alleviate some of the distrust in which Napoleon was held, "but he had always told the Emperor that His Majesty must be prepared for a refusal, and that he must not look upon such a refusal as a slight to himself."[1]

Drouyn de Lhuys' efforts to prepare his master for the failure of the congress idea seem, however, to have had little effect; nothing witnesses so convincingly to the sincerity of Napoleon's proposal than the effect upon him of its rejection. This effect impressed both Cowley and Metternich, neither of whom had thought at first that the proposal was a serious one, and both of whom soon changed their minds. "I have never seen the emperor so discouraged and making so little effort to conceal it," Metternich reported. Cowley concluded: "It is

1. Bóbr-Tylingo, "Un congrès européen manqué," 78; Spencer, Drouyn de Lhuys," 201; Cowley to Russell, Chantilly, private, November 12, 17, 1863, both in Russell Papers, 30/22, 59; Cowley to Russell, Paris, most confidential, December 15, 1863, in PRO, FO, 27, 1499: no. 1161.

right that I should state that since I have had the honor of knowing the Emperor, I have never seen him in so morose a mood and this I must add is the general opinion of those who hold intercourse with him. That His Majesty really believed in the success of a Congress it would now be unfair to doubt." Apparently those diplomats were not far off the mark who cautioned their governments not to treat Napoleon's congress proposal too cavalierly. "The act of which he has taken the initiative," Talleyrand reminded Bismarck, "is obviously the great work which he has always dreamed of accomplishing; it is the trophy that he wants for his reign." There is, as we have seen, much to justify this point of view. But it must still be asked why Napoleon should have chosen the autumn of 1863 and the occasion of a foredoomed Polish insurrection as the moment for passing from anticipation to action.[2]

Of course Poland was an embarrassment for him, but certainly no more so than Rome, for example, had been in the past. And while the congress proposal proved popular in France, this alone is hardly an explanation for it. Were there other, deeper reasons? Was this proposal the culmination of long frustrations and a feeling of time running out? It was toward the end of 1863, apparently, that the emperor's health began noticeably to deteriorate. Moreover, even a man as patient as Napoleon might have reached the conclusion by 1863 that a general congress could not be arranged by preliminary alliances or ententes, that only a direct appeal to public opinion might succeed in bringing about such a meeting. If this were so, the state of the Polish question in late 1863 could have seemed a good focus for such an appeal. It is also possible that, viewed from the perspective of the moment itself, the situation in Europe seemed more favorable to the emperor's project that it actually was. To begin, British public opinion favored the Polish cause and might be brought to support a congress at which something could be done for the Poles. At Vienna, there had been since 1860 at least a willingness to *talk* about sacrifices and compensations; Austria was as likely to accept a congress in 1863 as it had ever been or, perhaps, ever would be. Above all, the Russian attitude may have seemed especially promising to Napoleon. In early

2. Cowley to Russell, November 7, 1863, in PRO, FO, 27, 1498: no. 1061; Metternich to Rechberg, Paris, November 17, December 14, 1863, both in HHSA, PA IX, Fr. Ber., 1863, X–XII, Box 76, no. 49A-B, fols. 373–75; no. 59B, fols. 477v–78; Cowley to Russell, Paris, confidential, December 15, 1863, in PRO, FO, 27, 1499: no. 1160; Talleyrand to Drouyn de Lhuys, Berlin, November 9, 1863, in AMAE, CP, Prusse, 347:56, no. 110.

May, during the Polish crisis, a significant hint from Gorchakov was reported by the French ambassador. "If it should become necessary to adopt a broader base, he does not oppose the convocation of a congress, provided that its scope not be limited to the Polish question but rather that it encompass the whole political situation of Europe." The thought did not go unnoticed at Paris; in the archives the passage is marked. Montebello noted that the congress appeared to have been suggested to Gorchakov by the Italian ambassador at Saint Petersburg, Marquis Gioachino Pepoli, a friend and relative of Napoleon's. Neither Montebello nor Drouyn de Lhuys liked the idea, and it soon became evident that the Russians did not intend to propose a general congress. Pepoli, however, continued his efforts, and while Drouyn de Lhuys had earlier told the Russian ambassador that France would neither oppose such a congress nor take the initiative, it was after an interview with Pepoli, who had passed through Paris for the purpose, that Napoleon issued his invitation. Since the French emperor must have known that Berlin had earlier offered its support for a general congress, he might well have decided, on the strength of Gorchakov's attitude as reported by Pepoli, to assume the initiative that Saint Petersburg had failed to take. Certainly Morny and Drouyn de Lhuys would both argue later that this had been the case.[3]

And so, feeling that neither Russia nor Prussia would oppose the congress; hoping, perhaps, to sway the British government by a direct appeal to public opinion; and gambling that Vienna would not again interpose its veto, Napoleon launched his bombshell. His letter of November 4 and speech of the following day sketched the scope and purpose of the congress that he saw, in the context of the Polish question, as the only alternative to "war or silence." This alternative, "to submit the Polish cause to a European tribunal," Russia, too, could accept if the other questions disturbing Europe were similarly treated.

3. Case, *French Opinion on War and Diplomacy*, 183–84; Williams, *The Mortal Napoleon III*, 106–108; Montebello to Drouyn de Lhuys, Saint Petersburg, confidential, May 9, 1863, in AMAE, CP, Russie, 231:45; Montebello to Drouyn de Lhuys, Saint Petersburg, May 13, 1863, in AMAE, CP, Russie, 231:50–55, no. 28; Montebello to Drouyn de Lhuys, Saint Petersburg, confidential, September 10, 1863, in AMAE, CP, Russie, 232:116–19 (someone, probably Drouyn de Lhuys, has written across this dispatch: "la démarche de M. de Pepoli était toute spontanée. Je ne l'avais ni inspirée, ni connue à l'avance"); Pingaud, "Un projet de désarmement," 4; Metternich to Rechberg, Paris, private, January 7, 1864, in HHSA, PA IX, Varia, 1864, Box 79, fols. 1–6; Morny to Gorchakov, November 8, 1863, in Morny, *Une ambassade en Russie*, 234–35; Drouyn de Lhuys to Jacques Adolphe Cousseau, comte de Massignac, Paris, November 16, 1863, in AMAE, CP, Russie, 232:212–14, no. 73.

And why not! The treaties of 1815 had ceased to exist, "broken in Greece, in Belgium, in France, in Italy, as well as on the Danube." Britain had generously altered them by ceding the Ionian Islands to Greece, and Russia was "trampling them under foot at Warsaw." What, then, "could be more legitimate and more sensible, than to invite the powers of Europe to a congress where self-interest and resistance would disappear before a supreme arbitrament?" What would make more sense than to "sit down together, with no preconceived systems, no exclusive ambitions, animated solely by the thought of establishing an order of things founded henceforth on the true interest of rulers and peoples"? Public opinion demanded as much, and only by taking such a course could Europe combat "the subversive spirit of the extremist parties." At any rate, it was appropriate that the invitation come from a ruler who, "raised in a hard school," was least able "to ignore the rights of sovereigns and the legitimate aspirations of the peoples," a ruler, moreover, to whom ambitious projects had often been attributed and who wished to demonstrate that his only purpose was "to achieve the pacification of Europe without violence." It would be particularly appropriate that Paris, the capital from which so many signals of revolution had gone forth, "should be the seat of conferences destined to lay the foundations of a general pacification." And Napoleon concluded his speech: "This appeal will, I like to think, be understood by everyone. A refusal would give rise to the suspicion of secret projects that have to be hidden from sight. But even if the proposal should not be accepted unanimously, it would still have the great advantage of having called to Europe's attention the danger—and the way to safety. Two paths are open to us: One leads to progress by way of reconciliation and peace; the other, sooner or later, will take us fatalistically to war, as the consequence of an obstinate determination to maintain a crumbling past." The appeal to public opinion was obvious; implicit in the decision to unfold the congress idea in a speech before the French legislature, explicit in the speculation that a refusal would give rise to suspicions of secret projects. Besides, the congress invitations went out to *all* European rulers and governments, not just to the great powers. Was there a hope at Paris that the lesser sovereigns might tip the balance in favor of acceptance? Separate invitations were sent, for example, not only to the four lesser German kingdoms (Hanover, Bavaria, Saxony, and Württemberg) but also to the German Diet; and Drouyn de Lhuys urged these middle states to use their influence in the confederation to gain its "adhesion to the work of pacification proposed by His Imperial Majesty."[4]

In the weeks between the congress invitation and its rejection Paris was called upon to spell out in more detail the composition, scope, and authority of the proposed meeting. But requests for an agenda were firmly rebuffed. It would compromise the work projected by Napoleon, argued Drouyn de Lhuys, to determine in advance the questions that were to be discussed. Once topics began to be excluded, soon only Poland would remain, and then Russia would refuse to come. If the French emperor presumed to set an agenda, he would be accused of attempting to impose his own will; if he entered into agreement with a few powers, that would nullify the congress as a clearinghouse for all Europe's problems; and if he attempted to arrange matters in advance with *all* the governments, it would take more time and effort than would the congress itself. Nevertheless, some information was gained as to the scope that Napoleon envisaged for the meeting. Drouyn de Lhuys frequently asserted that France had no claims to make for itself, an assertion Metternich was willing to accept, insofar as it applied to Napoleon himself. "He has put Himself on a pedestal," Metternich wrote of the emperor, "where He admires Himself, and on the base of which He has inscribed 'rapprochement of my dynasty to the others—a friendly understanding and *disinterest pushed to the point of self-denial.*'" Poland, it was clear, would be a major item of discussion. After all, as Drouyn de Lhuys admitted to Cowley, "the state of Poland was the principal motive which had prompted the Emperor to make [his] appeal to Europe." Then there were the questions of Schleswig-Holstein, the Danubian Principalities, Rome, limitation of armaments, the antagonism between Austria and Italy. But did Napoleon mean to restrict the congress to a resolution of particular problems, or was there more in his mind? "Drouyn says," wrote Palmerston to Leopold I, "that the congress could take the treaties of 1815, examine them article by article, remove whatever requires removal and re-establish the rest as the 'treaty of 1863—

---

4. Napoleon III to the European sovereigns, Tuileries, November 4, 1863, in *La politique impériale,* 399–401; imperial address at the opening of the legislative session, Palais du Louvre, November 5, 1863, in *La politique impériale,* 407–410; Drouyn de Lhuys to French agents at Hanover, Munich, Dresden, Stuttgart, November 9, 1863, in AMAE, MD, 2126:80. The Diet was invited to decide how it wished to be represented at the congress (Bóbr-Tylingo, "Un congrés européen manqué," 83).

1864.'" And while Napoleon expressed his willingness to avoid "questions of a delicate nature," some suspected that, once he was seated at the conference table, his ambitions (and imagination) would soar.[5]

Certainly the French emperor intended that his congress be held at the highest level. He clearly showed his irritation when the king of Prussia deprecated a congress of princes ("we are not suited for discussing; we are made for approving or rejecting the result of the discussions of others"). The personal interchange of views among sovereigns, Drouyn de Lhuys argued, would have a great influence in favor of peace, and, he noted, Napoleon especially held to this approach, since the rulers were more apt to accept generous ideas than were their cabinets. But the French foreign minister suggested that, while the sovereigns would open the congress, their foreign ministers would then work out the application of principles, and after several weeks the task of detailing agreements would be handed over to the regularly accredited representatives at Paris. Probably Napoleon was the more determined to have a congress of sovereigns, since he could not see a principle of authority for the meeting other than its moral weight. He asked Count Ludwig von der Goltz how the Congress of Vienna had decided, and did not argue with the Prussian's answer that the invariable international custom was to seek unanimous decision, although, of course, moral pressure could usually bring the minority into line. When Cowley raised the question of enforcing the decisions of the congress, Napoleon simply replied that, if the meeting was conducted in a frank and disinterested spirit, the powers would agree, and enforcement would be unnecessary. "He counts on his skill," Metternich believed, "to draw some along with him, divide the others, and arrive *tant bien que mal* at more or less complete results." This was, as we have seen, a familiar approach of the emperor's, and it seems that in 1863 as on earlier occasions he put his hope in persuasion, but a sort of persuasion that the prestige of France and his own charm and reasonableness would endow with some of the force of mediation,

5. Goltz to Bismarck, Paris, confidential, November 14, 1863, in *APP*, IV, 146, no. 88; circular of Drouyn de Lhuys to French diplomatic agents, Paris, December [11 or 12], 1863, in AMAE, MD, 2126:93–96; Metternich to Rechberg, Paris, November 17, 1863, in HHSA, PA IX, Fr. Ber., 1863, X–XII, Box 76, no. 49A-B, fols. 373–75; Cowley to Russell, London, confidential, November 14, 1863, in PRO, FO, 27, 1498: no. 1075; Palmerston to Leopold I, Piccadilly, November 15, 1863, in Craven (ed.), *Lord Palmerston*, II, 627; Metternich to Rechberg, Paris, telegram, November 20, 1863, in Hallberg, *Franz Joseph and Napoleon III*, 338.

perhaps even of arbitration. The treaty of Paris of 1856, Drouyn de Lhuys recalled, had adopted the principle of mediation in the case of a dispute between Turkey and another signatory, and the Congress of Paris had agreed with Clarendon's wish that this principle be given an even wider application. Now Napoleon was going a logical step further. "He would not wait until dissensions have broken out in order to recommend the application to present circumstances of this wholesome principle, which is inscribed on the latest monument of European public law. His Majesty invited his allies, as of this moment, to exchange views and to reach an understanding."[6]

Unfortunately for Napoleon, the requests for amplification of his proposal were not serious. Although the secondary powers quickly accepted the congress, only the Dutch posing a condition (implicit) that Britain must accept the invitation, none of the great powers was eager to do so. On the other hand, those of the Continent had no intention of vying for the honor of being the first to say no. Gorchakov early informed Bismarck that Russia, having itself suggested a general congress in April, could not oppose the idea. In the end, Russia's response was to accept, provided all the other great powers did so, although Pepoli, whom Napoleon sent to Saint Petersburg after November 5 to confirm the supposed Russian promises concerning Poland, was soon made to understand that none had been given. Although Paris hinted at a wish for closer entente, Bismarck, who managed to appear an enthusiastic champion of the congress to the French ambassador Talleyrand, took essentially the same position and even seemed to hope that an anti-French coalition would be the result of Napoleon's "miscalculation." Clearly, Prussia and Russia were not eager to go to the conference table, but neither were they prepared to veto the emperor's proposal. Would Austria have done so if necessary? The Austrians, intending to hold on to both Galicia and Venetia and fearing that they might be isolated on these issues at the congress, had good reason to oppose such a meeting on principle. However, Rechberg chose to send a dilatory response to Paris (accepting in principle but insisting on an

6. Talleyrand to Drouyn de Lhuys, Berlin, November 14, 1863, in AMAE, CP, Prusse, 347:61v, no. 112; Goltz to William I, Compiègne, November 23, 1863, in APP, IV, 197–99, no. 130; Goltz to Bismarck, Paris, confidential, November 14, 1863, in APP, IV, 145–47, no. 88; Cowley to Russell, Paris, November 18, 1863, in PRO, FO, 27, 1498: no. 1086; Metternich to Rechberg, Paris, confidential, November 23, 1863, in HHSA, PA IX, Fr. Ber., 1863, X–XII, Box 76, no. 52B, fols. 395v–97; Drouyn de Lhuys to Cadore, Compiègne, November 23, 1863, in AMAE, CP, Angleterre, 727:85–86, no. 117.

agenda) and to rely on a British rejection. Probably he felt assured that Britain would not accept the congress. Had Britain unexpectedly done so, Vienna's position would have been difficult, and there is no certainty that Austria would then have found the courage to block the congress with another blunt rejection like that of 1859.[7]

On the other hand, Vienna's attitude may well have been decisive in shaping London's response. Most British leaders probably shared Victoria's initial reaction that the congress proposal was "an impertinence" and that no rulers should "lower themselves by going there." Cowley deluged the French foreign minister with good reasons why the congress idea was noble but impracticable. The congress could never agree, its decisions could not be enforced, no one would freely accept sacrifices not imposed by a defeat in war, compensation could not be arranged without despoiling someone, the congress would make things worse not better. Nevertheless, in his instructions to Cowley of November 7, Russell seemed to waver. Then, on November 18 the foreign secretary learned from Count Rudolf von Apponyi that Austria would not under any circumstances agree to give up Galicia or Venetia. That same day he received a persuasive letter from Palmerston, arguing against the congress. On the nineteenth the cabinet decided for a definitive rejection. The British government might well share France's opinion on many of the points in contention, Russell wrote, but "if the mere expression of opinions and wishes would accomplish no positive results, it appears certain that the deliberations of a Congress would consist of demands and pretentions put forward by some and resisted by others; and there being no supreme authority in such an Assembly to enforce the decisions of the majority, the Congress would probably separate, leaving many of its members on worse terms with each other than they had been when they met." To make the veto even more brutal, the British government permitted

7. Baron Alexander Redern to Bismarck, Saint Petersburg, telegram, November 8, 1863, in *APP*, IV, 118 n.; Count Guido von Thun-Hohenstein to Rechberg, November 25/13, 1863, in Hallberg, *Franz Joseph and Napoleon III*, 420 n.; Talleyrand to Drouyn de Lhuys, Berlin, November 7, 1863, in AMAE, CP, Prusse, 347:23–27, no. 109; Goltz to William I, Compiègne, November 23, 1863, in *APP*, IV, 198, no. 130; William I to Napoleon III, Berlin, November 18, 1863, in AMAE, CP, Prusse, 347:95–96; Oubril to Gorchakov, Berlin, confidential, November 29, 1863, in *APP*, IV, 226, no. 155; Rechberg to Metternich, private, December 8, 1863, in Hallberg, *Franz Joseph and Napoleon III*, 339; Francis Joseph to Napoleon III, Vienna, undated, in AMAE, MD, France, 2122:69–70, no. 27. The final Austrian rejection was based on the argument that no acceptable agenda had been agreed on.

the letter of rejection to be published in the *Times* before it was delivered at Paris.[8]

During the negotiations Drouyn de Lhuys had suggested that if some powers accepted the congress while others did not, the emperor would at least know who his friends were, and "the proposition of a congress could lead in that way to a new system of alliance." This was undoubtedly what the foreign minister hoped for, and it was probably all that he ever expected to gain from Napoleon's initiative. His approaches to Prussia and to Austria continued, and he seemed content to be done with the congress. It would be up to the emperor, he told Cowley at the end of November, to decide whether the powers who had accepted would be invited to a more restricted meeting. "This was evidently not said," noted the ambassador, "with the slightest idea that such would be the Emperor's decision." And yet, on December 8, French representatives were instructed to work for a conference of those sovereigns who had not rejected the congress, to be preceded by a meeting of foreign ministers. This proposal, wrote the Belgian minister, Beyens, "does not at all come from the thought of the minister of foreign affairs. . . . [It] belongs to the initiative and is the express will of the Emperor." If Cowley's information was correct, the French council of ministers' meeting of November 30 had decided that the question of a congress was at an end. This would mean that Napoleon's decision was taken in the first week of December. It was entirely against Drouyn de Lhuys' advice. The foreign minister admitted this and conceded that he would have much preferred to let the matter drop, trying simply for closer relations with the friendly powers. During these days at Paris and then Compiègne, Napoleon had withdrawn almost completely, even shutting out his foreign minister. His state of mind was reflected in his response on December 21 to the address of the Senate:

---

8. Victoria to Leopold I, Windsor, November 12, 1863, in *Victoria Letters, 1862–1878*, I, 114; Cowley to Russell, Paris, confidential, November 14, 1863, in PRO, FO, 27, 1498: no. 1075; Russell to Cowley, London, telegram, November 7, 1863, in PRO, FO, 27, 1498; Count Rudolf von Apponyi to Rechberg, London, November 18, 1863, in Temperley and Penson, *Foundations of British Foreign Policy*, 230–31, no. 71; Palmerston to Russell, November 18, 1863, in Temperley and Penson, *Foundations of British Foreign Policy*, 256–58, no. 86; Apponyi to Rechberg, London, November 22, 1863, in Temperley and Penson, *Foundations of British Foreign Policy*, 258–59, no. 87; Russell to Cowley, London, November 25, 1863, in AMAE, CP, Angleterre, 727: 98v–99v.

I wish with all my heart for the arrival of the moment when great questions which divide governments and people will be peacefully resolved by a European arbitrament [*arbitrage européen*]. This wish was also that of the head of my family, when he exclaimed at Saint-Helena: "To wage war in Europe is to wage civil war."

Cannot this great thought, which is today a utopia, become tomorrow a reality? However that may be, there is always honor in proclaiming a principle which tends to abolish the prejudices of another day. Let us unite our efforts to achieve this noble goal; and let us occupy ourselves with obstacles only to overcome them and with incredulity only to confound it.[9]

Nevertheless, our own incredulity is difficult to confound in the face of this imperial tilting at immovable obstacles. Perhaps Napoleon was influenced in his obstinacy by the fact that Prussia had accepted his congress proposal, Russia had not exactly rejected it, and Austria was still pondering its reply. But, in the end, there can be no satisfactory explanation of his action other than pure exasperation. Until December, 1863, the French emperor had followed two themes of foreign policy with great consistency, pursuit of a congress revision of the treaties of 1815 and adherence to the British alliance. That he had turned, in his *congrès restreint* proposal (the term was his own), from the latter in a forlorn attempt to salvage something of the former is an arresting indication of the strength of the congress idea in his thinking. It is clear from Cowley's reports that Napoleon blamed Britain not only for rejecting the congress but for trying to persuade the other powers to reject it as well. "So it seems we shall have no congress," he had snapped to Goltz. "Well, I shall have to change my alliances!" But there was no more hope for the limited congress than for the general one. The Austrian rejection of the latter, on grounds that could only be strengthened by the exclusion of Britain, crossed the *congrès restreint* circular in the diplomatic mails. Prussia at-

9. Goltz to Bismarck, Paris, confidential, November 8, 1863, in *APP*, IV, 126, no. 68; Cowley to Russell, Paris, telegram, November 28, 1863, in PRO, FO, 27, 1498; circular of Drouyn de Lhuys to French diplomatic agents, December 8, 1863, in AMAE, MD, 2126:98–98v; Beyens to the Belgian foreign minister, December 16, 1863, in Beyens, *Le Second Empire*, I, 339; Cowley to Russell, Paris, December 1, 1863, in PRO, FO, 27, 1498: no. 1117; Metternich to Rechberg, Paris, December 14, 1863, in HHSA, PA IX, Fr. Ber., 1863, X–XII, Box 76, no. 59B, fols. 477v–78; Cowley to Russell, Chantilly, private, December 15, 1863, in Russell Papers, 30/22, 59; Cowley to Russell, Paris, most confidential, December 15, 1863, in PRO, FO, 27, 1499: no. 1161; Cowley to Russell, Paris, private, December 25, 1863, in Russell Papers, 30/22, 59; Napoleon's reply, *La politique impériale*, 410–11.

tempted evasion, but the day after Napoleon's speech to the Senate, Gorchakov politely rejected the proposal. As Beyens had predicted: "To persist in summoning a congress more or less modified when Britain has categorically refused her co-operation on an earlier program and when there is every reason to anticipate the refusal of the other great powers, is to seek disappointment with a light heart." But is was hardly with a light heart that Napoleon must have surveyed the ruins of his hopes. Even before the definitive British rejection he had left Paris, and at Compiègne he appeared to Metternich to be "uneasy, very sad, discouraged, and bitter," a lion lurking in his den, unwilling to be enticed from it. After a brief visit to Paris, where those who saw him found his ill humor not at all improved, Napoleon returned to Compiègne. There, when Cowley finally brought up the matter of the British note of rejection, he replied in a tone more angry than the ambassador had ever heard him use. "I do not think," Cowley observed, "I ever saw the Emperor so morose or out of spirits." "Je ne vous parle pas de politique," Napoleon wrote several months later to his friend, Count Francesco Arese. "Tout est si sombre et si embrouillé que ce qu'il y a de mieux à faire, c'est de rester dans sa tente, l'arme au bras."[10]

By the time of his letter to Arese, the emperor's sulking had already become a matter of concern to Europe. On February 1, 1864, war had broken out between Denmark and the two major German powers over the question of Schleswig and Holstein. Two years earlier Napoleon had told Reuss that he considered this problem "as being within the province of a European Congress"; as we have seen, the question of the Elbe Duchies was destined to play a major role at the general congress, had it met, and even at the congrès restreint, where, according to Drouyn de Lhuys, it was to be the first topic discussed, followed by the questions of the Danubian Principalities and of Italy. In fact, the emperor had argued to Goltz that this problem was proof of the necessity of a congress. Why, then, should the atttitude of Paris toward the

10. Cowley to Russell, Paris, private, December 1, 1863, in Russell Papers, 30/22, 59; Gorchakov to Budberg, Saint Petersburg, December 22, 1863, in AMAE, CP, Russie, 232:278–80; Beyens to the Belgian foreign minister, December 16, 1863, in Beyens, Le Second Empire, I, 339; Metternich to Rechberg, Paris, November 23, 1863, in Salomon, Ambassade de Richard Metternich, 84; Cowley to Russell, Paris, private, December 1, 1863, Cowley to Russell, Compiègne, private, December 11, 1863, Cowley to Russell, private, December 13, 1863, all in Russell Papers, 30/22, 59; Napoleon III to Arese, Paris, March 27, 1864, in Grabinski, Un ami de Napoléon III, 221.

northern crisis have been one of such studied abstention during the first months of 1864?[11] Of course it was a difficult problem for Napoleon, caught between the London convention of May, 1852, which he was pledged to support, and the German nationality claims, which had his sympathy. Moreover, should French public opinion force him to intervene in the event that Denmark's existence appeared to be threatened, the result might well be a war with Germany, and the consequences of such a war would be incalculable. Only genuine alarm at Prussian ambitions would have simplified the problem, and reasons for such alarm did not yet exist, at least not to the extent of overriding Napoleon's aversion to a foreign policy based frankly on preservation of the status quo. Thouvenel as foreign minister had rejected both an intervention by France and Britain and the proposal by Sweden in January, 1862, of a great-powers conference. In fact, he had attempted to use the threat of European intervention to hasten a direct Danish-German settlement. Now Drouyn de Lhuys returned to this policy of nonintervention, justifying it by repeated reproaches to the powers for having rejected the general congress, which alone would have had the authority to solve so difficult a problem. Drouyn de Lhuys' sincerity in making use of such an argument may well be doubted, but it must have carried weight with Napoleon, smarting from Britain's "defection" during the Polish crisis as well as from Europe's dismissal of his congress proposal. Probably it was this imperial state of mind that permitted Drouyn de Lhuys to block several efforts between December, 1863, and March, 1864, to submit the Schleswig-Holstein question to a European conference.[12]

Confronted with Napoleon's *congrès restreint* proposal, Bismarck attempted on December 17 to persuade Paris that it would be preferable to have a special foreign ministers' conference at Paris that would concern itself only with the question of the Duchies. Although Bismarck had sought and received British approval of this initiative, he clearly had no great hope for the conference and was probably con-

11. Metternich to Rechberg, Paris, secret, January 15, 1862, in HHSA, PA IX, Fr. Ber., 1862, I–VI, Box 72, no. 3C, fol. 32v; Bóbr-Tylingo, "Un congrès européen manqué," 91; Goltz to Bismarck, Compiègne, very confidential, November 24, 1863, in APP, IV, 208, no. 137.

12. Thouvenel to Gramont, Paris, April 22, May 7, 1862, both in AMAE, CP, Autriche, 481:177–78, no. 34, 217v–19, no. 40; Drouyn de Lhuys to Emile Félix, comte de Fleury, Paris, December 9, 1863, in Fleury (ed.), Souvenirs, II, 274; Metternich to Rechberg, Paris, January 19, 1864, in HHSA, PA IX, Fr. Ber., 1864, I–X, Box 78, no. 5, fols. 46v–47.

cerned most of all with placating the emperor. For that same reason, no doubt, the rest of Europe quickly supported his proposal. London found that the objections to a general congress did not apply "to a conference limited in its scope to one object alone, upon which an understanding may be arrived at, or reasonably expected," and the British government accepted Paris as the meeting place, stipulating that the conference should be limited to the signatories of the 1852 treaty of London and, "if it were desired," of a representative of the German Diet. Both Sweden and Denmark urged the French government to accept, while Vienna proposed that France take the initiative.[13] Napoleon had been irritated, however, by the transparent attempt to pass off the proposed conference as a substitute for his general congress. He vetoed Paris as conference site, declined to take the initiative, and gave Drouyn de Lhuys his head to deal with Bismarck's proposal. The foreign minister thereupon returned to the great powers the same favor they had rendered Napoleon's general congress proposal. He did not reject the conference; he merely set conditions for it that were unlikely to be met, including maintenance of the political and military status quo before and during the conference and representation for the German Diet, while making clear at the same time French disdain for the whole idea. The general congress, at least, would have had the advantage of presenting a number of problems concurrently, argued the foreign minister, thus making transactions possible, and it offered some possibility of enforcement, since "a meeting of the Cabinets of Europe in Congress should result in the formation of a nucleus of common wills before which individual wills would most likely have yielded." At the end of January, Russell attempted to revive the conference idea, but Bismarck declined. The subsequent defeat and withdrawal of the Danes, however, once again brought the idea to the fore, especially at Saint Petersburg. Drouyn de Lhuys simply repeated the conditions that had successfully blocked the conference earlier. When Vienna, Saint Petersburg, and London agreed to waive the condition of a preliminary armistice (which Paris had made no real effort to secure), the French foreign minister tartly announced: "So far as we are

13. Talleyrand to Drouyn de Lhuys, Berlin, private, December 17, 1863, in AMAE, CP, Prusse, 347:217v–18; Russell to Cowley, December 22, 1863, in RA, J80/116; Bismarck to Goltz, Berlin, private, December 20, 1863, in *APP*, IV, 336–37, no. 241; Fleury to Napoleon III, telegram, December 24, 1863, in *Origines*, I, 2–4, no. 1; Russell to Count Albert von Bernstorff, London, confidential, December 19, 1863, in *APP*, IV, 327, no. 235; Gramont to Drouyn de Lhuys, Vienna, telegram, December 25, 1863, in AMAE, CP, Autriche, 485:271.

concerned, we have no interest at all in the opening of a Conference under the conditions as now proposed." Metternich would have added "or under any conditions."[14]

But already the situation had begun to change. While Napoleon must have found some satisfaction in Drouyn de Lhuys' use of the rejected congress idea, there is evidence that he was more favorable to a conference on the Duchies than was his foreign minister. He had not personally dissented when Cowley advanced the opinion in December, 1863, that the question required a conference and that such a meeting would not find a solution impossible. Goltz found the emperor less opposed to the conference than Drouyn de Lhuys had led him to believe, and Emile Félix, comte de Fleury, insisted that, on his return from Copenhagen (where he had been sent on special mission) in January, 1864, he had persuaded Napoleon to agree to a conference, only to have the foreign minister regain the upper hand. Besides, carping and sulking are not a foreign policy. With French public opinion as ardently pro-Danish as it was pacifistic, the emperor had little choice but conference diplomacy, even had that not been his own preference. Having assured Flahaut that he would not sulk any longer, Napoleon moved steadily toward the decision that he took in early March to accept the conference even without a preliminary armistice. Overruled, Drouyn de Lhuys duly proclaimed the new policy on March 11, although he was as much opposed to a conference as ever.[15]

Several days later, Ernest II presented to Napoleon the argument

14. Metternich to Rechberg, Paris, January 7, 1864, in HHSA, PA IX, Fr. Ber., 1864, I–X, Box 78, no. 1B, fol. 8; Goltz to Bismarck, Paris, private, December 26, 1863, in APP, IV, 354–55, no. 255; Metternich to Rechberg, Paris, telegram, December 27, 1863, in HHSA, PA IX, Fr. Ber., 1863, X–XII, Box 76, fol. 501; Drouyn de Lhuys to comte de Salignac-Fenelon (at Frankfurt), Paris, January 18, 1864, in Origines, I, 154, no. 93; Drouyn de Lhuys to Gramont, Paris, confidential, December 26, 1863, in Origines, I, 18–22; Talleyrand to Drouyn de Lhuys, Berlin, January 31, 1864, in Origines, I, 233–35, no. 153; Drouyn de Lhuys to French agents in London, Berlin, Vienna, and Saint Petersburg, February 15, 1864, in Origines, I, 306–307; no. 204; Metternich to Rechberg, Paris, telegram, no. 13, February 11, 1864, in HHSA, PA IX, Fr. Ber., 1864, I–X, Box 78, fol. 79; Drouyn de Lhuys to Talleyrand, Paris, March 4, 1864, in Origines, II, 76–77, no. 293; Metternich to Rechberg, Paris, February 28, 1864, in HHSA, PA IX, Fr. Ber., 1864, I–X, Box 78, no. 10B, fol. 111.

15. Cowley to Russell, Compiègne, confidential, December 11, 1863, in PRO, FO, 27, 1499: no. 1137; Goltz to Bismarck, Paris, private, December 26, 1863, in APP, IV, 354, no. 255; Cowley to Russell, Paris, January 14, 1864, in PRO, FO, 519, 231:88; Case, French Opinion on War and Diplomacy, 188–89; Cowley to Russell, Paris, March 1, 18, 1864, both in PRO, FO, 519, 231:115, 121; Drouyn de Lhuys to Dotézac, Paris, March 11, 1864, in Origines, II, 109, no. 320. Britain had once again proposed a conference, on February 23,

that France should propose before a European conference the solution of the Schleswig-Holstein question by means of "suffrage universel." The emperor replied that in his opinion conferences on the basis of the 1852 treaty would be useless; rather, he would proceed at the meeting "in the manner you have indicated," although he expected great opposition. The subsequent French proposals for a solution by plebiscite undoubtedly originated with Napoleon, as he himself admitted to both Cowley and Clarendon. It was, he told Cowley, the only possible solution; after all, he could hardly follow "one policy on the Eider and another on the Po." Nevertheless, the opposition that Napoleon had expected soon developed. Neither London nor Vienna was ready to accept this new principle of nationalities, which Drouyn de Lhuys in his instructions to the French ambassador at London had sweepingly pronounced "un principe fondamental de notre droit public." Russell, fearing that the nationalities idea would wreck the conference, sent Clarendon to Paris to discover if the emperor could be brought around. As it happened, Napoleon was not completely inflexible. He agreed that the plebiscite would be reserved as a last resort and he abandoned the position Drouyn de Lhuys had defended, that any plebiscite must involve all of Schleswig. But he refused to give up (perhaps against Drouyn de Lhuys' advice) the irreducible minimum of the nationalities principle—that the mixed frontier areas where both Danes and Germans lived should be partitioned by nationality and that the part of the Duchies to be separated from Denmark should be free to dispose of itself. Perhaps this restricted appeal to a plebiscite could have won grudging acceptance by the great powers, but the Danes were adamant in their rejection of partition. With the Prussian and Austrian rejection of Russell's proposal that Napoleon should arbitrate, the conference (which met in London June 9–25) lost all hope of success. The Danes were quickly overwhelmed and forcibly deprived of the Duchies, which would soon become a bone of contention between the two great German powers. "If we still believe," wrote Drouyn de Lhuys a year later in rejecting an Austrian suggestion that the conference on the Elbe Duchies be reconvened, "in the grandeur and usefulness of a general Congress, we cannot concede the same character and advantages to a combination of limited scope and doubtful success which would force us to participate in a debate from which we have wished to remain aloof."[16]

16. Ernest II, *Memoirs*, IV, 172, 179–80; Cowley to Russell, Paris, April 5, 1864, in PRO, FO, 519, 231:125; Clarendon to Russell, April 13, 1864, in Ollivier, *L'empire li-*

Perhaps during 1864 and 1865 as the contest between Prussia and Austria for dominance in Germany developed and sharpened, Napoleon *was* tempted to adopt a wholly egoistic foreign policy for France (not that his had ever been entirely altruistic), to seek the Rhineland, for example, through alliance with Prussia. Perhaps he would have liked to withdraw from all European problems that did not affect the vital interests of France. It was at this time that the French emperor, plagued by deteriorating health and growing political problems, returned to a more sedentary personal life, devoting himself to his history of Julius Caesar, published in 1865. And yet, the evidence is more convincing that he was trying, after the disappointments of 1863, to reassemble in his own mind the vision of European concert and of the destiny of France that had guided him until then. To the Corps législatif at its opening session in February, 1865, Napoleon alluded with regret to his abortive congress proposal: "At the time of your last meeting I hoped to see those difficulties which menaced the peace of Europe removed by a congress. It happened otherwise. I regret it, for the sword often decides questions without solving them, and the only foundation for a lasting peace lies in the gratification, by agreement of the rulers, of the true interests of the peoples." In March he outlined for the English journalist, Thornton Hunt, a plan for an "International Council" that could regulate European affairs. Perhaps these events were in his mind when, on the eve of a visit to Algeria in May, 1865, he prepared his political testament. "Power," he advised the prince imperial, "is a heavy burden, because one cannot always do the good one would wish, and because one's contemporaries rarely do one justice."[17]

Probably Napoleon continued to regard a general congress as the only exit for Europe from its problems. Increasingly, too, such a congress must have appeared one of the few options left open to him by a

---

béral, VII, 87; Drouyn de Lhuys to La Tour d'Auvergne, Paris, March 20, 1864, in *Origines*, II, 145, no. 349; Metternich to Rechberg, Paris, April 19, 1864, in HHSA, PA IX, Fr. Ber., 1864, I–X, Box 78, no. 16C, fols. 197–97v; Drouyn de Lhuys to La Tour d'Auvergne, March 29, 1864, in *Origines*, II, 191–92, no. 384; Cowley to Russell, Paris, June 5, 1864, in PRO, FO, 519, 13:47; Drouyn de Lhuys to La Tour d'Auvergne, Paris, confidential, May 8, 1864, in *Origines*, II, 356, no. 499; Drouyn de Lhuys to Gramont, Paris, confidential, August 1, 1865, in *Origines*, VI, 367, no. 1470.

17. Metternich to Rechberg, Paris, reserved, June 26, 1865, in HHSA, PA IX, Fr. Ber., 1865, Box 81, no. 32B, fols. 59v–60; Metternich to Rechberg, Paris, December 2, 1865, in HHSA, PA IX, Fr. Ber., 1865, Box 81, no. 49C, fols. 239–39v; address of Napoleon III, February 15, 1865, in *Oeuvres de Napoléon III*, V, 225; Ollivier, *L'empire libéral*, VII, 379.

public opinion that rejected war while clamoring that something must be done for "French dignity." At the beginning of 1864, Cowley expected that Napoleon would soon bring forward again his plan of a congress, perhaps proposing in regard to Schleswig-Holstein that they be joined to Germany while Denmark, Sweden, and Norway formed a Scandinavian kingdom. In August, Metternich believed that the emperor wanted to solve the Roman question and "to profit from the first incident in order to resurrect the idea of a Congress." Bismarck showed his awareness of Napoleon's state of mind by dangling the lure of a general congress, in order, no doubt, to prevent a conference that might resolve the Schleswig-Holstein problem. "People have become accustomed to the idea of a Congress," he told the French ambassador. Wouldn't Napoleon consider renewing his proposal now that it would no longer meet with the same obstacles? By the summer of 1865, rumors abounded, which could be traced without great difficulty to Berlin. At Hanover the French minister's heart beat with pride when a confidant of Bismarck's told him: "I am convinced that Austria and Prussia, realizing the impasse in which they have engaged themselves, will finally return to the idea of a Congress, and will beg the Emperor Napoleon to convoke it at Paris." Goltz believed that Napoleon would use an Austro-Prussian war in order to bring about a general congress. But Drouyn de Lhuys, for all his propagandist use of his master's "noble thought," showed no interest in reviving the proposal. France, he made it known, would not again risk a snub, by taking the initiative. But Metternich thought there was hope at Paris that another power might take up the idea and that there had already been a trial balloon. At any rate, it seems likely that when Napoleon thought of a congress in these years, Italy was at the center of his thoughts. The September Convention of 1864, by which France committed itself to evacuate Rome within two years and Italy to prevent an attack on the pope, was not a solution to the Roman question, merely a postponement. Moreover, one of its objectives was to turn attention from Rome to Venetia, and a transaction in regard to Venetia would involve precisely those intricate adjustments that in the past had caused the French emperor to prefer conference diplomacy. At the end of 1864 he told Metternich that his intentions in regard to Italy were very simple—to promote a peaceful solution of the Venetian question between Italy and Austria "by means of friendly terms with Italy, through political contrivances, or in consequence of a system of compensations." A year later, Drouyn de Lhuys told the Spanish ambassador that in the event of disturbances at Rome "the ques tion could cease to be an Italian one and change into a question of European order or balance." Such was the situation when, in February, 1866, the overthrow of Prince Couza, ruler of the Danubian Principalities, opened the door once again to the sort of large transaction of which Napoleon was so fond.[18]

18. Case, *French Opinion on War and Diplomacy*, 161; Cowley to Russell, Paris, January 31, 1864, in PRO, FO, 519, 231:97; Metternich to Rechberg, Paris, August 21, 1864, in HHSA, PA IX, Fr. Ber., 1864, I–X, Box 78, no. 30B, fols. 374v–75; Talleyrand to Drouyn de Lhuys, Berlin, February 20, 1864, in *Origines*, I, 343, no. 224; *Origines*, VI, 367 n. (on the rumors in 1865); Comte Gustave Armand Henri de Reiset to Drouyn de Lhuys, Hanover, August 1, 1865, in *Origines*, VI, 371, no. 1472; Goltz to Bismarck, Paris, confidential, August 4, 1865, in Oncken (ed.), *Rheinpolitik*, I, 48–51, no. 20; Metternich to Rechberg, Paris, reserved, July 19, 1865, in HHSA, PA IX, Fr. Ber., 1865, Box 81, no. 34B, fol. 91v; memorandum of Metternich, regarding a conversation of November 29, 1864, with Napoleon, in *Origines*, V, 126, no. 1074; marquis de Lema to the Spanish minister of state, Paris, October 24, 1865, in AMAE, MD, Papiers Rouher, II.

CHAPTER 13

Crisis in Germany
The Congress Proposal
of 1866

The events of 1866 as they affected France may be studied from the point of view of Franco-German relations or from that of Franco-Italian relations. But while both are essential viewpoints, neither singly nor together do they fully illuminate the role of Napoleon III, his motives and objectives. Significantly, the starting point of French involvement in the crisis of that year was not Germany or Italy but the Danubian Principalities. Napoleon had long hoped that Austria might be brought to accept an exchange of Venetia for the Principalities. His plans had been frustrated more than once, but in early 1866, optimism again appeared, both at Florence and in the mind of Gramont, the French ambassador at Vienna. In early February, Turin and Vienna unofficially discussed the possibility of an exchange. Francis Joseph remained adamantly opposed, but there were some in the Austrian capital who were more flexible. Under these circumstances the overthrow on February 23 of Prince Couza, ruler of the two Principalities, introduced into a formerly frozen situation a degree of fluidity. "The policy which has guided France in the Principalities, is, I think, becoming apparent," wrote Cowley. "They have supported Couza, thinking he would go on, until they could come to terms with Austria and make some exchange of the Principalities against Venetia. Whatever negotiations may be undertaken now, we shall have this undercurrent at work."[1]

---

1. On the Franco-German aspect, see Pottinger, *Napoleon III and the German crisis;* on the Franco-Italian aspect of the crisis, see Bush, *Venetia Redeemed.* Cowley to Clarendon, Paris, January 19, 1866, in PRO, FO, 519, 13:368; Henry George Elliot to Clarendon, Florence, February 2, 1866, in PRO, FO, 45, 85:34; Bush, *Venetia Redeemed,* 42–43; Cowley to Clarendon, Paris, February 25, 1866, in PRO, FO, 519, 232:105.

As it happened, an ambassadorial conference was already meeting at Paris to ratify the work of the European commission on the Danube. It seemed to the Russian ambassador at London that this meeting might well be broadened to consider the problem of the Principalities. Paris, which in 1861 had shown no enthusiasm for such a conference and had encouraged Austria to reject it (Was Napoleon unwilling, before the time was ripe, to risk losing his best hope for an exchange of Venetia?), now proved amenable. The invitation to a conference to meet at Paris went out to the great powers and to Italy on February 27. Cowley was convinced from the beginning that the French government was interested in the Principalities primarily as a means of getting Venetia for Italy. In fact, Drouyn de Lhuys had already hinted at London that an exchange of Venetia for the Principalities would be an excellent solution to the problem. Before the end of February, there were rumors in several quarters that the conference would become a congress that would proceed to a general pacification, linking the German, Italian, and Eastern questions. It was in this atmosphere that, on the evening of February 28, the Italian ambassador at Paris, Nigra, had a significant conversation with Napoleon.[2]

General Alfonso La Marmora, the Italian president of council and a longtime friend of Napoleon's wanted to follow a pro-French policy, but events were rapidly isolating him and threatening to force his government into dependence upon Prussia. He had therefore accepted at once Nigra's suggestion of February 24 that the idea of a Venetian-Principalities exchange be revived. Nigra, however, was more interested in recruiting Napoleon's support for an Italian-Prussian alliance against Austria (thus persuading La Marmora) than in promoting a territorial exchange in which he had no real faith. There can be no certainty, then, as to who said what to whom during the interview between the minister and the emperor. But Nigra's account does not conflict with what we know of Napoleon's attitudes and actions either before or after the conversation. The minister informed Napoleon of what he must already have known, Prussia's overtures at Flor-

---

2. La Tour d'Auvergne to Drouyn de Lhuys, London, February 24, 1866, in *Origines*, VII, 324, no. 1789; Metternich to Rechberg, Paris, July 8, 1861, in HHSA, PA IX, Fr. Ber., 1861, VII–XII, Box 70, fols. 77–77v; Cowley to Clarendon, Paris, February 25, 1866, in PRO, FO, 519, 13:395–400, no. 215; La Tour d'Auvergne to Drouyn de Lhuys, London, confidential, February 27, 1866, in *Origines*, VII, 343, no. 1811; Benedetti to Drouyn de Lhuys, Berlin, February 28, 1866, in *Origines*, VII, 345–47, no. 1814; Meroux de Valois to Drouyn de Lhuys, Kiel, February 28, 1866, in *Origines*, VII, 348–49, no. 1816; Malaret to Drouyn de Lhuys, Florence, March 16, 1866, in *Origines*, VIII, 9–10, no. 1899.

ence to gain Italian support in the growing conflict between the two great German powers. He marshaled arguments favoring the exchange of Venetia for the Principalities—arguments for which the emperor certainly had no need. And Napoleon made two proposals: that France or Britain or both, rather than Italy, should present the proposition of an exchange at Vienna; and that, to force a favorable Austrian decision, Italy should incite Prussia to war and should put itself in condition to do so. He was agreeable to drawing out as long as possible the conference on the Principalities so that it might charge itself with the necessary arrangements. And this time he did not raise, as in the past, the question of approval by the population of the Principalities. In a word, concluded Nigra, three points were agreed upon: "1. Italy should incite Prussia to war and in case of need should find herself ready to do so; 2. the emperor will present the proposal [of an exchange of Venetia for the Danubian Principalities] at Vienna in the way he thinks most prudent; 3. in the meantime the conference will be drawn out at length."[3]

Two major questions confronted the conference on the Principalities that convened at Paris on March 10—union and a foreign prince. Both were vital to Napoleon's plans and both were opposed by Russia. Saint Petersburg wanted an assembly of each Principality to meet and vote separately, hoping that Moldavia, at least, might choose to separate. Britain vacillated, but Paris, maintaining the "voeux des populations" argument, insisted on a single assembly and a foreign prince. Drouyn de Lhuys would have preferred a compromise, trading abandonment of the foreign prince for conference acceptance of unity. But Napoleon stood firm, and as long as he did, agreement was impossible. Probably it was on the emperor's instructions that Drouyn de Lhuys, who had forcefully implied before the conference that no single power had the right to thwart the otherwise unanimous will of Europe when "le caractère européen d'une question est manifeste," now bluntly announced that "if . . . the Conference should prefer the principle of separation, the Emperor would say that his opinions were not to be guided by the opinions of a Conference, and that he should abide by his own views." This was certainly an uncharacteristic argument, and Cowley, who detected the shadow of the Venetian question in Nigra's enthusiastic support for the idea of a foreign prince, smelled a rat. And then, on

3. See Bush, *Venetia Redeemed*, 44–45. For the conversation between Napoleon III and Nigra, see Nigra to General Alfonso La Marmora, Paris, private and confidential, March 1, 1866, in Colombo *et al.* (eds.), *Carteggi di Nigra*, 156–60.

April 12, although the British government had at last come down on the side of allowing the people of the Principalities to have a foreign prince if they wished, Napoleon declared that this demand could be abandoned for the present. The way was open to a compromise that would end the conference.[4]

The link between Napoleon's tactics at the conference and his effort to bring Austria to accept an exchange of Venetia for the Principalities seems obvious. On March 6, Drouyn de Lhuys had launched the campaign at London. He admitted the difficulties. Compensation would have to be found for Turkey, and the right of the people of the Principalities to self-determination must not be sacrificed to "les convenances de l'Europe." And yet, "what seems difficult or even impossible in the present state of things can change aspect if the circumstances were themselves to take another turn." In a private letter of the same day the foreign minister was more explicit. In the event of a war of Prussia and Italy against Austria, Vienna would perhaps take quite a different view of the proposed exchange than it had in the past. "But might not this combination serve as well to prevent the conflict if adopted in time?" Apparently Drouyn de Lhuys, although he was not to be informed until the end of the month of the Prussian-Italian alliance negotiations and of Napoleon's encouragement of them, understood the emperor's intentions. In London, however, there was no enthusiasm. Although the French ambassador, Henri Godefroi, prince de La Tour d'Auvergne, had reported that both Clarendon and Russell had long favored such an exchange of territory and that Clarendon had referred to Drouyn de Lhuys' earlier suggestion that the crisis in the Principalities might be turned to Italy's advantage, Clarendon was in fact strongly opposed to the cession of the Principalities to Austria. He

---

4. Cowley to Clarendon, Paris, March 13, 1866, in PRO, FO, 519, 13:434, no. 312; Metternich to Count Alexander von Mensdorff-Pouilly-Dietrichstein, telegram, no. 10B, March 13, 1866, in HHSA, PA IX, Fr. Ber., 1866, I–V, Box 82, fols. 191–91v; Cowley to Clarendon, Paris, March 12, 1866, in PRO, FO, 519, 232:121–22; Drouyn de Lhuys to La Tour d'Auvergne, Paris, March 3, 1866, in Origines, VII, 364, no. 1832; Cowley to Clarendon, Paris, March 13, 1866, in PRO, FO, 519, 13:434, no. 312; Cowley to Elliot, Paris, March 27, 1866, in PRO, FO, 519, 232:153; Cowley to Clarendon, Paris, secret, April 2, 1866, in PRO, FO, 519, 13:482, no. 405; Cowley to Clarendon, Paris, most confidential, April 12, 1866, in PRO, FO, 519, 13:501, no. 451. The compromise was that there should be one assembly at Bucharest, which would have "faculté pour les députés de voter séparément." If union were agreed to, the assembly would elect a native hospodar. The Paris conference, which was unable to prevent a foreign prince (Charles of Hohenzollern) from being elected hospodar in May with Napoleon III's secret support, adjourned on June 25 (Ollivier, L'empire libéral, VIII, 41, 84–85; Mosse, The Rise and Fall of the Crimean System, 145–54).

replied to the French proposal on March 9 that Britain saw too many obstacles to the plan (Russian resistance, Austrian reluctance, Turkish refusal, and anti-Austrian sentiment in the Principalities) to take the initiative.[5]

Saint Petersburg, encouraged by Bismarck, was indeed adamant. "Unacceptable—even to the point of war," scrawled the czar across a telegram recounting the rumor of a Venetia-Principalities exchange. Nor was the atmosphere at Vienna more promising, despite rumors, which proved groundless, and intimations, which had no sequels. When Eugénie, probably at Napoleon's request, broached the matter to Metternich about March 12, arguing that Russia was too weak to resist effectively, the ambassador's reaction was so violent that the official Austrian rejection written on March 16 by the foreign minister, Count Alexander von Mensdorff-Pouilly-Dietrichstein, could have come as no surprise. On March 17, Nigra informed his government that Napoleon, faithful to his promise, had tried to obtain a territorial exchange but had failed. Five days later, the emperor accepted Metternich's stipulation that the question of Venetia would not be raised again unless in connection with a general redrawing of boundaries in Europe. In this context, Napoleon's decision to permit the conference on the Principalities to complete its work can be seen as his admission that the conference could not usefully undertake the task of resolving the Venetian question. His first initiative in the developing German crisis had centered, then, not on Germany but on Italy, where lay, no doubt, his greatest concern.[6]

5. Drouyn de Lhuys to La Tour d'Auvergne, Paris, March 6, 1866, in *Origines*, VII, 379–80, no. 1850; Drouyn de Lhuys to La Tour d'Auvergne, Paris, private, March 6, 1866, in *Origines*, VII, 381, no. 1851; Pottinger, *Napoleon III and the German Crisis*, 71; La Tour d'Auvergne to Drouyn de Lhuys, London, confidential, February 27, 1866, in *Origines*, VII, 343, no. 1811; La Tour d'Auvergne to Drouyn de Lhuys, London, March 6, 1866, in *Origines*, VII, 384–85, no. 1854; La Tour d'Auvergne to Drouyn de Lhuys, London, confidential, March 9, 1866, in *Origines*, VII, 395–96, no. 1865. On Clarendon's opposition to the exchange (he thought Drouyn de Lhuys' intent was to dismember Turkey), see Millman, *British Foreign Policy*, 28–30. However, the British government *did* informally advise Austria to give up Venetia, which may account for La Tour d'Auvergne's confusion. A strong case can be made against this British refusal to support a proposal that might have prevented the war (Ramsay, *Idealism and Foreign Policy*, 164–71).

6. Bush, *Venetia Redeemed*, 50; Talleyrand to Drouyn de Lhuys, Saint Petersburg, March 14, 1866, in *Origines*, VII, 343, no. 1811; Pottinger, *Napoleon III and the German Crisis*, 73–76; Nigra to La Marmora, Paris, March 17, 1866, in La Marmora, *Un peu plus de lumière*, 133. Writing from the viewpoint of Franco-German relations, Pottinger suggests that this was in fact Napoleon's *second* initiative; his first (at the beginning of March) having been a bid for the Rhine through alliance with Prussia.

Napoleon could not avoid considering as well the position that France would take in the quarrel between Austria and Prussia. Probably he would have tried to convert the conference into a congress that would link a Venetia-Principalities exchange and other questions to the German dispute, attempt to reconcile the proposed exchange of territory with the principle of nationalities, and thus seek a solution short of war. But now that there was to be no congress, it was necessary to decide. Apart from a true neutrality, which neither French opinion nor his own concept of the role of Bonapartist France in the world would have condoned, Napoleon's choices were three: to preserve the status quo by making war impossible; to gain Venetia for Italy and territory for France by participating in a war against Austria; or to use the threat of conflict (or, if necessary, the war itself) in order to move Europe along the paths of revision, concert, and satisfaction of nationalities that he had long charted. Preservation of the status quo held no charms for the French emperor. The status quo in 1866 meant still the preservation of those treaties of 1815 that had been made against France; it meant continued Austrian control of Venetia and the reproach of promises unredeemed; it meant the dominance of conservative Austria over "liberal" Prussia, the official denial of the principle of nationalities, and a Metternichian interpretation of the concert of Europe. Certainly Cowley's indictment was just. Napoleon did not sufficiently fear a war because, had he done so, he could easily have prevented one. Already he had rejected a British proposal that France and Britain should protest against the impending conflict on the grounds that "protest would be futile unless backed by threats and that France was not prepared to threaten." A month later he would make equally short shrift of Clarendon's suggestion that the neutral powers present a moral appeal for peace in the name of the protocol of Paris of 1856.[7]

But if Napoleon was not yet ready to make the preservation of peace for its own sake his main objective, did this mean that he was willing to wage war for a national objective? Certainly if he had to choose between Austria and Prussia, his preference would be the latter. There was the ring of truth in his words to Goltz, Prussia's ambassador to France: "Even in the eventuality of the struggle taking on dimensions

---

7. Cowley to Clarendon, Paris, most confidential, April 12, 1866, in PRO, FO, 519, 13:502–505, no. 451; Cowley to Clarendon, Paris, April 2, 3, 1866, both in PRO, FO, 519; 232:165, 166; Clarendon to Cowley, London, secret and confidential, May 2, 1866, in Origines, IX, 440, no. 2218.

that are unforeseeable at this time, I am convinced that I could always reach an understanding with Prussia whose interests in a host of questions are identical with those of France, while I see no ground on which I would ever meet with Austria." And yet the French emperor cultivated both German powers. He talked of neutrality to Vienna and approved an important loan to Austria and the negotiation of a Franco-Austrian commercial treaty, while to Prussia he said, in effect, "Tell me what it is you want of me and what you will offer for my services." This refusal to take the initiative, despite his obvious sympathy for Prussia, was disconcerting at Berlin. By March, Bismarck, who had himself failed during a stay at Biarritz in October, 1865, to discover anything of Napoleon's intentions except that he was most concerned with the Italian question and would not enter into alliance with Austria, felt impelled to have William I write to the French emperor to ask that he be more explicit. But when Goltz lifted the veil to reveal a bit of Bismarck's plans for Germany, Napoleon merely indicated that in such an eventuality he would need compensation, possibly the frontier of 1814. His reply to William was completely noncommittal: "If serious events arise in Germany, my express intention is to observe neutrality while preserving with Your Majesty's government the friendly relations which we have long enjoyed. If later, as a result of extraordinary circumstances the balance of Europe were to change, I would ask that Your Majesty and I examine together the new bases in order to guarantee the interests of my country." Undoubtedly Napoleon, after his interview with Goltz on March 5, knew that Prussia could not offer German territory to France as compensation. Several days later, Bismarck told him so explicitly. Would Napoleon have used an acceptable Prussian offer in order to launch a general war in Europe? Cowley clearly doubted it. "I still hold to the opinion," he wrote to Clarendon, "that he will not go to war for any acquisition of territory, tho' if a favorable opportunity occurred, he will get what he can by negotiation." It was the same opinion that the ambassador had expressed in 1864 and again at the end of 1865.[8] In fact, the only evidence we have that Napoleon seriously considered a war in alliance with Prussia is in the explanations he himself offered of why he had rejected such an adventure. There the matter must rest.

8. Goltz to Bismarck, Paris, confidential, February 17, 1866, in Oncken (ed.), *Rheinpolitik*, I, 90, no. 33; Pottinger, *Napoleon III and the German Crisis*, 15–71; William I to Napoleon III, Berlin, March 3, 1866, in Oncken (ed.), *Rheinpolitik*, I, 92–93, no. 35 (the draft is in Bismarck's hand); Goltz to Bismarck, Paris, very confidential, March 6,

Goltz had speculated in August, 1865, that if war threatened between Austria and Prussia the French emperor would have to choose between two roles. On the one hand, he could act to gain compensation for France; on the other, he could, as arbiter of the European peace, summon a congress. Napoleon had himself recognized this choice, as he later confirmed to Nigra. "The Emperor hesitated for a long time between two courses of action, that is, between the peaceful solution of the Congress and an alliance with Prussia and with us, an alliance founded on the cession of some Rhine province. But the overtures made to Prussia in this respect had not been accepted. Therefore, the Emperor decided in favor of the Congress." If "overtures" were seriously made before the decision for the congress was taken, no evidence of them survives. Whether Napoleon would have been tempted to war by a daring Prussian initiative, a "golden bridge" for France to the Rhine, we cannot know, for such an offer was not made. What we do know with certainty is that by early April he had turned his back on war[9] and that before the end of the month he would bring forward the idea of a European congress. What hope was there, after so many disappointments, of persuading Austria to accept such a meeting before a war had been fought? The answer has to be sought in the Prussian-Italian alliance negotiations of March and April, 1866, and especially in the French emperor's role in them.

By mid-March, as Napoleon knew, Prussia was actively seeking an

---

1866, in Oncken (ed.), *Rheinpolitik*, I, 94–98, no. 37; Napoleon III to William I, Paris, March 7, 1866, in Oncken (ed.), *Rheinpolitik*, I, 99, no. 38; Bismarck to Goltz, Berlin, telegram, March 9, 1866, in Oncken (ed.), *Rheinpolitik*, I, 105, no. 41; Cowley to Clarendon, Paris, April 13, 1866, in PRO, FO, 519, 232:183; Cowley to Russell, Paris, February 23, 1864, in PRO, FO, 519, 231:112–13; Cowley to Clarendon, Compiègne, December 2, 1865, in PRO, FO, 519, 232:50–54.

9. Goltz to Bismarck, Paris, confidential, August 4, 1865, in Oncken (ed.), *Rheinpolitik*, I, 48–51, no. 20; Nigra to La Marmora, Paris, May 28, 1866, in Colombo *et al.* (eds.), *Carteggi di Nigra*, 166. Metternich wrote of Napoleon: "Er glaubt nicht an den Krieg und sagte, ce serait une trop grosse affaire" (Metternich to Mensdorff, Paris, telegram, April 5, 1866, in Oncken (ed.), *Rheinpolitik*, I, 123, no. 57). And again: "L'Empereur m'a dit qu'il ne croyait pas à la guerre, que c'était une trop grosse affaire pour que l'une ou l'autre des puissances adverses prisse la résolution de marcher en avant. Quant à lui, il était décidé à maintenir une stricte neutralité en tant que les intérêts de la France ne seraient pas compromis" (Metternich to Mensdorff, Paris, reserved, April 9, 1866, in Oncken (ed.), *Rheinpolitik*, I, 127–28, no. 60). Cowley believed that Napoleon "would not be sorry if hostilities broke out" but would do nothing to encourage a rupture (Cowley to Clarendon, Paris, April 10, 1866, PRO, FO, 519, 232:176–77). Later he reported, after a conversation with Napoleon, "He seemed to have made up his mind to peace" (Cowley to Clarendon, Paris, April 24, 1866, in PRO, FO, 519, 232:191). This did not mean, of course, that Napoleon was certain the war between Prussia and Austria could be prevented.

offensive and defensive alliance with Italy. Florence wanted such an alliance for a fixed period of time. Bismarck, however, preferred a vaguer treaty, without date. Consulted by Nigra on March 21, the French emperor advised Florence to "sign a treaty with Prussia, however vague and noncommittal it may be, for it is very desirable to furnish M. de Bismarck with the necessary means to push the King to war." And yet, when Bismarck on March 27 proposed a treaty binding Italy to go to war with Austria if Prussia were itself to do so within three months, Napoleon withdrew all official support, telling Nigra and Arese (whom La Marmora had sent to assure himself of the emperor's intentions) that an alliance of the sort proposed was "useful," but that he spoke "as a friend and without any responsibility." Moreover, Benedetti, the French ambassador at Berlin, advised the Italian delegation there on April 6 *not* to sign, but to have another project worked out to present after Prussian mobilization. Although there are the usual unresolvable contradictions lying in the way of a full and complete understanding of French policy, it seems obvious that Napoleon did not approve of the Prussian-Italian alliance initialed on April 8. It gave too much leverage to Bismarck, placing Italy, and therefore France, in too much jeopardy. This attitude, coupled with his earlier decision against war and his subsequent one for a congress, strongly suggests that Napoleon was continuing the policy he had adopted at the beginning of the crisis. The alliance that he preferred would lead not to war but to negotiation. Already, on March 10, Metternich was informed "at the Tuileries" that, while France could not prevent Italy from entering into an alliance with Prussia, Austria could always seek an understanding based on compensations and that the door would be left open to such an entente. If Vienna understood its own interests, Napoleon insisted a month later to Cowley, Austria would "make friends" with Italy at once and then there would be no war. Perhaps much of the uncertainty persisting in regard to the French emperor's role in these alliance negotiations can be dispelled with the acceptance of the thesis that for Napoleon the major function of any agreement between Prussia and Italy was to frighten Austria to the conference table. If the congress failed and war there must be, to have Italy and Prussia together would even the odds and increase the chances that Venetia could be wrested from Austria in a peace settlement over which France would preside.[10]

10. On Napoleon's role in the negotiations, see Bush, *Venetia Redeemed*, 49, 52–55, and Pottinger, *Napoleon III and the German Crisis*, 80–81. Metternich to Mensdorff, Paris, telegram, no. 26, March 10, 1866, in HHSA, PA IX, Fr. Ber., 1866, I–V,

Certainly a congress proposal was widely anticipated during March. At the beginning of the month Drouyn de Lhuys had referred once again to Napoleon's initiative of almost three years before:

> Undoubtedly it is desirable that any attack on the European order should be met at once by the opposition of all of Europe. . . . But this role of guardian of the peace . . . does not belong to any single power; it can only be exercised in a general way. And it is this mutual guarantee that the emperor hoped to establish in proposing two years ago the reunion of a European congress. If His Majesty's initiative was not appreciated then, the state of insecurity throughout a great part of Europe has proved only too well since then how farsighted this generous thought was.

Although the French foreign minister firmly rejected the idea of an initiative by France, arguing that those who had now learned from experience should take the first step, Goltz detected in Napoleon, who had referred to the fact that any territorial exchanges decided upon after the war had begun would have to be agreed upon by a congress, the same state of mind that had led to the 1863 proposal. On April 23, in the course of a court ball, Napoleon suggested to the Prussian ambassador that war could be avoided and the goals of the Prussian-Italian alliance achieved through a revival of the congress proposal he had made two years earlier. The emperor badly wanted to avoid having to take the initiative. On April 28 he hinted unsuccessfully to Metternich that Vienna might want to do so; and when several days later he approached Cowley, without Drouyn de Lhuys' knowledge, he was remarkably circumspect, sending La Valette, the minister of the interior, to make sure that in proposing a congress Napoleon would not again be humiliated by a British refusal. Part of this tactic, perhaps, was the emperor's studied emphasis, in his first conversation about the congress with Cowley, on the difficulties in its path. However, this was also a time when he seems genuinely to have doubted whether war could be avoided. Nevertheless, on May 2, Drouyn de Lhuys requested the French ambassadors to the great powers to sound confidentially the opinions of those courts in regard to a congress, and while the foreign minister tried hard to attribute the idea of a congress to Cowley (to such an extent that the Englishman was moved to label him an "unscrupulous liar"), obviously the initiative was Napoleon's. On May 8, Drouyn de Lhuys instructed the French representa-

---

Box 82, fols. 179–79v; Cowley to Clarendon, Paris, April 10, 1866, in PRO, FO, 519, 232:177–78.

tives at London and Saint Petersburg to persuade those capitals to join France in proposing to Prussia, Austria, Italy, and the German Confederation "a common deliberation of all the great powers" concerning the cession of Venetia to Italy (with compensation for Austria), the fate of the Elbe Duchies, and German reform.[11]

Napoleon wanted "un congrès sincère," Ollivier later argued of the emperor's role, and he hoped that it would succeed. Cowley, who at first believed the congress was merely a sop to public opinion, came on balance to feel that it was a serious proposal. As early as May 1 the ambassador noted that Napoleon "seemed sincerely anxious to turn the notion of a congress to good account." Moreover, by the end of the first week in May, the French emperor apparently believed, after several days of doubt, that this could be done and war avoided. "He told Rothschild last night," Cowley wrote on the eighth, "that he thought peace would be preserved by means of a congress—that much would depend upon the English Government, and La Valette and Fould have both told me that he is confident of the success of a congress." A week later the Englishman was even more certain that Napoleon sincerely wanted a congress and that he preferred peace to war. Goltz agreed, arguing that the French emperor was "seriously engaged" in arranging the congress, that it would meet, and that Prussia must accept. Nigra, Beyens, Metternich, and others all testified to Napoleon's sincerity and optimism. It would be, the emperor told Emile de Girardin, "a disgrace if the Plenipotentiaries assembled in Paris should not be able to prevent such a massacre as a war would produce." Napoleon's obvious disappointment at the subsequent failure of the congress is further evidence of his sincerity.[12]

11. Drouyn de Lhuys to Gramont, Paris, March 6, 1866, in *Origines*, VII, 383, no. 1852; Drouyn de Lhuys to d'Astorg, Paris, March 16, 1866, in *Origines*, VII, 4, no. 1894; Goltz to William I, Paris, reserved, March 17, 1866, in Oncken (ed.), *Rheinpolitik*, I, 111–15, no. 49; Goltz to William I, Paris, April 25, 1866, in Oncken (ed.), *Rheinpolitik*, I, 142–43, no. 71; Metternich to Mensdorff, Paris, telegram, no. 60, April 28, 1866, in HHSA, PA IX, Fr. Ber., 1866, I–V, Box 82, fol. 418; Cowley to Clarendon, Paris, secret and confidential, May 1, 1866, in PRO, FO, 519, 13:532–38; Cowley to Clarendon, Paris, May 1, 1866, in PRO, FO, 519, 232:197; Drouyn de Lhuys to La Tour d'Auvergne, Paris, May 12, 1866, in *Origines*, IX, 105, no. 2322; Drouyn de Lhuys to Gramont, Paris, telegram, May 11, 1866, in *Origines*, IX, 94, no. 2314; Metternich to Mensdorff, Paris, telegram, May 11, 1866, in Oncken (ed.), *Rheinpolitik*, I, 193, no. 99; Drouyn de Lhuys to French representatives at London and Saint Petersburg, confidential, May 8, 1866, in *Origines*, IX, 53–54, no. 2278.

12. Ollivier, *L'empire libéral*, VIII, 147; Cowley to Clarendon, Paris, May 27, 1866, in PRO, FO, 519, 232:251; Cowley to Clarendon, Paris, secret and confidential, May 1, 1866, PRO, FO, 519, 13:537; Cowley to Clarendon, Paris, May 8, 1866, in PRO, FO,

A similar conclusion can be drawn from the actions of French diplomacy during April and May. Almost from the moment of the signing of the treaty with Prussia, the Italian government came under pressure from Paris to avoid any aggressive action. "It was hardly worth asking my advice," Napoleon acidly told the Italian ambassador on May 1, "in order to do exactly the opposite of what I counselled." On May 5 the emperor asked Nigra if Italy could break its engagement with Prussia; when Florence declined on a point of honor, Napoleon remarked "that in order to gain time he would do everything possible to bring up again for consideration the idea of a congress." On May 6 in a speech at Auxerre, the French emperor alluded to revision; this, coupled with new reminders in the preceding days to Prussia that France would demand compensation if any major changes occurred in Europe, can only be interpreted either as a bid for alliance with Prussia or as an effort to frighten Bismarck out of launching a war. But the objections to the first thesis are serious. Napoleon had no reason to believe that the situation that had dissuaded him in March from seriously contemplating an alliance with Prussia had changed (as indeed it had not). Why, then, should he have made another effort? Why did he not inform Florence of his desire for a Franco-Prussian alliance? Why did he not speak clearly to Bismarck (who, after all, could not wage a war if France were opposed) rather than content himself with hinting again at a Prussian initiative concerning compensation (May 1) and sending an emissary (May 5) who may or may not have spoken in the emperor's name? Moreover, the chronology is wrong. On May 2, Drouyn de Lhuys instructed his agents to begin soundings for a congress that he, the foreign minister, opposed. On the sixth, the day of the Auxerre speech, Napoleon promised Nigra that he would bring the congress idea forward; and by May 8 the emperor was fully committed to peace and to the congress. Could this position be ascribed to the failure of French opinion, following Auxerre, to rally to a war policy? Surely a period of not quite two days is too short a time for any meaningful reading of public opinion. The

---

519, 232:210; Goltz to Bismarck, Paris, confidential, May 8, 1866, in V. Wellesley and Sencourt (eds.), *Conversations with Napoleon III*, 264–66; Nigra to La Marmora, Paris, telegram, May 28, 1866, in La Marmora, *Un peu plus de lumière*, 267; Metternich to Mensdorff, Paris, telegram, June 1, 1866, in Oncken (ed.), *Rheinpolitik*, I, 247, no. 128; Cowley to Clarendon, Paris, May 25, June 4, 1866, both in PRO, FO, 519, 232:244, 269–73; Nigra to La Marmora, Paris, telegram, June 4, 1866, in La Marmora, *Un peu plus de lumière*, 293–94.

possibility that Bismarck himself noted, that Napoleon wanted to frighten Prussia out of precipitating a war, remains the most likely explanation of an admittedly confused series of events and is strengthened by the emperor's remarks to Goltz of May 8.[13]

Napoleon's initiative of the congress against the advice of his foreign minister, the many witnesses to his apparent sincerity, his own words (including a defense of the congress in a meeting of the council of ministers on May 18), his efforts to dissuade Italy and Prussia from precipitating hostilities, all attest to the accuracy of Ollivier's judgment. The French emperor wanted a congress, and he hoped that it would succeed. Historians have been inclined to search for reasons why Napoleon should have turned to conference diplomacy in 1866. In reality, however, it would have required more explanation had he not. His fear of the uncertainties of war, his desire to promote European solutions to European problems, his penchant for congresses, his determination to avoid another French military involvement in Italy,[14] his awareness of the state of opinion in France against war, his realization from an early date that Bismarck could not or would not freely offer German territory to France as compensation, and his matter-of-fact reluctance to see a great war erupt in Europe with no guarantee of

13. Metternich to Mensdorff, Paris, reserved, April 9, 1866, in Oncken (ed.), *Rheinpolitik*, I, 127–28, no. 60; Nigra to La Marmora, Paris, private, April 25, 1866, in Colombo *et al.* (eds.), *Carteggi di Nigra*, 165–66; Nigra to La Marmora, Paris, May 1, 1866, in La Marmora, *Un peu plus de lumière*, 201–202; La Marmora to Nigra, Florence, telegram, May 5, 1866, in La Marmora, *Un peu plus de lumière*, 217; Nigra to La Marmora, Paris, telegram, May 7, 1866, in La Marmora, *Un peu plus de lumière*, 224. La Marmora had himself suggested that the congress might be a way to prevent war until the Prussian-Italian alliance expired on July 8. This was apparently the first time Napoleon or Drouyn de Lhuys talked with Nigra about a congress. It followed a conversation between Metternich and Napoleon in which the ambassador suggested that if France and Italy remained neutral and Austria could win adequate compensation in a war with Prussia, Austria would give up Venetia. Goltz to Bismarck, Paris, confidential, May 8, 1866, in V. Wellesley and Sencourt (eds.), *Conversations with Napoleon III*, 261. For development of the thesis that Napoleon seriously sought a Franco-Prussian-Italian alliance but withdrew following the Auxerre speech, see Pottinger, *Napoleon III and the German Crisis*, 108–126.

14. Cowley to Clarendon, Paris, May 4, 1866, in PRO, FO, 519, 13:542–44; meeting, May 18, 1866, in Oncken (ed.), *Rheinpolitik*, I, 210, no. 112A. "Shall I tell you now why I have decided to call for a congress? All right, it's because the war, now imminent, frightens me today by the great proportions which it threatens to assume" (Metternich to Mensdorff, Paris, May 23, 1866, in Oncken (ed.), *Rheinpolitik*, I, 228–30, no. 120). Bush (*Venetia Redeemed*, 58–59) argues convincingly that Napoleon's commitment to the congress was increased when Austria unexpectedly mobilized on its Italian front about April 26. If the war began *in Italy* and the Italians were defeated, Napoleon might have to intervene.

advantages for France—all were natural reasons that he should have initiated a congress proposal at the end of April and worked consistently thereafter for its success.

But one qualification is necessary. In the spring of 1866, Napoleon was no more ready than he had ever been to accept a concert of Europe whose purpose was to defend the status quo or a congress whose efforts would be restricted to preventing war. Nothing better illustrates this than his Auxerre speech. Three days before, Adolphe Thiers, in a masterly effort, had defended the treaties of 1815 with reference to Germany. In his reply, Napoleon made clear that he did not share this dedication to France's "traditional policy." And to emphasize the point he added to the *Moniteur* report of the speech a paragraph destined for immediate notoriety. The people of the Yonne, he said, "know, as do the great majority of the French people, that their interests are mine and that I detest as they do those treaties of 1815 which today some people would make the sole basis of our foreign policy." In particular, Napoleon was determined that the congress (or war) must finally resolve the Venetian question. If Vienna could be persuaded to accept in advance the principle of a cession to Italy, so much the better. These efforts (May 4–8) failed, since Austria insisted on adequate compensation (Silesia) as well as the promise of French and Italian neutrality, and since Italy felt that its alliance with Prussia could not be broken with honor. Even had the Franco-Austrian negotiations succeeded, however, Napoleon must have intended, as Mensdorff suspected, that they would serve as prelude to the congress, which alone could arrange the required compensations. The emperor made no secret of his determination. "For himself," he told Cowley, "he must say that the annexation of Venetia to Italy must prove the first item of any arrangement to which he could consent either in a Congress or in a more limited understanding"; otherwise, he would leave his son sitting on a barrel of gunpowder. To Metternich he was even more blunt: "I have just one interest in the whole affair, that is to be done with the Italian question by means of the cession of Venetia. If this cession can be brought about by the peace, I shall do all possible to further it; if not, I shall profit from any opportunities which the war between Austria and Prussia may afford me in this direction."[15]

15. Mensdorff wrote: "Si le Gouvernement français s'est prévalu de vos entretiens intimes avec l'Empereur Napoléon pour nous représenter aux autres Puissances comme prêts à admettre en principe que nous devons céder Venise je n'hésite pas à qualifier ce procédé d'un abus de confiance. . . . Si le Gouvernement français a eu recours à de semblables moyens pour amener la réunion du Congrés, nous ne nous trouvons guère en-

Small wonder, then, that Italy, thus reassured, accepted the congress while it was still in the rumor stage. The other powers were not so eager. London, always fearful of French designs, preferred, as we have seen, a pronouncement for peace by France, Russia, and Britain in the name of the protocol of Paris of 1856; London would at any rate insist, as a condition for accepting the congress, on "the necessity of precisely defining beforehand the purposes for which it is convoked." Saint Petersburg, wanting to risk neither a rupture with Prussia nor an Austrian gain in the Near East, shared this lack of enthusiasm, but Gorchakov made the tactical error of shielding himself behind an anticipated British veto. Instead, Clarendon accepted on May 9 a preliminary meeting at Paris of the British and Russian ambassadors with Drouyn de Lhuys.[16]

This meeting, convened on the fifteenth, began at once to consider a tentative invitation to the congress drafted by Drouyn de Lhuys, which was to be addressed by the neutral great powers to Austria, Prussia, Italy, and the German Confederation:

> The purpose of these deliberations is self-evident to all. The Venetian question, that of the Duchies, federal reform, these are the three questions now posed, the solution of which through diplomatic channels would forestall the redoubtable extremities which, with reason, alarm Europe. The discussion would thus be concerned with the cession of Venetia to Italy (taking into account compensations which Austria would require and guarantees which would have to be given as to the temporal power of the Holy See), with the definitive settlement of the fate of the Elbe Duchies, and, finally, with the reform of the Germanic Pact, inasmuch as it might concern the European balance of power.

---

couragés à y compter sur une attitude bienveillante de la France. . . . Nous ne pouvons pas admettre que vos conversations intimes avec l'Empereur Napoléon deviennent le point de délibérations officielles au sein du Congrès" (Mensdorff to Metternich, Vienna, May 25, 1866, in Oncken (ed.), *Rheinpolitik*, I, 236–37, no. 123). Cowley to Clarendon, Paris, secret and confidential, May 5, 1866, in PRO, FO, 519, 13:545; Cowley to Clarendon, Paris, May 7, 1866, in V. Wellesley and Sencourt (eds.), *Conversations with Napoleon III*, 258; Metternich to Mensdorff, Paris, confidential, May 21, 1866, in Oncken (ed.), *Rheinpolitik*, I, 219, no. 116.

16. On May 11, La Marmora announced that Italy would come to the congress but would not disarm (Bush, *Venetia Redeemed*, 63). See also Clarendon to Loftus, London, private, May 3, 1866, in Clarendon Papers, C-145, 45–46; La Tour d'Auvergne to Drouyn de Lhuys, London, telegram, May 9, 1866, in *Origines*, IX, 77–78, no. 2299. The idea of a meeting was one Drouyn de Lhuys had advanced (Cowley to Clarendon, Paris, May 11, 1866, in PRO, FO, 519, 232:212; Drouyn de Lhuys to Talleyrand, Paris, confidential, telegram, May 5, 1866, in *Origines*, IX, 17, no. 2246) in response to Clarendon's suggestion of a joint appeal for peace by the neutral powers.

These were the points of discussion that Napoleon himself had several times suggested to Goltz. Several objections were raised at once to the wording. London rejected the inclusion of Rome on the agenda, on the grounds that the question did not constitute a threat to European peace, and Drouyn de Lhuys yielded, knowing that Russia and Italy were also opposed to a discussion of Rome. Gorchakov suggested that the Venetian question (Austria did not admit that there was such a thing) should be tactfully disguised as the "différend italien." It was further agreed that disarmament would not be required, but merely suggested. Thus modified, the letters of invitation to a congress to meet on June 12 went out on May 24.[17]

For every power but Austria the invitation was a formality. Even Bismarck, in the face of the agreement of the neutral states and the attitude of his ally, Italy, had accepted the congress on May 19, abandoning the delaying tactics that he had followed until then. Benedetti, however, had no illusions. "The congress and peace," he wrote of Bismarck, "would upset all his plans at the moment when he believes their realization at hand." Berlin continued to hope for the failure of the congress. Even if Austria should accept, Bismarck told the Italian ambassador, "all that will lead to nothing; only we shall have time to complete our armaments and from the Congress we shall go on to war." At London and Saint Petersburg, too, there was little optimism.[18] But in *Revue des deux mondes* (May 31), Eugène Forcade, no admirer of diplomatic conclaves, embraced this one with hope, noting the uniqueness of a congress held *before* a war and in order to prevent a conflict. In a sense the mediation proposal of the Congress of Paris of 1856, which Clarendon had himself stopped short of invoking in the German crisis, was to be given its first application but, at the insis-

17. Drouyn de Lhuys to London and Saint Petersburg, May 16, 1866, in *Origines*, IX, 145–47, no. 2355; La Tour d'Auvergne to Drouyn de Lhuys, London, telegram, May 18, 1866, in *Origines*, IX, 179, no. 2377; Talleyrand to Drouyn de Lhuys, Saint Petersburg, telegram, May 21, 1866, in *Origines*, IX, 210, no. 2400; Drouyn de Lhuys to French representatives at Vienna, Berlin, Florence, Frankfurt, May 24, 1866, in *Origines*, IX, 248–49, no. 2433.

18. Benedetti to Drouyn de Lhuys, Berlin, private, April 25, 1866, in *Origines*, VIII, 322–23, no. 2127; Benedetti to Drouyn de Lhuys, Berlin, private and confidential, May 4, 1866, in *Origines*, IX, 3–4, no. 2238; Benedetti to Drouyn de Lhuys, Berlin, confidential, May 29, 1866, in *Origines*, IX, 305–306, no. 2481; Giulio-Camillo, Count Barral di Monteauviard, to La Marmora, Berlin, May 19, 1866, in La Marmora, *Un peu plus de lumière*, 251; Millman, *British Foreign Policy*, 21; Charles-Roux, *Alexandre II, Gorchakov et Napoléon III*, 381.

tence of Napoleon, within the context of a European congress. What sort of meeting did the French emperor envisage, and what did he expect from it?

It would meet, of course, at Paris. Drouyn de Lhuys had proposed this in the preliminary conference, and there was no serious objection. In fact, so great still was Napoleon's prestige that there was even talk of holding the meeting at Vichy, if his health required him to go there. And it would be a congress, not a conference. There was the usual confusion over these terms, but as Napoleon's preferences concerning the form and scope of the meeting became known it was obvious that he inclined toward the one whose representation and mandate would deserve the weightier title. This may even have been true for the agenda. Certainly suspicion continued that the emperor, despite his willingness to limit in advance the topics for discussion, would not necessarily be bound very strictly by this limitation once the congress met. Especially there were rumors that he hoped to reorganize Italy. After all, it was on Napoleon's instructions that Drouyn de Lhuys had tried, at the preliminary conference, to link Rome with the Venetian question. It was certainly true in the matter of rank of plenipotentiaries and the number of states represented. At the preliminary conference Drouyn de Lhuys represented the professional diplomat's point of view in suggesting a meeting of himself with the representatives at Paris of the great powers, Italy, and the German Confederation, the latter to participate only in discussions of the German question. But Cowley, who very much wanted Clarendon to come and who did not like or trust Drouyn de Lhuys, had no difficulty in persuading Napoleon that the foreign ministers should represent their countries. The ambassador even proposed that Napoleon should preside over the congress, an idea that seemed to impress the emperor and that he promised to consider. At the end of the month the foreign ministers had accepted and Napoleon was preparing the opening address, amid speculation that he might convoke the congress in person. Moreover, he had by that time thrown a wrench into Drouyn de Lhuys' tidy plans by instructing his foreign minister to argue for the inclusion of Spain. It appears that Napoleon had promised the former Spanish ambassador at Paris that Spain would be invited to any future congress. Perhaps in this matter he was trying to be agreeable to the empress, who had, in fact, first raised the question, for 1866 was a particularly difficult time in their relationship. But the tact remains that he persisted, that he was willing to have Spain admitted to the congress even if, as seemed likely, Portugal and Sweden would then have to be invited as well.[19]

On the other hand, Paris had once again yielded to British objections concerning the authority of the congress. On May 8, Drouyn de Lhuys had given it as his opinion that the three neutral great powers should announce "their firm intention" of resolving the problems before the congress. British protest against "coercion" followed, and Cowley took the matter directly to Napoleon, who hoped that if France, Britain, and Russia could agree "there would be a better chance of inducing the more interested governments to agree." Napoleon, however, insisted that Drouyn de Lhuys' "firm intention to resolve" meant only "that the three Powers, if they agreed in their views as to these questions, should state to the Congress that in their opinion they were questions which ought not to be left unsettled and that they should invite a serious examination of them with a view to their settlement."[20]

Obviously Napoleon's hopes for the congress rested on his ability to persuade the other powers to accept his program. But what were his views concerning the major problems, and what expedients could he offer for their solution? In the matter of the "différend italien," which was Napoleon's main concern, his minimum program was the cession of Venetia to Italy or even, perhaps, to Europe. To gain a guarantee of the pope's position at Rome by Europe, or at least by the Catholic powers, was also highly desirable. The French emperor had no commitment to Italian unity and would undoubtedly have welcomed "spontaneous movements" in the peninsula (especially in the south) that would have permitted the congress to substitute a confederal or-

19. Cowley to Clarendon, Paris, May 31, 1866, in PRO, FO, 519, 232:265; Cowley to Clarendon, Paris, secret and confidential, May 12, 1866, in PRO, FO, 519, 13:551; Cowley to Clarendon, Paris, most confidential, May 14, 1866, in PRO, FO, 519, 13:558; Bloomfield to Clarendon, Vienna, private, May 25, 1866, in PRO, FO, 356, 39; Cowley to Clarendon, Paris, May 18, 1866, in PRO, FO, 519, 232:231; Cowley to Clarendon, Paris, May 22, 1866, in V. Wellesley and Sencourt (eds.), Conversations with Napoleon III, 272; Nigra to La Marmora, Paris, May 31, 1866, in La Marmora, Un peu plus de lumiére, 270; Cowley to Clarendon, Paris, June 1, 1866, in PRO, FO, 519, 232:266; Metternich to Mensdorff, Paris, telegram, June 3, 1866, in Oncken (ed.), Rheinpolitik, I, 250, no. 131; Cowley to Clarendon, Paris, June 4, 1866, in PRO, FO, 519, 232:272.

20. Drouyn de Lhuys to French representatives at London and Saint Petersburg, confidential, May 8, 1866, in Origines, IX, 53–54, no. 2278; Cowley to Clarendon, Paris, secret and confidential, May 12, 1866, in PRO, FO, 519, 13:551–52.

ganization.[21] All of these were objectives he had sought persistently for almost twenty years.

Compared with the Italian problem, the German question was certainly secondary in the emperor's mind, but that does not mean he was disinterested. Although the official invitation to the congress implied that Europe was only concerned with Germany if changes there threatened the European balance of power, Napoleon gave to this European right of intervention a very broad interpretation, insisting that "since the German Confederation formed a constituent part of European treaties, therefore the European Powers could not be denied the right to veto any change of its organization having an effect on its foreign relations." At Berlin, France was blamed for drawing Britain in this direction. The French emperor might have been content, the Venetian problem resolved, to accept the status quo in Germany. But he would have insisted that any changes in the organization of Germany must receive the sanction of the congress. As for the nature of those changes, he had certain preferences. Prussia might be allowed to annex the Elbe Duchies, except for the northern district, which would be given to Denmark following a plebiscite, and perhaps Prussia could be allowed to "round itself out" with some other German acquisitions as well, including Saxony. In a word, Prussian hegemony might be established in northern Germany, while the south German states would be encouraged to form a closer union among themselves. In fact, Napoleon's preference was obviously for a tripartite Germany, a north Germany under Prussian hegemony, a south German confederation, and a still-powerful Austria. These, too, were ideas he had long nurtured.[22]

But what about France? Would France gain nothing from the congress except renewed prestige? "He would be satisfied," Nigra had concluded of Napoleon's state of mind, "with a peaceful solution, which would give him no territorial gain, but which would have as its

21. Nigra to La Marmora, Paris, May 28, 1866, in Colombo et al. (eds.), Carteggi di Nigra, 168; Bush, Venetia Redeemed, 66.

22. Goltz to Bismarck, Paris, confidential, May 8, 1866, in V. Wellesley and Sencourt (eds.), Conversations with Napoleon III, 263, 261; Bernstorff to William I, London, May 19, 1866, in Oncken (ed.), Rheinpolitik, I, 215–16, no. 114; Goltz to William I, Paris, reserved, May 11, 1866, in Oncken (ed.), Rheinpolitik, I, 192, no. 98; Nigra to La Marmora, Paris, May 11, 1866, in Origines, IX, 93 n.; project of address for the opening of the congress, May 29, 1866, in Origines, IX, 298–303, no. 2479; Napoleon III to Drouyn de Lhuys, June 11, 1866, in Ollivier, L'empire libéral, VIII, 186–89.

result the liberation of Venetia." Probably the emperor would have regarded the congress as successful had it done no more than settle the Venetian question, and in that case he would have asked nothing for himself. But if Prussia, for example, were to make major territorial gains through either war or negotiations, Napoleon would of necessity claim compensation for France. When he reminded Berlin of this during the first week of May in his speech at Auxerre, he was perhaps acting to discourage Bismarck from launching a war; he was most certainly spelling out the realities of the situation; and he was probably preparing his position for the congress, if it met, or for the war that would follow its failure. All in all, Nigra's judgment was discerning: Napoleon had no great enthusiasm for annexations, but his aversion was not insurmountable. It would be a matter of degree. French statements of disinterest in advance of the congress made it perhaps difficult and certainly embarrassing to advance territorial demands on the basis of slight changes in the organization of Germany. But events quickly indicated what compensation Napoleon would ask for major gains by another great power. As early as June 16 he made clear to London that, if Prussia won control of northern Germany, France would need compensation; and when this event seemed inevitable after Sadowa, he first proposed the establishment of an independent Rhenish buffer state and then, when that was refused, a return to the boundaries of 1814. There seems no reason to question the sincerity of Napoleon's own analysis in the letter he wrote Drouyn de Lhuys after the congress had failed. "You were to declare, in my name, that I would reject all ideas of territorial increase, as long as the balance of power in Europe remained unbroken. Indeed we could not envisage an extension of our frontiers unless the map of Europe happened to be modified to the exclusive advantage of one great power and unless the adjacent provinces asked, by means of free expression of their wishes to be annexed to France." The necessity, under which the French emperor would find himself at the congress, of balancing his personal inclination toward disinterest against the need of claiming compensation if the balance of power were altered (What, for that matter, would constitute an "alteration"?) was one of the two great obstacles to the success of the meeting. The other was the question of compensation for Austria.[23]

23. Nigra to La Marmora, Paris, May 28, 1866, in Colombo et al. (eds.), Carteggi di Nigra, 166; Nigra to La Marmora, Paris, May 24, 1866, in La Marmora, Un peu plus de

Napoleon recognized the difficulty of this problem, seeing it as "the pivot on which the deliberations turn." From the beginning he had admitted Austria's right to claim adequate compensation for the loss of Venetia. Poland was not to be considered, especially since raising the Polish question would bar Russia from the conference. Three possible compensations for Venetia remained: Silesia, Bosnia-Herzegovina, and the Principalities. At Vienna, only Silesia sparked interest. Compensation in the East would not do, said Mensdorff, it must be in Germany. Napoleon's initial reaction, as reported by Cowley, was sensible: "He does not seem to object to Austria retaining Silesia if she can get it, via Venetia, but he asks with reason how can any proposal of the kind be made in congress with a chance of success." Yet the emperor told Metternich, after Austria's rejection of the congress, "I would have proposed that Prussia should cede to you a great part of Silesia, with permission to indemnify herself in the North of Germany; and I would have supported any extension of Austria on the East." Probably, however, this lure of Silesia was more bait than substance, and Napoleon's real hope lay in the East.[24] There the chief problem was not Austrian reluctance but Russian truculence. Gorchakov had threatened to go to war rather than to let Vienna have the Principalities. The resistance of Saint Petersburg might not be so great, however, to acquisition of Bosnia and Herzegovina by Austria, in which case another use might be found for the Principalities. Nigra thought, for example, that Napoleon intended them to compensate German princes dispossessed as a result of Prussian expansion. Besides, there were ways of smoothing ruffled feathers. A strengthening of Serbia, some relaxing of the restrictions of the Black Sea treaty of 1856, a cession to Russia of some part of Bessarabia might make Saint Petersburg more tractable. Bosnia and Herzegovina were, the emperor told Goltz, the only compensation he could suggest for Austria. "This would provide the Dalmatian coast-line with a hinterland which would enable Austria to defend it against Italian attacks." On May 25,

---

lumière, 261–62; Millman, *British Foreign Policy*, 37–38; Napoleon III to Drouyn de Lhuys, June 11, 1866, in Ollivier, *L'empire libéral*, VIII, 188.

24. Metternich to Mensdorff, Paris, telegram, May 5, 1866, in Oncken (ed.), *Rheinpolitik*, I, 160, no. 80; Goltz to Bismarck, Paris, confidential, May 8, 1866, in V. Wellesley and Sencourt (eds.), *Conversations with Napoleon III*, 262–63; Bloomfield to Clarendon, Vienna, private, May 17, 1866, in PRO, FO, 356, 39; Cowley to Clarendon, Paris, May 1, 1866, in PRO, FO, 519, 232:197; Metternich to Mensdorff, Paris, June 6, 1866, in V. Wellesley and Sencourt (eds.), *Conversations with Napoleon III*, 275.

Goltz suggested and Napoleon approved the idea that Italy might purchase Bosnia to give to Austria. Probably, then, Napoleon's real hopes for compensation were indicated in the May 29 draft of the speech with which the French plenipotentiary was to open the congress. Turkey had vast territories but badly needed money. Why should Turkey not, for "a considerable monetary compensation," provide the needed compensation, especially as this could be done without any real weakening of its frontiers? The congress "would have . . . to contact the Ottoman Porte to express to it the wish of the cabinets; and Europe, which has made so many sacrifices, on so many occasions, to help Turkey, could reasonably expect that she would, in turn, in a noble spirit of gratitude, contribute to the common good by agreeing to an arrangement so much in keeping with the general interest."[25]

There were expedients, then, but obviously a spirit of self-sacrifice would have to prevail. "Even if peace were preserved for the moment," Napoleon told Cowley, "he did not see how these questions were to be settled peaceably unless all parties were willing to make sacrifices for peace." Would it be France's "sacrifice" to accept a certain enlargement of Prussia and Italy without territorial compensation? Later, when Napoleon's failure to secure compensation was attacked, he defended, in retrospect, his precongress position, arguing "that having united England and Russia who could by no possibility obtain any material advantage in Europe to aid him in the work of peace, it was right that he should disclaim all intention of turning their co-operation to his own profit and that moreover as no satisfactory arrangement would have been made without some redistribution of territory, he could only hope to arrive pacifically at that redistribution by showing that he was consulting general interests and not those of France in proposing it." However that might be, the French emperor undoubtedly planned to rely on a redoubtable arsenal of persuasion—persuasion of logic (Did he not represent better than any other sovereign the irresistible ideas of the day?), persuasion of personality (Had not he dominated the great congress of 1856?), and, finally persuasion that commands respect because of the power behind

25. Talleyrand to Drouyn de Lhuys, Saint Petersburg, May 8, 1866, in Charles-Roux, *Alexandre II, Gorchakov et Napoléon III*, 378; Nigra to La Marmora, Paris, May 11, 1866, in *Origines*, IX, 93 n.; Goltz to Bismarck, Paris, confidential, May 8, 1866, in V. Wellesley and Sencourt (eds.), *Conversations with Napoleon III*, 262–63; Goltz to William I, Paris, reserved, May 25, 1866, in Oncken (ed.), *Rheinpolitik*, I, 234, no. 122; project of address for the opening of the congress, May 29, 1866, in *Origines*, IX, 302–303, no. 2479.

it (Was not France, if it chose to exert itself, the most powerful nation of the Continent?). And so, when pressed by Cowley to explain how he proposed to deal with the problem of compensation for Austria, Napoleon replied, "That must be the business of the Congress. . . . It is one of those questions that can be best ventilated in Congress and . . . the ventilation of it may produce some results." Later, when Austria had rejected the meeting, he explained his regret to Cowley. "He had been quite prepared . . . for the refusal of Austria to cede Venetia, but he had hoped that she would have waited to say so in Paris, and that the compensation to which he admitted she was justly entitled, might have been treated dans les coulisses." Obviously Napoleon was convinced of the usefulness of conference diplomacy. "If no other result was obtained," he told Cowley, "all parties would [be] obliged to vider leurs sacs." Later he explained that, in order to find solutions to the problems threatening to bring on war, "I thought it necessary to approach them openly, to disengage them from the veil of diplomacy which covered them, and to give serious consideration to the legitimate wishes of sovereign and peoples."[26]

As the date of the congress approached, Napoleon must have contemplated the sort of solutions that would emerge if those "legitimate wishes" were indeed consulted: Venetia ceded to Italy, the work of liberation completed, and his credit restored in the peninsula; Schleswig-Holstein given to Prussia, but the nationalities principle safeguarded by a plebiscite in the northern district; Prussia allowed to "round itself out" and to dominate the north of Germany; Austria compensated in the East for the loss of Venetia, but preserved as a great power and restored to its true historical role as Europe's vanguard against the Turk; the south German states encouraged to confederate, thus establishing a tripartite Germany; Europe's supervision of the German situation firmly established and perhaps extended to Rome as well by a guarantee of the pope; the concert of Europe solidly established in the form that Napoleon had envisaged since his earliest writings; and France secure in its moral dominance of Europe if not rewarded, as well, by some modest tangible gain such as a rectification of its military frontier (the boundaries of 1814). Was it only a pipe

26. Cowley to Clarendon, Paris, secret and confidential, May 5, 1866, in PRO, FO, 519, 13:545; Cowley to Clarendon, Paris, most confidential, June [18], 1866, in PRO, FO, 519, 14:10–11; Cowley to Clarendon, Paris, May 11, June 4, May 29, 1866, all in PRO, FO, 519, 232:215, 270, 257; Napoleon III to Drouyn de Lhuys, June 11, 1866, in Ollivier, L'empire libéral, VIII, 188.

dream? Apparently London, haunted by the nightmare of a successful manipulation of the congress by Napoleon, did not think so. Nor did Bismarck, in his extreme reluctance to see the congress meet. Nor did Gorchakov, in his secret encouragement of Austria to decline the invitation. Nor, finally, did the Austrian government, in rejecting the congress at the expense of giving up its long effort to be completely in the right in the duel with Bismarck.[27]

Ironically, Napoleon's persistent doubts about Vienna's intentions had been lulled toward the end of May. "He said," reported Nigra, "he thought that Austria, alarmed at the idea of being the only one to refuse, would perhaps decide to accept." Eugène Forcade, in Revue des deux mondes (May 31), expressed the certainty that Austria would not reject the conference and that Turkey would provide the required compensation. Metternich advised his government to come to Paris and defend its views there, since the congress would then certainly fail. Obviously Mensdorff and Francis Joseph did not share this optimism, for, having lost the opportunity to squelch the congress idea at its inception out of fear of offending Napoleon, they now in effect vetoed the meeting by requiring, as was decided on May 31 and as Metternich informed Napoleon on June 3, that all of the powers rule out in advance the possibility of a territorial aggrandizement by one or more of them.[28]

It was 1859 repeated. As then Cavour so now Bismarck was saved by the incompatibility of the Austrian Empire with those ideas that Napoleon intended to advance in congress and the success of which Vienna must certainly have feared, for otherwise there could have been no reason to reject Metternich's advice and to veto the congress so brutally. Mensdorff admitted as much: "To cede a province, and especially a province so important . . . would be an act of suicide that

27. Ramsay, Idealism and Foreign Policy, 182–85, 189, 200–207; Fletcher, The Mission of Vincent Benedetti, 71–73; Bush, Venetia Redeemed, 67.

28. Nigra to La Marmora, Paris, May 24, 1866, in La Marmora, Un peu plus de lumière, 261–62; Metternich to Mensdorff, Paris, confidential, May 21, 1866, in Oncken (ed.), Rheinpolitik, I, 220, no. 116. In the official Austrian dispatch the crucial condition was "qu'on excluera des délibérations toute combinaison qui tendrait à donner à un des Etats invités aujourd'hui à la réunion un agrandissement territorial ou un accroissement de puissance" (Mensdorff to Metternich, Vienna, June 1, 1866, in Oncken (ed.), Rheinpolitik, I, 250 n. There was also an Austrian proviso that the pope be invited to the congress (Ollivier, L'empire libéral, VIII, 159–62). Clark (Franz Joseph and Bismarck, 430–32) states that Mensdorff on May 30 had already prepared a response with sufficient reservations to threaten the congress, and Francis Joseph, probably influenced by Maurice Esterhazy, gave the final intransigent tone.

would forever displace Austria from her great-power rank." No one doubted that the Austrian reply was a veto. "I consider this dispatch," Napoleon told Metternich, "equivalent to a refusal; for it is evident that, if there is to be no question of territorial revisions intended to prevent the recurrence of the war, the meetings of the conference would be superfluous." On June 12, Napoleon obtained from Vienna the promise that, in return for French neutrality, Italy would receive Venetia even if Prussia lost the war. Three weeks later, on July 3, Austria was decisively defeated at Sadowa.[29]

---

29. Mensdorff to Metternich, Vienna, reserved, June 1, 1866, in Oncken (ed.), *Rhein-politik*, I, 251–52 n.; Metternich to Mensdorff, Paris, June 6, 1866, in V. Wellesley and Sencourt (eds.), *Conversations with Napoleon III*, 275.

CHAPTER 14

Decision and Disillusionment
From Sadowa to the Conference on Luxemburg
1866–1867

Europe anxiously awaited the French response to Prussia's unexpectedly decisive victory. Would Napoleon insist on territorial compensation? Would he permit Bismarck to impose peace terms or would he ally with Austria (actually or in effect) to limit Prussian gains? Would he, in a word, persevere in his neutrality, making no demands, or would he intervene? Conventional historical wisdom states that French failure to intervene in the German quarrel after Sadowa was a fatal error by which France lost forever the opportunity of preventing Prussian dominance in Europe. As a statement of what was to happen, the appraisal is sound, but it is not very useful in helping us understand the decisions made at Paris between July 3 and 11. Bismarck's post-1866 policies and successes were not yet data upon which Napoleon could draw. Many possibilities existed that, had they been realized, would have altered an outcome that seems inevitable only in hindsight. In light of what the French emperor could have known, and of what we can know of his policies and of his state of mind, we can easily understand why at least two courses of action—extortion of territory and alliance with Austria—were unacceptable to him in July, 1866.

In his open letter to Drouyn de Lhuys of June 11, Napoleon had flatly stated that France would contemplate additions to its territory only if "neighboring provinces should demand annexation by a free vote." And Cowley reported: "In conversations which I have had the honour to have with H.M. he has more than once expressed himself as convinced that neither the Rhenish provinces nor Belgium desired annexation to France." Before the war Goltz was convinced that Napoleon had abandoned all thought of acquiring the left bank of the Rhine or even a small extension of territory there. Even Heinrich von

Sybel admitted the probable sincerity of the French emperor's words to Goltz: "It would be a miserable gain to win a little strip of territory that would arouse against me the national wrath and hatred of all Germany." And, Napoleon might well have added, that would repudiate the principle of nationalities, bring about an irreparable break with Britain, and leave France isolated in a hostile Europe. Nothing that he could have known or reasonably anticipated in those first weeks of July, 1866, would have justified such a policy. "I dare not of course take upon myself to give further assurances in regard to the future," wrote Cowley on July 9, "but I can conscientiously express the opinion that an extension of territory is not now contemplated by the Emperor and is not coveted by France."[1]

An alliance with Austria raised equal difficulties. In fact, such an alliance would require a fear of Prussia so great as to leave no alternative to adoption of a frankly conservative foreign policy. However flexible Vienna might have been immediately after Sadowa, in the long run (and, having set his face against Prussia, Napoleon would have been bound to Austria for the long run) Austrian policy could only be conservative. This Hübner had seen clearly in May, 1862: "The politics of *faits accomplis* leads," he then wrote, "to the dissolution of European society. Respect for the treaties is a necessity of life for us. It was to defend the treaties that Austria alone dared to draw the sword in 1859. She has remained in her role of a conservative power. That or nothing will save us." Such an alliance would reverse almost twenty years of Napoleonic foreign policy. It would represent a denial of the Napoleonic idea and of the principle of nationalities. More, it would require France to become a defender of the new status quo. Napoleon not only would abandon his position at the head of the "ideas of the time" but would necessarily march against them. In July, 1866, this was still inconceivable, if only because there seemed, as yet, no reason to fear unduly the consequences of Austria's defeat. Quite the contrary. "I believed," the French emperor wrote to Francis Joseph shortly after the beginning of the war, "that it was not without a certain satisfaction that I witnessed the dissolution of the German Confederation organized mainly against France." When the Austrian emperor protested that this confederation had never caused France any

---

1. Napoleon III to Drouyn de Lhuys, June 11, 1866, in Ollivier, *L'empire libéral*, VIII, 188; Cowley to Edward Henry Stanley, Paris, July 9, 1866, in PRO, FO, 519, 14:37–38; Cowley to Stanley, Paris, confidential, June 19, 1866, in PRO, FO, 519, 14: 13; Heinrich von Sybel, *The Founding of the German Empire*, V, 246.

trouble, Napoleon replied, one suspects, with a certain irony: "What the Emperor says about the German Confederation is perfectly correct; I cannot complain of the hostility of the Diet and I wished in my letter only to make reference to the date of its institution." But the date was enough. To those who warned him of the dangers of Prussian aggrandizement, Napoleon invariably replied, even after Sadowa, that he preferred a strong Prussia "to the continued existence of the Germanic Confederation which he considered had been a standing menace to France." Ollivier would have us believe that, upon receiving the telegram informing him of Prussia's victory, Napoleon expressed his satisfaction in the way that was habitual to him—by pinching the end of his moustache. The pinch may have been apocryphal, but there was at least some occasion for it. Austria had already yielded up to him all it had to give—the promise of Venetia for Italy. Sadowa meant the attainment of still other goals long sought by or acceptable to him: the annexation of Schleswig-Holstein by Prussia, the destruction in Germany of the treaties of 1815, the forcible turning of Austria's attention from Germany and Italy toward the East. Most important, Sadowa could be seen as a victory for the principle of nationalities, and that principle, in turn, could be used to prevent a unitary (and therefore dangerous) Germany and perhaps even to gain in due course an adequate compensation for the increased power of Prussia.[2]

Clearly Napoleon regarded Prussia's cause as consonant with the principle of nationalities. In his letter of June 11 he had spoken of "the desires of Germany, demanding a political reconstitution more in keeping with her general needs." The strengthening of Prussia in the north had become, he said, "a necessity which could not be disputed." And when Cowley asked Drouyn de Lhuys why his master favored Prussia's program even though Austrian dominance in Germany had kept the peace, the foreign minister replied that the emperor was submitting to a necessity. "H.M. was convinced that the time was come when the claims of Prussia must be attended to, and as he would not prevent their realisation he thought it best to define a limit to them." To La Valette, Napoleon reflected after Sadowa that he saw the dangers of Prussian expansion, but even could he have prevented it he

2. Hübner to Rechberg, Paris, May 9, 1862, in HHSA, PA IX, Varia, 1862, I–VI, Box 72, fols. 126–30; Napoleon III to Francis Joseph, June 17, 1866, in Salomon, *Ambassade de Richard Metternich*, 127; Metternich to Mensdorff, Paris, secret, June 29, 1866, in Oncken (ed.), *Rheinpolitik*, I, 284, no. 161; Cowley to Stanley, Paris, July 26, 1866, in PRO, FO, 519, 233:52; Ollivier, *L'empire libéral*, VIII, 410.

would not have done so: "The aspirations for German unity and independence might have been stifled for the moment but could not have been eradicated and if stifled on one spot would make themselves heard on another. It is a fire that would ever be bursting out afresh." Moreover, a limit might be set to Prussian expansion by the same consideration that made Bismarck's initial success desirable in Napoleon's mind—the principle of nationalities. The essence of that principle was freedom to choose. Because a people spoke the same language did not require them to unite if this was not their wish. Louis Napoleon had lived and studied in southern Germany. Clearly he doubted the wish and will of the Germans to form a unitary state. Already, before the war, Germans had approached him to ask his support for a south German confederation, and he had bluntly stated on June 11: "For our part, we would have desired for the secondary States a closer union, a more powerful organization, a more important role." Napoleon wanted a tripartite, federal Germany, and Prussia's victory could be considered a giant step in that direction.[3]

And yet, for all of this, the French emperor obviously regarded the days following Sadowa as a period of crisis. He gave very serious thought to armed intervention and later regretted that he had not sent a French force to the Rhine. The reason is obvious. The peace settlement that seemed likely to emerge from Austria's overwhelming defeat was far from perfect in Napoleon's eyes. In the first place, it would not be complete. Rome, northern Schleswig, and the status of the south German states were unlikely to be satisfactorily dealt with. Nor was it clear what limits, if any, Prussia would set to its ambitions once Austria was excluded from Germany. Never, Napoleon had told Cowley, would he "permit the formation of a Great German Power uniting under one sceptre a population of 70 millions." And even if, as did in fact prove to be the case, Bismarck chose the side of moderation, what guarantees could there be that this moderation would continue? Too much depended on the will of one man and the policy of one state. Perhaps most important of all, the settlement would have been made without the active participation of France, and France would not have received even modest compensation, a fact that French

3. Napoleon III to Drouyn de Lhuys, June 11, 1866, in Ollivier, *L'empire libéral*, VIII, 188; Cowley to Clarendon, Paris, most confidential, June 18, 21, 1866, both in PRO, FO, 519, 14:10, 19; Cowley to Stanley, Paris, most confidential, September 18, 1866, in PRO, FO, 519, 14:97–98; Cowley to Clarendon, Paris, confidential, April 20, 1866, in PRO, FO, 519, 13:520–22.

public opinion might reasonably be expected to regret once there had
been time for reflection. And that is why immediately after Sadowa
such serious consideration was given at Paris to the possibility of a
French intervention in the German quarrel. But before the outcome
of that debate is noted, an observation is necessary. If France were not
to content itself with extorting territory from Prussia and if France
were not to ally itself with Austria, then Paris could hardly presume
to impose its will alone on the combatants. Nothing we have seen of
Napoleon's attitude toward the role of France within Europe could
lead us to believe, at any rate, that he contemplated this, nor is it
likely that Britain and Russia would have permitted it. What form,
then, could French intervention have taken? At the end of 1866, a
French Foreign Office note for an outline of the situation hinted at the
answer: "Considered in part," it read, "these results [of the war], which
create a completely new situation in Europe, would not fulfill all the
ideas for which the Emperor's Government would have endeavored to
win acceptance in a meeting previous to the war." Or following it?
The inevitable outcome of armed French intervention must have
been not a French mediation but a European congress. Napoleon had
worked sincerely for such a congress before hostilities began; and one
would certainly have followed a protracted conflict. In fact, as early as
June 3 the emperor told Metternich he would be grateful if Austria
were to support the idea of inviting Spain "zur eventuellen Kon-
ferenzen als Grossmacht." Through Drouyn de Lhuys he continued to
voice his conviction that changes in the federal constitution of Germany must receive the sanction of Europe. Immediately after Sadowa,
Cowley anticipated a congress invitation (with grave misgivings), and
Drouyn de Lhuys, in reply to Goltz's question, obviously considered a
congress or conference to be in the normal course of things. The day
before, Goltz had pleased Napoleon (or so the ambassador thought) by
proposing Paris as the site for such a meeting. "We have lost nothing
yet, Sire," one of Napoleon's intimates, General Fleury, is supposed to
have exclaimed upon hearing the news of Sadowa. "On the contrary,
now or never is your chance to reconstruct the map of Europe."[4]

4. Cowley to Clarendon, Paris, most confidential, June 18, 1866, in PRO, FO, 519,
14:8; Note pour l'exposé de la situation, December 27, 1866, in Origines, XIII, 382, no.
3977; Metternich to Mensdorff, Paris, telegram, June 3, 1866, in Oncken (ed.), Rheinpolitik, I, 250, no. 131; Cowley to Clarendon, Paris, June 23, 1866, in PRO, FO, 519,
14:23; Cowley to Clarendon, Paris, July 5, 1866, in PRO, FO, 519, 233:23–24; Goltz to
Bismarck, Paris, confidential, July 5, 1866, in Oncken (ed.), Rheinpolitik, I, 307–308,
no. 177; Goltz to William I, Paris, July 4, 1866, in Oncken (ed.), Rheinpolitik, I, 301, no.
173, 302 n.

In many ways, in fact, the situation was more favorable to the congress in July than it had been in May. Russia, eager to assert Europe's right of intervention in the German question, would propose a gathering on July 24. Austria, having lost its last Italian province, no longer had anything to fear from a European conclave and much, perhaps, to gain. Italy might welcome a European intervention that would save the humiliation of receiving Venetia from France, to whom Austria had surrendered it. Britain was resigned to accepting an invitation subject to conditions that in the past would have been fully to Napoleon's taste: all the great powers to attend, the decisions of the congress to be binding, and all questions raised by the war to be considered, although Edward Henry Stanley, who had succeeded Russell as foreign secretary, admitted that these conditions were designed to be unacceptable to Prussia and that before setting them he had made sure of Berlin's refusal. The congress, Bismarck declared, would deny Prussia the advantages it had won; rather than accept, he would cross the Main and continue the war. A European congress in July, 1866, could, then, have given Napoleon the opportunity to remedy the defects he saw in the peace settlement. Moreover, it would have been the logical culmination of a policy and of a method that he had followed with great persistence since 1849. Persuasion had failed; intrigue had failed; now the threat of force might succeed. Certainly, in view of Bismarck's attitude, only force could bring Prussia to the conference table. This was what French armed intervention would have achieved, and what the failure to intervene lost.[5]

That failure resulted from the conjunction of three factors: French unpreparedness, both military and in terms of public opinion; Bismarck's moderation; and (more arguably) Napoleon's health. "In congresses as in war," Pierre Magne, a key minister of Napoleon III's, would advise, "fortune likes to smile on those who are strong and resolute." And France, in the summer of 1866, was neither. Despite the optimism of Marshal Jacques Louis Randon, the minister of war, Napoleon soon realized, as he himself told both Count Friedrich Ferdinand von Beust and Cowley, that the army was not ready for war. As for the figures cited on July 5 by Randon, it is perhaps enough to recall that he was soon replaced and the admittedly urgent work of reorganizing the French army confided to Marshal Adolphe Niel, who, as late as the spring of 1867, would counsel against war on the

5. See Mosse, *The European Powers and the German Question*, 238–46, for Russia's July 24 proposal. Millman, *British Foreign Policy*, 34–35; La Tour d'Auvergne to Drouyn de Lhuys, July 31, 1866, in *Origines*, XI, 321, no. 3242.

grounds of French unpreparedness. Nor was public opinion, which had been strongly pacifistic since 1863, prepared for a conflict. And what would be the effect upon that opinion if Italy were to stand fast with Prussia and the emperor were then shown ready to wage war against his own creation because of the consequence of an alliance that he himself had encouraged Florence to accept? In these circumstances Bismarck's moderation proved decisive. By July 11 it was known in Paris that Prussia, uncertain of French intentions, would halt at the Main and offer reasonable terms to Austria. For Napoleon, the choice must now have seemed to be between two gambles. Armed intervention would involve great risk for a major prize. Cooperation with Prussia avoided the immediate risk, but offered much more problematic gains. Had the emperor been a younger man, more vigorous, more firmly seated at home, and in better health,[6] he would perhaps have followed his own star against all odds. Instead, he chose to speculate on the rising star of another. Probably this seemed to Napoleon just another tack in a long, patient course. The goals he had been unable to reach with the help first of Britain and then of Russia he would try for again in cooperation with Prussia. He could not have known how quickly time was running out or how completely the initiative had passed from his hands.

This new phase of French foreign policy did not begin at once, however. For the next month Drouyn de Lhuys apparently conducted affairs with a freedom that the emperor did not usually allow his foreign ministers. Drouyn de Lhuys easily disposed of Saint Petersburg's bid for collective action in the German question. Would Russia, he innocently inquired, care to discuss the logical consequence of such an action, that is, recourse to arms? The answer was a hasty no. The foreign minister then rejected Paris as the site of a congress, and he threw so much cold water on the whole idea, working diligently against it in private, that Bismarck's rejection of Russia's invitation

---

6. The decision against intervention, which emerged from a series of meetings held at Paris on July 4 and 5, could have been reversed at any time in the week that followed (see Pottinger, *Napoleon III and the German Crisis*, 156–61; Fletcher, *The Mission of Benedetti*, 82 n.; Case, *French Opinion on War and Diplomacy*, 208–209). Pierre Magne to Napoleon III, confidential, July 20, 1866, in *Papiers et correspondance*, I, 241; Beust to Mensdorff, Paris, July 11, 1866, in Oncken (ed.), *Rheinpolitik*, I, 334–36, no. 204; Cowley to Stanley, Paris, July 11, 1866, in PRO, FO, 519, 233:32–35; Rothan, *Souvenirs diplomatiques*, 264–65; Case, *French Opinion on War and Diplomacy*, 209–215. On Napoleon's illnesses in August, 1865, and July, 1866, see Williams, *The Mortal Napoleon III*, 109–119.

ended the matter. Gorchakov's final effort—a proposal that the signatories of the Vienna treaties "reserve their rights," in principle, to participate in the changes to be effected in Germany—was rejected by the British government with Drouyn de Lhuys' approval and assistance. This was in the first week of August. Already, on July 29, Paris had demanded of Prussia that France receive the boundaries of 1814 as well as the Bavarian and Hessian territories on the left bank of the Rhine, and that Prussian troops be withdrawn from Luxemburg. Whether Napoleon or Drouyn de Lhuys was more responsible for this compensation demand, which Bismarck of course rejected, remains an academic question, since France had only one foreign policy—that of the emperor. And, in fact, France regained a foreign policy worthy of the name only with the unexpected return to Paris on August 7 of Napoleon from Vichy, where his illness had taken him. The temptation is great to agree with Cowley, who concluded, after reviewing these events: "Such inconsistencies . . . can only be accounted for by great weakness somewhere, and I begin to think that the illness under which [the emperor] is suffering, which has something to do with the bladder, affects his head, which I am told is sometimes the case, although it is not dangerous." However that may be—and opinion remains divided on the degree to which Napoleon's illness affected his decisions—on August 11 in an interview with Goltz, Napoleon repudiated his foreign minister with uncharacteristic brusqueness. The next day he set the keynote for a new policy toward Prussia. "France's true interest," he wrote to La Valette, the minister of the interior, "lies not in a meagre increase of territory but in helping Germany to establish herself in a manner most favorable to our interests and to those of Europe." On the twentieth, Drouyn de Lhuys' resignation was accepted. Since his successor, Moustier, was in Constantinople, La Valette served as the interim foreign minister.[7]

The policy adopted by Napoleon after August 11, revealed in the following weeks by pronouncements such as La Valette's circular of September 16 as well as by the continuing Franco-Prussian negotiations, may be briefly summarized. France would accept Prussian aggrandizement as being compatible with the principle of nationalities

7. Drouyn de Lhuys to Talleyrand, Paris, July 7, 1866, in *Origines*, X, 347, no. 2899; Cowley to Stanley, Paris, July 23, 29, 1866, both in PRO, FO, 519, 14:63–64, 72–73; Millman, *British Foreign Policy*, 35; Goltz to Bismarck, Paris, telegram, August 11, 1866, in Oncken (ed.), *Rheinpolitik*, II, 51, no. 267; Napoleon III to La Valette, August 12, 1866, in *Origines*, XII, 70–71, no. 3385.

and therefore with the best interests of France and Europe. Napoleon would seek only such compensation as would not too openly violate the principle of nationalities and that could be gained by negotiation. And France would ally itself with Prussia. Of course, this alliance was motivated to a great extent by the desire to win compensation. Paris proposed, in fact, that its basis should be one of mutual assistance. France would annex Luxemburg and guarantee recent Prussian gains; Prussia would agree to help if at some time in the future French efforts to annex Belgium were opposed by Britain. Later, at Bismarck's request, France agreed not to oppose a federal Germany. None of this necessarily contradicted the principle of nationalities, although in the case of Belgium, political necessity might well have tempted Napoleon to anticipate and encourage a proannexationist sentiment in that linguistically divided state, which had, after all, existed for less than forty years. In fact, political necessity had already begun to weigh heavily against principles.[8]

Yet Napoleon evidently intended to persevere as well as he might in the way that had so long guided him before the dominance of France and the stability of his own regime had come into question. "Everything has an end in this world," he had told La Valette. "M. Bismarck with his arrogant and violent temper will pass away, his old king will pass away, and I will pass away, but let you and me have the satisfaction before we go, of feeling that we have made the attempt to lay the basis of a new order of things, to do away with natural animosities, to replace jealousies by confidence and to promote the general happiness of mankind." At the end of the year the French Foreign Office somewhat wistfully concluded: "Prejudices are disappearing, nations are coming closer together and every day we understand more fully that the system of economic solidarity inaugurated since 1860 [the Cobden-Chevalier commercial treaty] will not have been an empty word."[9] Ironically, just three weeks earlier Napoleon had failed in his first effort to use the proposed Franco-Prussian alliance as a means to reactivate his version of the concert of Europe.

In August, 1866, the French emperor faced other problems than Germany, in particular that of Rome. By mid-December, France

8. On these negotiations, see Fletcher, *The Mission of Benedetti*, 123–36; see also draft of a proposed Franco-Prussian treaty, August 23, 1866, in Oncken (ed.), *Rheinpolitik*, II, 95, no. 297.

9. Cowley to Stanley, Paris, most confidential, September 18, 1866, in PRO, FO, 519, 14:97–98; Note pour l'exposé de la situation, December 27, 1866, in *Origines*, XIII, 382–83, no. 3977.

would have completed the evacuation of its troops from Rome under the terms of the September Convention. Napoleon's concern was reflected in the reference to a guarantee of papal sovereignty that he presumably added in his own hand to a draft of La Valette's circular of September 16. A European solution of the Roman question still appealed to him. When at the end of November the Spanish premier wondered if it might not be a good idea to convoke at Paris a conference of all the Catholic powers, the French ambassador replied that "as all the major European powers had a more or less sizeable number of Catholic subjects, it seemed that it was only by means of a general Congress that the question, because of its European character, could find a fitting solution." Napoleon must have been encouraged, therefore, when in October the Prussian minister at Rome, Count Harry Arnim von Suchow, convinced the French chargé "that he was supposedly empowered to suggest to the French Representative at Rome an idea which the Cabinet at Berlin did not wish to bring forward openly at Paris—that of a European understanding for the benefit of the Holy See." And Arnim gave it as his personal opinion that after the powers had reached agreement in principle at Paris they should assemble a conference at Rome to work out the details, including reforms. Presumably as a step toward such a solution, the Prussian representative announced to the pope that his government, considering the conservation of the Holy See to be a European interest, tendered its good offices and that he was charged with making the same declaration in the name of the Russian emperor.[10]

If Napoleon was pleased at this apparent Prussian initiative, he was probably not surprised, since Moustier, who had taken up his duties as foreign minister on October 2, had suggested to Goltz later in the month that France and Prussia might cooperate in "establishing the foundations of an agreement to safeguard and assure in the future" the papal power. In view of Arnim's actions, however, and Goltz's favorable reception of the French overture, the emperor must have been disagreeably surprised when Berlin at once disavowed its representative at Rome. Bismarck's exact role in these events remains a mystery, but the sequel was to show clearly that Napoleon still hoped, as 1866

10. Circular of La Valette to the diplomatic agents of the emperor, September 16, 1866, in *Origines*, XII, 304, no. 3598; Case, *French Opinion on War and Diplomacy*, 221 n.; Baron Henri Mercier de l'Ostende to Moustier, Madrid, November 29, 1866, in *Origines*, XIII, 192, no. 3840; Ernest, comte Armand, to Moustier, Rome, October 30, 1866, in *Origines*, XIII, 36, no. 3712; Armand to Moustier, Rome, telegram, November 12, 1866, in *Origines*, XIII, 85, no. 3749.

neared its end, for an alliance with Prussia that would assist him in finding a European solution for the problem of Rome. Arnim, while drawing back, continued to offer encouragement. The initiative, he advised, "belonged to the Emperor and . . . Prussia would not outdistance France but . . . she would go as far." Besides, he argued, an accord between Prussia and France would be better than a European agreement, since only those two powers were in a position effectively to aid the pope. On November 25, Moustier sent to Benedetti from Compiègne a projected Franco-Prussian convention on the Roman question. The accompanying letter left no doubt as to Napoleon's initiative. "You recently asked me," Moustier wrote, "how you should follow up the idea of an entente of Prussia and France concerning Roman affairs. During my stay at Compiègne, the Emperor ordered me to give form to these ideas at once, and I am sending you the project that I have drawn up and that His Majesty was kind enough to approve as corresponding perfectly to his thought. Count Goltz, whom His Majesty has consulted several times and who has helped me in this work, is sending it as well to his Government and recommends its adoption." Obviously Napoleon was genuinely concerned to prevent complications at Rome following the withdrawal of French troops. "The Emperor attaches the greatest importance to the immediate signature of this convention," Moustier continued, "because a delay could allow us to be outstripped by events and could compromise everything that it is our aim to safeguard, as much in the interest of Italy as in that of the Holy Father." But there was more. "His Majesty considers this entente as a happy prelude to the more intimate relations that he wishes to see established between the two Governments." Relations, the foreign minister hinted, that could lead, as well, to a satisfactory solution of the compensation problem.[11]

The convention, as proposed, began with the statement that both France and Prussia agreed that the pope's independence could be assured only if he "will continue in liberty and security to exercise his rights of sovereignty over his States." Moreover: "They also think that, aside from any religious consideration, the maintenance of his sovereignty constitutes today a real European interest." To the end of

11. Confidential note [in Moustier's hand] on the *démarche* made to the pope by the Prussian representative at Rome, [November 14, 1866], in *Origines*, XIII, 93, no. 3759; Benedetti to Moustier, Berlin, telegram, November 16, 1866, in *Origines*, XIII, 99–100, no. 3767; Armand to Moustier, Rome, November 17, 1866, in *Origines*, XIII, 115–16, no. 3779; Moustier to Benedetti, Compiègne, private, November 25, 1866, in *Origines*, XIII, 151–52, no. 3805.

assuring the pope's position, France and Prussia would guarantee his temporal power, persuade him to carry out necessary reforms, and use their good offices between Rome and Florence. But that this convention was meant to be more than a Franco-Prussian entente is explicit in Article 5: "The said Parties desire and reserve in advance the adhesion of all the Powers who, guided by the same principles, would be disposed to work together towards the same goal, and they will agree with them, in the event, on the arrangements which would seem to be of a nature to assure in a still more efficacious manner the object of the present convention." One such arrangement, Moustier pointed out, might be a papal budget made up of contributions from all states having Catholics in the population. At any rate, Paris and Berlin would decide when and how such a general European agreement would be sought. From the first, Benedetti had held out little hope, despite the optimism at Paris, that Bismarck would accept the French proposal. His presentiment was quickly confirmed. Prussia would not join a guarantee of the pope's temporal power. And while Bismarck, having rejected the convention on December 6, continued to talk of "good offices," it was abundantly clear before the end of December that he had no intention of entering into any agreement with France concerning Rome. "I decidedly am inclined," Benedetti wrote, "to believe that M. de Bismarck does not attach, or is not in a position to attach to the accord that we have proposed to him, the value that we ourselves place on it." For Berlin, the Roman question was not Europe's problem. It was simply another embarrassment for the French emperor, the prolonging of which would be in Prussia's interest. Besides, Bismarck could not ignore the possibility that Paris' real motive in seeking to involve Prussia at Rome was to alienate Prussia from its Italian ally. Napoleon's disillusionment with the course that he had chosen must now have begun in earnest. But the rejection of his Roman convention would soon prove to be only the beginning of a bitter awakening to the new reality of European politics.[12]

In his telegram reporting the final failure of the convention, Benedetti had concluded: "As for the other project, it has entered into explanations which do not lead me to hope for success—at least for the moment." He was referring, of course, to the French bid for Luxem-

12. Project of convention, November 25, 1866, in *Origines*, XIII, 153–54, no. 3806; Moustier to Benedetti, Compiègne, private, November 25, 1866, in *Origines*, XIII, 152, no. 3805; Benedetti to Moustier, Berlin, private, December 14, 1866, in *Origines*, XIII, 277, no. 3915.

burg, which Benedetti had first raised with Bismarck on August 17. A week later, the ambassador's gloom had deepened: "I have conceived some doubts that I cannot hide from you and if I had to put into words what seems to me the most reasonable hypothesis, I would say that they are resolved not to accept our projected treaty, but that they are trying to hide it from us." Within three months, on April 1, 1867, Bismarck, after having long encouraged France to acquire Luxemburg by propaganda in the duchy and agreement with The Hague, publicly drew back during a Reichstag interpellation. Napoleon, who had already negotiated a treaty of cession with the Dutch king (from which the latter now hastily withdrew), seemed to have no choice between war and a humiliation so complete as to threaten his regime. For one week the French emperor seriously considered war. The cession of Luxemburg to France was an "irrevocable act," Moustier asserted, and Bismarck must show the moral authority and the courage necessary "to set for German patriotism limits which it cannot exceed without wounding the patriotism of others." As for Napoleon, "His Majesty, strong in his right and his moderation, is ready for any eventuality. The country would rise as one man if Germany were to make proof of a spirit of expansion and of intolerance such as the one whose symptoms you describe to me. The smaller Luxemburg, the less France could tolerate that the possibility of her peacefully making even so tiny an acquisition should be contested." To Goltz, the emperor's tone was calm and moderate, but firm. He played the themes of national honor and of dynastic necessity. France and Prussia, he said, were in the position of "two friends, who happen to disagree in a café and find themselves obliged to fight, they do not exactly know why." But of course there *was* a reason: "his own existence as Sovereign of France would be imperilled," Napoleon stated, "if he were to submit to such a rebuff." War appeared inevitable.[13]

Nevertheless, there were strong arguments against asserting French claims until they led to the point of hostilities. Was Luxemburg worth a war? In the event of a conflict between Prussia and France, would not Italy seize the opportunity to act at Rome and Russia in the East? Besides, the attitude of the Dutch king made a clear "moral" stand

13. Benedetti to Moustier, Berlin, telegram, December 19, 1866, in *Origines*, XIII, 305, no. 3942; Benedetti to Moustier, Berlin, private, December 26, 1866, in *Origines*, XIII, 375–78, no. 3976; Moustier to Benedetti, Paris, telegrams, March 31, April 1, 1867, both in *Origines*, XV, 215–16, no. 4517, 222, no. 4524; Cowley to Stanley, Paris, April 4, 1867, in PRO, FO, 519, 233:216–20.

difficult. On April 3 he asked that negotiations be suspended. Most important, France was not ready to fight. France had no allies, and the reorganization of its army under Marshal Niel, which had been prompted by Sadowa, had barely begun. According to Cowley, Niel told the emperor that a war with Germany was out of the question; the army would need eight months to get ready. By April 5 the decision against war had been taken. It was confirmed by a meeting of the council of ministers on the sixth. But if not by war, then how could the French government avoid a capitulation so complete and obvious as to precipitate a crisis of the regime?[14]

The route had, in fact, been signaled on several occasions. As early as November, 1866, The Hague had threatened to carry its protest against the maintenance of a Prussian garrison in Luxemburg "before the tribunal of the European Powers." Later, when the Dutch king, having agreed to cede Luxemburg to France, began to worry about Prussia's reaction, he spoke of having the matter regulated by the signatories of the Belgian neutralization treaty of 1839. On that occasion Moustier demurred, asserting that Belgium had nothing to do with the question. But Saint Petersburg disagreed, and Napoleon himself did not seem to question the legality of a consultation of the 1839 signatories so much as its propriety, telling Goltz after the crisis had erupted "that we might have consulted the Powers concerned in the treaty; but we could scarcely do that after we had paid so little attention to the treaty in Denmark." Goltz, who had already at the end of March proposed to Berlin a conference as one way out of the problem, insisted that such a consultation was an excellent idea and that if France must proceed to a formal signing of the treaty of cession, a clause should be added "by which its operation should depend upon the ratification of Prussia, or upon the verdict of a European council." After all, he added on April 2, "once we were all seated round a green table it would be most improbable that we should set Europe in a blaze over such a comparative trifle." Napoleon avoided commitment, but, in his dilemma, he must certainly have been impressed by these arguments, especially since Benedetti had received hints at Berlin that Prussia "could make concessions to Europe which, because of national pride, it could not accord to intimidation." Cowley,

14. Millman, *British Foreign Policy*, 65; Cowley to Stanley, Paris, April 9, 1867, in PRO, FO, 519, 233:232; Moustier to Benedetti, Paris, telegram, April 5, 1867, in *Origines*, XV, 287, no. 4587; procès-verbal of the sitting of the council of ministers, April 6, 1867, in *Origines*, XX, 469–70, no. 18 (Appendix I).

hearing of Goltz's interview with the emperor, wrote that he would
not be surprised "if something like a Congress or Conference were to
be proposed for settling the Luxemburg question."[15]

In fact, if the British ambassador's information was correct, the majority of the ministers who decided on April 6 against war also recommended an appeal to a conference or a congress of the great powers.
Napoleon had remained noncommittal, perhaps even opposed. The
following day, however, he summoned Cowley to the Tuileries, justified his own handling of the Luxemburg matter, admitted the danger
of war, and concluded: "It had been suggested to him, that an appeal
be made to the Great Powers. He was most desirous to maintain the
peace of Europe, and if the Great Powers could prevail on Prussia to
give him satisfaction or could suggest any mode of settling this question, he would be too glad to adopt it." The next morning a meeting of
the ministers confirmed the emperor's decision to appeal to the 1839
signatories, and Moustier communicated it that same day to the legislature. To preserve peace and maintain its honor, France would appeal
to the concert of Europe. Moustier was careful to specify that under
these circumstances, the initiative must be left to Europe, with
whom it was now the intention of the French government to negotiate. The powers were asked to rule upon the morality and the legality
of Prussia's actions, to "call her back to the paths of justice and of
moderation," and to prevail upon Prussia "to renounce claims which
no longer have any foundation since she has herself destroyed the
treaties on which they were based, without asking first for the approval, or later the sanction of Europe."[16]

---

15. Note of Benedetti, Berlin, [probably November 16], 1866, in *Origines*, XIII, 104,
no. 3769; Charles Baudin to Moustier, The Hague, telegram, March 21, 1867, in *Origines*, XV, 124, no. 4407; Moustier to Baudin, Paris, telegram, March 28, 1867, in *Origines*, XV, 181, no. 4473; Talleyrand to Moustier, Saint Petersburg, private and confidential, April 3, 1867, in *Origines*, XV, 276, no. 4572; Goltz to Bismarck, April 2,
1867, in V. Wellesley and Sencourt (eds.), *Conversations with Napoleon III*, 322–25;
Goltz to Bismarck, Paris, telegram, March 30, 1867, in Oncken (ed.), *Rheinpolitik*, II,
267–68, no. 387; Benedetti to Moustier, Berlin, private, April 3, 1867, in *Origines*, XV,
270, no. 4569; Cowley to Stanley, Paris, April 4, 1867, in PRO, FO, 519, 233:220.

16. Cowley to Stanley, Paris, confidential, April 9, 1867, in PRO, FO, 519, 14:180–
81; Cowley to Stanley, Paris, April 7, 1867, in PRO, FO, 519, 233:226–27; Cowley to
Stanley, Paris, April 8, 1867, in PRO, FO, 519, 14:176–78; Moustier to Baudin, Paris,
telegram, April 10, 1867, in *Origines*, XV, 351–52, no. 4642; procès-verbal of the sitting of the council of ministers, April 10, 1867, in *Origines*, XX, 471, no. 19 (Appendix
I); Moustier to La Tour d'Auvergne, Paris, private and confidential, April 11, 1867, in
Origines, XV, 368, no. 4657; Moustier to La Tour d'Auvergne, Paris, telegram, April 21,
1867, in *Origines*, XVI, 92–93, no. 4764.

On this occasion, for the first time, appeal was made to the European concert to prevent a war that France itself feared, not, as in 1859 or 1866, to work out the changes that alone could prevent a war in which France might choose to participate rather than endure indefinitely a state of affairs that was, in its opinion, outmoded, unjust, and dangerous. The change in Napoleon's concept of the concert of Europe had begun. It was not yet complete, however. In 1867, as on earlier occasions, he would not accept a settlement that merely preserved the status quo. To the powers, and especially to Britain, Paris turned for some concession that would save French honor and avert war. On April 18, Cowley offered Britain's good offices. Napoleon, whose personal interest in London's reactions is attested to by the direct communication to him of La Tour d'Auvergne's dispatches, remarked on that occasion that "he did not look to terms or expressions, but what he desired was that Her Majesty's Government should endeavour to come to some understanding with the Governments of Austria and Russia to advise Prussia to settle the Luxemburg question amicably." Whether war could, in fact, be averted would depend on the emperor's decision as to what honor would require. From London, Vienna, and Saint Petersburg came suggestions. Luxemburg might be ceded to Belgium, after destruction of its fortress; the duchy might remain with the Dutch king, who would raze the fortress and promise not to cede Luxemburg to any power; or the fortress might be razed and the Luxemburgers left free to decide to which country they wished to belong. These were Stanley's suggestions. Beust, the Austrian foreign minister, tentatively offered Vienna's mediation on one of two bases. Luxemburg could remain with Holland after Prussian troops had been withdrawn; or the duchy could be ceded to Belgium, which would then return to France the fortresses it lost in 1815 by the Second Peace of Paris.[17]

Although Napoleon had begun by rejecting any suggestion that the Luxemburg fortress be demolished and had indicated a pronounced aversion to the idea of neutralization, on April 10 the council of ministers decided to negotiate with the great powers for the withdrawal of the Prussian garrison on condition that the fortress be razed. That

17. La Tour d'Auvergne to Moustier, London, April 18, 1867, in *Origines*, XVI, 50–51, no. 4734 (at top, in ink, "Copiée pour l'Empereur"); Cowley to Stanley, Paris, April 18, 1867, in PRO, FO, 519, 233:242–49; La Tour d'Auvergne to Moustier, London, confidential, April 8, 1867, in *Origines*, XV, 334–35, no. 4624 (at top, in ink, "Copiée pour l'Empereur").

same day Cowley was approached by General Fleury, who, in the emperor's name, gave him to understand "that the Luxemburg question might be settled by the destruction of the fortress, or the neutralization of the country." Moustier obviously continued his efforts to influence Napoleon to prefer the Austrian-Russian combination, by which Belgium would receive Luxemburg and give compensation to France, and he succeeded to the extent that on the thirteenth the council of ministers agreed to accept this solution if the other powers all agreed. But the emperor's hesitation was brief. On April 16 he informed Metternich of his final decision against Beust's proposal, and thereafter Moustier's instructions to his agents emphasized a single French condition, evacuation of the fortress by Prussia. "France had acquired a right with regard to Luxemburg," Napoleon told Metternich. "Prussia is in possession of the fortress—well then what could be simpler for France than to give up this right on condition that Prussia give up her occupation." He would ask that the fortress be razed "in order to anticipate a like request which Prussia might make." As for Beust's proposal: "Despite all the good will towards us which I find in [it], I have decided to reject it provisionally. . . . We must not complicate this question, Belgium and Holland could cause difficulties and I do not wish to give the impression of having followed a policy of conquest or aggrandizement while negotiating the Luxemburg question."[18]

Napoleon's decision to "limit his demand to satisfying the honour of France" and to accept a Prussian evacuation of Luxemburg as sufficient for honor might have seemed to lessen the need for a conference, and, in fact, France did not insist on one. But aside from the fact that the European concert was accustomed to manifest itself in con-

18. Benedetti to Moustier, Berlin, telegram, March 31, 1867, in Origines, XV, 212, no. 4511; Cowley to Stanley, Paris, April 7, 1867, in PRO, FO, 519, 233:223–29; Cowley to Stanley, Paris, April 8, 1867, in PRO, FO, 519, 14:176–79; Cowley to Stanley, Paris, April 9, 1867, in PRO, FO, 519, 233:232–34; procès-verbal of the sitting of the council of ministers, April 10, 1867, in Origines, XX, 471, no. 19 (Appendix I); Cowley to Stanley, Paris, April 11, 1867, in PRO, FO, 519, 233:235; Moustier to La Tour d'Auvergne, Paris, private and confidential, April 11, 1867, in Origines, XV, 369, no. 4657; Moustier to La Tour d'Auvergne, Paris, confidential, telegram, April 12, 1867, in Origines, XV, 386–87, no. 4670; procès-verbal of the sitting of the council of ministers, April 13, 1867, in Origines, XX, 472, no. 20 (Appendix I); Metternich to Beust, Paris, April 14, 1867, in Oncken (ed.), Rheinpolitik, II, 319–20, no. 421; Moustier to La Tour d'Auvergne, Paris, telegram, April 15, 1867, in Origines, XVI, 12, no. 4700; Metternich to Beust, Paris, telegram, April 16–17, 1867, in Oncken (ed.), Rheinpolitik, II, 334–35, no. 429; Metternich to Beust, Paris, April 18, 1867, in Oncken (ed.), Rheinpolitik, II, 336, no. 430.

ferences, there was another reason for such a meeting. One week before the French emperor's assertion to Cowley that, if Prussian troops were not withdrawn quickly from Luxemburg, war would be inevitable, Bismarck had instructed Bernstorff at London that German opinion and national feeling would not permit the separation of Luxemburg from Germany or evacuation of the fortress. Such a direct confrontation lent special weight to Bismarck's assertion that Prussia "could . . . make . . . to the United Powers concessions which she could not make to a single Power." The distinction would be most easily maintained at the conference table. Moreover, a conference protocol would strengthen French claims to having appealed successfully to Europe on an issue of European "law," and would prevent any of the great powers from feeling neglected. Perhaps all of these considerations were in Gorchakov's mind when he proposed on April 21, in a conversation with Talleyrand, the French ambassador, that a conference be called to meet in London to decide if Prussia's right to station troops in Luxemburg was still valid. Knowing that Bernstorff was proclaiming Prussia's refusal to evacuate Luxemburg and that Bismarck had shown a willingness to consider a conference, Paris accepted on April 27.[19]

Already, however, an obstacle had arisen. Fearful above all of involving Britain in the quarrel, Stanley announced on April 25 that his government "would consent to participate in a Conference, on the express *condition* that the Powers most directly interested in the questions to be discussed should declare themselves ready to accept the decision of the Congress as final." It would be difficult if not impossible for him to make such a statement, Napoleon replied, since France must insist upon evacuation by Prussia. "He should but deceive if he allowed it to be supposed that he could be satisfied with or accept any

19. The emperor told Cowley: "Let that garrison be withdrawn on what conditions you please. Give the fortress over to the Grand Ducal troops declaring the country neutral. Cede the Grand Duchy to Belgium, or destroy the fortress altogether. One arrangement might please me more than another, but I will not put a veto upon any one of them—all I declare is that I will not accept any territorial acquisition for France" (Cowley to Stanley, Paris, April 19, 1867, in V. Wellesley and Sencourt (eds.), *Conversations with Napoleon III*, 338–40). Cowley to Stanley, Paris, April 28, 1867, in PRO, FO, 14:192–95; Millman, *British Foreign Policy*, 71 n., 74 n., 79; La Tour d'Auvergne to Moustier, London, telegram, April 27, 1867, in *Origines*, XVI, 206, no. 4852; Fletcher, *The Mission of Benedetti*, 176; Talleyrand to Moustier, private, April 21, 1867, in *Origines*, XVI, 107, no. 477 (at top, in blue pencil, "Envoyé copie à l'Empereur"); La Tour d'Auvergne to Moustier, London, April 17, 1867, in *Origines*, XVI, 33, no. 4717 (at top, in ink, "Copiée pour l'Empereur"); Moustier to French agents in Vienna, London, and Saint Petersburg, telegram, April 27, 1867, in *Origines*, XVI, 207–208, no. 4855.

other solution, but he was quite ready on the other hand to give his promise to agree to whatever conditions the conference might think it right to impose, either in respect to the neutralization of the Grand Duchy or to dismantling or razing the fortress." Bismarck, who, influenced perhaps by letters to William I from both Queen Victoria and the Russian emperor, had abandoned his opposition in principle to the withdrawal of Prussian troops from Luxemburg, opposed both an arbitral conference and a preliminary agreement, but he indicated that he considered it inevitable that Prussia would have to evacuate the fortress. Informed that Eugène Rouher and Goltz were agreed on details, Stanley decided to yield and did so officially on April 30. That same day Napoleon characteristically wrote personally to thank Cowley, who, almost deaf and in financial difficulties, was about to leave the post he had held since 1852: "My dear Lord Cowley, I thank you for the good news you have given me. I am happy to think that if a peace that is honorable for us is preserved, I shall owe it in part to the good offices of the English government."[20]

But immediately there was a new problem. Bismarck's own condition for the conference was publicly revealed on April 27 in a press release from Berlin to Bremen stipulating that any solution must involve "substitution for the [Prussian] right of garrison at Luxemburg of guarantees for the security of Germany, and the placing of Luxemburg under the protection of Europe." Once again Paris offered no objection. To Metternich's suggestion that Prussia might withdraw from Luxemburg at Holland's request if neutralization under European guarantee followed, Napoleon replied: "If you succeed in winning acceptance for such an arrangement, you will have rendered me a service of gratitude," and he added that his experience "in another quarter" would serve as a lesson for him. Stanley, however, was extremely reluctant to commit his government to a guarantee. A "plan of agreement" drawn up by him in the first days of May at the request of La Tour d'Auvergne and Brunnow, and submitted "confidentially for the approval of the interested Courts," conspicuously avoided the issue. Moustier, who still hoped that France might someday gain

20. La Tour d'Auvergne to Moustier, London, confidential, April 25, 1867, in Origines, XVI, 181, no. 4826; Cowley to Stanley, Paris, most confidential, April 29, 1867, in PRO, FO, 519, 196; Benedetti to Moustier, Berlin, April 22, 1867, in Origines, XVI, 119, no. 4782; Benedetti to Moustier, Berlin, telegram, April 27, 1867, in Origines, XVI, 203, no. 4851; Benedetti to Moustier, Berlin, April 27, 1867, in Origines, XVI, 212, no. 4860; Cowley to Moustier, Paris, April 30, 1867, in Origines, XVI, 249–50, no. 4893; Millman, British Foreign Policy, 81 n.

compensation from Belgium in return for the eventual annexation of the duchy to that country, agreed with Stanley's argument that, if all the great powers promised not to violate Luxemburg's neutrality, this would be equivalent to a guarantee, But, then, Moustier was also ready to accept a formal guarantee; the important thing was to settle the dispute. Bismarck, however, stood firm, professing the darkest suspicions of British intentions. Prussia would not participate in the conference unless promised that Europe would guarantee the duchy's neutrality. Since the conference depended upon it, the foreign secretary declared his willingness to agree at the conference to a compromise proposed by Brunnow and agreed to by Bernstorff that would substitute a collective guarantee for one that would be exercised individually and separately. This, once more, was acceptable to Napoleon, if only the conference would meet at once and conclude its deliberations quickly.[21]

Meanwhile the usual problems involved in organizing an international meeting had been resolved. It would be at the ambassadorial level, would discuss only Luxemburg (Prussia, Austria, and Britain having rejected a discussion of such other matters as the treaty of Prague and the troubles in Crete), and would include representatives of Belgium and of Italy. The former was to be invited as a signatory of the 1839 treaty and as a onetime part of the Dutch kingdom, on particular insistence of London, which also felt that Italy, in view of its new status, ought to be admitted "to express her opinion in a council which proposes to consolidate the peace of Europe." As for Napoleon, at the top of a note in which Italy's ambassador reminded Moustier of the latter's promise to support the Italian bid for an invitation, he wrote: "We must accept the English proposal and admit Italy and Belgium." Obviously he had no particular interest in expanding the conference, and he had earlier doubted that Italy had any right to be

21. Benedetti to Moustier, Berlin, telegram, April 27, 1867, in *Origines*, XVI, 204–205, no. 4850; Metternich to Beust, Paris, April 27, 1867, in Oncken (ed.), *Rheinpolitik*, II, 365–66, no. 451; Millman, *British Foreign Policy*, 82–89; La Tour d'Auvergne to Moustier, London, confidential, telegram, May 3, 1867, in Oncken (ed.), *Rheinpolitik*, II, 308, no. 4945; Cowley to Moustier, Paris, translation, May 3, 1867, in Oncken (ed.), *Rheinpolitik*, II, 310, no. 4947; La Tour d'Auvergne to Moustier, London, confidential, May 3, 1867, in Oncken (ed.), *Rheinpolitik*, II, 309, no. 4946; Moustier to La Tour d'Auvergne, Paris, telegram, May 5, 1867, in Oncken (ed.), *Rheinpolitik*, II, 328–29, no. 4967; La Tour d'Auvergne to Moustier, London, confidential, May 6, 1867, in *Origines*, XVI, 347–49, no. 4987 (at top, in ink, "Copiée pour l'Empereur"); Moustier to La Tour d'Auvergne, Paris, telegram, May 7, 1867, in *Origines*, XVI, 353–54, no. 4994.

invited, although he probably did not quite share Beust's opinion that "one rogue more or less is neither here nor there" or Bismarck's profound suspicion of Britain's motives. Nor did Napoleon on this occasion support Spain's pretensions. Finally, it was decided that the formal invitation should be sent by The Hague, as Prussia and Britain preferred, rather than collectively from Saint Petersburg, London, and Vienna, as Gorchakov had proposed. Paris, in its desire for haste, would have adopted either plan. In fact, so eager was the French government to be done with the matter that on the same day on which the Dutch king sent out invitations to the conference, Moustier notified Cowley of French acceptance.[22]

Although so little had been left to the ambassadors at London to decide[23] that Moustier rejected La Tour d'Auvergne's request for instructions, the conference that assembled under Stanley's chairmanship at 10 Downing Street on May 7 did not complete its work without further complication and alarm. Even before the foreign secretary responded (as he had planned) to the wish of the conference for a collective guarantee by moving an adjournment in order to consult his government, Bismarck rattled the saber at Berlin. If peace were not assured within three days, he announced, the Prussian army would be mobilized. Whether Bismarck genuinely feared a French attack or was merely hoping to jolt Stanley into action, his threat was unnecessary.

22. Cowley to Moustier, Paris, May 2, 1867, in *Origines*, XVI, 287, no. 4928; Nigra to Moustier, Paris, May 2, 1867, in *Origines*, XVI, 287–88, no. 4929; Cowley to Stanley, Paris, April 28, 1867, in PRO, FO, 519, 14:195; Cowley to Stanley, May 1, 1867, in PRO, FO, 519, 232:265; Gramont to Moustier, Vienna, confidential, May 5, 1867, in *Origines*, XVI, 338–40, no. 4977; Benedetti to Moustier, Berlin, May 4, 1867, in *Origines*, XVI, 318–22, no. 4960 (at top, in ink, "Copiée pour l'Empereur"); La Tour d'Auvergne to Moustier, London, telegrams, April 27, 29, 1867, both in *Origines*, XVI, 206, no. 4852, 234, no. 4878; Benedetti to Moustier, Berlin, telegram, April 27, 1867, in *Origines*, XVI, 205, no. 4851; Moustier to French agents in Vienna, London, and Saint Petersburg, telegram, April 27, 1867, in *Origines*, XVI, 207–208, no. 4855; Moustier to Cowley, Paris, May 1, 1867, in *Origines*, XVI, 268, no. 4911.

23. The official British note of acceptance predicated the understanding that Berlin and Paris "désirent . . . voir s'ouvrir la discussion sur les bases de la neutralisation de la forteresse, ce qui implique comme une conséquence nécessaire le retrait de la garnison prussienne qui l'occupe en ce moment et la renonciation de la France à toute prétention sur le Duché ou la forteresse" (Cowley to Moustier, Paris, translation, April 30, 1867, in *Origines*, XVI, 250, no. 4893). To this the French government fully adhered (Moustier to La Tour d'Auvergne, Paris, telegram, May 2, 1867, in *Origines*, XVI, 284, no. 4925), while Bismarck's instructions to Bernstorff were a model of concision: "Neutrality guaranteed and evacuation, nothing more, without reservations, without reserves, without requests for indemnity or stay of proceedings" (Gramont to Moustier, Vienna, confidential, May 5, 1867, in *Origines*, XVI, 338–40, no. 4977).

Although France was arming, its motives were defensive. The council of ministers had decided on April 27 against a defense loan, and Metternich reported on May 9 that Prussian fears were exaggerated, since French efforts were aimed at attaining full *peacetime* strength. Napoleon personally had given assurances to Goltz at the end of April, and he now repeated them. Under the circumstances, Moustier's indignation had the ring of sincerity: "The allegations made against us are absurd in the extreme. . . . [Prussian] mobilization would be an act of aggression which nothing would justify, and we would be obliged to call it to the attention of an indignant Europe." As for Stanley, he did what he had intended to, announcing at the second session of the conference that Britain would agree to a collective guarantee of Luxemburg's neutrality. This meeting also decided that the question of the duchy's continued membership in the Zollverein was not within the competence of the conference and began consideration of a timetable for Prussian evacuation. No agreement proved possible in the third session (May 10). Paris could not accept Bismarck's suggestion of three months, especially since it almost immediately became "at least three months." Brunnow once again provided a formula. Evacuation would begin immediately after the exchange of ratifications of the treaty; only the minimum of troops necessary to safeguard the war matériel and expedite its removal would remain behind; and the whole operation would be accomplished as soon as possible. Napoleon told Cowley that he had instructed La Tour d'Auvergne to agree to this arrangement and added that he personally would have accepted Bismarck's three-month proposal except for the effect that it would have had on French opinion. Early in the evening of the eleventh, the treaty was signed.[24]

The conference on Luxemburg had accomplished the only task it set for itself. The peace of Europe had been maintained. Otherwise,

24. Moustier to La Tour d'Auvergne, Paris, May 5, 1867, in *Origines*, XVI, 329–31, no. 4969; Millman, *British Foreign Policy*, 87; procès-verbal of the sitting of the council of ministers, April 27, 1867, in *Origines*, XX, 473, no. 23 (Appendix I); Metternich to Beust, Paris, May 9, 1867, in Oncken (ed.), *Rheinpolitik*, II, 385, no. 468; Goltz to Bismarck, Paris, telegram, April 29, 1867, in Oncken (ed.), *Rheinpolitik*, II, 373, no. 457; Metternich to Beust, Paris, May 9, 1867, in Oncken (ed.), *Rheinpolitik*, II, 385, no. 468; Rothan, *Souvenirs diplomatiques*, 382–87; Moustier to Benedetti, Berlin, telegram, May 9, 1867, in *Origines*, XVI, 381, no. 5019; circular of Moustier, Paris, May 9, 1867, in *Origines*, XVI, 382–84, no. 5020; La Tour d'Auvergne to Moustier, London, May 9, 1867, in *Origines*, XVI, 400–402, no. 5029; La Tour d'Auvergne to Moustier, London, telegram, May 10, 1867, in *Origines*, XVI, 404, no. 5034; Cowley to Stanley, Paris, confidential, May 13, 1867, in PRO, FO, 519, 14:209.

there was little cause for rejoicing. Stanley exerted himself to prove that the collective guarantee was meaningless. Moustier continued to hope that Luxemburg would somehow, someday become Belgian, with consequent compensation for France. The Prussian army made its last days in the fortress the occasion of deliberate provocation, continuing maintenance work until almost the last moment, while Bismarck refused to accept a three-month time limit for withdrawal. French opinion accepted peace with relief but otherwise treated the settlement with disdain. And so, the atmosphere of mutal suspicion between Berlin and Paris deepened rather than dissipated. Yet, thanks largely to French moderation and to the continued existence of a sense of European concert, a war had been avoided that neither protagonist wanted but toward which considerations of honor, prestige, and public opinion might inexorably have led, had there been no exit from the cul-de-sac.[25] A diplomatic conference, mused Forcade in *Revue des deux mondes* (May 14), had been shown to be still "bonne à quelque chose." And he speculated hopefully that, a semblance of Europe's collective authority having been reestablished, governments would perhaps find once again a taste for working together to resolve dangerous questions before they could lead to conflict. This was still far, however, from the scope and function that Napoleon had long imagined for the concert of Europe and toward which he would turn yet again, and for one last time, as 1867 drew to its close.

25. Millman, *British Foreign Policy*, 90–92; Metternich to Beust, Paris, May 6, 1867, in Oncken (ed.), *Rheinpolitik*, II, 379, no. 461; Moustier to Benedetti, Paris, telegram, May 11, 1867, in *Origines*, XVI, 413, no. 5044; Mahon to Moustier, Eich, May 12, 1867, in *Origines*, XVI, 430–31, no. 5057; La Tour d'Auvergne to Moustier, London, May 12, 1867, in *Origines*, XVI, 433–36, no. 5061; Case, *French Opinion on War and Diplomacy*, 232–33.

CHAPTER 15

Rome Again
The Congress Proposal
of 1867

After the failure in December, 1866, to have a conference on Rome, it had still seemed possible that the threat of a congress might prove useful in holding Florence to the terms of the September Convention. Such did not prove to be the case, however. As bands of Garibaldians raided papal territory virtually unchecked in October, 1867, and as Garibaldi himself threatened at any moment to escape from the island of Caprera, where he had been confined by the government of Urbano Rattazzi, Napoleon instructed Moustier from Biarritz: "According to the news which you send me, I think it necessary to write to M. Rattazzi that he seems unable to prevent the invasion of Roman territory and to carry out the Convention on his own." And in that case, concluded the emperor, "we would be obliged to take steps." Napoleon also wrote directly to Victor Emmanuel, warning him that if the September Convention were violated, a French expeditionary force would have to be sent. Under these circumstances, Nigra, at Paris, regarded the congress less as a threat than as a means of escape. The French council of ministers was to meet on October 16. On the fifteenth, Nigra advised his government, by telegraph, to occupy papal territory ("to establish order"), while proposing, with France in agreement, "a Congress of the great Powers which would meet at Florence to settle definitively the Roman Question." The response was not encouraging. Italy would probably not reject a congress if proposed by France but would prefer to avoid such a meeting, since it would be unlikely to "produce favorable results." Nigra, however, wished above all else to avoid French intervention. On October 14 he had, while arguing Italy's need to occupy papal territory in the interest of order, concluded that French intervention would be, of all possible solutions, "the most dangerous." And so, he now wrote to Moustier, not only would an Italian occupation of the Papal States be carried out in such a way as to leave the issue of sovereignty uncompromised and to ensure the independence of the pope, but "Italy would furthermore accept, I think, a Congress of the Powers to settle the Roman question definitively."[1]

Although Nigra's note was received in time to be read at the meeting of the French council of ministers on the sixteenth, it failed of its purpose. Only La Valette and Baroche opposed intervention. Rouher argued in favor of a strong policy, and Napoleon concluded the debate by accepting this principle. He could hardly have done otherwise, in view of recent setbacks and the state of public opinion, which had favored the withdrawal of French troops but held Napoleon personally responsible for the pope's safety. Nevertheless, the congress suggestion had not gone unnoticed. The next day, Moustier's reply to Nigra was approved: "It is at the same time decided that a circular will be addressed to our Agents close to the great Powers. This circular will explain 1) that we are intervening solely because of the urgency and peril of the situation in order to maintain the status quo; 2) that we intend neither to continue our occupation indefinitely nor to resolve on our own the Roman question; 3) that we are prepared to initiate [provoquer] conferences in order to arrive at a definitive solution which will bring about the disappearance of this difficult question from the chessboard of Europe." France would accept a congress, Moustier explained, would even be disposed to employ all its influence to bring such a meeting about, and for that reason no change in the status quo (e.g., an Italian occupation) would be tolerated until the congress could be convoked. In fact, the initiative of a congress had now passed into French hands, if indeed it had not always been there. Nigra vigorously combated Moustier's thesis that Italy had proposed the congress. He had, the ambassador maintained, merely expressed his opinion that Florence would accept such a meeting; it was Rouher who, on October 15, had proposed a conference "as being his personal idea." Perhaps the authorship ascended even higher. Certainly Napoleon gave his immediate and entire support to the in-

1. Malaret to Moustier, confidential, December 21, 1866, in *Origines*, XIII, 337, no. 3955; Napoleon III to Moustier, Biarritz, telegram, October 11, 1867, in *Origines*, XVIII, 403–404, no. 5766; Nigra to [Italian foreign minister] Campello, Paris, telegram, October 15, 1867, in *Origines*, XIX, 421 n.; Campello to Nigra, Florence, telegram [sent 5 A.M.], October 16, 1867, in *Origines*, XIX, 419 n.; Nigra to Moustier, Paris, October 16, 1867, in *Origines*, XIX, 5, no. 5800.

volvement of Europe. As early as October 21 he told Goltz that he "would be satisfied with a simple declaration from the Italian Government that they intended to respect the September Convention; and that he will be ready to enter into common deliberations for an equitable solution to the question." To the papal nuncio, on October 24, he "suggested the convocation of a European Congress with a view to obtain a general guarantee of the status quo of the Pope's temporal sovereignty." And to Victor Emmanuel he wrote two days later: "Moreover, it is not my intention to prolong the occupation; when order is re-established, I will do everything possible to induce the powers to settle a question which interests the whole of Europe." The circular arguing the case for a congress was sent out on October 28.[2]

But first it was necessary to reestablish order. Rattazzi's resignation on the twentieth precipitated a political crisis at Florence. Four days later, the French government decided upon the immediate dispatch of an expeditionary force to Città Vecchia, a resolution that was kept despite the descent upon Paris of Pepoli and La Marmora and the intention of the new Italian government under Count Luigi Federigo Menabrea to send troops into the Papal States should French forces land. On November 3 the new French Chassepot rifles were initiated in battle. French and papal troops routed the Garibaldians at Mentana. From Paris, Beyens reported reaction to the news: "We were so low that tonight we felt the same satisfaction as though we had achieved the definitive and complete solution of the Roman question. The Emperor, M. de Moustier, the nuncio and the Italian minister are equally joyful . . . at finding themselves again confronting the grave difficulties of 1864. Now all efforts will be directed toward the Congress question." There was, certainly, a sense of return to familiar scenes. One year before, Napoleon had sought a European solution of the Roman question with Prussian assistance. Now his hopes apparently turned, however forlornly, to London. But Cowley was gone, entered into retirement after fifteen years at the Paris post. His successor,

2. Rouher's notes on the meetings of the council of ministers, October 16, 17, 1867, in *Origines*, XIX, 1–3, no. 5796, 8, no. 5803; Case, *French Opinion on War and Diplomacy*, 168–70; Moustier to Villestreux [French chargé át Florence], Paris, confidential, October 18, 1867, in *Origines*, XIX, 20, no. 5819; Nigra to Moustier, Paris, December 5, 1867, in *Origines*, XIX, 419–21, no. 6179; Sir Augustus Paget to Stanley, telegram, October 22, 1867, in PRO, FO, 45, 108: no. 90; Fane to Stanley, Paris, confidential, October 25, 1867, in PRO, FO, 27, 1669: no. 753; Napoleon III to Victor Emmanuel, October 26, 1867, in Ollivier, *L'empire libéral*, X, 146; circular, October 28, 1867, in *Origines*, XIX, 102–104, no. 5908.

Lord Richard Lyons, had hastened to Paris at the end of October with a sincere desire to be of help to the French but with a confessed lack of ideas. Perhaps this change of personnel explains why the emperor's approach to Britain was now made indirectly through Florence.[3]

On November 6, Menabrea presented a proposal to the British representative at Florence that, by its timing and nature, could have been made only with the consent if not the connivance of Napoleon.

> He had [Menabrea told Paget] information on which he could rely, that the Emperor was quite ready to agree to an arrangement, which might be accepted by Italy, but which His Imperial Majesty, owing to the account he had to take of the feelings of an influential party in France, would not venture to propose.
>
> Neither could the Italian Government on their side propose it.
>
> The arrangement to which he alluded, was that by which the Leonine quarter of the City of Rome should be assured in full sovereignty to the Pope, with certain other provisions suitable to the dignity of the temporal Power, and with every guarantee in regard to Civil List and spiritual authority, which should befit the Head of the Catholic Church.
>
> The plan in question is not a new one, and is said to have [been] for some time under the consideration of the Emperor.
>
> Such a basis, His Excellency said, if proposed by a friendly Power, could be accepted by both France and Italy as a settlement of the whole question.

What he really wanted, Menabrea explained, was that if Paris proposed a solution Florence could not accept, the British government would bring forward the alternative proposal, arguing that it might work and that they would be prepared to discuss it. And he concluded by repeating that he had "the most positive, though confidential grounds" for knowing that this proposal would be acceptable to France. Whether it would have been acceptable to France is open to question, but the evidence suggests that the proposal was acceptable to Napoleon and that there had been a conspiracy between the emperor and Florence to which his foreign minister was not a party. "His information entitled him to say," repeated Menabrea three days later, "that all that the Emperor wished for, was to have a plan of settlement laid before him by another government, which he was quite ready to adopt, but which in view of the difficulties of his position as regards the clerical party in France, he was not able himself to propose." When Paget

---

3. Count Luigi Federigo Menabrea to Nigra, Florence, October 28, 1867, in *Origines*, XIX, 113, no. 5918; Beyens to [?], Paris, November 5, 1867, in Beyens, *Le Second Empire*, II, 284; Lord Richard Lyons to Stanley, Paris, November [8], 1867, in RA, J83/13.

asked if the minister was "perfectly certain" that Napoleon would accept such a proposal, Menabrea took from his drawer a telegram of Nigra's. It was, reported the ambassador, as nearly as possible in the following words: "The Emperor is most favorably inclined towards the solution of the Roman question. He would even grant to us the Vatican City plan, but because of his position he cannot propose it. He wishes it suggested to him by a friendly Power." Menabrea did his best to persuade Paget: "The Roman question . . . was essentially an European question, and in this light it ought to be taken up by H.M. Government. So long as it was unsettled, the peace of Europe might be disturbed at any moment, and His Majesty's Government, being interested in the maintenance of peace, were consequently and evidently interested in the settlement of the relations between Rome and Italy. They had it in their power to contribute in an eminent degree towards this settlement now—would they not do so?"[4]

Perhaps Nigra had misunderstood Napoleon's meaning, but it should be remembered that the French emperor had himself studiously avoided using the term *temporal authority* of the pope and might well have accepted a settlement more favorable to Italy (a useful ally against Prussia) than to the papacy if he could have made it appear that in so doing he was bending to the will of Europe. French opinion, which almost unanimously had approved of Mentana, might not have accepted such a *volte-face* even so, for Rouher as government spokesman had on more than one occasion pledged support for the pope's temporal power, and both he and Napoleon well understood at the end of 1867 the danger of offending the Catholic party, given the growing opposition on the Left. The issue did not arise, however, for it was soon evident that Britain had no enthusiasm for a congress and would certainly not take the initiative there. Stanley had given advance warning of this attitude as early as October 19, and the French chargé's reports from London continued to reflect the British government's determination to stand clear. By November 9, the day on which Moustier's circular formally launched the congress idea, Florence had decided that there was nothing to be hoped for from the British government and therefore nothing to be hoped for from the congress. General La Marmora, who had talked with Napoleon at Compiègne on November 5, concluded that "the object of His Imperial Majesty in convoking a Conference is to impose a still more disadvantageous ar-

4. Paget to Stanley, Florence, secret, November 7, 9, 1867, both in PRO, FO, 45, 108.

rangement on Italy than that which now exists, and to place this arrangement under the sanction and guarantee of the European powers." Although Napoleon continued to want a congress, Italian agents began to work quietly against it, for example, d'Azeglio at London and Count Edoardo di Launay at Berlin, and poor Moustier was at a loss to explain this change of attitude at Florence—strong circumstantial evidence that he had known nothing of the conversations between the emperor and Nigra. France, argued Moustier in his circular, had for the moment saved the pope, but to be truly effective France's efforts must be shared "by the other Governments, no less interested in making the principles of order and stability prevail in Europe." Therefore, France did not doubt that the European governments would speedily accept the proposal to unite in conference for the examination of the grave questions involved. "It is in a calm and attentive study of the facts that this assembly, by its nature beyond the reach of secondary consideration, will find the foundation of a work to which we should not at this time attempt to ascribe limits, neither to prejudice the results."[5]

With the exception of Austria, however, none of the other great powers showed any enthusiasm for the congress, and all insisted, as a minimum, that limits *should* be ascribed in advance. Beust had been at Compiègne in the first days of November and was thereafter an ardent champion of the congress. He had had "his head turned," wrote Bloomfield, "and is bent on doing everything in his power to promote the views of France." In fact Beust, who was cultivating Paris in his quarrel with Bismarck and who represented a Catholic state bordering Italy, sounded almost Napoleonic in his confidence "that round a green table happy ideas would be exchanged and that the result of a Conference would be an arrangement 'à l'aimable.'" Florence, however, demanded "a reasonable prospect of a solution which would be acceptable to Italy, or at least not place her in a worse position," and presented a long list of questions for "clarification." Menabrea also

5. Case, *French Opinion on War and Diplomacy*, 169–70, 172–73; Baron Georges Napoléon Baude to Moustier, London, October 19, 1867, in *Origines*, XIX, 33, no. 5830 (at top, in ink, "Copiée pour l'Empereur"); president of the council of ministers to Paget, Florence, private, November 9, 1867, in PRO, FO, 45, 108; Paget to Stanley, Florence, confidential, November 9, 1867, in PRO, FO, 45, 108; Baude to Moustier, London, telegram, November 11, 1867, in *Origines*, XIX, 220, no. 6023; Benedetti to Moustier, Berlin, telegram, November 12, 1867, in *Origines*, XIX, 222–23, no. 6029; Moustier to Villestreux, Paris, telegram, November 12, 1867, in *Origines*, XIX, 221, no. 6026; circular of Moustier, Paris, November 9, 1867, in *Origines*, XIX, 199–201, no. 6005.

wanted all of the great powers to attend and France to withdraw from papal territory before the congress met. Stanley bluntly insisted that the congress would certainly fail if the powers did not agree before-hand on principles, leaving only details to be settled at the conference table. Moreover, he wanted the most interested parties to agree "to adhere, within certain limits, to the decisions which the Conference would formulate," although he subsequently softened this condition in conversation with the French ambassador. Gorchakov insisted upon the setting of a program in advance, and Bismarck found that the French plan of bringing the powers together before having dis-cussed a program and reached agreement on general bases was "an in-ternational innovation" that Prussia could not accept. By the end of November, Moustier's list of those governments whose attitude could be construed as an acceptance of the congress was singularly unim-pressive: Austria, Bavaria, Württemberg, Hesse-Darmstadt, Baden, Sweden, Denmark, Luxemburg, Portugal, and Spain.[6]

And yet, the diplomatic exchange had become an elaborate minuet from which the congress might well emerge intact if for no other rea-son than that no one wished to play the role of spoiler. Italy ardently desired to see the congress frustrated, but, as the Italian ambassador at Berlin admitted, "would not be permitted to decline." Saint Pe-tersburg did not expect the congress to meet, but intended to come if the other powers did. As for Prussia: "If," Bismarck had told Benedetti as early as November 9, "I had the honor of being Foreign Minister to the Emperor Napoleon, I would not hesitate to suggest to His Majesty that he renounce such a plan." Aside from all the good arguments that the North German chancellor could find against the congress, he ob-viously did not want to help France pull its chestnuts from the fire, having "no wish to be called in to repair the mistakes of others . . . to extricate France and Italy from the confusion which they had them-selves created." Moreover, he was genuinely irritated by the fact that

6. Bloomfield to Stanley, Vienna, private, November 19, 1867, in PRO, FO, 356, 40; Menabrea to Nigra, Florence, telegram, November 12, 1867, in *Origines*, XIX, 229, no. 6040; Menabrea to Nigra, Florence, translation, November 19, 1867, in *Origines*, XIX, 284–88, no. 6080; Paget to Stanley, Florence, November 22, 1867, in PRO, FO, 45, 109: no. 182; Stanley to Lyons, London, translation, November 18, 1867, in *Origines*, XIX, 269–72, no. 6074; Talleyrand to Moustier, Saint Petersburg, November 10, 16, 1867, both in *Origines*, XIX, 214, no. 6016, 257, no. 6065 (at top, in ink, "Copiée pour l'Em-pereur"); Benedetti to Moustier, Berlin, telegram, November 29, 1867, in *Origines*, XIX, 374, no. 6149; Moustier to Comte Eugène de Sartiges, Paris, November 27, 1867, in *Origines*, XIX, 360–61, no. 6138.

Moustier had sent separate invitations to Bavaria, Saxony, Württemberg, Baden, Hesse-Darmstadt, and, for that matter, Luxemburg. But Bismarck clearly looked to London in determining his final attitude, and he would not decline the congress if "others and especially England accepted the invitation." The circle closed, then, in the British Foreign Office, where Stanley's attitude toward the operation of the concert of Europe—or at least toward the conference aspect of it— was, as revealed by his statement to the House of Commons, completely antithetical to that of Napoleon: "A Conference is an excellent means of giving formal and solemn satisfaction to settled facts. But in the case where there is a fundamental disagreement, not on questions of detail, but of principle, I cannot make myself believe that it suffices, in order to bring about a rapprochement, to gather several Ambassadors together. I ought to add that, in a question which does not directly touch English interests, we would not want to risk, by our attitude, allowing ourselves to be drawn into complications which could arise."[7] Nevertheless, the British foreign secretary did not reject the congress; rather, he assumed that the conditions he had set would make the meeting impossible. It was time, therefore, for Paris to define more clearly its thinking in regard to the mechanics, scope, and—above all—the purpose and utility of the congress.

Neither the authority nor the site of the meeting posed a problem. Moustier had from the first tended to play down the thought of coercion. The gathering, he said, "should be a conference rather than a congress," and issues should not be submitted to a vote without the consent of the interested parties. Moreover, France would accept any meeting place that suited "the convenience of the Powers." There was, perhaps, a slight French preference for Rome, but Russia, having broken off relations with the papal government, opposed meeting there, as did the pope himself. Munich was a possibility. Paris was not suggested as a site, either directly or indirectly. There was more difficulty in deciding on participants, but the Italian government's opposition to a congress of Catholic powers, and the pope's distaste for a congress of great powers only, left little choice, and on October 24,

7. Benedetti to Moustier, Berlin, November 14, 1867, in *Origines*, XIX, 239, no. 6050; Talleyrand to Moustier, Saint Petersburg, telegram, November 22, 1867, in *Origines*, XIX, 325, no. 6108; Benedetti to Moustier, Berlin, November 10, 1867, in *Origines*, XIX, 207, no. 6013; Fletcher, *The Mission of Benedetti*, 192, 193, 195; Loftus to Stanley, Berlin, November 2, 1867, in PRO, FO, 64, 624: no. 456; Baude to Moustier, London, November 20, 1867, in *Origines*, XIX, 299, no. 6091.

Napoleon assured the papal nuncio that he was contemplating a general congress, not one of Catholic states only. "The question was one which was of importance to all the Powers," Moustier declared. "All were concerned in the maintenance of peace and order—all had more or less Catholic subjects, who were deeply interested in the maintenance of the independence of the Head of their Church."[8]

While Bismarck felt that inviting all the European states to a congress was contrary to custom and would make a successful outcome more difficult to achieve, it seems likely that Napoleon believed just the opposite, although this does not make it any easier to determine what outcome he favored or expected. On the one hand, there is some evidence that the emperor still hoped that Europe would "impose" upon him a solution more favorable to Italy than to the pope. At least he vaguely formulated, in a conversation with Lyons, the hope that the preservation of papal temporal power could be reconciled with the assimilation of the papal territory to Italy. Earlier, Baron Joseph de Malaret had told Menabrea that "the Emperor attached great value to the meeting of the Conference as the only means of arriving at an understanding upon the question at issue. Being at Rome as the Guardian and Protector of the Pope, it was impossible for His Imperial Majesty to make a proposal to the Italian Government which was likely to be acceptable but that His Imperial Majesty was quite prepared to accept such an arrangement as should be judged best by the Powers of Europe." Moustier was even more explicit: "If France acted alone, she must virtually be the advocate of the Holy See. She could not herself propose, she could not prevail upon the Pope to accept conditions so favorable to Italy as those which would probably be obtained from a Conference." Lyons, for his part, thought that Napoleon would be willing to make considerable concessions to Italy, if he could be shielded from responsibility by appearing to yield not to Italy but to the "voice of Europe." The ambassador felt that what Napoleon intended was what Moustier had more than once suggested: "The Pope to remain at Rome as Sovereign—His subjects to have all the rights and privileges of Italian subjects—and his States to be garrisoned by Italian troops." On the other hand, Stanley's refusal to make at the

8. Lyons to Stanley, Paris, November 1, 1867, in PRO, FO, 27, 1669: no. 33; Moustier to Malaret, Paris, November 27, 1867, in *Origines*, XIX, 358, no. 6136; Moustier to La Tour d'Auvergne, Paris, November 29, 1867, in *Origines*, XIX, 373, no. 6148; Fane to Stanley, Paris, confidential, October 25, 1867, in PRO, FO, 27, 1669:753; Lyons to Stanley, Paris, confidential, October 28, 1867, in PRO, FO, 27, 1669: no. 12.

congress a proposal favorable to Italy left little hope that one could be effectively advanced. Besides, whatever Napoleon's personal views might have been, his government was compromised. Not only had Moustier called attention to the keen interest that all Catholics had "in the maintenance of the independence of the Head of their Church" but he had made use of the legalistic argument that "the triumph of the aggression directed against the Pontifical Government would be fatal to the principles of order and conservation in Europe." Thus encouraged, Benedetti assured the Prussian king that France would not tamper with the pope's temporal power (*toucher au pouvoir temporel*).[9]

It seems likely, in fact, that the emperor had come reluctantly to accept what he had assured the papal nuncio (probably insincerely at that time) on October 24, that the congress would be convoked "with a view to obtain a general guarantee of the status quo of the Pope's temporal sovereignty." Eugénie, who, significantly, advocated the congress as strongly as the *Italianissime* Prince Napoleon opposed it, informed Lyons on November 11 that she thought the status quo would be the proper basis for a conference, since this would be a compromise between the pope's demand for a restoration of his lost territories and Italy's demand for Rome. It might be impossible to satisfy the pope at the expense of Italy or Italy at the expense of the pope, argued Talleyrand at Saint Petersburg, but it was urgent "to find from a calm and attentive study of the facts a modus vivendi which Europe can advise, notify, if needs be impose upon the parties in litigation." Moustier professed not to believe in "an eternal settlement," but hoped that "a means of peaceful coexistence" might be worked out "under the impulsion of the great authority of the Powers met together and safeguarding all situations as well as legitimate susceptibilities." Moreover, it was decided at Paris that, if the congress met, the French troops would be withdrawn from Città Vecchia.[10]

9. Benedetti to Moustier, Berlin, November 29, 1867, in *Origines*, XIX, 375–78, no. 6150 (at top, in ink, "Copiée pour l'Empereur"); Lyons to Stanley, Paris, private, November 16, 1867, in RA, J83/34; Paget to Stanley, Florence, November 19, 1867, in PRO, FO, 45, 108: no. 173; Lyons to Stanley, Paris, November 14, 1867, PRO, FO, 27, 1669: no. 78; Lyons to Stanley, Paris, private, November 26, 1867, in Lyons Papers, RC2 (reference supplied by Richard Millman); Lyons to Stanley, Paris, confidential, October 28, 1867, in PRO, FO, 27, 1669: no. 12; Moustier to Benedetti, Paris, November 4, 1867, in *Origines*, XIX, 164, no. 5970: Benedetti to Moustier, Berlin, November 17, 1867, in *Origines*, XIX, 262, no. 6067.

10. Fane to Stanley, Paris, confidential, October 25, 1867, in PRO, FO, 27, 1669: no. 753; Lyons to Stanley, Paris, November 11, 1867, in RA, J83/34; Talleyrand to Mous-

But whether the congress was to please Italy or Rome or neither, whether it was to work out a definitive solution or merely establish a modus vivendi that would stabilize a precarious situation until time could work its appeasement, Napoleon appeared to be convinced that the difficulty of reaching an acceptable solution would "be very much diminished if the Powers of Europe would meet in conference to consider the matter." For one thing, it would be easier for both France and Italy to accept whatever solution was thought necessary if it were the work of a congress. "France," affirmed Moustier, "on her side, would readily defer to the general voice, and would not be disposed to maintain her own views so absolutely as she would be obliged to do, if she were left to bear all the responsibility alone." As to the Italian government, it "would have less difficulty in reconciling its own people to a moderate solution, recommended by the united voice of Europe, than to a solution insisted upon by France alone." Before such a body, both Florence and Rome might prove more moderate. And even if this were not so, the congress could hope to achieve much through the exercise of what Napoleon called its "moral influence." At any rate, Moustier insisted that "it is indeed beyond all question that the concessions which may be expected from the parties in order to arrive at a definitive arrangement will be more easily granted to an arbitration proceeding from the wisdom of Europe than to a more limited and consequently less authorized initiative." Besides, it was just possible that in a European assembly expedients might be discovered that would otherwise be missed, especially if the discussions were to be as free-wheeling as possible, uninhibited by a restrictive agenda or preliminary commitments. In fact, to devise an agenda in advance would be, in Moustier's opinion, "to outstrip the work of the Conference," since the bases of a settlement were "to emerge only from a preliminary examination on the part of the Conference itself." At the very least, "even if the stated aim were not completely reached, from this sincere study in depth undertaken by the Powers, there would necessarily emerge new information and new insights which would further justify the usefulness of our proposal."[11]

---

tier, Saint Petersburg, November 16, 1867, in *Origines*, XIX, 258, no. 6065 (at top, in ink, "Copiée pour l'Empereur"); Lyons to Stanley, Paris, confidential, November 7, 1867, in PRO, FO, 27, 1669: no. 48; circular of Moustier, Paris, December 24, 1867, in *Origines*, XX, 69, no. 6257; procès-verbal of the sitting of the council of ministers, November 23, 1867, in *Origines*, XIX, 325, no. 6110.

11. Lyons to Stanley, Paris, confidential, November 7, 1867, in PRO, FO, 27, 1669: no. 48; Lyons to Stanley, Paris, November 14, 1867, in PRO, FO, 27, 1669: no. 78; Lyons

Of course, there was yet another reason for French aversion to an agenda. As Benedetti argued, with admirable finesse, if it were necessary to bring Rome and Florence together by virtue of mutual concessions, "it was fitting to explain oneself only before the assembled Representatives, the Court of Rome and the Italian government being able, once Europe was assembled, to consent to arrangements which a legitimate sensitivity would not allow them to accept even in principle at preliminary negotiations." In view of the attitude of the papal government, such optimism seemed excessive. The nuncio had already warned Napoleon "that the Pope would scarcely accept a guarantee of the status quo which would necessarily imply a sanction of the usurpations already consummated on the ancient patrimony of the Church." Consequently, when Antonelli, the papal secretary of state, accepted the congress on November 19, he added that the pope would raise there "the question of law and of principle with respect to the provinces taken from the Church States." Did this mean that the papal government would withdraw from the congress if the pope's rights to his lost provinces were not reaffirmed? At London, Berlin, Saint Petersburg, and Vienna, such was assumed to be the case. In fact, the issue was unclear, because Antonelli apparently spoke in one manner with the French ambassador, Comte Eugène de Sartiges, and in another with representatives of the other powers. Certainly the pope had no enthusiasm for the congress and did not believe that in the present state of opinions and passions it could bring peace to Italy, but he was not therefore resolved to be completely intransigent. Nevertheless, the demand for an agenda had been persistent, and now it was reinforced by a legitimate doubt as to the pope's attitude.[12]

Moustier responded by attempting to shift responsibility. Since the papal government wanted to preserve the status quo and Italy wanted to change it, Florence should be requested to prepare a tentative program. "A declaration from Italy of its wants, would be a proper basis

---

to Stanley, Paris, private and confidential, November 16, 1867, in RA, J83/34; Moustier to Benedetti, Paris, November 4, 1867, in Origines, XIX, 165, no. 5970; Moustier to Baude, Paris, November 8, 1867, in Origines, XIX, 190, no. 6000; Moustier to Villestreux, Paris, telegram, November 13, 1867, in Origines, XIX, 232, no. 6045; Moustier to Benedetti, Paris, November 4, 1867, in Origines, XIX, 165, no. 5970.

12. Benedetti to Moustier, Berlin, November 14, 1867, in Origines, XIX, 240, no. 6050; Fane to Stanley, Paris, confidential, October 25, 1867, in PRO, FO, 27, 1669: no. 753: Sartiges to Moustier, Rome, telegram, November 19, 1867, in Origines, XIX, 255, no. 6064; Sartiges to Moustier, Rome, November 20, 1867, in Origines, XIX, 301, no. 6092.

for the deliberations of the Conference; and the Powers assembled in consultation could insist upon its being modified or adjourned." And so Moustier formally requested that Florence prepare a program for the congress. In his dispatch the foreign minister also replied to Menabrea's earlier questions. He affirmed that Italy would have an equal deliberative voice (as would the pope); that there would be no decision by vote (except "d'une manière partielle, et comme conséquence d'un accord commun et du consentement des parties intéressées"); that, therefore, no advance agenda was needed; that all the powers had been invited (and France had no preference as to a meeting place); and that French evacuation of Rome would depend on whether the conference met. Thus summoned, the Italian government accepted the charge, if grudgingly. Stanley, however, was only partly appeased—if Florence did submit a proposal, that would be a step forward, but many more such steps would be necessary. Even more important was Prussia's attitude, since the congress could not, in the French view, be held without Prussia. When Bismarck suggested (he did not propose) at the end of November that a preliminary conference be held in Paris, Moustier must have realized that his space for maneuver had become very limited.[13]

Probably Bismarck really hoped by the preliminary conference to prove once and for all the impracticality of the congress. But he had the support of Saint Petersburg and could anticipate the sympathy of London, where Baron Georges Napoleon Baude, the French chargé, had become convinced that Stanley's insistence on some sort of agreement in advance could be satisfied by a preliminary conference. While Moustier deliberated, apparently with an open mind, Beust tried once more to be helpful. He was convinced, he said, that if the French government continued to insist on a congress without preliminary agreement, it would have its way. Why not, then, propose the congress, have it accepted in principle by the powers, and set a date and place, leaving an interval of perhaps a month? This interval could be used "to seek *secretly* and *confidentially* a basis for agreement with the Cabinets, so as to create points of similarity, to define the questions and to prepare a program." On December 7, Moustier wrote to

13. Lyons to Stanley, Paris, November 21, 1867, in PRO, FO, 27, 1670: no. 101; Moustier to Malaret, Paris, November 27, 1867, in *Origines*, XIX, 359, no. 6136; La Tour d'Auvergne to Moustier, London, November 29, 1867, in *Origines*, XIX, 383, no. 6153; Lyons to Stanley, Paris, confidential, December 12, 1867, in PRO, FO, 27, 1671: no. 160.

Gramont at Vienna: "I have replied [in an interview with Goltz] that if we had the hope of Prussia's assent to the proposal developed in my circular of the 9th November, we would be very inclined to be party to a preliminary understanding of the great Courts, and it could be . . . agreed that before the meeting of the Plenipotentiaries at the time and place which would be established by common accord, there would be at Paris a preliminary and confidential negotiation among the Representatives of Austria, France, Britain, Prussia and Russia." It was Moustier's intention to fix February as the date of the congress, without awaiting the results of the preliminary conference. In thus adopting, or, rather, adapting, Beust's proposal, Moustier meant to avoid two pitfalls in Bismarck's suggestion. As France envisaged the preliminary conference it would not have power either to decide if the congress should meet or to determine what role the secondary states should play there. The preliminary conference would, in fact, follow rather than precede agreement on the time and place of the congress. By an adroit maneuver, the French foreign minister had seemingly compromised the only effective argument advanced against the congress (its lack of a preliminary program) and had kept alive the possibility of testing whether the powers, gathered at a conference table, could find some means of putting to rest the vexatious Roman question.[14]

Even before the doubtful effectiveness of Moustier's tactic could be tested, however, another and more serious obstacle to the convening of a congress appeared. On December 2, debate began in the French Legislative Body on the question of Rome. On the fourth, Thiers, in a masterly speech that won an acclamation from the deputies, demanded of the government a strong propapal statement. Rouher, who followed him the next day to the tribune, was carried along by the current and proceeded (in the phrase of La Gorce) from deviation to deviation to the famous peroration: "Well, we state, in the name of the French Government, Italy will not take possession of Rome. France will never tolerate this violence to her honor and her catholicity." Then, having left the tribune, the minister of state suddenly re-

14. Talleyrand to Moustier, Saint Petersburg, telegram, December 2, 1867, in *Origines*, XIX, 409, no. 6170; Baude to Moustier, London, telegram, November 12, 1867, in *Origines*, XIX, 244, no. 6032; Gramont to Moustier, Vienna, December 1, 1867, in *Origines*, XIX, 396, no. 6165; Moustier to Gramont, Paris, December 7, 1867, in *Origines*, XIX, 433, no. 6191; Talleyrand to Moustier, Saint Petersburg, December 7, 1867, in *Origines*, XIX, 441, no. 6197.

turned to declare that by Rome he meant the whole papal territory. Perhaps Rouher, who was sometimes carried away by his own eloquence, went further than he had intended. The emperor shortly afterward offered a gentle reprimand: "En politique," he advised the orator, "il ne faut jamais dire jamais!" Of course, Rouher had stated no more than the truth; Napoleon certainly could not allow Italy to seize Rome. And it is true that almost at the same moment Menabrea was assuring the Italian parliament that his government "ne peut aller à Rome par la violence." In retrospect, however, the *jamais* of December 5 may be regarded as symbolic of a turning point in Second Empire history. Unsuccessful in placating the opposition by reforms, confronted by a resurgence of revolutionary sentiment, the goverment would once again court the Right, offering to the Catholic party, among other concessions, a guarantee of the status quo at Rome. Abroad, the reaction to Rouher's speech was immediate and decisive. At Florence it was accepted as "the funeral oration of the Conference." "Maintenant," Menabrea exclaimed to Malaret, "la Conférence est impossible!" He was convinced that, France having declared its intention to maintain the integrity of papal territory, the congress would meet only to ratify the pope's temporal power. Gorchakov agreed, pointing out that Europe had no interest in helping France to make a new September Convention, the original having been, indeed, "an act of impotence." On December 10, Italy officially rejected the congress.[15]

Napoleon did not seem to accept Rouher's speech as the end of his hopes. Clarendon, who saw him on the eighth, sensed no change in his attitude toward the congress and in fact felt obliged, in response to the emperor's inquiry whether Britain would take part in the preliminary conference, to argue vigorously against the idea of such a meeting. It was not until the eighteenth that Lyons was led to believe that Napoleon had abandoned the congress, at least for the moment, and even then he was far from sure. If we are to believe Metternich, the emperor as late as mid-January greeted word that Berlin had decided

15. *Origines*, XIX, 419 n.; La Gorce, *Histoire du Second Empire*, V, 309–314; Case, *French Opinion on War and Diplomacy*, 173; Malaret to Moustier, Florence, telegram, December 6, 1867, in *Origines*, XIX, 430, no. 6187; Paget to Stanley, Florence, December 7, 1867, in PRO, FO, 45, 109: no. 208; Malaret to Moustier, Florence, December 7, 1867, in Ollivier, *L'empire libéral*, X, 232; Talleyrand to Moustier, Saint Petersburg, December 7, 1867, in *Origines*, XIX, 442, no. 6197; Menabrea to Nigra, Florence, telegram, December 10, 1867, in *Origines*, XX, 2–3, no. 6209.

to accept the congress (a now meaningless gesture) with the exclamation: "Nous allons joliment traiter les canailles d'Italiens!" Moustier must have had fewer illusions. Despite his insistence that nothing had changed and that, if he could have all the plenipotentiaries together, it would not take him three-quarters of an hour to bring them to agreement, he early reminded Talleyrand that France had no wish "to precipitate the resolutions of the Cabinets." Indeed, these resolutions had already been taken—against the congress. On December 19, perhaps reflecting Napoleon's decision, Moustier assured the British ambassador that Paris was in no hurry. Efforts to bring the congress about would not be relaxed but "perhaps it would be adviseable to allow a month or more to elapse, in order to give time for excitement to subside." As for the preliminary conference, France now wanted to avoid a formal assembly that might be used to "strangle" the congress. "On the other hand he [Moustier] should be quite ready to exchange ideas with the several Cabinets and to give explanations with a view of smoothing difficulties. Nor should he be averse to an entirely confidential and informal meeting of the Representatives of the Great Powers at Paris, as a preliminary to the Congress." The obituary had been pronounced.[16]

Within the context of that intense and wholly egoistic nationalism that would soon shape all European diplomacy, there is only one way to regard Napoleon's bid for a congress on the Roman question in 1867. It was naïve, futile, and hopeless from the start. In the words of an end-of-the-century English historian, the powers "were being asked to discuss a question on which they were certain to differ, and the sole reason given for summoning a Conference was that the Emperor disliked bearing the responsibility which he had assumed. Why should we be asked to bear it for him? It must have been a congenial task for a man of Lord Stanley's temperament to throw cold water upon the

16. Clarendon to Stanley, Paris, private, December 9, 1867, in RA, J39/117; Lyons to Bloomfield, Paris, private, December 18, 1867, in PRO, FO, 356, 33; Lyons to Stanley, Paris, private, December 19, 1867, in RA, J83/49; Fletcher, *The Mission of Benedetti*, 196; Moustier to Malaret, Paris, telegram, December 9, 1867, in *Origines*, XIX, 447–48, no. 6200; Beyens to Brussels, Paris, December 13, 1867, in Beyens, *Le Second Empire*, II, 286; Moustier to Talleyrand, Paris, December 9, 1867, in *Origines*, XIX, 458, no. 6202; Lyons to Stanley, Paris, December 19, 1867, in PRO, FO, 27, 1671: no. 181. The demise was officially admitted on December 24, in a circular that recognized the need of "postponing" the congress and concluded: "Nous continuerons donc cet échange d'idées tant avec les Gouvernements directement intéressés qu'avec les différentes Cours, en vue de préparer la réunion des Plénipotentiares" (circular of Moustier, Paris, December 24, 1867, in *Origines*, XX, 68–69, no. 6257).

vague and slipshod proposals of the unlucky Emperor." Such was, as well, the sentiment of Ollivier, writing in the same era.[17]

But Rome *was* a European problem; "Europe" in 1867 still had existence, if an increasingly tenuous one; and the failure to find a reasonable solution to the Roman question then, perhaps along the same lines as were applied successfully sixty-two years later, was a not insignificant part of that complex of events that eventually would bring about the confrontation between a unified and dominant Germany and its neighbors, including Britain. Certainly the difficulties facing the congress were great, but it does not at all appear from an examination of the evidence that its convocation was impossible or that, once convoked, its failure was inevitable. With Italy committed to preparing a program, Prussia committed to a preliminary conference, Austria committed to the support of French policy concerning Rome, and neither Stanley nor Gorchakov eager, for all their misgivings, to deliver the coup de grâce, Moustier's attempt to use the preliminary conference as a means of securing the congress might have succeeded. In the end it was not Prussian *Realpolitik*, British caution, Russian indifference, or even papal-Italian antagonism that made the congress impossible. Rouher's *jamais* was most certainly the decisive event. And it happened as it did largely as a result of tensions within a beleaguered political system. Perhaps, then, it would not be absurd to argue that if Napoleon failed in 1866 to present the German problem, and in 1867 the Roman question, to the consideration of a European congress, this cannot be explained simply by invoking the judgments of a later era, or even of our own. The explanation is surely to be found in large part in the divisions within France itself and in the problems created for any French government by an apparently endemic political instability and by the unwillingness of Frenchmen in the 1860s to make their military means commensurate with national aspirations. By 1868, in fact, these weaknesses, and the failures following from them, would bring about a significant change in Napoleon's attitude toward and expectations for the concert of Europe.

17. Newton, *Lord Lyons*, I, 181; Ollivier, *L'empire libéral*, X, 179.

CHAPTER 16

The Conservative Concert
German and Eastern Questions
1868–1869

The gravity of the German question for France after 1867 did not end Napoleon's interest in the concert of Europe. While the concert was not the sole source of security, it was at least one of several possible shields against the impending danger. European intervention could take a number of forms. A congress, by placing the settlement of 1866 (treaty of Prague) under European supervision, might reassure France and provide an environment within which the German states could move gradually and in accordance with the principle of nationalities toward unity. At the very least, appeal might be made to the mediation of Britain, perhaps in cooperation with one or more other great powers. Or, if all else failed, it might still be possible to find in conference diplomacy, and, especially, in Clarendon's mediation proposal of 1856, a precedent for the peaceful solution of crises as they arose. And, of course, a general limitation of armaments would make war less likely. Even the prolonged alliance negotiations that occupied a good part of the energy of French diplomacy from the end of 1866 were not entirely separable from an appeal to Europe. The flirtation with Prussia was initiated, as we have seen, in the context of a proposed congress on Rome and abandoned in the acrimony surrounding the conference on Luxemburg. Approaches to Russia were inescapably linked with the Eastern question, in regard to which bilateral action would have been difficult if not impossible. And, as events soon proved, the ultimately abortive Franco-Austrian alliance negotiations were destined not to stray far, even in the days of hope, from the context of conference diplomacy.

The courtship between Paris and Vienna had begun soon after Bismarck's uncooperative attitude in the Roman question became evident. It accelerated in April, 1867, during the Luxemburg crisis, with a first French alliance bid. Napoleon announced himself ready to accept what he called an "active alliance," that is, one with precise objectives that could lead to war with Prussia. Whether he would have used such an alliance as a means to war or as an incentive to negotiation is impossible to say, because neither Beust nor Francis Joseph was free, in the new amalgamation of the Austrian and Hungarian realms, to enter into a contract whose major aim would be to restore Austria to its pre-1866 position in Germany at the cost of a new conflict with Prussia. When the French and Austrian emperors met in August, 1867, at Salzburg, no more was decided (if we can believe Beust) than that the status quo should be preserved, east as well as west. But that, of course, was of great significance in itself. That the French emperor could now contemplate an alliance designed to preserve the status quo indicated a major change in his foreign policy, a change that coincided at home with the turn toward the Catholic Right, symbolized, as we have seen, by Rouher's *jamais* in regard to Rome.[1]

Indeed the change was to be signaled on many occasions during the following year. Even the most astute observers seemed convinced of Napoleon's peaceful intentions. In November, 1867, he had declared: "We must openly accept the changes that have come about on the other side of the Rhine, and proclaim that as long as our interests and our dignity shall not be threatened, we shall not interfere in those changes which are wrought by the will of the people." When Benedetti insisted on the need for a strong French stand in southern Germany, Moustier's response was obviously in the spirit of his master: "At this moment the general well-being which is linked to the keeping of the peace in Europe must be placed before all questions. Our firm resolve, expressly stated, to refrain from interfering in purely German affairs . . . has had unquestionable results." And Napoleon himself expressed to Lyons the opinion that "the safest course with respect to Germany, was to abstain from all interference; that the best chance of lessening the power of Prussia, was to leave the discontent of the annexed Provinces to work by itself."[2]

1. Metternich to Beust, Paris, January 7, 1867, in Oncken (ed.), *Rheinpolitik*, II, 163–65, no. 328; Metternich to Beust, Paris, telegram, February 3, 1867, in Oncken (ed.), *Rheinpolitik*, II, 194, no. 342; Mosse, *The European Powers and the German Question*, 259–61; Beust to Metternich, Vienna, confidential and reserved, April 27, 1867, in Oncken (ed.), *Rheinpolitik*, II, 361–65, no. 450; memorandum of Beust, [about August 23], 1867, in *Origines*, XVIII, 205–206 n.

2. Gorchakov to Bismarck, Saint Petersburg, private, July 9, 1867, in *Origines*, XVII, 385, no. 5384; Lyons to Bloomfield, Paris, private, May 20, 1868, in PRO, FO, 356, 33;

And then, in July, 1868, Napoleon, who had already assured Metternich that if France and Austria could agree on a specific aim (but déterminé) they could "by themselves" keep the peace of the world, fully embraced the consequences of this new foreign policy based on maintaining the status quo. He would like, he told the Austrian, to reach an agreement with Vienna "concerning a congress which would consecrate the present *status quo*, limiting it to boundaries determined upon together." A congress of this nature, bruited since 1866 in the imperial entourage (Cowley reported in 1866, for example, "Fould continues anxious and uneasy and wants a pacific Congress"), was a possibility that had stirred Bismarck's apprehension both during the Luxemburg crisis and, later, during the efforts to secure a congress on Rome at the end of 1867. Now Napoleon had bid for just such a meeting. Long an indefatigable, in fact, an incorrigible advocate of Europe's vocation to revise and reform in accordance with the ideas of the time, he had come full circle, returning to the concept of the concert of Europe as guarantor of the status quo, a concept that had prevailed from 1815 to 1856 and that he himself had since done much to destroy. From being an avowed enemy of the treaties of 1815 he had become a defender of the sanctity of those of 1866. "His object," he would tell Clarendon, "was to calm public opinion in France, and the means of doing this were to be a sort of collective confirmation by Europe of the Treaty of Prague."[3]

It had long been evident what program France would bring to the sort of congress that Napoleon had now proposed. Moustier summarized it in the midst of the Luxemburg crisis: a plebiscite in northern Schleswig in accordance with the treaty of Prague; right of the south

---

Lyons to Stanley, Paris, private, May 28, 1868, in RA, J83/63; Lyons to Clarendon, Paris, very confidential, March 2, 1869, in PRO, FO, 27, 1749; address of Napoleon III to the French legislature, November 18, 1867, in Origines, XIX, 310 n.; Moustier to Benedetti, Paris, January 26, 1868, in Origines, XX, 263, no. 6390; Lyons to Stanley, Paris, private, March 19, 1868, in RA, J83/56.

3. Metternich to Beust, Paris, confidential and secret, July 3, 1868, in Oncken (ed.), *Rheinpolitik*, III, 9, no. 611; Metternich to Beust, Paris, secret, telegram, July 20, 1868, in Oncken (ed.), *Rheinpolitik*, III, 12–13, no. 615; Cowley to Stanley, Paris, November 13, 1866, in PRO, FO, 519, 233:142–44; Felix, Count Wimpfen, to Beust, Berlin, April 8, 1867, in Rothan, *Souvenirs diplomatiques*, 374 n.; Lyons to Stanley, Paris, private, December 19, 1867, in RA, J83/49; Lyons to Stanley, Paris, October 20, 1868, in RA, J83/73. Clarendon later recalled of the same conversation: "The sole danger to peace, according to the emperor, consists in an infraction of the *status quo*, for if the present state of affairs is not maintained . . . the irritation of France, and above all that of the army, would know no bounds [ni peines ni limites]" (Clarendon to Victoria, London, October 28, 1868, in Oncken (ed.), *Rheinpolitik*, III, 52, no. 641).

German states to form a confederation and to determine their position in regard to Prussian Germany; and restriction of Prussian activity to the boundaries determined at Prague. In regard to Schleswig, the attitude of the Prussian government made it impossible for French diplomacy to raise that question unilaterally without risk of a rupture. As for southern Germany, Bismarck professed complete agreement with the moderate stand taken by Napoleon in June, 1867. The French government, Cowley explained, accepted the treaty of Prague. "On the other hand they expect that southern Germany shall be allowed to reconstruct herself as the states may think best for their own interests, that the southern fortresses shall not be occupied by northern troops, and that Austria shall not be further molested." But the remodeling of the Zollverein in that same month (which brought it within hailing distance of a political union by admitting deputies from the south German states to the North German parliament), and the military alliances between Prussia and the south German states made secretly by Bismarck in August, 1866, and announced during the Luxemburg crisis, gave the lie to these professions. Moreover, the marked lack of success attending efforts within southern Germany to move toward confederation, noted by La Valette in early 1869, indicated that hope for a solution acceptable to France worked out by the Germans themselves was unrealistic. Yet it was equally clear that French intervention would not be tolerated by Prussia. Neither, perhaps, would an intervention by Europe, but there, at least, lay some hope of escape from the dilemma confronting French diplomacy. If Napoleon frankly stipulated Prussian extension south of the Main River as casus belli, then opinion in Germany would soon lead to war. If, on the other hand, the French government announced its willingness to permit the union of southern and northern Germany in accordance with the principle of nationalities, the effect in French military and political circles would be embarrassing to the regime—if not fatal. And such an announcement would, besides, violate the understanding reached with Austria at Salzburg. Such, at least, was Rouher's assessment of the situation in September, 1867. In these circumstances, the congress alone promised a chance of solving without war the problems so vexing to France.[4]

4. Moustier to Gramont, Vienna, very confidential, April 21, 1867, in *Origines*, XVI, 95–97, no. 4767; Cowley to Stanley, Paris, confidential, June 14, 1867, in PRO, FO, 519, 14:222–23; La Valette to Benedetti, Paris, February 15, 1869, in *Origines*, XXIII, 249, no. 7232; Rouher to Napoleon III, Cerçay, September 27, 1867, in *Papiers et correspondance*, I, 371–78.

Certainly Napoleon was serious in his congress suggestion. The usual pamphlet appeared at Paris, this one entitled *Congrès ou la guerre*, and in a conversation with Metternich on August 19 the French emperor advanced a thought that must be regarded as symbolic of the drastic alteration that events had forced in his attitude toward the concert of Europe. He was ready, Napoleon told Metternich, to have the congress meet in Vienna! "Although the Congress of Vienna has not been favorable to us," he added, "it gave Europe thirty years of peace—that's a good omen—and we must not forget that the other meetings of this kind, at Paris, Zurich, etc., were not *very successful.*" Beust, who had, of course, preferred a "passive" to an "active" alliance, was not much concerned with securing the congress for Vienna. He did not believe, moreover, that the other powers would accept the preservation of the status quo as the basis of the meeting, and he therefore hoped to substitute the regulation of a general disarmament. The Austrian argument was that to have the congress discuss a limitation and guarantee of the status quo would be a direct *halte-là* to Prussia; Britain and Russia would see this at once, and the Germans would be indignant. But if the purpose of the meeting were to be a general disarmament, the danger would be averted and Napoleon would win the gratitude of all peoples. Moreover, this gratitude would be strengthened when the moderation of French conditions was known. Metternich apparently won Rouher over to this point of view and flattered himself that he had also persuaded Napoleon. But the latter countered Metternich's arguments with sound ones of his own. He had, he assured the ambassador, "but one objection to disarmament—that is the *fear of a trap.*" Besides, "with Prussia's organization . . . *she can pretend to disarm and still be in a state of readiness!* And, furthermore, *disarmament* is but a *word* today when the ranks are filled in the twinkling of an eye." Rouher had talked with him concerning the Austrian proposal, the emperor later told Metternich, but there was the danger that, once disarmament was mentioned, opinion in France would force him into extreme reductions that Prussia, with its different military system, would not really reciprocate. "You understand," he added, "I don't wish to play the dupe!"[5]

5. Metternich to Beust, Paris, private, August 19, 1868, in Oncken (ed.), *Rheinpolitik*, III, 19–22, no. 622; memorandum of Beust [end of July, 1868], in Oncken (ed.), *Rheinpolitik*, III, 14–15, no. 617; Metternich to Beust, Paris, telegram, September 4, 1868, in Oncken (ed.), *Rheinpolitik*, III, 22, no. 624; Metternich to Beust, Paris, private, August 19, September 14, 1868, both in Oncken (ed.), *Rheinpolitik*, III, 20, no. 622, 24, no. 628.

Did Napoleon hope, in fact, that the Austrians could be persuaded to play that role? After all, if a congress met on the basis of disarmament and failed, it would simply fail. But if a congress to guarantee the status quo should come to no good end, it might serve the alternative—that of an "active" alliance. There is some evidence that the thought had occurred to both Napoleon and his minister of state. However, when Rouher's promised memorandum was prepared, it proved to be no more than a thinly disguised reassertion of the French position that, at the congress, definition and guarantee of the status quo should be primary concerns. The memorandum stipulated a reduction of French and Prussian effectives to 250,000 men for ten years. Russia, Italy, and Austria-Hungary were to be invited to follow suit. But Prussia would have to guarantee the release of men from the reserves as well and formally pledge itself for the ten years to respect the status quo in Germany as created by the treaty of Prague. And when Clarendon, during an October visit to Paris, expressed grave reservations concerning disarmament, Napoleon's last hesitations on that score seem to have disappeared. "He demonstrated to me," the emperor later told Metternich, "using what I admit are excellent arguments, that the sole result of disarmament proposals would be to make war more inevitable."[6]

Moreover, although Napoleon raised the subject of a congress during dinner with Clarendon at Saint-Cloud on October 19, he did not insist upon it as the only acceptable means of action by Europe. The danger, he said, was that, despite his own and William I's pacific intent, should Prussia cross the Main, sentiment in France would force a war. "Therein lies the danger and it is to end it that I desire a true understanding with Prussia, either by means of a congress or by the good offices of united Powers. I wish to justify before France the measures necessary in order to re-establish confidence based upon a well-founded conviction that peace is no longer threatened." And this would require "some new diplomatic actions, some official renewal of the guarantees of the Treaty of Prague." The guarantee was the thing, not the method of attaining it. This attitude of the French emperor is

6. Metternich to Beust, Paris, private, August 19, 1868, in Oncken (ed.), *Rheinpolitik*, III, 20, no. 622; Vitzthum to Beust, Paris, secret, September 14, 1868, in Oncken (ed.), *Rheinpolitik*, III, 26–27, no. 629; Vitzthum to Beust, Paris, telegram, September 24, 1868, in Oncken (ed.), *Rheinpolitik*, III, 33, no. 633; Vitzthum to Beust, Paris, secret, September 25, 1868, in Oncken (ed.), *Rheinpolitik*, III, 33–37, no. 634; Metternich to Beust, Paris, private, October 28, 1868, in Oncken (ed.), *Rheinpolitik*, III, 54, no. 642.

summarized in Clarendon's account to Gladstone of the interview of
October 19:

> I had a conversation of two hours with the Emperor and was able to report
> to him the highly pacific language held by the King of Prussia—he was
> much pleased and suggested a congress for the settlement of existing diffi-
> culties, and when after much discussion he was induced to admit the inex-
> pediency of such a course he said that England, either alone or in conjunc-
> tion with other powers, might render an immense service to the cause of
> peace by applying such a pressure on France and Prussia as would induce
> them by their acts to dispel the apprehensions of war.

That, as Lyons informed Stanley, was no new thought.

> This idea . . . has, as you know, been vaguely suggested to me more than
> once by men more or less in the Emperor's confidence. It has never been
> hinted at by Moustier in speaking to me. The Emperor appears, however, to
> have dwelt a good deal upon it with Lord Clarendon, and even to have
> [entered] a little upon details. He seems to have relished the idea of other
> great powers being united with England in a sort of mediation, but I did not
> gather that he had any matured plan, or any distinct notion of the way in
> which practical effect could be given to his wishes. His object was to calm
> public opinion in France, and the means of doing this were to be a sort of
> collective confirmation by Europe of the Treaty of Prague, and a sort of
> pressure to be exercised by Europe on France and Prussia, which could
> compel them, or rather enable them, to diminish their military prepara-
> tions and take effectual steps to restore public confidence.

Although Clarendon informed his party leader, Gladstone, that he
had discouraged this line of thought as being impracticable, there is
reason to believe he may not have been all that dampening.[7]

Clarendon was perhaps the only really important British statesman
who was more sympathetic to France than to Prussia, and he might be
expected to have presented a more kindly ear than was then being offered by the pro-Prussian Stanley. In fact, Napoleon told Metternich
that his guest thought the diplomatic intervention of Britain would
suffice to guarantee the status quo and added: "I did not refuse to examine his proposition and I count on seeing it come about and on

7. Clarendon to Gladstone, private, November 16, 1868, in Gladstone Papers, Add.
MS 44133, no. 129–32 (reference supplied by Richard Millman); Lyons to Stanley,
Paris, October 20, 1868, in RA, J83/73. In April, 1868, Moustier had had Lyons ask the
British government to say a word at Berlin in discouragement of Prussian designs on
the south German states but Stanley had refused (Millman, British Foreign Policy,
111).

profiting some day from its success." With prompting from Metternich, Napoleon also agreed that it was "only in the sense of a real status quo, *libérateur pour l'Allemagne du Sud*" that he would understand a guarantee of this nature. Rouher told the Austrian ambassador that Clarendon had proposed a choice: "England's guarantee of the status quo in Germany, or a guarantee by all the powers, or, finally, a secret treaty between Prussia and France defining and reciprocally guaranteeing the *status quo*." Rumors of European intervention, perhaps led by Britain, appeared in the French press toward the end of the year, reinforcing the possibility that the emperor really did hope for some arrangement with London.[8]

By December, 1868, however, Napoleon must have had few illusions about the possibility of European intervention. Prussian opinion had reacted violently against the idea. Disarmament had been definitively ruled out, Napoleon telling Metternich that he had found it *"impossible* to embark upon this course which was *dangerous for him* and *advantageous to Prussia"*; British mediation now seemed "a snare"; and the congress was, as the emperor wrote to Clarendon, at least for the moment "inexpedient."[9] And yet, to what alternatives could he turn? His attempt to reform the French army had largely failed in the face of a public opinion that would accept neither the necessity of major changes nor the sacrifices they would entail. His efforts to arrange an alliance with Austria-Hungary were frustrated by basic incompatibilities in the foreign policy aims of the two governments. It was at this juncture that important changes of personnel occurred. In Britain, the November elections made Clarendon foreign secretary (on December 9, in the first Gladstone ministry); at Paris, on December 17, La Valette returned to the Quai d'Orsay (Moustier had had a heart attack). Whether coincidentally or not, by the end of the month Napoleon turned once again to the congress idea.

Victor Emmanuel had sent his aide-de-camp, the Hungarian General Stefano Türr, to Paris. The emperor received him on December

8. Millman, *British Foreign Policy*, 102–103, 106–108, 112; Metternich to Beust, Paris, private, October 28, 1868, in Oncken (ed.), *Rheinpolitik*, III, 54, no. 642; articles by P. David, *Journal des débats*, November 27, December 7, 1868, in *Origines*, XXII, 354 n.

9. Benedetti to Moustier, Berlin, confidential, December 12, 1868, in *Origines*, XXII, 351–55, no. 7058 (the response was to the articles in *Journal des débats*); Metternich to Beust, Compiègne, private, December 2, 1868, in Oncken (ed.), *Rheinpolitik*, III, 72–73, no. 649; Clarendon to Lyons, London, December 18, 1868, in Newton, *Lord Lyons*, I, 207–208.

31, and the two talked of a triple alliance. "Although we do not have a war upon our doorsteps," Napoleon remarked, "I think it well, against all eventualities, to conclude an offensive and defensive alliance between Austria, Italy, and France. I think it right that Austria ask for territorial compensation and I am ready to work towards the reaching of a complete accord among the three powers." And then, according to Ollivier, he added: "This would ensure peace for Europe and above all would safeguard the small States. If the three courts were to succeed in establishing the foundations of an agreement, I should try to reach an understanding with the Queen and with some English statesmen in order to have England's support. In this way we shall perhaps succeed in assembling a congress of the European sovereigns." Subsequently Napoleon discussed the idea with Nigra and Metternich at Fontainebleau and wrote about it to Victor Emmanuel. Nor had the hope of a British or European mediation been completely abandoned. At the end of January, 1869, La Valette repeated to Lyons the French position "that any marked step of Prussia towards annexing [the south German states] would so excite public opinion in France, that whatever might be the wishes of the Government, war would be inevitable." But then the foreign minister ventured a further thought. "Could a third Power, England for instance, speak with effect? He doubted this—and certainly it would not do for France to ask any Power to speak." Lyons inquired what such a third power could say. "M. de la Valette answered that the only arrangement that could make a settlement of the German question, satisfy France, and restore confidence in peace—was the Neutralization of the States south of the Main. Their military connection with Prussia should be dissolved, and they should be placed on the same footing as Belgium. He was fain however to admit that he had very little hope that either England or any other Power could obtain this from Prussia." It was all very vague. But clearly Paris continued to want a European solution to a terrible problem that the emperor did not really believe he could solve alone. Neither congress nor mediation seemed practicable. Even Clarendon now argued that the unification of Germany was inevitable and the French government should prepare its people to accept it. Yet the concert of Europe remained, if increasingly uncertain and feeble. At this moment it was brought to new life by a sudden rekindling of the long-smoldering Cretan problem.[10]

10. General Stefano Türr to Beust, January 6, 1869, in *Origines*, XXIII, 135, no. 7165; Ollivier, *L'empire libéral*, XI, 204–205; Lyons to Clarendon, Paris, private and

The revolt against Turkish control that broke out on the island of Crete (Candia) in September, 1866 (there had been earlier uprisings in 1841, 1852, and 1863), was destined to become the pivot of French policy in the East. Since 1849 Napoleon had consistently held that the Eastern question could not be resolved by any single great power or even by several great powers together, but only by Europe. He had obviously believed as well, however, that Europe should "solve" the question by disposing of Turkish territory as its interests required. Sadowa did not destroy the first of these attitudes but was destined to alter the second. In September, 1866, the basic dichotomy of French policy toward Turkey remained. On the one hand, Napoleon scarcely concealed his contempt for the Turks and his personal belief that they must displace themselves as required by European and Christian interests; on the other hand, pronouncements from Paris continued to offer support for the preservation of the Ottoman Empire. Turkey, Napoleon told La Valette in September, 1866, must have an independent existence; and seven months later he assured Cowley that "he sincerely desired the conservation of the Ottoman Empire." In fact, Moustier had brought with him to the Quai d'Orsay, from his ambassadorship at Constantinople, a policy that could have embraced both conservation and disintegration under the euphemism of "reform." French policy, he insisted, was to favor "everything which could contribute to the softening of manners, the progresss of civilization, the development of all moral and material improvements," to encourage "reforms in the Administration generally, and improvements especially in the Army and Navy," to promote "the fair and equal treatment of all classes," to aid in "the construction of roads and ports, and other measures for advancing the material prosperity of Turkey." These reforms should be encouraged by the collective action of the powers. And, of course, it might very well prove that the sultan would be required to make sacrifices in turn, particularly in the direction of ridding himself of rebellious provinces that were a source of weakness rather than of strength.[11]

---

confidential, January 26, 1869, in Clarendon Papers, C-146, 145–50; Clarendon to Lyons, London, private, January 27, 1869, in Clarendon Papers, C-148, 90–92.

11. Debidour, *Histoire diplomatique de l'Europe*, II, 325–69; Cowley to Stanley, most confidential, Paris, September 18, 1866, April 29, 1867, both in PRO, FO, 519, 14:196–98, 98; Driault, *La question d'Orient*, 187–89, 190–202; Moustier to Talleyrand, Paris, January 23, 1867, in *Origines*, XIV, 169, no. 4106; Lyons to Stanley, Paris, confidential, October 28, 1867, in PRO, FO, 27, 1669: no. 15; Cowley to Stanley, Paris, confidential, October 6, 1866, in PRO, FO, 519, 14:104–106, no. 317.

From September, 1866, until the spring of 1867, Napoleon appears to have flirted with the idea of gaining Russian support against Prussia by himself supporting the dismemberment of Turkey in the name of reform. Probably he hoped, too, that Austria-Hungary could be caught by such a policy. In December, 1866, he proved amenable to the Russian suggestion that Crete be separated from the Ottoman Empire (the Cretans had already declared their annexation to Greece) and that full encouragement be given to Rumanian, Serbian, Bulgarian, and Hellenic nationalism. It was Napoleon and not the Russian ambassador (with whom he talked at Compiègne) who insisted that Crete should be annexed to Greece rather than simply granted autonomy and that Greece should be enlarged in other ways as well— at Turkish expense. He was advising the cession of Crete, Napoleon would later tell Cowley, "for the same reasons that he had counselled the abandonment of Venetia to Austria—viz: that Candia was a source of weakness to the Turkish Empire."[12]

Whether the French emperor also considered substituting an entente à trois or à deux for European action in the Eastern question is less clear. Certainly he opposed, at the end of 1866, Beust's idea of a general congress of 1856 signatories, remarking uncharacteristically that "plusieurs cuisiniers gâtent la sauce." "The immediate examination of the whole Eastern question by the representatives of *all the great powers*," he told Metternich, "would only lead to quarrels, to a more profound schism, perhaps even to desperate acts on the part of Turkey, and to a menacing re-emergence of revolutionary demands against which we would be powerless, in view of the difference of opinion which would manifest itself among the cabinets." Earlier La Valette, then acting foreign minister, had received coldly Gorchakov's September 1 bid for collective action by Europe on behalf of the Cretans; later (in March, 1867) Moustier would continue to resist such collective action, just as, several months earlier, he had looked to an understanding between France and Russia as the chief instrument for persuading the Porte to give up Crete in return for a guarantee of "all the conditions of security and vitality." More likely, however, Napoleon saw an agreement with Russia or with Russia and Austria as a preliminary step, after which, as he told Metternich in January, "in case difficulties should present themselves and it should be necessary

12. Charles-Roux, *Alexandre II, Gorchakov et Napoléon III*, 402–403; Moustier to Talleyrand, Paris, January 23, 1867, in *Origines*, XIV, 169–71, no. 4106; Cowley to Stanley, Paris, March 14, 1867, in PRO, FO, 519, 233:192–95.

to consult in order to circumvent them, a [general] conference at Vienna [could seem] entirely natural." When Cowley later argued that Turkey would never agree to give up Crete, the emperor replied that he thought otherwise, "provided all the Powers would unite in giving the same advice." In fact, early in January, Moustier had proposed at London that the powers should collectively advise the Porte to evacuate the Belgrade fortress and grant local autonomy to Crete. But Britain, if she would no longer fight to preserve the Ottoman Empire, was unwilling to contribute to its disintegration, and Napoleon's flirtation with despoliation in the name of reform was destined to be brief. Its objective, the enlisting of Russian help against Prussia, proved unattainable, because Russia would not make in advance the pledge that alone might have steeled Napoleon to accept an irrevocable break with Britain.[13] Under these circumstances, the spring of 1867 witnessed a steady reorientation of French policy in the East from one of revision to one of defending or at least supervising the status quo.

At the beginning of April, 1867, Moustier dropped his resistance to Russia's proposal of "a collective démarche at Constantinople with a view to ending the bloodshed" and at the same time began backing away from the idea of a Turkish cession of Crete. Probably Gorchakov still assumed that the one would lead inevitably to the other. He wanted the five great-power ambassadors at Constantinople to meet, concert their language, and then, in an audience with the Porte, insist (but without the threat of force) that the Cretans be consulted as to their wishes. But the French foreign minister immediately undertook a campaign to force Turkey into effective action in Crete by the device of threatening European action. When this effort foundered on Turkish intransigence, and both Vienna and London expressed reserve concerning Moustier's draft of a collective note calling for consultation of the Cretans, he set about modifying the French position accordingly. By mid-May, the Luxemburg crisis having demonstrated how little support France could expect from Russia in the German question, Paris was ready to accept an inquest by the sultan's commissioners, "avoiding an appeal to the popular vote," although the powers would answer for the sincerity of the inquiry. When even this modest proposal proved unacceptable to the Porte, and therefore to

13. Metternich to Beust, Paris, January 12, 1867, in Oncken (ed.), *Rheinpolitik*, II, 178–79, no. 333; Moustier to Talleyrand, Paris, January 23, 1867, in *Origines*, XIV, 169–71, no. 4106; Cowley to Stanley, Paris, March 14, 1867, in PRO, FO, 519, 233:193; Millman, *British Foreign Policy*, 59–62.

London and to Vienna, Moustier agreed simply to end negotiations, disengage the responsibility of the powers, and leave the sultan to his own devices vis-à-vis his rebellious subjects.[14]

The French note was delivered at Constantinople in October, 1867. Several months earlier, at Salzburg, Napoleon had, as we have seen, pledged himself to the defense of the status quo, east as well as west. A year later, Vienna declined the French offer of an "active" alliance in the East and in Germany, as Napoleon probably had expected and perhaps had wished. At any rate, if Vienna would not accept an adventurous policy, there remained only the alternative of invoking the action of the concert in defense of existing treaties. The first French draft of a proposed Franco-Austrian-Italian alliance recognized this in March, 1869, by defining the purpose of the alliance in the East as the preservation of Turkey combined with defense of Christian interests and, in western Europe, "la sincère exécution et le maintien du traité de Prague." "We want to safeguard the authority of the Sultan," Moustier announced in January, 1868. "We want to keep the Eastern question on the peaceful terrain of the European concert." And he told Lyons: "It had . . . always been the policy of France to maintain concert between the Powers of Europe. . . . By uniting to a certain extent with Russia and inducing most of the other Powers to adopt the same policy, the Government of France had done something to uphold the 'European Concert.'" Now France would attempt to consolidate the Ottoman Empire by encouraging, in cooperation with other powers, the implementation of necessary reforms. Napoleon took the same line in his conversations with foreign diplomats, although with a somewhat less optimistic nuance. Vitzthum reported: "It is in this imminent danger, in the impotence of the Sultan to save himself, that the Emperor of the French can detect the starting point for common action between all the Powers and not only signatories of the Treaty of 15th April 1856. 'Let us invite them all to consult with us,' said the Emperor, 'the replies that we may receive will give us the measure of the sincerity of those who wish to help us save Turkey.'" Such was the situation when, on December 2, 1868, the Porte, encouraged by Vienna, unexpectedly broke off diplomatic relations with Greece on the issue of Greek aid to the Cretan rebels and, nine days later, sent

14. Moustier to Talleyrand, Paris, April 8, 1867, in *Origines*, XV, 328–29, no. 4618; Talleyrand to Moustier, Saint Petersburg, telegram, April 22, 1867, in *Origines*, XVI, 131, no. 4787; Moustier to Gramont, Paris, May 18, 1867, in *Origines*, XVII, 54, no. 5120.

an ultimatum to Athens, threatening to expel all Greeks from the Ottoman Empire.[15]

Moustier was amazed and angered at this Turkish action, which seems to have caught him completely by surprise. His immediate response, under orders of the emperor, was to appeal for concerted action of the 1856 signatories to prevent a conflict between Greece and Turkey, a conflict that seemed imminent after Athens rejected the Turkish ultimatum on December 15. Gorchakov proved amenable; he proposed a mediation by all the great powers and, pending its accomplishment, immediate action by the three guarantor powers of Greece (France, Britain, and Russia) to prevent violence. As for Beust, from an initial response that was decidedly unenthusiastic for intervention, he moved quickly under French persuasion to favor an entente of the 1856 signatories. In fact, reported Gramont on the eleventh, "the Cabinet of Vienna is quite prepared to take part in a Conference towards this end." It was, however, Bismarck who first raised in a formal manner the possibility of a conference. Prussia, he said, would support an invocation of the mediation protocol of 1856. Moreover, the Prussian representative at Paris was to inquire whether France was disposed to accept a conference at Paris of the six signatories of the 1856 treaty. Probably Bismarck's proposal was prompted by a desire to be agreeable to Russia, for Gorchakov was at the same time engaged in similar overtures at London. Clarendon did not favor a conference, fearing that it might reopen the whole Eastern question, but unlike Stanley he was willing to meet France halfway. Paris clearly liked Bismarck's suggestion, as Lyons amply demonstrated in his reports, concluding "that there is great rejoicing over the prospect of the Conference at the Tuileries." On December 21, La Valette formally stated French approval in an interview with Lyons: "The Marquis de la Valette told me this afternoon that the Emperor was decidedly in favor of acceding to the Prussian Proposal that a Conference of the Six Powers should be held at Paris in order to effect a reconciliation between Turkey and Greece. He had, he said, made known to the Emperor the objections which I had stated, and His Majesty had given them careful consideration, but had nevertheless come to the conclu-

15. First French draft project, March 1, 1869, in Oncken (ed.), *Rheinpolitik,* III, 124–25, no. 671 (supp. 1); Moustier to Talleyrand, Paris, January 3, 1868, in *Origines,* XX, 122, no. 6290; Lyons to Stanley, Paris, confidential, October 28, 1867, in PRO, FO, 27, 1669: no. 15; Vitzthum to Beust, January 19, 1868, in V. Wellesley and Sencourt (eds.), *Conversations with Napoleon III,* 346.

sion that they were outweighed by the advantages which a Conference might be expected to produce."[16]

But what advantages? Insofar as the crisis involving Greece and Turkey was concerned, La Valette's arguments in favor of the conference were "that it would render a suspension of active measures compatible with the dignity of the Porte which would yield only to the counsels of all the Great Powers; that it would render it easy to prevent, vi et armis, if necessary, all communications between Greece and Crete during the negotiations . . . that in fact not only the dignity of the Porte but the amour propre of the other Powers concerned would be best consulted by allowing the settlement to be made by the united voice of Europe." The three guarantor powers might, as London suggested, settle the matter if they were unanimous, but could Russia, with its pro-Greek stance, be brought to support representations at Athens? And then, suddenly, with the admission that he was ignorant of all the details of the question and that Moustier was too ill to help him, La Valette plunged into a remarkable defense of the conference:

There were . . . considerations of a higher order than any he had yet mentioned, which had great influence with him. He was convinced that the mere assembling of a Conference of the Six Powers, to consult in common on any measure for securing tranquillity, would have the best possible effect. Nothing would in his opinion contribute so much to the maintenance of peace—nothing he was certain would do so much towards re-establishing in France the confidence which had been so shaken. There were perhaps very few questions upon which there would be a sufficient accord among the Powers to render such a Conference possible. It would, he thought, be a most grave error to lose the present opportunity. A Conference ad hoc strictly limited to the matter in hand seemed perfectly safe. It was as a man responsible to God and his Country who deprecated above all things a war which would lead to frightful slaughter and be injurious alike to France and to the Imperial Dynasty, that he so earnestly sought to obtain the assent of Her Majesty's Government to a measure which he conscientiously believed to be more than any other calculated to secure to Europe the blessings of peace and tranquillity.

16. Moustier to Talleyrand, Paris, telegram, December 7, 1868, in Origines, XXII; 328, no. 7035; Talleyrand to La Valette, Saint Petersburg, telegram, December 19, 1868, in Origines, XXIII, 8, no. 7084; Gramont to Moustier, Vienna, telegram, December 11, 1868, in Origines, XXII, 348, no. 7054; telegram communicated by Solms (Prussia's chargé at Paris) to La Valette, December 18, 1868, in Origines, XXIII, 12 n.; Lyons to Clarendon, Paris, private, December 27, 1868, in Clarendon Papers, C-146, 54–55; Lyons to Clarendon, Paris, confidential, December 21, 1868, in PRO, FO, 27, 1712: 1069.

It was a strange plea. "M. de L's arguments in favour of the Conference," observed Clarendon, "though they do some credit to his imagination shew that his reasoning faculties are not much developed." Yet La Valette's reasons seem obvious from our more favorable perspective. For him, and presumably for Napoleon as well, the Eastern question in 1868–1869 owed its importance to its association with the overwhelming problem of Franco-German relations, and he saw the proposed conference in a much broader context than that of a quarrel between Greece and Turkey. "Speaking . . . for himself," La Valette had told Lyons, "he had no hesitation in declaring to Count Solms that in principle he was entirely in favour of referring all international disputes to the decision of the general voice of Europe. This was the system laid down by the Congress of Paris, and he was anxious that it should be acted upon as much as possible."[17]

So important to France was the symbolic role of the conference that La Valette was willing to settle the Greco-Turkish dispute even before the meeting took place and to agree in advance that no proposal of cession should be made. On December 22, Lyons was able to inform Clarendon of the base that France would propose for the conference: "That the subject of Crete and its internal administration should be excluded from discussion; that the Bands of volunteers should be dissolved; that Greece should prevent sending of arms, etc., to Crete; that Cretan emigrants should be allowed to return and helped to do so; that possibly the European powers might establish a naval patrol and attend to return of the emigrants; that there should be no indemnity or trials and punishments; that friendly relations should be reestablished between Turkey and Greece; that the Conference should meet at once and have one or at most two sittings." No clearer indication of French willingness to work through conference diplomacy for the preservation of the status quo was possible. And yet La Valette offered even further reassurance. Nothing, he told Lyons, should be done to compromise the integrity of the Ottoman Empire or to interfere in its administration. Britain thus reassured, the only remaining obstacle to the meeting of a conference was disagreement over the role of the two litigants, Turkey and Greece. One solution would have been, as Gorchakov urged, to exclude both, but Paris believed that the

17. Lyons to Clarendon, Paris, confidential, December 20, 21, 1868, both in PRO, FO, 27, 1712:1062, 1069; Clarendon to Lyons, London, private, December 22, 1868, in Clarendon Papers, C-148, 18v; Lyons to Clarendon, Paris, confidential, December 20, 1868, in PRO, FO, 27, 1712:1062.

participation of the Porte was indispensable, and the Russian government had made clear that in such a case it would insist that Greece be
admitted on exactly the same footing as Turkey. At first, Paris had
seemed to incline readily to the exclusion of Greece, but when La Valette sought orders from Napoleon, the emperor insisted "that it
would not be advisable that, while Turkey was admitted, Greece
should be altogether excluded." In terms of "diplomatic forms and
precedents," there might indeed be grounds for not inviting Athens to
send a representative, he admitted, but "the common sense view of
the question was that Greece, as a party concerned, ought to have
a full hearing, public opinion, without weighing nice distinctions
would be formed by the dictates of common sense; and much of the
benefit to be derived from the Conference would be lost if the fairness
of its proceedings and the justice of its decisions were not apparent to
all." Paris really would have preferred the admission of Greece *à voix
délibérative*. But as the Porte would then not have come, or would have
walked out, that was impossible. The French government therefore
proposed the admission of Greece without a vote (*à titre consultatif*),
after the conference should have convened. Despite some objections,
the proposal was accepted. Athens, however, at the last moment declined to participate on such terms. The telegrams of invitation went
out on January 2. The British government having already accepted (if
with bad grace), as had, in effect, the others, the conference met in
Paris on January 9 and in seven meetings devised a declaration calling
upon Athens not to furnish any further aid to the rebellion.[18] After
some delay, the Greek government fell into line. Within a few months
the insurrection had been crushed.

In November, 1863, Drouyn de Lhuys had asked, regarding Napoleon's proposal for a general congress, "Does it follow . . . that the governments will always be condemned to leave to the judgment of force
solutions that their wisdom could have carried out? It seems to us to

18. Lyons to Clarendon, Paris, confidential, December 21, 1868, in PRO, FO, 27,
1712:1069; Lyons to Clarendon, Paris, private and confidential, December 22, 1868, in
Clarendon Papers, C-146, 26–29; La Valette to La Tour d'Auvergne, Paris, confidential,
December 28, 1868, in *Origines*, XXIII, 83–84, no. 7132; Lyons to Clarendon, Paris,
January 15, 1869, in PRO, FO, 27, 1746:77; Lyons to Clarendon, Paris, private and confidential, December 22, 1868, in Clarendon Papers, C-146, 26–29; Lyons to Clarendon,
Paris, December 27, 1868, in PRO, FO, 27, 1712:1092 (and January 15, 1869, in PRO,
FO, 27, 1746:77); La Valette to Benedetti, Paris, telegram, December 25, 1868, in *Origines*, XXIII, 59–60, no. 7117. For protocols of the conference and text of the declaration, see *Archives diplomatiques*, IV, 1665–1700. The conference was attended by the
great powers who had signed the treaty of Paris of 1856 and by Italy.

be otherwise. It seems to us to be worthy of our day that we should sincerely try to prevent any eventuality of war by a friendly mediation and to reaffirm the peace by giving it a truly valid base in public law, that is, a base that has been unanimously agreed to by the powers." Surely it was no coincidence that La Valette, in his telegram of invitation to the conference on Crete, seized, as had his predecessor six years before, on the protocol of Paris of 1856, which enjoined the parties to a dispute to accept mediation. But Drouyn de Lhuys was defending then the idea of the concert of Europe as Napoleon III would have had it be. That events had ended the dream, La Valette's opening words for the conference were designed to show. The meeting, he would announce, was in conformity with the 1856 mediation proposal:

> The spirit of this proposal at once settles beyond a doubt the functions of this Conference, which makes the first practical application of it. The Conference cannot come to resolutions restraining the freedom of action of the Nations, to whom it offers its good offices. Legitimately it can only examine the state of the case, say which party appears to be in the right, and propose the basis of a reconciliation, which is the object of all its wishes. The Powers represented form not a Tribunal whose business it is to pronounce a sentence—but a friendly arbitration whose impartial opinion binds the Parties only by the liberty it leaves them, and the total absence of any other sanction than the moral sanction which must belong to a declaration of the Public Opinion and so to speak of the conscience of Europe.[19]

Above all the French government sought in the conference of January, 1869, a precedent for the effective mediation by Europe of disputes likely to lead to war. This is apparent in the open resort to propaganda, involving not only the use of the *Livres jaunes* but also the tribunal of the Legislative Body. "Though La Valette did not say so," wrote Lyons on January 16, "he was evidently extremely anxious to come to a conclusion to be announced in the speech of the Emperor at the opening of the session on the day after tomorrow." And the am-

19. Drouyn de Lhuys to Gramont, Paris, November 25, 1863, in AMAE, CP, Autriche, 485:196v–97, no. 100. La Valette's telegram of invitation began: "Le Cabinet de Berlin, se référant au protocole du 14 avril 1856, a proposé que les Puissances signataires du traité de Paris fussent appelées à se réunir en Conférence pour rechercher les moyens d'apaiser le différend qui s'est élevé entre la Turquie et la Grèce. Nous avons adhéré à cette proposition, et nous l'avons immédiatement recommandée à l'assentiment de toutes les Cours" (La Valette to French agents at the courts signatory of the treaty of 1856, Paris, telegram, January 2, 1869, in *Origines*, XXIII, 107, no. 7151). Lyons to Clarendon, Paris, private and confidential, January 4, 1869, in Clarendon Papers, C-146, 82–91. Lyons was reporting the speech as La Valette proposed to make it.

bassador concluded. "If what we have done suffices to furnish a Paragraph in the Imperial Speech tomorrow, the real object of the Conference may perhaps be said to be attained." The paragraph was duly inserted. "The Conference," announced the emperor on the eighteenth, "which has just taken place to avert [étouffer] an imminent clash in the East, is a great action, the importance of which we must appreciate [dont nous devons apprécier l'importance]." If the imperial words were somewhat Delphic, those of the foreign minister were less so. "Its results [those of the conference] will have been of equal significance from another point of view. The Paris Conference, by enacting the wish formulated by the Congress of 1856, has proved in a specific incident, how fruitful diplomatic action by the Powers could be, when applied along the lines initiated by the Emperor some years ago [1863] in regard to general questions. In this respect, too, it constitutes an important action and the success which has crowned its efforts may be seen as a propitious omen of the progress yet to be accomplished, we hope, in this new direction." Neither Lyons, who carefully documented the conference because he saw it as the first practical application of Clarendon's mediation proposal, nor Clarendon, who wanted evidence of Bismarck's appeal to the protocol of 1856 in case of future misconduct on Prussia's part, appears to have noted the significant alteration, in French hands, of that protocol. Whereas Clarendon had spoken in 1856 of the mediation of a third power, La Valette had now made the thought serve, as it were, the Napoleonic idea of conference diplomacy, even, one might argue, of a "congress system" the function of which would be to preserve the peace of Europe. But by 1869 the hour was late; a dispute between Greece and Turkey was in no sense equivalent to a dispute between France and Prussia; and there is an ironic ring to the unanimous wish expressed at the conclusion of the conference on Crete that "the work of peace accomplished by virtue of and in the spirit of the Protocol of the 14th April 1856 will stand as a precedent which will be more and more invoked in such differences as can be settled by a common deliberation."[20]

20. Lyons to Clarendon, Paris, private, January 16, 1869, in PRO, FO, 27, 1746: 120–25; imperial address at the opening of the legislative session, January 18, 1869, in Origines, XXIII, 169 n.; circular of La Valette to French agents, Paris, February 22, 1869, in AMAE, MD, 2126:318 (this document does not appear in Origines); Lyons to Clarendon, Paris, private, February 25, 1869, in Clarendon Papers, C-146; Lyons to Clarendon, Paris, March 9, 1869, in PRO, FO, 27, 1750:271.

Epilogue
The Vanquished European
1870–1873

The conference on Crete was the last major initiative of French diplomacy. Moreover, it was completely unsuccessful in creating a precedent for the peaceful solution of disputes by the European community. France continued to seek an alliance with Austria-Hungary and with Italy, but this project was fatally handicapped by Vienna's unwillingness or inability to take a stand against Prussia and by Italy's demand that Rome should be the price of its acquiescence. Occasionally there were glimpses of the old sweep of ideas: Iberian union; "Scandinavianism"; a united Europe; European mediation in the German question; major exchanges of territory. Napoleon continued to nurture, for example, a scheme by which the Polish question could be resolved and Austria and Russia drawn into an alliance. It involved the cession of Congress Poland by Russia to Austria, in return for Austrian Galicia and its three million Ruthenians. But the reality was far different. Thus when the efforts of a French railway company (with government encouragement) to acquire two Belgian lines resulted in a crisis during the spring of 1869 that was caused partly by Brussels' clumsiness and partly by acute French suspicion of Prussia, La Valette found it necessary to turn violently against any thought of European intervention (in this case, Belgium's hint of a conference of the signatory powers of 1839): "Belgium indict France before Europe! We will not go! I am of a peaceful, very peaceful, turn of mind, but in such a case I should advise the Emperor to resist, even if this meant sacrificing his last man and his last coin! I am beginning . . . to get tired of intervention." The dispute was eventually settled by talks between Paris and Brussels, France making the major concessions. The swing to conservatism was complete. "Wherever we look," Ollivier assured the legislature on July 1, 1870, "we see no irritating questions en-

gagod, all of tho oabinoto undorotand that tho troatioo muot bo ro
spected."[1] In fact, on that same day rumors had reached Paris of the
Hohenzollern candidacy for the throne of Spain.

This final crisis of the regime requries little elaboration here.
Bismarck, for his own reasons, had contrived to have Leopold of
Hohenzollern-Sigmaringen, a relative of William I's, invited to assume the crown of Spain, unclaimed since the overthrow of Queen
Isabella in 1868. Word reached Paris, where a parliamentary government with Emile Ollivier as premier had been installed since April.
France could not, of course, accept a Prussian prince on the Spanish
throne. On July 6 the French foreign minister, Gramont, said so publicly in the Legislative Body. And this time, there would be no appeal
to Europe. France accepted a gage that was assumed to have been deliberately thrown down to the state. Neither Napoleon nor his advisers could escape the conclusion that the regime itself might disappear if this latest Prussian provocation, whether real or apparent, were
not met head on. To risk denying a throne to his son and to destroy,
perhaps, the Napoleonic idea to which he had devoted his life and in
which he continued to see the best hope of France and of Europe were
unthinkable to the emperor. And for what purpose? To avert a war
that this further humiliation, and perhaps even the replacement of
the imperial regime by a republic, would only make inevitable. La
Gorce has argued that the declaration Gramont read to the chamber
in the afternoon of July 6 was a "first act of war, rather than an invitation to negotiate." Certainly this declaration placed the decision for
peace or war in Bismarck's hands. And yet Gramont's explanation
seems irrefutable. He was sorry, he told the British ambassador, that
his words had been so severe. "Milder language," he admitted, "would
have rendered it more easy to treat both with Prussia and with Spain."
But: "The nation was . . . so strongly roused upon this question, that
its will could not be resisted or trifled with. . . . Nothing less than
what he had said would have satisfied the public. His speech was in
fact, as regarded the interior of France, absolutely necessary; and diplomatic considerations must yield to public safety at home."[2]

    1. Vitzthum to Beust, Paris, private and secret, July 4, 1869, in Oncken (ed.), *Rhein-politik*, III, 211–12, no. 714 (and Metternich to Beust, Paris, secret, May 14, 1870, in Oncken (ed.), *Rheinpolitik*, III, 349–51, no. 811; Prime Minister H. J. W. Frère-Orban to Foreign Minister Van der Stichelen, Paris, April 26, 1869, in *Origines*, XXIV, 429–31, no. 10 (Appendix II); Millman, *British Foreign Policy*, 123–45; Lyons to the foreign secretary, Paris, July 1, 1870, in PRO, FO, 27, 1805: no. 668.
    2. On the Hohenzollern candidacy and outbreak of the war, see especially Steefel,

It is this sense of powerlessness on the part of the government that gives to the final act of the Second Empire its quality of epilogue. By April, 1870, Napoleon, broken by illness, retained only two aspects of his former power. He could still appeal to the nation through plebiscites, while ministers remained responsible to him as well as to the Legislative Body. The emperor could no longer control or initiate; perhaps he could not even influence events. He could only react to the mood of the country as he interpreted it and, having reacted, helplessly observe the results of his actions. There is, in all of this, a tragic irony. War was destined to erupt over precisely the sort of question of "law" and European order that the concert might have been expected to resolve. It is at least conceivable that if Napoleon's congress proposal of 1863 had been accepted, even without noticeable results, he would have dared, in spite of all, to risk a congress proposal in 1870. Certainly his own predilection remained for conference diplomacy and an appeal to Europe. On July 9, Girardin, perhaps the most influential of Second Empire publishers, had written in *La Liberté*: "No conference! Rather a congress where might has equity as judge, where France, claiming neither the left bank of the Rhine, nor the port of Antwerp, will content itself with requiring the destruction of the fortresses which menace her, fortresses constructed on territory whose possession for all time was assured us by the congress of Rastadt." Other newspapers also spoke of congress or conference, and Ollivier wrote to the emperor on the eleventh that voices from both Left and Right in the legislature had been raised to assert that "the Hohenzollern affair should be considered as merely an incident, and even if its solution should be favorable one must not stop there but rather raise the question of the treaty of Prague and resolutely place Prussia between an accepted congress or war." On the twelfth, under the influence of French opinion, Napoleon decided to seek further assurances from Berlin than the reported renunciation by Charles Anthony of his son Leopold's candidacy. The question of the emperor's judgment in this decision, which led to the Ems telegram and to war,

---

Bismarck; Dittrich, *Bismarck, Frankreich und die Spanische Thronkandidatur der Hohenzollern*; Bonin (ed.), *Bismarck and the Hohenzollern Candidature for the Spanish Throne*; Fester, *Briefe, Aktenstücke und Regesten*; Halperin, "The Origins of the Franco-Prussian War Revisited," 83–91. For a persuasive statement of the thesis that French public opinion left the government no choice but to meet the Prussian challenge head-on, see Case, *French Opinion on War and Diplomacy*, 241–69. See also La Gorce, *Histoire du Second Empire*, VI, 222; Lyons to Granville, Paris, July 7, 1870, in PRO, FO, 1805: no. 698.

will probably never be resolved. But a strong argument can be made that public opinion was decisive, that Napoleon felt he had no other choice, and that he was right. Certainly his subsequent actions would leave little foundation for the only credible counterthesis: that he was determined to humiliate Prussia for dynastic reasons or to have war in order to strengthen his regime. On the thirteenth, Ollivier secured a reversal of this policy, the cabinet agreeing eight to four that even if William did not offer additional assurances the matter would be considered closed. Whether the country would have agreed is doubtful, and whether Bismarck, with Gramont's declaration of July 6 in his pocket, would have been thus caught is even more so. But it is apparent that the French emperor was desperately trying to find the least that he could do without losing the country. On the fourteenth, Gramont's initially strong stand having at least ended (apparently) the immediate possibility of a Hohenzollern becoming king of Spain, Napoleon flirted one more time with the idea of a congress.[3]

Before the first council meeting of that day, word had reached Paris of Bismarck's publication of the Ems telegram. The incident is well known. William I had telegraphed to Bismarck an account of the conversation he had had with the French ambassador at Ems concerning the demand for additional assurances. Bismarck edited the telegram to make the encounter seem more acrimonious than it was and, to assure that France would perceive the insult, he published this edited version in the newspapers and circularized it to Prussian diplomatic agents although negotiations were still officially in progress. The council quickly agreed that Prussia had insulted France and was seeking to provoke a conflict. Unanimously the ministers decided to call up the reserves. Around 4:30, the minister of war, who had insisted that the army was ready, left to sign the necessary orders. It was then that a dispatch from Benedetti arrived, indicating that the ambassador had not, as the published telegram implied, been insulted by William. The ministers, who had been meeting for over five hours, were weary. If we can believe the account of La Gorce, Gramont suggested that a congress could now take the place of the additional assurances that France had demanded. "At this word 'congress,' which so often had resounded in his public declarations, the Emperor came to life again: 'That's it! that's it!' he exclaimed." And, according to Charles Louvet,

3. Oncken (ed.), *Rheinpolitik*, III, 410, no. 858; Ollivier to Napoleon III, July 11, 1870, in Oncken (ed.), *Rheinpolitik*, III, 417, no. 867.

a member of the council: "Either as a result of the nervous strain, or because of a sudden return of joy, his emotion expressed itself in tears." The suggestion was agreed to by all. At once the work of drawing up a statement began. After many drafts, Ollivier found an acceptable formula. "Finally, in talking, I found a turn of phrase that seemed to be a happy one. 'Quick! Go and write that down in my cabinet,' the Emperor told me, striking me on the arm, and at the same moment two tears rolled down the length of his cheek." The statement, which Ollivier described as having "une forme oratoire et pathétique," has been lost, but presumably it resembled his later recollection: "We would declare that for the present the question was sufficiently resolved by the King's approval of the withdrawal of the prince of Hohenzollern, and in order to assure the future, we would address ourselves to Europe, so that, assembled in Congress, she would solemnly confirm the international law already tacitly admitted, by which any prince belonging to the ruling family of a great power is forbidden, without preliminary agreement, to mount a foreign throne." Perhaps Napoleon was thinking in even more ambitious terms, because he told Metternich immediately after the council meeting, "We are ready to accept a congress in which all the questions in dispute would receive a definitive solution in the interest of a lasting peace."[4]

By his own account, Ollivier almost at once repented of the congress idea. "A barbarian had just slapped us," he would later write, "with such force that the entire world felt it, and that Germany first of all and even before the appeal of her king, was on her feet, and we would try to find out if this resounding blow could be removed from our cheek by a conference!" He had approved the congress, Ollivier recalled, as had all those present, but "I blush in describing this failure of courage, which does little honor to us." Once in the open air, after the council meeting, the chimera dissipated: "There was just one long chorus of astonishment and blame." At Saint-Cloud, Napoleon underwent a similar experience. Informed of the congress proposal, Eugénie responded dryly, "I doubt that that will accord with the feelings of the legislature and of the country." When Marshal Edmond Leboeuf, the minister of war, arrived and seemed willing to accept the congress, the empress' response was more vehement: "What! You, too, you ap-

4. La Gorce, *Histoire du Second Empire*, VI, 292; Ollivier, *L'empire libéral*, XIV, 364–71; Metternich to Beust, Paris, telegram, July 14, 1870, in Oncken (ed.), *Rheinpolitik*, III, 439–40, no. 888.

prove this *lâcheté!* If you want to dishonor yourself, don't dishonor
the emperor!" Obviously Napoleon and Ollivier were not swayed
merely by the opinions of their families and friends. They could and
did anticipate public reaction on the basis of past experience and they
shared and reflected the national sensibilities of their own day. An
individual, Ollivier reasoned, might turn the other cheek, but not a nation. By the time the council reassembled at Saint-Cloud in the evening of the fourteenth, Napoleon seemed resigned to the situation.
"On reflection," he presumably told his chief minister, "I don't find
the declaration that we've just agreed on to be very satisfactory." And
he added: "You see in what sort of situation a government can sometimes find itself. If we didn't have an avowable reason for war we
would still have to accept a conflict in order to follow the wishes of
the country." Did he, even so, persist in advocating the congress?
Gramont implied as much to Metternich: "I am the one who opposed
the idea of a congress. The emperor, after having seen you [*i.e.*, at the
conclusion of the first council meeting] entered the Council and read
us a declaration which he had drafted and which he showed you. It
wasn't without difficulty that we dissuaded him from speaking of a
congress, but when he saw that I would resign rather than accept the
idea, he yielded."[5] He yielded, if we may believe the accounts, by suddenly leaving the room as the moment came to vote. The next morning, July 15, at 9 A.M., the council met once again at Saint-Cloud and
decided unanimously for war.

But if Napoleon had now abandoned the idea of a congress to avert
war, he may still have hoped that by a congress the conflict could be
shortened. Less than an hour after the formal council decision he suggested to the special Austrian emissary, Vitzthum, that Vienna take
the initiative of such a proposal.[6] "The emperor said . . . that it would
be good if Austria and Italy would offer their mediation in the conflict. . . . The emperor would be inclined to leave to us (and Italy) the
initiative of proposing a congress which the ministers will not talk

---

5. Ollivier, *L'empire libéral*, XIV, 369–73; Metternich to Beust, Paris, private, July
31, 1870, in Salomon, *Ambassade de Richard Metternich*, 256. Sybel, who confused
the two council meetings, had Gramont exclaim: "Sire, si vous nous parlez encore une
fois de Congrès, je jette mon porte-feuille à vos pieds" (Ollivier, *L'empire libéral*, XIV,
365 n.). One council member later testified that Napoleon began the meeting by reading a statement that concluded with a plea for a peaceful solution (*Origines*, XXVIII,
350).
6. Ollivier, *L'empire libéral*, XIV, 393. For Vitzthum's recollection (1873) of this
meeting, see Oncken (ed.), *Rheinpolitik*, III, 440–42.

about in the legislature." But, added Napoleon, "this must not prevent us from fighting." The next day he approved having the Italian government join its efforts to those of Vienna. Nigra telegraphed: "To make the alliance of Italy and Austria with France easier, the Emperor approves the idea that Italy and Austria offer their mediation to the belligerent powers. The bases would be the territorial *status quo* consecrated by the treaties and the engagement of France and Prussia to exclude from the throne of Spain all members of the reigning French and Prussian families." Whether Napoleon saw this merely as a means to an alliance or sincerely hoped that a congress could follow a battle or two, it is certain that Paris no longer would accept European intervention before a war, and that only a French victory could make such an intervention practicable once the conflict had begun.[7] Less than seven weeks later, Napoleon was a prisoner in Germany and the Second Empire had been toppled by a popular uprising at Paris.

Imprisoned at Wilhelmshöhe following his surrender at Sedan, Napoleon remained as convinced of the rightness of his cause as he had been in the prison of Ham some twenty-five years before. To a German journalist, hired by the London *Times* to interview him, he recalled the first Napoleon's goal of promoting the unity of Europe, the "transformations" in Italy and Germany being only first steps toward a single European confederation. But Bismarck, complained the former emperor, preferred to exacerbate old antagonisms in order to further Prussian ambitions. "The Napoleonic idea today has succumbed," he admitted, "but history will judge which of the two [views] was the more just, the more worthy for civilization and for humanity." "Do you know what this dream of a united Germany will cost you?" he asked one of his captors. "A price which, I hope, will cure once and for all those who surrender themselves to fantasies of power. In spite of herself—and I really think that it *will* be in spite of herself—Prussia, in twenty or thirty years will find herself obliged to be-

---

7. Metternich to Beust, Paris, telegram, July 15, 1870, in Oncken (ed.), *Rheinpolitik*, III, 440, no. 890; Vitzthum to Count Gyula Andrássy, Brussels, January 16, 1873, in Oncken (ed.), *Rheinpolitik*, III, 440–42, no. 891-A; Nigra to Marquis Emilio Visconti Venosta, Paris, private and reserved, telegram, July 16, 1870, in *I documenti diplomatici italiani*, XIII, 100, no. 175. In the early evening of the fifteenth, Gramont unequivocally rejected a congress; his conversation with Vitzthum lasted just five minutes. France, he told the emissary, would overthrow any government that attempted to prevent the war, and he would himself resign if the congress were insisted upon (Gramont to Vitzthum, April 22, 1878, in Ollivier, *L'empire libéral*, XVI, 580–84; Vitzthum to Gramont, April 20, 1878, in Ollivier, *L'empire libéral*, XVI, 578–80).

come aggressive. And then all her diplomatic skill, all the worth of her armies will be futile. Europe will crush her. Then she will realize what the dreams of Bismarck have cost her." At Chislehurst, in the last months of his life, Napoleon returned to one of his most persistent ideas. The occasion was a visit in November, 1872, by the English journalist, Thornton Hunt, to whom, in March, 1865, the emperor had presented the advantages of an "International Council," the mission of which would be "to watch over the affairs of Europe, to follow out and study the different phases through which the mutual relations between various states might pass, and to give to treaties their true interpretation." Urged by the journalist to write a book on the subject, Napoleon asked one of his courtiers, the comte de La Chapelle, to begin research. "The day will come," Hunt had written, "when the world will rejoice at the inauguration of that institution in which civilization is still wanting . . . and when that time arrives, if memory still exists among men, mankind will recognize that Napoleon III . . . was the founder of this court of legislation and of judicial appeal for nations."[8] In early January, 1873, Louis Napoleon died in the course of a series of operations for removing the bladder stone that had tormented him during the last years of his reign.

Historians have doubted whether the Second Empire had a foreign policy worthy of the name. La Gorce gave up his efforts to establish a "logical order." Renouvin ended by excluding from consideration "the idea of a firm and logical directing thought [pensée directrice]." And Taylor has concluded of Napoleon's foreign policy: "He was a mixture of idealist and conspirator; consistent only in one thing—he could never resist the temptation to speculate." To Bismarck, the French emperor had "a set of fixed ideas" but never knew where they would take him. Cowley, however, in January, 1869, ended with the conviction that, while Napoleon had his own way of doing things, he knew perfectly well where he wanted to go. After the passage of a century, some historians have returned to this point of view. "In short," Roger Williams has argued, "any analysis of Second Empire policy must centre in the Emperor's own plans, and the student must always remember that contrary opinions, entrenched opposition, and the force of logic, acted only as a suspensive veto upon imperial decision."[9]

8. Williams, The Mortal Napoleon III, 31–32; Sencourt, Napoléon III, un précurseur, 348–49. For the text of the "International Council" proposal, and Hunt's comment, see La Chapelle (ed.), Posthumous Works of Napoleon III, 252–56.
9. La Gorce, Histoire du Second Empire, I, 421; Renouvin, "La politique extérieure

If, indeed, we center our analysis "in the Emperor's own plans" as revealed by words and actions over more than a quarter of a century, it becomes reasonable to assert that Napoleon did not lack a foreign policy; if anything, he had too much of one. Certainly he was intelligent enough to see that after 1856 two "French" foreign policies were open to him. Had he chosen to maintain the status quo and therefore the relative grandeur of France, he could have enlisted the sympathy of both Britain and Austria. If, on the other hand, he preferred to secure territory for France, the ambitions of Prussia in Germany, of Sardinia in Italy, and of Russia in the East would almost have guaranteed success to a patient and frankly opportunistic policy. But to preserve the status quo would be to oppose the "ideas of the day" and to leave to his son a legacy of unsolved and dangerous problems. And to grasp for territory would be to perpetuate distrust and tension in Europe for an objective that never appeared to him to be of much importance. Napoleon III was, far more than his uncle, a French patriot. He had a sense of French prestige and he fully accepted the concept of *la grande nation*, never doubting, apparently, that France within its present boundaries was already large and powerful enough and that France had the will and the strength to promote a foreign policy the essence of which was the reconciliation and the harmony of three goals—promotion of a sort of French moral hegemony in Europe, satisfaction of nationalities, and encouragement of European concert. Of these goals, the first two were dependent on the last, just as, Napoleon hoped, the first would follow inevitably from success in achieving the other two. That Europe was neither happy nor peaceful Napoleon knew; that Europe would be more content when all its peoples had received the right of self-determination was for him a general guide. But above all it was necessary that Europe work out its problems and its destiny in concert, beginning with the destruction of the treaties of 1815 and of the Metternichian principles upon which they stood. The purpose of the concert of Europe was not to preserve the status quo but to modify it, to anticipate problems before they could undermine the peace, and to find solutions to them. Through this concept of European concert, the nationalities would be set on their way to ultimate satisfaction, French prestige (and perhaps the 1814 military frontiers) would be re-

du Second Empire," n.p.; Taylor, *The Struggle for Mastery in Europe*, 25; Renouvin, *Histoire des relations internationales*, 273; Sencourt, *Napoléon III, un précurseur*, 285; Williams, "Louis Napoleon," 220.

stored and enhanced, and Europe would be spared "civil war" and enabled itself to constitute a third force between the United States and Russia.

The wisdom of this foreign policy appears more clearly, perhaps, when we consider the alternatives. If a king rather than an emperor had followed the Second Republic in France, he might well have avoided the disasters of 1870, but he would certainly have done so at the cost of passing on to his successor a legacy of every existing problem, made worse by years of neglect. And a republic of the Left could only with the greatest difficulty have skirted the twin dangers of revolutionary war in Europe and civil war at home. The Second Empire was, arguably, for France at mid-century a necessity. From it came twenty years of relative stability, internal peace, economic revolution, a modernized Paris, social reform, and one of the most remarkable political evolutions of modern times—from dictatorship to parliamentary democracy without revolution. As for the foreign policy of those twenty years, its objectives seem difficult to fault from our perspective of more than a century. Nationalities *was* an idea whose time had come, and the proper, the only response was to seek to guide rather than to exploit, oppose, or ignore it. The problems of the emerging modern world, the challenge to Europe inherent in the development of the United States and of Russia were, as Napoleon III foresaw, beyond the control of a single European great power. Nor was this foreign policy doomed to failure. Almost forty years ago Robert Binkley argued that for a moment, at least, after the Crimean War, the concert of Europe conceived as "a legislative authority and a conference procedure" did exist. As for Napoleon III: "To interpret [his] dreams . . . as mere bargaining proposals to win for France additional Rhineland territory is to miss the meaning and the tragedy of the man's role in history. In 1863 he was perhaps the last genuine European who stood in a place of authority, a successor to Metternich, a precursor to Woodrow Wilson," a man whose vision was of a Europe "that would accept confederation of the various national areas, and defer to the authority of the concert as expressed in a congress."[10]

Of course, the foreign policy of the Second Empire did fail. Napoleon III destroyed the Metternichian concert but he could not reshape it as he had wished. And when Prussian nationalism, following the example already given by Cavour in Italy, shook loose from the control of Europe and became, at least in the minds of Frenchmen, a men-

10. Binkley, *Realism and Nationalism*, 162, 260, 304.

ace to France, the emperor could not reconstruct against Germany the conservative pre-1856 concert that the conquerors of his imperial predecessor had erected against France. However, without subscribing entirely to Binkley's theory of "the crisis of federative polity" in Europe, we can share his aversion to arguments of historical determinism. "There are moments in history the whole record of which is not disclosed except in an estimate of what never came to be." Napoleon III failed in his attempt to incline the balance of tensions that constitute what we call Europe one way rather than another, and since that failure historians have generally refused to believe that he was serious or, at any rate, that his efforts deserve to be taken seriously. It is understandable that, in Binkley's words, "when the spirit of *Realpolitik* had once become a dogma of a foreign office, diplomats became incapable of understanding that any other spirit could exist."[11] But historians should be more supple. They have a responsibility to assure that our judgment of the past not be influenced unduly by premises that have themselves been shaped by past events. Because the foreign policy of the Second Empire expired in the midst of ultimate weakness and futility, it does not follow that it was destined to fail or that it deserved to fail.

In fact, there were real and concrete reasons for the collapse of Napoleon III's foreign policy. Outside of France, his name, vital to political success within the country, was a burden to him. He was never really trusted and often he was feared. Nowhere was this more true than in Britain, whose friendship and cooperation he sought. Traditional British policy of refusing to concert in advance of problems becoming crises was reinforced by this implacable suspicion that saw a French plot in every conference proposal. At Vienna, suspicion of plots was unnecessary to harden an obdurate resistance to Napoleon's foreign policy. Already a historical anachronism, the Austrian Empire depended for its existence upon maintenance of treaties and of the status quo. The principle of nationalities and elevation of the authority of "Europe" over existing treaties were alike anathema to Francis Joseph and to his advisers. The efforts Napoleon made to move these obstacles to his plans only served to create further obstacles. Plom-

---

11. By "federative polity," Binkley meant the tendency toward agglomeration, as evidenced by Napoleon III's "paper Confederation of Italy," for example, and Francis Joseph's attempted federal reorganization of his empire (see *Realism and Nationalism*, 299–301). The concept of "Europe" embraces much more than a mere congeries of sovereign states. See Curcio, "Le problème historique," in *L'Europe du XIXe et du XXe siècle*, ed. Max Beloff *et al.*, I, 157–58.

bières, the war against Austria, and the annexation of Nice and Savoy deepened distrust of the Second Empire throughout Europe and especially in Britain, strengthened Austrian determination to resist the "new principles," and, most fatefully, reconfirmed in European affairs the principle of might makes right. In the face of these tensions, congresses and conferences seemed weak reeds indeed. Doubtless most diplomats would have agreed with Guizot's cynicism: "A congress has often been talked about—and the possibility of submitting the question of peace to a deliberation by Europe. Congresses are fine for regulating the results of the past, not for determining the future. . . . When it is a matter of the future . . . they are useless and serve only to irritate the causes of disorder and conflict."[12] Moreover, as a statesman Napoleon III had serious faults. Insistent that the control and even the day-to-day direction of foreign policy should be in his hands, he was impatient of detail and of solid preparation. He neglected to read important dispatches, and the gaps in his understanding were often considerable. Sometimes, too, he dissipated his energy in the pursuit of chimeras, and that energy was increasingly undermined after 1865 by the serious illness from which he suffered.

None of these factors, however, made failure inevitable; they merely assured that success would be difficult. Napoleon III, whatever his lapses, was not a hopeless idealist, nor was he always a dreamer. The achievements of his early reign attest to his ability to act realistically and effectively. And besides, as one of his ablest ministers, Victor Duruy, was later to remark, it is not a disability to dream, for dreaming is often necessary to arrive at an ideal. In the end, British pragmatism, Austrian realism, and Prussian *Realpolitik* alike failed dismally. Vienna feared French policies because they threatened its existence; less than fifty years after the collapse of those policies, the Hapsburg Empire had, nevertheless, ceased to exist. Britain dreaded the stirring up of trouble and feared long-range commitments in Europe; within half a century of the fall of the Second Empire, the march of nationalism on the Continent had drawn Britain into a bloodbath from which it would never fully recover. Bismarck saw Napoleon III's ideas as a barrier to German unity under Prussian control; in less than a century, the overwhelming success of Bismarckian policy would itself contribute to the unmaking of Germany and the passing of Prussia's heartland under the military control of Soviet Russia. The for-

12. Pingaud, "Un projet de désarmement," 16.

eign policy of the Second Empire failed not because it was wrong-headed but because it was based upon inadequate power. The crisis came in 1866. Then, after Sadowa, was the moment, if ever, for decisive action. Of course, the French emperor had been extraordinarily unlucky in the outcome of the Prussian-Austrian conflict and was handicapped at the crucial moment by illness and by the complications of an unnecessariy devious diplomacy. But none of this would have mattered had France possessed the will and force required for the task its ruler had set. Moreover, Caesarean democracy, by its very dependence on public opinion and its marriage to *la volonté nationale*, had proved incapable of summoning whatever reserves of strength the nation did possess. Twice Napoleon III proposed military reform, once after the 1859 war with Austria, and again after Sadowa. Twice the proposals were rejected by a people who wanted grandeur without cost and predominance without effort. In this sense, then, it would be more just to recognize that through his will, personality, and diplomacy, Napoleon III gave France twenty years of dominance to which it was no longer entitled than to condemn him for losing that dominance in the end.[13]

An overwhelming indictment remains. As ruler of France, Napoleon III failed to measure means to ends and to provide for national security. But if this ultimate failure cannot be excused, it ought not blind us to the achievements of French foreign policy between 1851 and 1870—the halting for a generation of Russian expansion, the inclusion of Turkey within the concert of Europe, the liberation of Italy, the unification of Rumania, the pacification of Syria, the extension of the French empire, and the building of the Suez Canal. Nor should it cause us to forget that even in his failures, Napolcon III was more often right than wrong, although frequently a generation or more ahead of his time. Such was the case in regard to his preference for confederation in Italy, his advice to the pope to renounce all but the symbols of temporal sovereignty, his support of a tripartite Germany, his championing of the cause of free trade, of nationalities, and of an Arab kingdom of Algeria, his efforts to turn Austrian attention toward the Danube Basin and the East and to draw Britain into Europe, his desire to keep the Turkish question a European one, and, above all, his sense of European unity and concert in the face of the modern age,

---

13. Typical is the charge that "as an exercise in the dissipation of national power, security, and prestige, Napoleon's performance following the Crimean War is almost unparalleled" (Schroeder, *Austria, Great Britain, and the Crimean War*, 423).

which had just begun. We are left, then, with a final irony. It is possible that, had Napoleon III been the man his enemies took him for, he would be remembered today as one of the most successful of French rulers. Such a man would not have asked of Europe more than he could seize or of France more than it could give. That a reign of almost twenty years should have ended in chaos and failure is a tragedy on the Greek scale, rendered more moving still by the personal qualities of the man. "He was good," Thirria has written, "thoroughly good; history will not forget that, and in condemning, even in cursing the ruler, it will render homage to the man."[14] Perhaps, however, this judgment is only partly right. Today it seems doubtful that, as a ruler, Napoleon III deserved the abuse once heaped upon him. Girardin has suggested that if we still lived in the days when princes were identified by epithets, then it is as Napoléon le bien intentionné that this third Napoleon should be remembered. But there is another epithet more fitting still, because it expresses not only the tragedy of the ruler but the broader tragedy of the era in which he lived. He was a complicated man, a man of many contradictions; and yet, through his life may be traced a few consistent themes, and none more tenacious than his belief in an entity called Europe. Beyond his failure, there would lie a hundred years in which "Europe" would no longer exist. Surely history will remember him, in light of that tragic century, as the vanquished European.

14. Thirria, Napoléon avant l'Empire, I, vii.

Bibliography

PRIMARY SOURCES

ARCHIVES

Archives du Ministère des Affaires Étrangères, Paris
  Correspondance politique
  Mémoires et documents
Bodleian Library, Oxford
  Papers of George William Villiers, earl of Clarendon
Haus-, Hof-, und Staatsarchiv, Vienna
  Politische Aktenstücke, Frankreich
Public Record Office, London, Foreign Office
  Diplomatic Correspondence with the Paris Embassy
  Papers of Henry Richard Charles Wellesley, earl of Cowley
  Papers of John Arthur Douglas Bloomfield
Public Record Office, London, Gifts and Deposits
  Papers of Lord John Russell
Royal Archives, Windsor, Files J39, J77, J80, J82, J83

PRINTED DOCUMENTS

Archives diplomatiques: Recueil mensuel international de diplomatie, d'histoire et de droit international. Paris, 1861–.
Die auswärtige Politik Preussens, 1858–1871: Diplomatische Aktenstücke. Edited by the Historischen Reichskommission, under the direction of Erich Brandenburg, Otto Hoetzsch, and Hermann Oncken. 10 vols. Oldenburg, 1933–1939.
British and Foreign State Papers, Compiled by the Librarian and Keeper of the Papers of the Foreign Office. London, 1836–.
I documenti diplomatici italiani. 1st series, 1861–1870. Rome, 1952–.
Documents diplomatiques: Livres jaunes. Paris, 1861–.
Oncken, Hermann, ed. *Die Rheinpolitik Kaiser Napoleon III. von 1863 bis 1870 und der Ursprung des Krieges von 1870/71: Nach den Staatsakten von Österreich, Preussen und den süddeutschen Mittelstaaten.* 3 vols. Stuttgart, 1926.

Les origines diplomatiques de la Guerre de 1870–1871. 29 vols. Paris, 1910–1932.

Temperley, Harold, and Lillian M. Penson. *Foundations of British Foreign Policy from Pitt (1792) to Salisbury (1902) or Documents, Old and New.* Cambridge, 1938.

LETTERS, SPEECHES, AND MEMOIRS

Benson, Christopher Arthur, and Viscount Esher, eds. *The Letters of Queen Victoria: A Selection from Her Majesty's Correspondence Between the Years 1837–1861.* First series of the official publication of Victoria's letters. 3 vols. New York, 1907.

Beust, Count Friedrich Ferdinand von. *Memoirs.* Translated from the German. 2 vols. 2nd ed. London, 1887.

Beyens, Baron Eugène. *Le Second Empire vu par un diplomate belge.* 2 vols. Paris, 1924–1926.

Bonaparte, Louis Napoléon. *Des idées napoléoniennes.* 6th ed. London, 1860.

Buckle, George Earle, ed. *The Letters of Queen Victoria: A Selection from Her Majesty's Correspondence and Journal Between the Years 1862 and 1878.* Second series of the official publication of Victoria's letters. 2 vols. London, 1926.

Cavour, Count Camillo Benso. *Il carteggio Cavour-Nigra dal 1858 al 1861.* Edited by the governmental Commissione Reale Editrice dei Carteggi Cavouriani. 4 vols. Bologna, 1926–1929.

———. *Il carteggio Cavour-Salmour.* Bologna, 1936.

———. *Cavour e l'Inghilterra: Carteggio con V. E. d'Azeglio.* 2 vols. in 3 parts. Bologna, 1933.

———. *La liberazione del Mezzogiorno e la formazione del Regno d'Italia: Carteggi di Camillo Cavour con Villamarina, Scialoja, Cordova, Farini, ecc.* 4 vols. Bologna, 1949–1954.

———. *La questione Romana negli anni 1860–1861: Carteggio del Conte di Cavour con P. Pantaleoni, C. Passaglia, O. Vimercati.* 2 vols. Bologna, 1929.

Colombo, Adolfo, et al., eds. *Carteggi e bibliografia di Costantino Nigra.* Turin, 1930.

Craven, Augustus, ed. *Lord Palmerston: Sa correspondance intime pour servir à l'histoire diplomatique de l'Europe de 1830 à 1865.* 2 vols. Paris, 1878–1879.

Discailles, Ernest. *Un diplomate belge à Paris, 1830–1864.* Vol. 3 of Académie Royale de Belgique, *Mémoires,* 2nd series. Brussels, 1908.

Emerit, Marcel, ed. *Lettres de Napoléon III à Madame Cornu.* Paris, 1937.

Ernest II, Duke of Saxe-Coburg-Gotha. *Memoirs.* 4 vols. London, 1888–1890.

Fleury, Général Emile F., comte de, ed. *Souvenirs du Général Comte Fleury, 1837–1867.* 2 vols. 3rd ed. Paris, 1897–1898.

Gooch, G. P., ed. *The Later Correspondence of Lord John Russell, 1840–1878*. 2 vols. London, 1925.

Hauterive, Ernest d', ed. *Napoléon III et le Prince Napoléon: Correspondance inédite*. Paris, 1925.

Hübner, Count Joseph Alexander von. *Neuf ans de souvenirs d'un ambassadeur d'Autriche à Paris sous le Second Empire, 1851–1859*. 2 vols. Paris, 1904.

La Chapelle, comte de, ed. *Posthumous Works and Unpublished Autographs of Napoleon III in Exile*. London, 1873.

Las Cases, comte de. *Le mémorial de Sainte-Hélène: Première édition intégrale et critique, établie et annotée par Marcel Dunan de l'Institut*. In the Flammarion series Les grands mémoires. 2 vols. Paris, 1951.

Loftus, Lord Augustus. *Diplomatic Reminiscences* [1837–1879]. 4 vols. London, 1892–1894.

Mallarmé, Camille. "Napoléon III et Villafranca (avec des lettres inédites)." *Revue hebdomadaire*, no. 10 (March 7, 1925), 41–42.

Malmesbury, third earl of. *Memoirs of an Ex-Minister: An Autobiography*. Tauchnitz edition, 3 vols. in 1. Leipzig, 1885.

Morny, duc de. *Une ambassade en Russie, 1856: Extrait des mémoires du duc de Morny*. Edited by Paul Ollendorff. Paris, 1892.

Napoleon III. *Oeuvres de Napoléon III*. 5 vols. Paris, 1856–1869.

———. *La politique impériale exposée par les discours et proclamations de l'Empereur Napoléon III depuis 10 décembre 1848 jusqu'en juillet 1865*. Paris, 1865.

Nesselrode, comte A. de. *Lettres et papiers du chancelier Comte de Nesselrode, 1760–1856*. 11 vols. Paris, n.d.

Papiers et correspondance de la famille impériale. 2 vols. Paris, 1870–1872.

Persigny, Fialin, duc de. *Mémoires . . . publiés avec des documents inédits, un avant-propos et un épilogue*. 2nd ed. Paris, 1896.

Pirri, Pietro, ed. *Pio IX e Vittorio Emanuèle II dal loro carteggio privato*. 5 vols. Rome, 1944–1951.

Raindre, Gaston. "Les papiers inédits du Comte Walewski: Souvenirs et correspondance (1855–1868)." *Revue de France* (January–February, 1925), 74–104, 485–510; (March–April, 1925), 39–56; (May–June, 1925), 281–305; (July–August, 1925), 82–96, 311–25.

Rothan, Gustave. *Souvenirs diplomatiques: L'affaire du Luxembourg, le prélude de la Guerre de 1870*. 3rd ed. Paris, 1883.

Schazmann, Paul-Emile. *Napoléon III, précurseur de la Société des Nations*. Paris, 1937.

Strachey, Lytton, and Roger Fulford, eds. *The Greville Memoirs, 1814–1860*. 7 vols. London, 1938.

Thouvenel, Louis, ed. *Pages de l'histoire du Second Empire d'après les papiers de M. Thouvenel, 1854–1866*. Paris, 1903.

———. *Le secret de l'Empereur, correspondance confidentielle et inédite échangée entre M. Thouvenel, le duc de Gramont et le général comte de Flahaut, 1860–1863*. 2 vols. Paris, 1889.

————. *Trois années de la question d'Orient, 1856–1859, d'après les papiers inédits de M. Thouvenel*. Paris, 1897.

Tocqueville, Alexis de. *Souvenirs: Texte établi, annoté et préfacé par Luc Monnier*. Vol. 12 of *Oeuvres complètes*. Edited by J. P. Mayer. Paris, 1964.

Vitzthum, Count Karl Friedrich. *St. Petersburg and London in the Years 1852–1864: Reminiscences of Count Charles Frederick Vitzthum von Eckstaedt*. Translated from the German. 2 vols. London, 1887.

Wellesley, F. A., ed. *Secrets of the Second Empire, Private Letters from the Paris Embassy: Selections from the Papers of . . . First Earl Cowley* [1852–1867]. New York, 1929.

Wellesley, Sir Victor, and Robert Sencourt, eds. *Conversations with Napoleon III: A Collection of Documents, Mostly Unpublished and Almost Entirely Diplomatic, Selected and Arranged with Introductions*. London, 1934.

SECONDARY SOURCES

BOOKS

Bapst, Edmond. *Les origines de la Guerre de Crimée: La France et la Russie de 1848 à 1854*. Paris, 1912.

Barker, Nancy Nichols. *The French Experience in Mexico, 1821–1861: A History of Constant Misunderstanding*. Chapel Hill, 1979.

Baumgart, Winfried. *Der Friede von Paris, 1856: Studien zur Verhältnis von Kriegführung, Politik und Friedenswahrung*. Munich, 1972.

Binkley, Robert C. *Realism and Nationalism, 1852–1871*. New York, 1935.

Bóbr-Tylingo, Stanislaw. *Napoléon III, l'Europe et la Pologne en 1863–1864*. Rome, 1963.

Bock, Carl H. *Prelude to Tragedy: The Negotiation and Breakdown of the Tripartite Convention of London, October 31, 1861*. Philadelphia, 1966.

Bonnin, Georges, ed. *Bismarck and the Hohenzollern Candidature for the Spanish Throne: The Documents in the German Archives*. London, 1957.

Bourgeois, Emile, and Emile Clermont. *Rome et Napoléon III, 1849–1870: Etude sur les origines et la chute du Second Empire*. Paris, 1907.

Bratianu, G. I. *Napoléon III et les nationalités*. Paris, 1934.

Bush, John W. *Venetia Redeemed: Franco-Italian Relations, 1864–1866*. Syracuse, 1967.

Case, Lynn M. *Edouard Thouvenel et la diplomatie du Second Empire*. Translated from the English. Paris, 1976.

————. *Franco-Italian Relations, 1860–1865: The Roman Question and the Convention of September*. Philadelphia, 1932.

————. *French Opinion on War and Diplomacy During the Second Empire*. Philadelphia, 1954.

Case, Lynn M., and Warren F. Spencer. *The United States and France: Civil War Diplomacy*. Philadelphia, 1970.

Charles-Roux, François. *Alexandre II, Gorchakov et Napoléon III*. Paris, 1913.

Clark, Chester Wells. *Franz Joseph and Bismarck: The Diplomacy of Austria Before the War of 1866*. Cambridge, Mass., 1934.

Collins, R. W. *Catholicism and the Second French Republic, 1848–1852*. New York, 1923.

Corley, T. A. B. *Democratic Despot: A Life of Napoleon III*. London, 1961.

Debidour, Antonin. *Histoire diplomatique de l'Europe depuis l'ouverture du Congrès de Vienne jusqu'à la fermeture du Congrès de Berlin (1814–1878)*. 2 vols. Paris, 1891.

Dittrich, Jochen. *Bismarck, Frankreich und die Spanische Thronkandidatur der Hohenzollern: Die "Kriegschuld Frage" von 1870*. Munich, 1962.

Driault, Edouard. *La question d'Orient depuis ses origines jusqu'à la paix de Sèvres*. 8th ed. Paris, 1921.

East, W. G. *The Union of Moldavia and Wallachia, 1859: An Episode in Diplomatic History*. Cambridge, 1929.

L'Europe du XIXe et du XXe siècle (1815–1870): Problèmes et interprétation historiques. Edited by Max Beloff *et al.* 6 vols. Paris, 1964.

Fester, Richard. *Briefe, Aktenstücke und Regesten zur Geschichte der Hohenzollernschen Thronkandidatur in Spanien*. 2 vols. Leipzig, 1911.

Fitzmaurice, Lord Edmond. *The Life of Granville George Leveson Gower, Second Earl Granville, 1815–1891*. 2 vols. London, 1905–1906.

Fletcher, Willard Allen. *The Mission of Vincent Benedetti to Berlin, 1864–1870*. The Hague, 1965.

Goriaïnow, Serge. *Le Bosphore et les Dardanelles: Étude historique sur la question des Détroits d'après la correspondance diplomatique déposée aux Archives Centrales de Saint-Pétersbourg et à celles de l'Empire [c. 1798–1878]*. Paris, 1910.

Grabinski, Comte Joseph. *Un ami de Napoléon III: Le Comte Arese et la politique italienne sous le Second Empire*. Paris, 1897.

Guichen, vicomte de. *La Guerre de Crimée (1854–1856) et l'attitude des puissances européennes*. Paris, 1936.

Hallberg, Charles W. *Franz Joseph and Napoleon III, 1852–1864: A Study of Austro-French Relations*. New York, 1955.

Hanna, Alfred Jackson, and Kathryn Abbey Hanna. *Napoleon III and Mexico: American Triumph over Monarchy*. Chapel Hill, 1971.

Harcourt, Bernard, Comte d'. *Les quatres ministères de M. Drouyn de Lhuys*. Paris, 1882.

Henderson, Gavin Burns. *Crimean War Diplomacy and Other Historical Essays*. Glasgow, 1947.

Henry, Paul. *Napoléon III et les peuples: À propos d'un aspect de la politique extérieure du Second Empire*. Paris, 1943.

Holbraad, Carsten. *The Concert of Europe: A Study in German and British International Theory, 1815–1914.* New York, 1970.

Isser, Natalie. *The Second Empire and the Press: A Study of Government-Inspired Brochures on French Foreign Policy in Their Propaganda Milieu.* The Hague, 1974.

Jomini, Alexandre de. *Diplomatic Study on the Crimean War (1852–1856): Russian Official Publication.* Translated from the French. 2 vols. London, 1882.

Kukiel, M. *Czartoryski and European Unity, 1770–1861.* Princeton, 1955.

La Gorce, Pierre François Gustave de. *Histoire du Second Empire.* 7 vols. Paris, 1894–1904.

———. *Napoléon III et sa politique.* Paris, 1933.

La Marmora, Alfonso. *Un peu plus de lumière sur les événements politiques et militaires de l'année 1866.* Paris, 1874.

Lane-Poole, Stanley. *The Life of the Right Honourable Stratford Canning, Viscount Stratford de Redcliffe, from his Memoirs and Private and Official Papers.* 2 vols. London, 1888.

Mange, Alyce Edythe. *The Near Eastern Policy of the Emperor Napoleon III.* Illinois Studies in the Social Sciences, XXV. Urbana, 1940.

Martin, Sir Theodore. *The Life of His Royal Highness, the Prince Consort.* 5 vols. London, 1875–1880.

Matter, Paul. *Cavour et l'unité italienne.* 3 vols. Paris, 1922–1927.

Maxwell, Sir Herbert Eustace. *The Life and Letters of George William Frederick, Fourth Earl of Clarendon.* 2 vols. London, 1913.

Millman, Richard. *British Foreign Policy and the Coming of the Franco-Prussian War.* New York, 1965.

Molinari, M. G. *Napoléon III publiciste: Sa pensée cherchée dans ses écrits—Analyse et appréciation de ses oeuvres.* Brussels, 1861.

Mollat, G. *La question romaine de Pie VI à Pie XI.* 2nd ed. Paris, 1932.

Monicault, Gaston de. *La question d'Orient: Le traité de Paris et ses suites (1856–1871).* Paris, 1898.

Mosse, W. E. *The European Powers and the German Question, 1848–1871: With Special Reference to England and Russia.* Cambridge, 1958.

———. *The Rise and Fall of the Crimean System, 1855–1871: The Story of a Peace Settlement.* New York, 1963.

Newton, Lord. *Lord Lyons: A Record of British Diplomacy.* 2 vols. London, 1913.

Ollivier, Emile. *L'empire libéral: Études, récits, souvenirs.* 17 vols. Paris, 1895–1915.

Pottinger, E. Ann. *Napoleon III and the German Crisis, 1865–1866.* Cambridge, Mass., 1966.

Puryear, Vernon John. *England, Russia, and the Straits Question, 1844–1856.* Berkeley, 1931.

Ramsay, A. A. W. *Idealism and Foreign Policy: A Study of the Relations of Great Britain with Germany and France, 1860–1878*. London, 1925.

Reinach, Joseph. *Napoléon III et la paix*. Paris, 1921. Reprint from *Revue historique*, CXXXVI (1921), 161–219.

Renouvin, Pierre. *Histoire des relations internationales: Le XIXᵉ siècle, 1ᵉʳᵉ partie, l'Europe des nationalités et l'éveil de nouveaux mondes*. Paris, 1954.

Riker, T. W. *The making of Roumania: A Study of an International Problem, 1856–1866*. London, 1931.

Salomon, Henry. *L'ambassade de Richard de Metternich à Paris*. Paris, 1931.

Schefer, Christian. *La grande pensée de Napoléon III: Les origines de l'expédition du Mexique, 1858–1862*. Paris, 1939.

Schroeder, Paul W. *Austria, Great Britain, and the Crimean War: The Destruction of the European Concert*. Ithaca, N.Y., 1972.

Sencourt, Robert. *Napoléon III, un précurseur*. Translated from the English. Paris, 1935.

Simpson, F. A. *Louis Napoleon and the Recovery of France, 1848–1856*. London, 1923.

Steefel, Lawrence. *Bismarck, the Hohenzollern Candidacy, and the Origins of the Franco-German War of 1870*. Cambridge, Mass., 1962.

Sybel, Heinrich von. *The Founding of the German Empire by William I*. Translated from the German. 7 vols. New York, 1890–1898.

Taylor, A. J. P. *The Italian Problem in European Diplomacy, 1847–1849*. Manchester, 1934.

———. *The Struggle for Mastery in Europe, 1848–1918*. New York, 1954.

Temperley, Harold W. V. *England and the Near East: The Crimea*. New York, 1936.

Thirria, Hippolyte. *Napoléon III avant l'Empire*. 2 vols. Paris, 1895–1896.

Williams, Roger L. *Gaslight and Shadow: The World of Napoleon III, 1851–1870*. New York, 1957.

———. *The Mortal Napoleon III*. Princeton, 1971.

ARTICLES, THESES, AND DISSERTATIONS

Barker, Nancy Nichols. "Austria, France, and the Venetian Question, 1861–1866." *Journal of Modern History*, XXXVI (1964), 145–54.

Bernardy, Françoise Chalamon de. "Un fils de Napoléon, le Comte Walewski, 1810–1869." Thesis, Sorbonne, 1951.

Blumberg, Arnold. "The Demise of Italian Federalism, 1859." *Historian*, XVIII (1955), 57–82.

Bóbr-Tylingo, Stanislaw. "Un congrès européen manqué (1863)." *Polish Review* (Summer, 1960), 77–94.

Boutenko, Victor. "Un projet d'alliance franco-russe en 1856, d'après des documents inédits des archives russes." *Revue historique*, CLV (1927), 277–325.

Cummings, Raymond. "The French Effort to Block Garibaldi at the Straits, 1860." *Historian*, XXXI (1969), 211–32.

Echard, William E. "Conference Diplomacy in the German Policy of Napoleon III, 1868–1869." *French Historical Studies*, IV (1966), 239–64.

————. "Louis Napoleon and the French Decision to Intervene at Rome in 1849: A New Appraisal." *Canadian Journal of History*, IX (December, 1974), 263–74.

Gooch, Brison D. "A Century of Historiography on the Origins of the Crimean War." *American Historical Review*, LXII (October, 1956), 33–58.

Goriaïnow, Serge. "Les étapes de l'alliance franco-russe, 1853–1861." *Revue de Paris*, XIX, pt. 1 (1912), 1–28, 529–44, 755–76.

Hagg, Harold Theodore. "The Congress of Paris of 1856." Ph.D. dissertation, Iowa State University, 1936.

Halperin, S. William. "The Origins of the Franco-Prussian War Revisited: Bismarck and the Hohenzollern Candidacy for the Spanish Throne." *Journal of Modern History*, XLV (1973), 83–91.

Handelsman, Marceli. "La Guerre de Crimée: La question polonaise et les origines du problème Bulgare." *Revue historique*, CLXIX (1932), 271–315.

Hauterive, Ernest d'. "Mission du Prince Napoléon à Varsovie (1858)." *Revue des deux mondes*, XLV, 7th per., ser. 13 (June 15, 1928), 823–54.

Jennings, Lawrence C. "French Diplomacy and the First Schleswig-Holstein Crisis." *French Historical Studies*, VII (1971), 204–225.

Ollivier, Emile. "Napoléon III: Son dessein international." *Revue des deux mondes*, CXLVI (1898), 49–54.

Pingaud, Albert. "Napoléon III et ses projets de confédération italienne." *Revue historique*, CLV (1927), 333–36.

————. "La politique extérieure du Second Empire." *Revue historique*, CLVI (1927), 41–68.

————. "Un projet de désarmement de Napoléon III, 1863." Reprint from *Institut de France: Séances et travaux de l'Académie des Sciences Morales et Politiques, compte-rendu*, II (November–December, 1931).

Renouvin, Pierre. "Le mouvement des nationalités en Europe dans la seconde moitié du XIXᵉ siècle." Mimeograph, Cours de Sorbonne, n.d.

————. "La politique extérieure du Second Empire." Mimeograph, Cours de Sorbonne, 1940.

Roloff, Gustav. "Frankreich, Preussen, und der Kirchenstaat im Jahre 1866: Eine Episode aus dem Kampfe zwischen Bismarck und Napoleon." *Forschungen zur brandenburgischen und preussischen Geschichte*, LV, pt. 1 (1939), 103–133.

Rothan, Gustave. "La mission de M. de Persigny à Berlin en 1850." *Revue des deux mondes*, XCIII, pt. 1 (May, 1889), 43–68.

Spencer, Warren F. "Edouard Drouyn de Lhuys and the Foreign Policy of the Second Empire." Ph.D. dissertation, University of Pennsylvania, 1955.

————. "The Mason Memorandum and the Diplomatic Origins of the Declaration of Paris." In Nancy N. Barker and Marvin L. Brown, Jr., eds., *Diplomacy in an Age of Nationalism.* The Hague, 1971.

Sumner, B. H. "The Secret Franco-Russian Treaty of 3 March 1859." *English Historical Review,* XLVIII (1933), 65–83.

Temperley, Harold W. V. "The Treaty of Paris and Its Execution." *Journal of Modern History,* IV (1932), 387–414, 523–43.

Thouvenel, Louis. "Paris et le congrès en 1856." *Revue de Paris,* III, pt. 6 (1896), 599–627.

Vidal, César. "La IIᵉ République et le Royaume de Sardaigne en 1849." *Rassegna storica del Risorgimento* (January–December, 1950), 505–530.

Williams, Roger. "Louis Napoleon: A Tragedy of Good Intentions." *History Today,* IV (April, 1954), 219–26.

Index